NCLE from ANOTHER WORLD

V

Hotondoshindeiru

A Man Who Survived

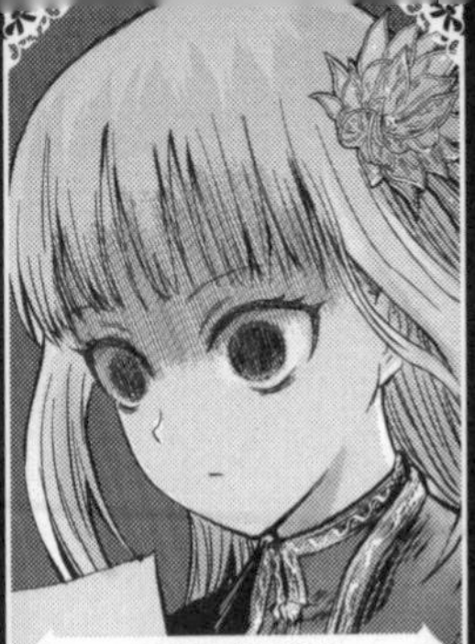

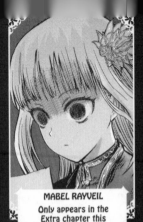

MABEL RAYVEIL

Only appears in the Extra chapter this volume. Has a ring.

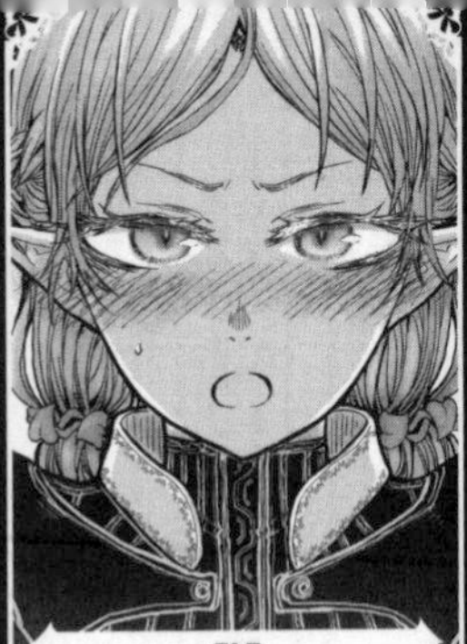

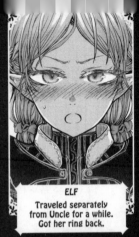

ELF

Traveled separately from Uncle for a while. Got her ring back.

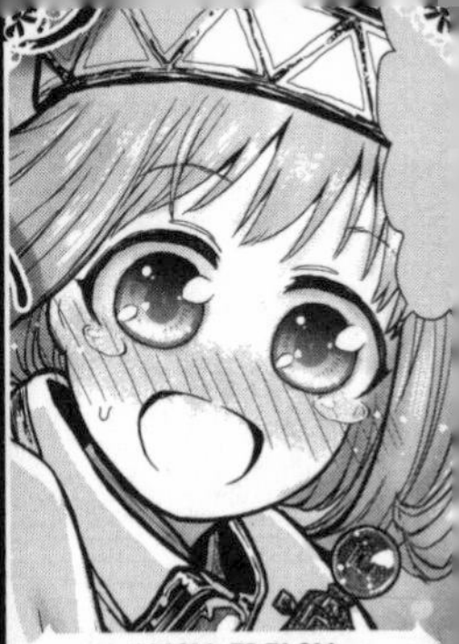

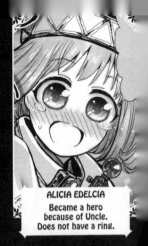

ALICIA EDELCIA

Became a hero because of Uncle. Does not have a ring.

THE STORY SO FAR Uncle heads to the royal capital to find out why Alicia was made a hero. There, he learns of a dark plot in the shadows. He summons the most powerful creature of all and shatters the dark chains binding the plotters, then goes on to transform into a giant dragon for added entertainment value. Except, now he can't turn back. His rescuer turns out to be none other than the tsundere elf!

CONTENTS

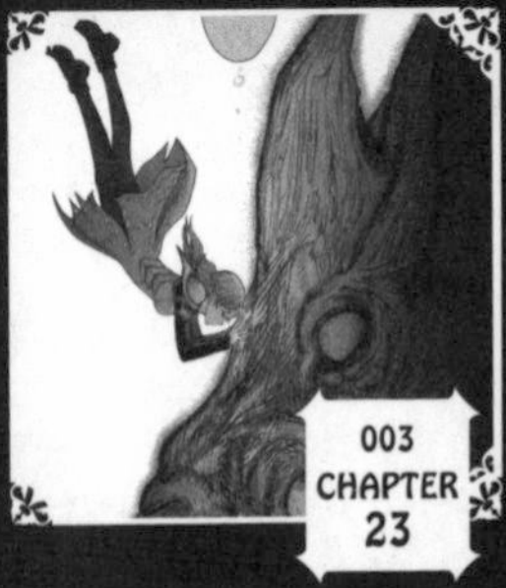

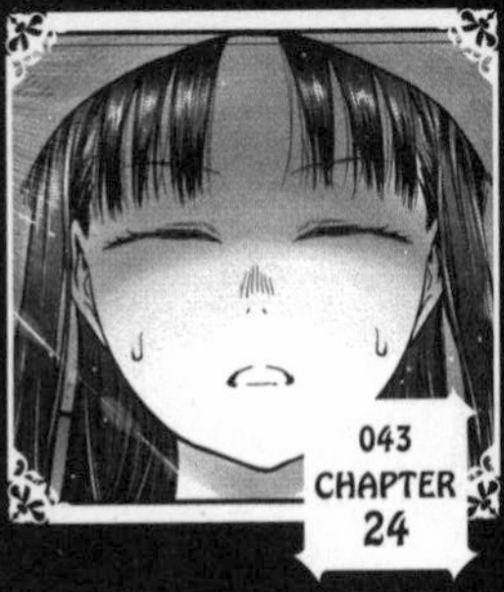

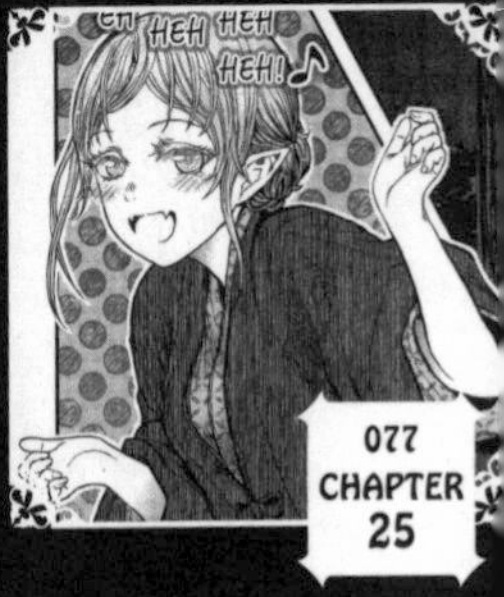
HEH HEH HEH!♪

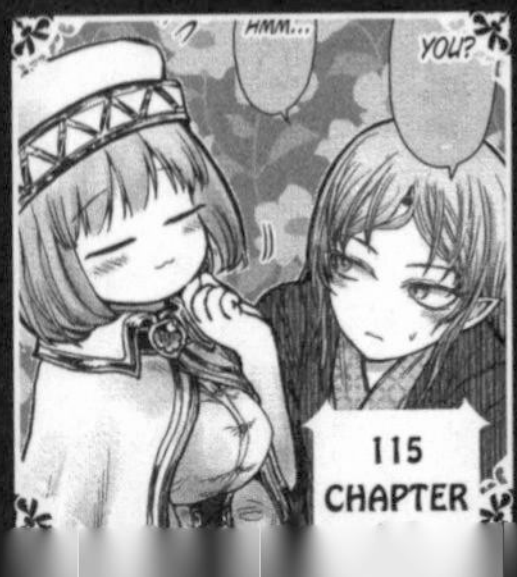
HMM...
YOU?

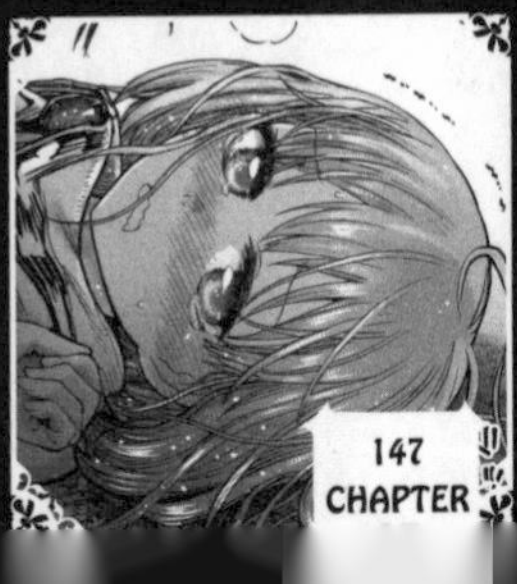

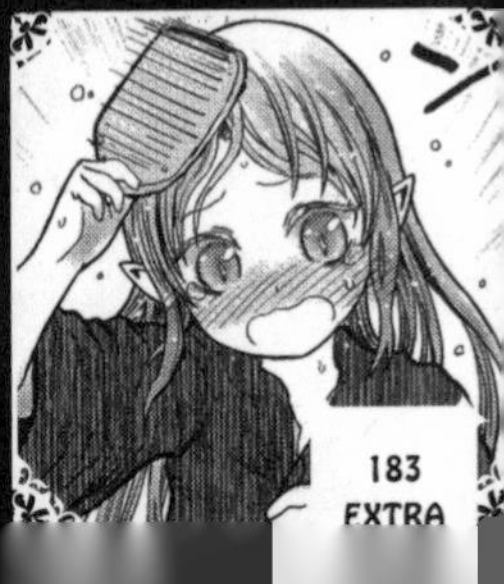

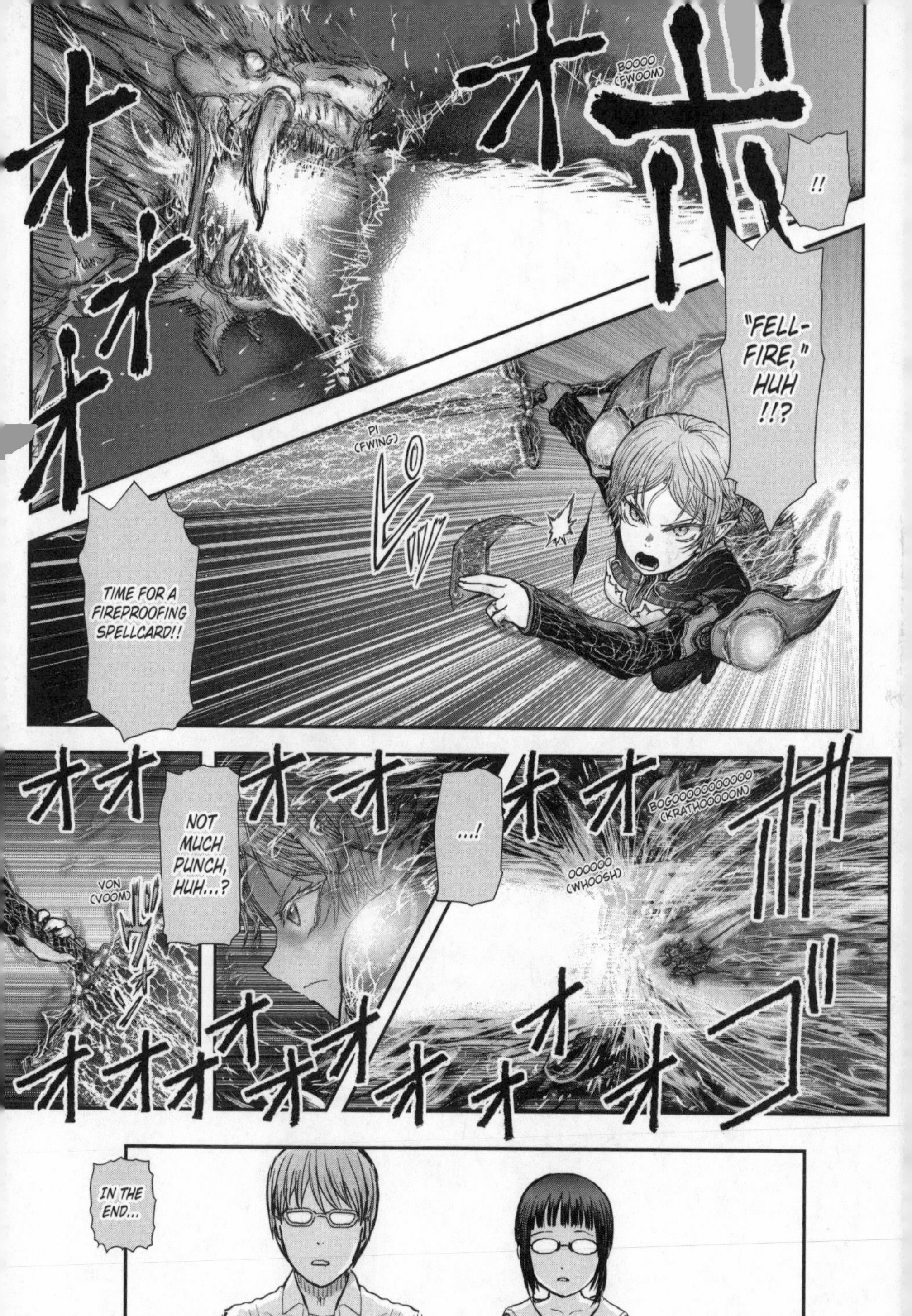
BOOOO (FWOOM)
!!
"FELL-FIRE," HUH!!?
PI (FWING)
TIME FOR A FIREPROOFING SPELLCARD!!
BOGOOOOOOOOOOO (KRATHOOOOOM)
...!
OOOOOO (WHOOSH)
NOT MUCH PUNCH, HUH...?
VON (VOOM)
IN THE END...

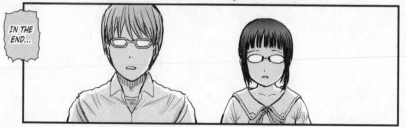

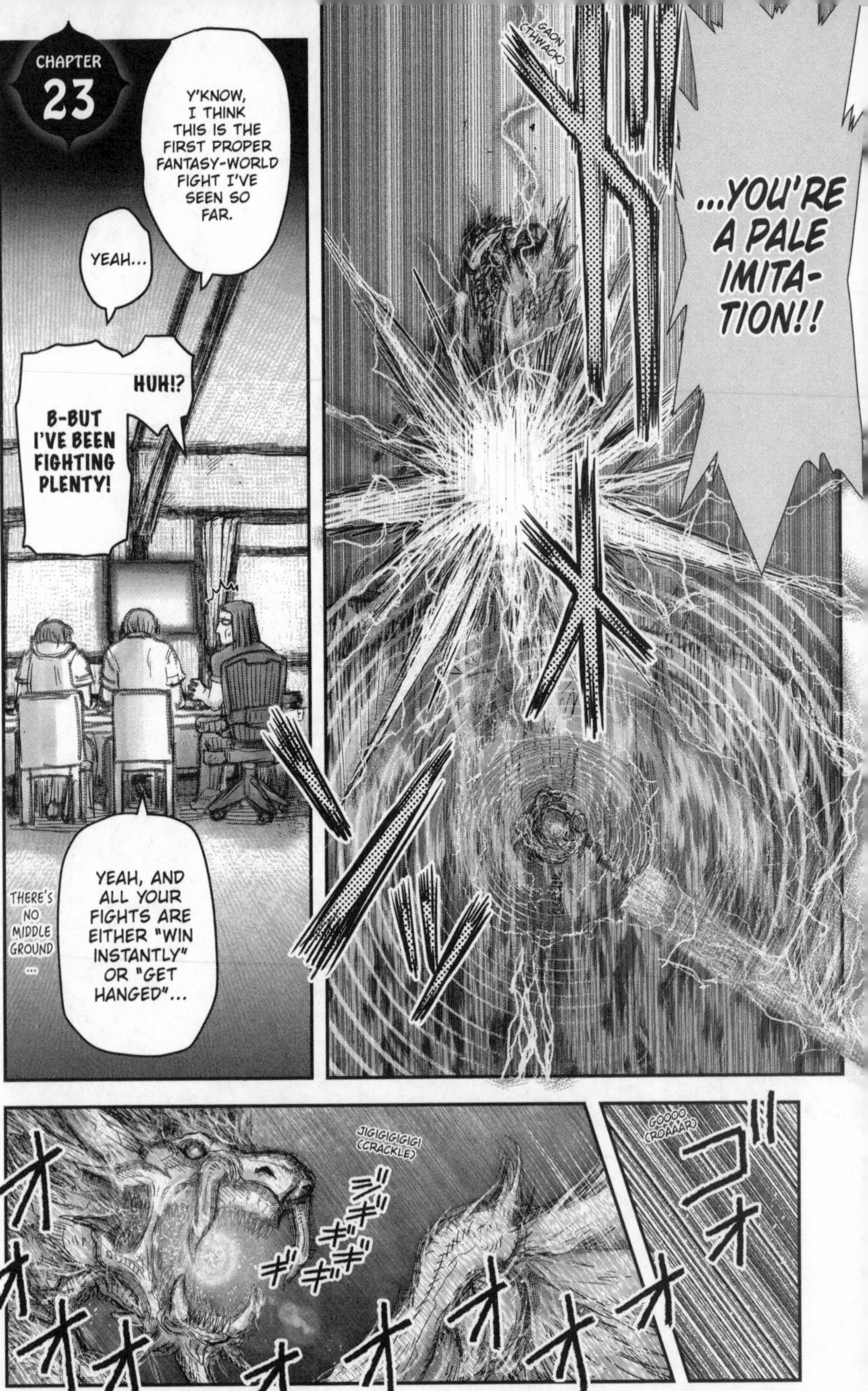
GAON (THWACK)
...YOU'RE A PALE IMITATION!!
CHAPTER 23
Y'KNOW, I THINK THIS IS THE FIRST PROPER FANTASY-WORLD FIGHT I'VE SEEN SO FAR.
YEAH...
HUH!?
B-BUT I'VE BEEN FIGHTING PLENTY!
YEAH, AND ALL YOUR FIGHTS ARE EITHER "WIN INSTANTLY" OR "GET HANGED"...
THERE'S NO MIDDLE GROUND...
GOOOO (ROAAAR)
JIGIGIGIGI (CRACKLE)

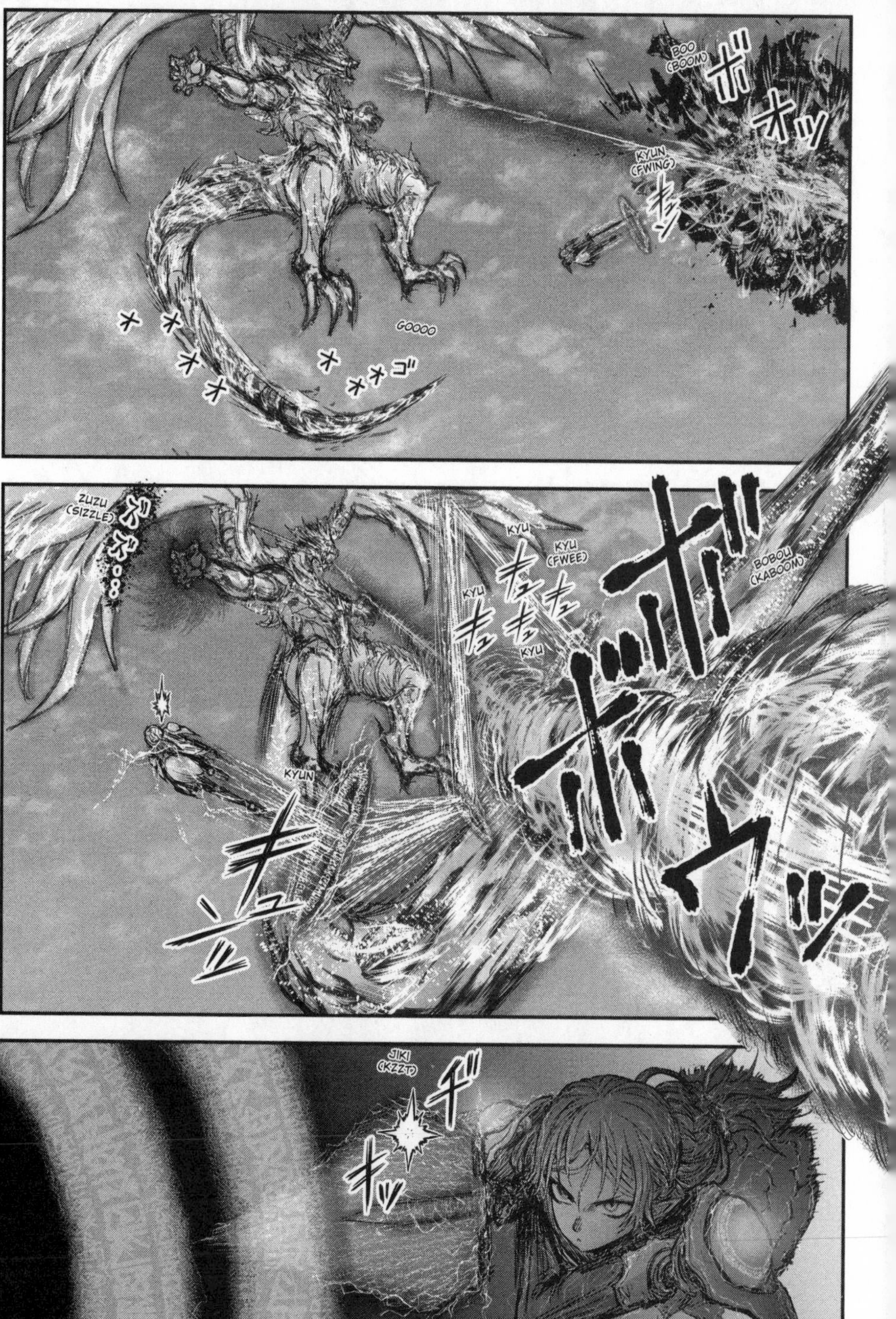
BOO (BOOM)
KYUN (FWING)
GOOOO
BOBOU (KABOOM)
KYU (FWEE)
KYU
KYU
KYU
ZUZU (SIZZLE)
KYUN
JIKI (KZZT)

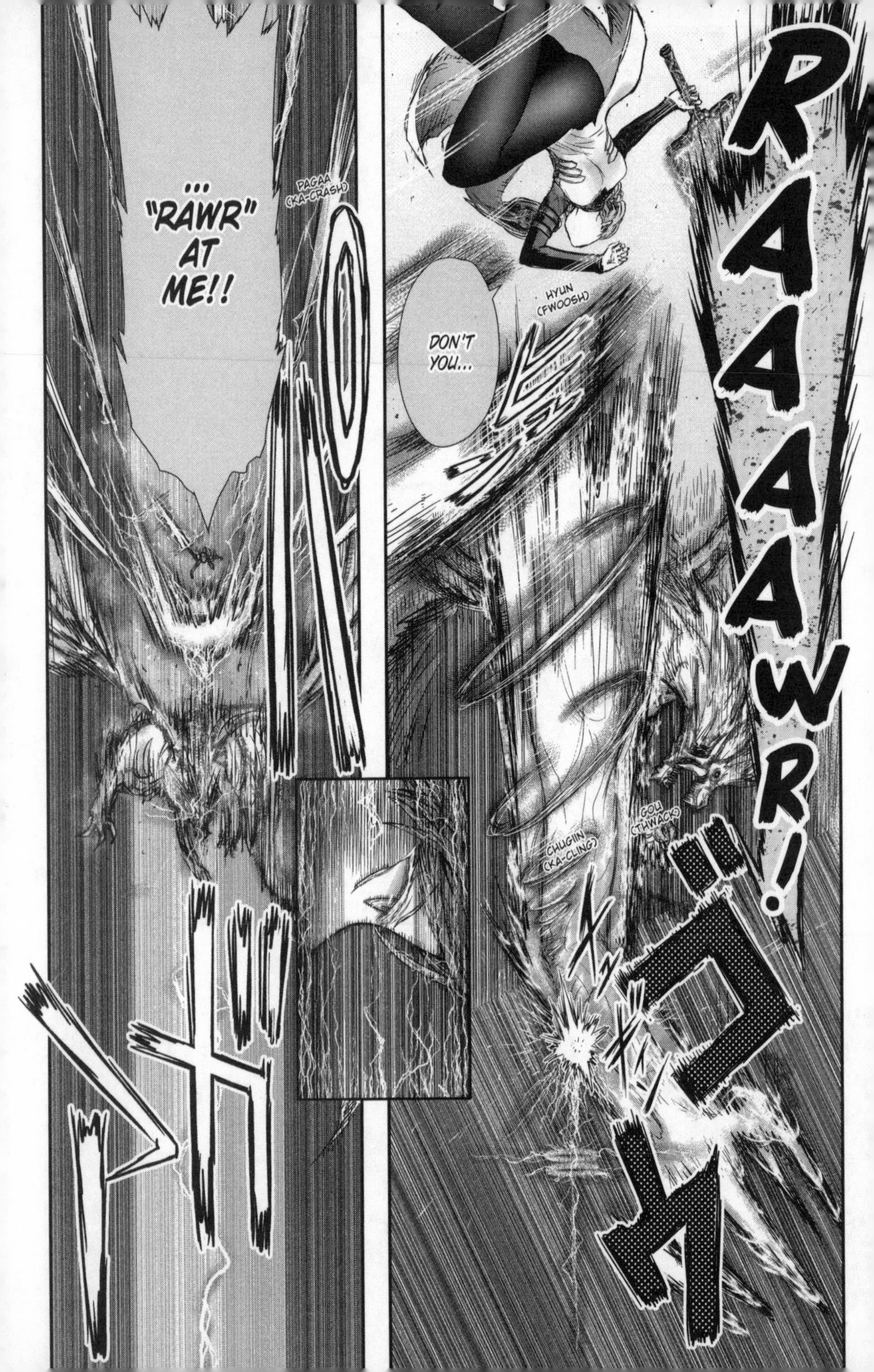
RAAAAWR!!
HYUN (FWOOSH)
DON'T YOU...
GOU (THWACK)
CHUGIIN (KA-CLING)
PAGAA (KA-CRASH)
..."RAWR" AT ME!!

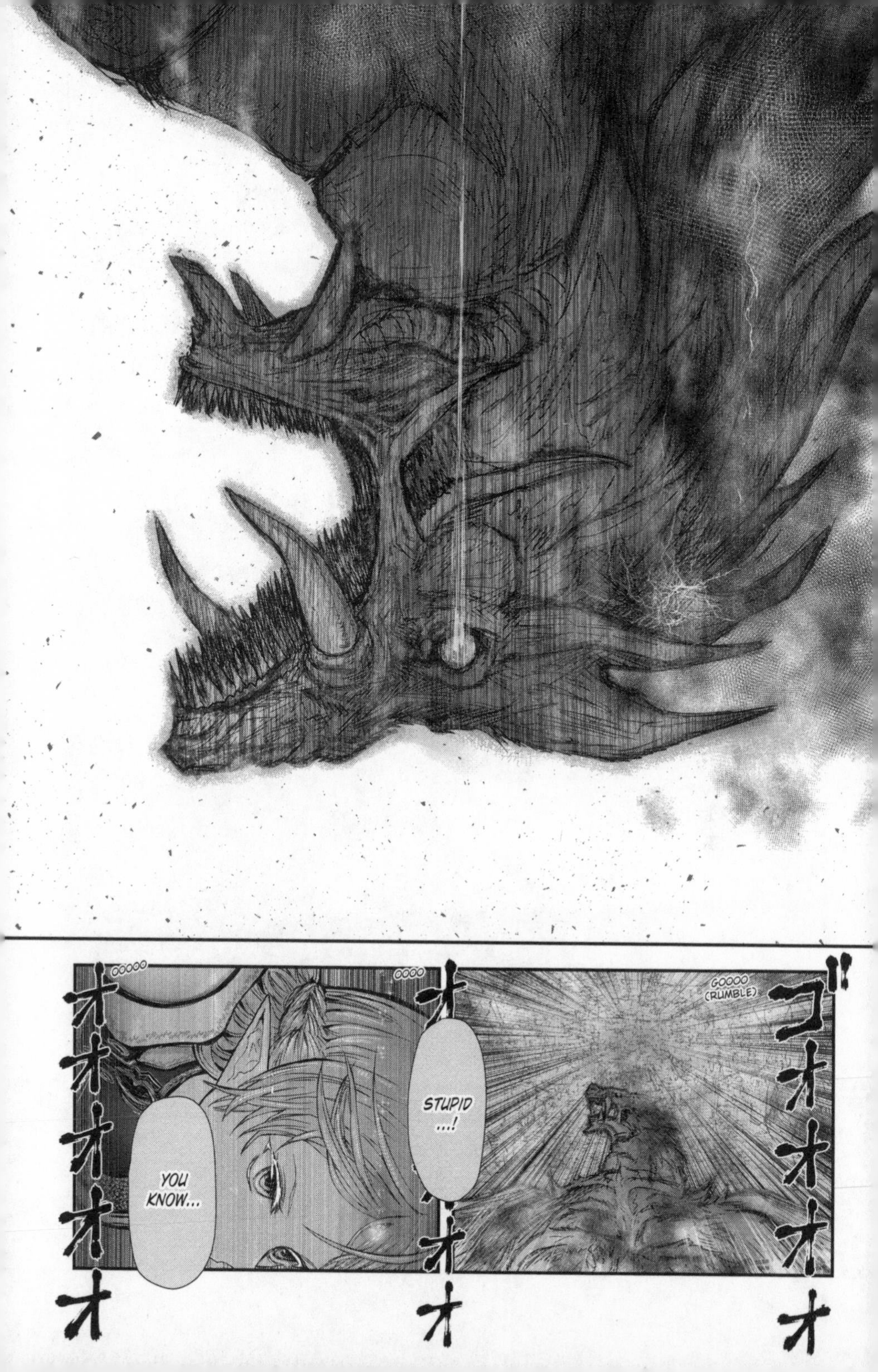
ゴオオオーオ
GOOOO (RUMBLE)
オオオ
OOOO
STUPID ...!
YOU KNOW...
オオオオオオ
OOOOO

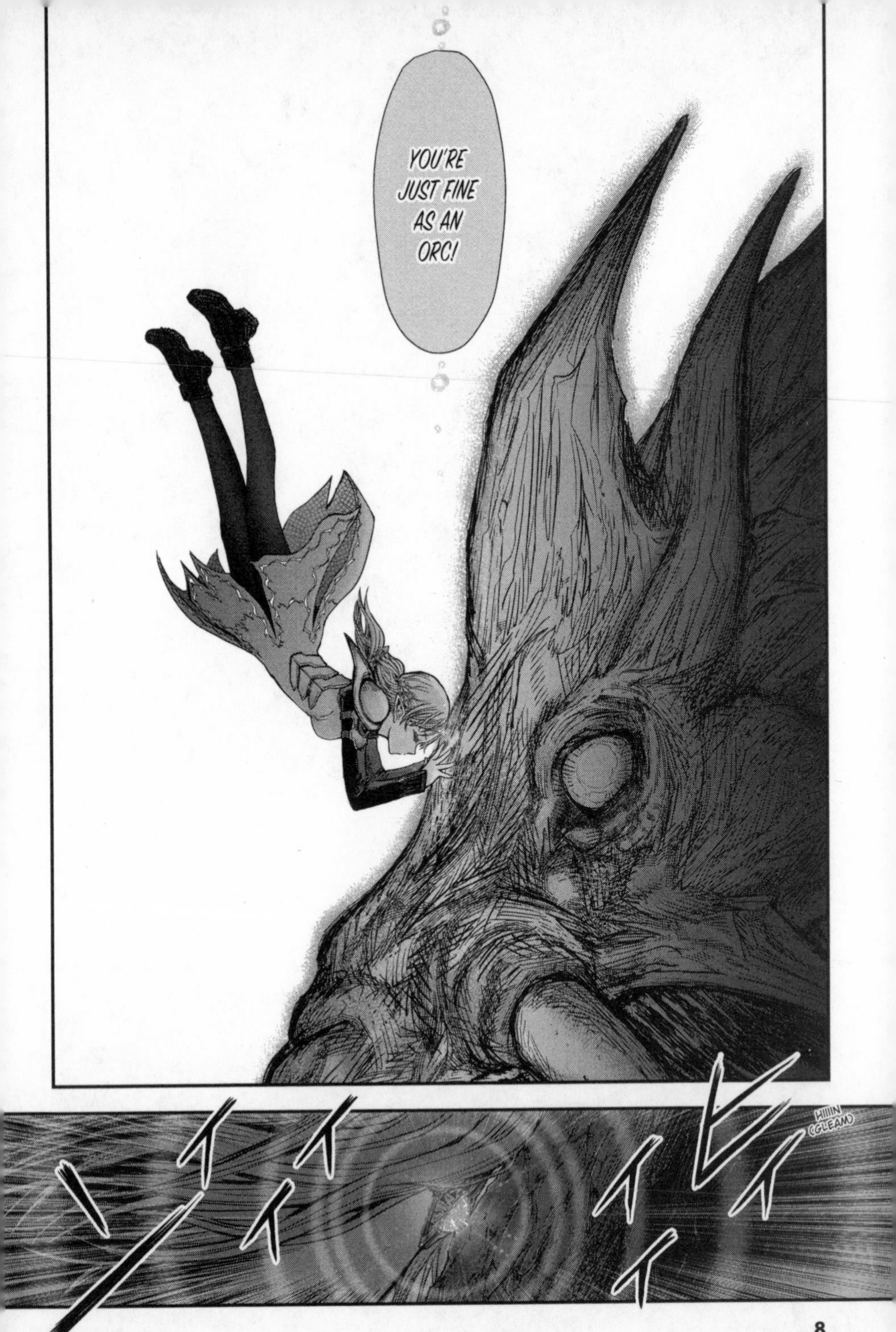
YOU'RE JUST FINE AS AN ORC!
HIIIIN (GLEAM)

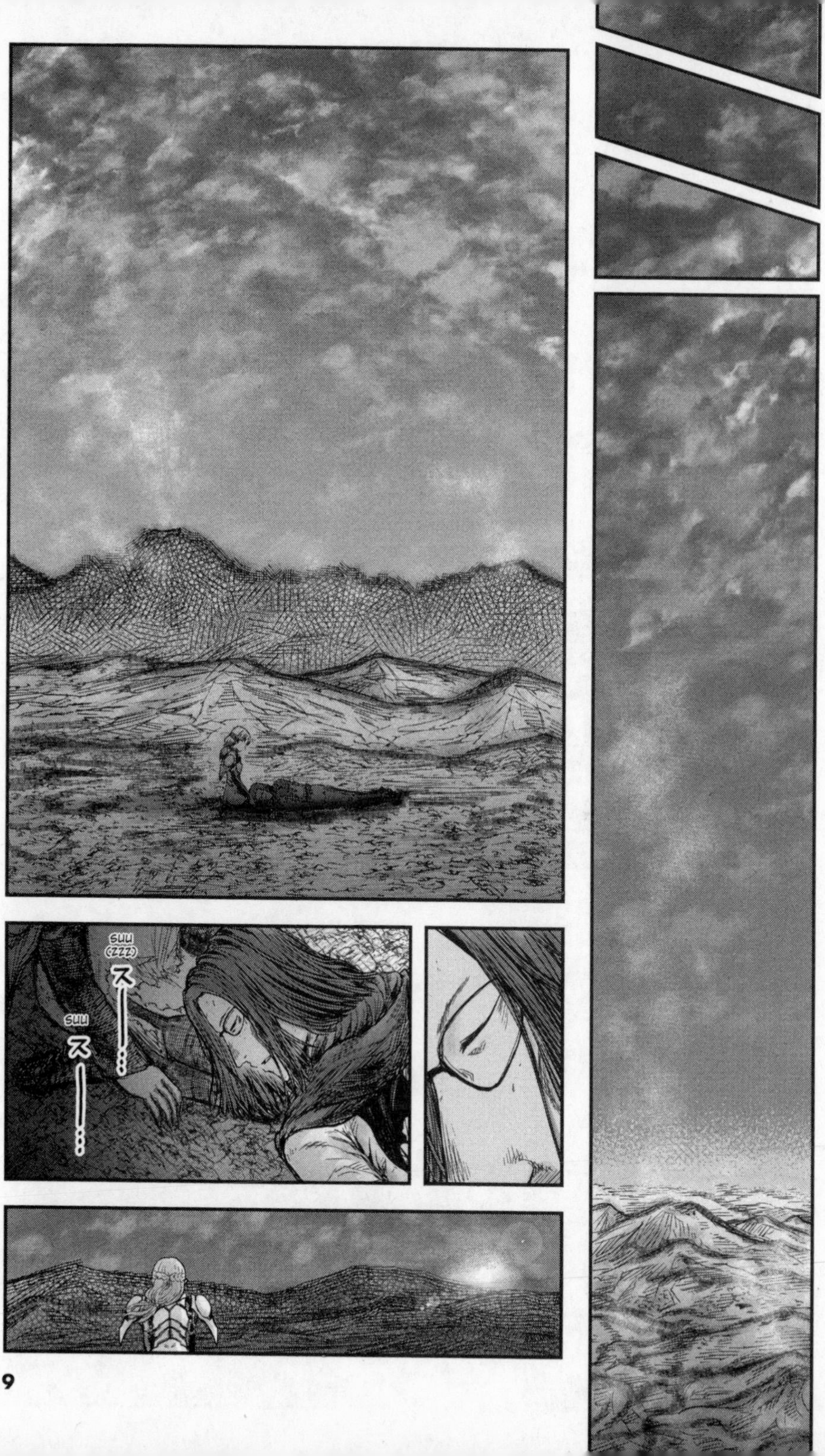
SUU (ZZZ)
ス――…
SUU
ス――…

!?

WELL, WELL, WELL...

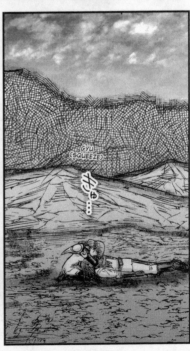

GYU
(SQUEEZE)

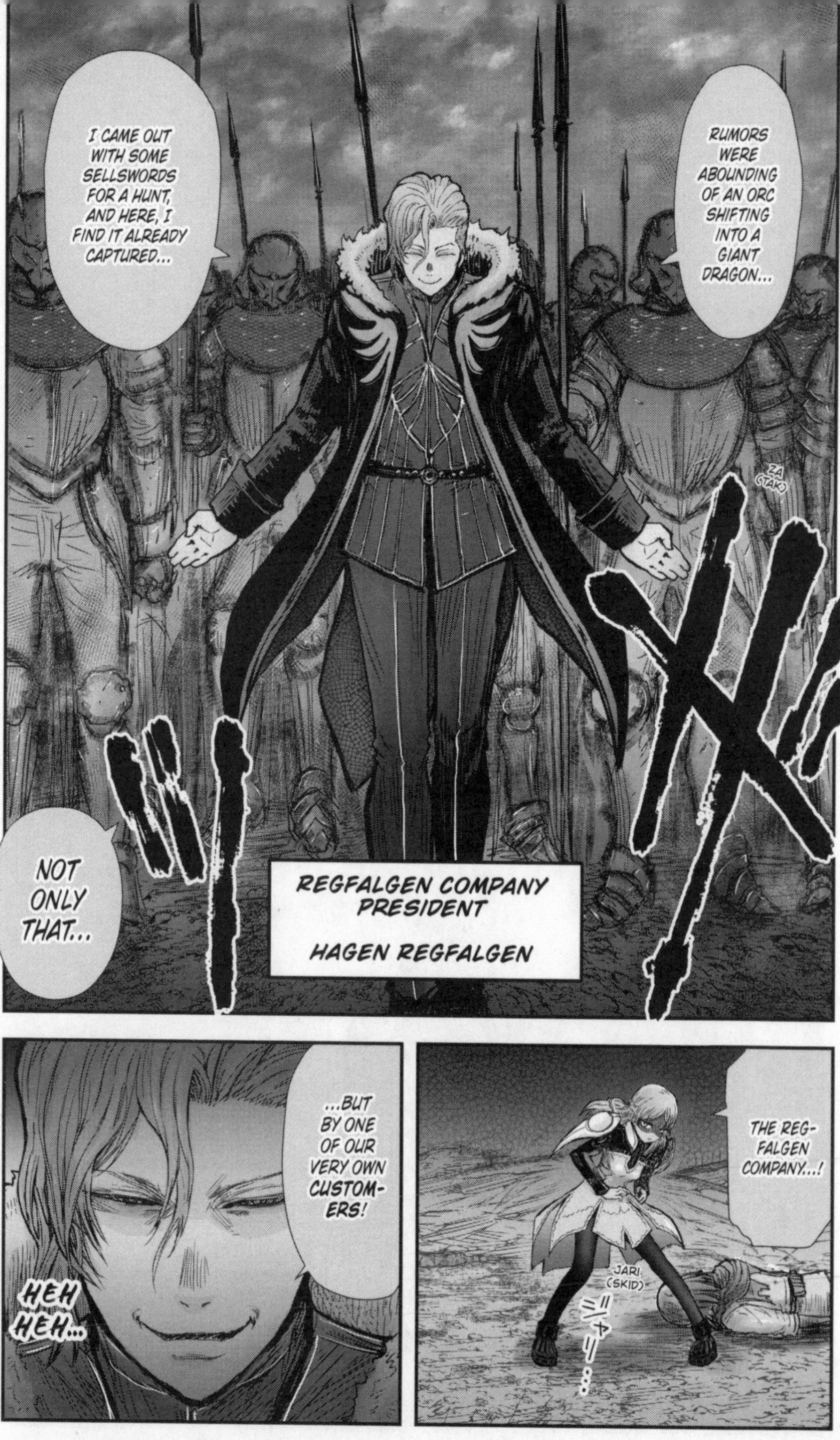
RUMORS WERE ABOUNDING OF AN ORC SHIFTING INTO A GIANT DRAGON...
I CAME OUT WITH SOME SELLSWORDS FOR A HUNT, AND HERE, I FIND IT ALREADY CAPTURED...
ZA (TAK)
REGFALGEN COMPANY PRESIDENT
HAGEN REGFALGEN
NOT ONLY THAT...
THE REG-FALGEN COMPANY...!
JARI (SKID)
...BUT BY ONE OF OUR VERY OWN CUSTOM-ERS!
HEH HEH...

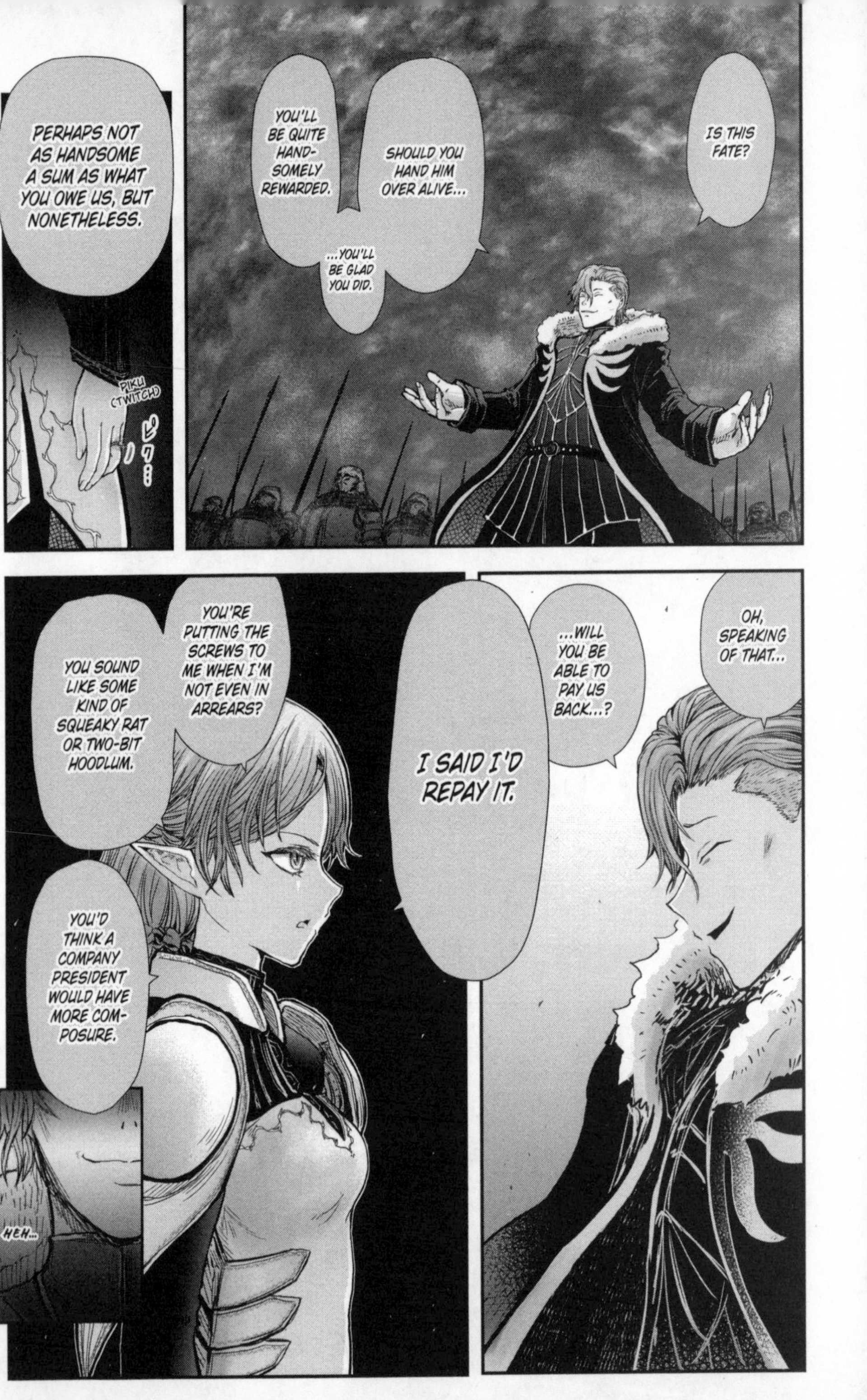
IS THIS FATE?
SHOULD YOU HAND HIM OVER ALIVE...
YOU'LL BE QUITE HAND-SOMELY REWARDED.
...YOU'LL BE GLAD YOU DID.
PERHAPS NOT AS HANDSOME A SUM AS WHAT YOU OWE US, BUT NONETHELESS.
PIKU (TWITCH)
OH, SPEAKING OF THAT...
...WILL YOU BE ABLE TO PAY US BACK...?
I SAID I'D REPAY IT.
YOU'RE PUTTING THE SCREWS TO ME WHEN I'M NOT EVEN IN ARREARS?
YOU SOUND LIKE SOME KIND OF SQUEAKY RAT OR TWO-BIT HOODLUM.
YOU'D THINK A COMPANY PRESIDENT WOULD HAVE MORE COM-POSURE.
HEH...

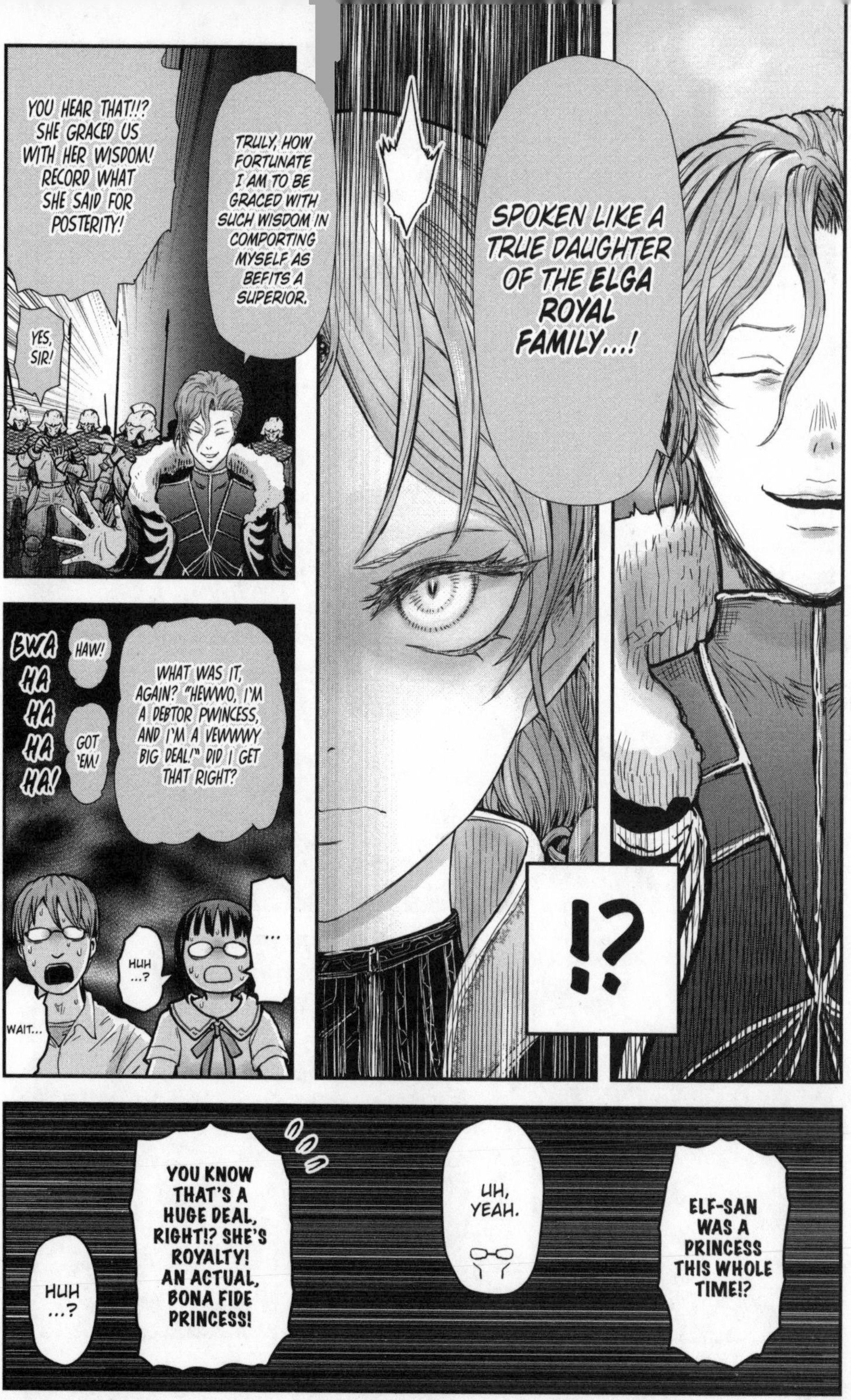

SPOKEN LIKE A TRUE DAUGHTER OF THE ELGA ROYAL FAMILY...!
!?
TRULY, HOW FORTUNATE I AM TO BE GRACED WITH SUCH WISDOM IN COMPORTING MYSELF AS BEFITS A SUPERIOR.
YOU HEAR THAT!!? SHE GRACED US WITH HER WISDOM! RECORD WHAT SHE SAID FOR POSTERITY!
YES, SIR!
WHAT WAS IT, AGAIN? "HEWWO, I'M A DEBTOR PWINCESS, AND I'M A VEWWWY BIG DEAL!" DID I GET THAT RIGHT?
HAW!
GOT 'EM!
BWA HA HA HA HA!
...
HUH ...?
WAIT...
ELF-SAN WAS A PRINCESS THIS WHOLE TIME!?
UH, YEAH.
YOU KNOW THAT'S A HUGE DEAL, RIGHT!? SHE'S ROYALTY! AN ACTUAL, BONA FIDE PRINCESS!
HUH ...?

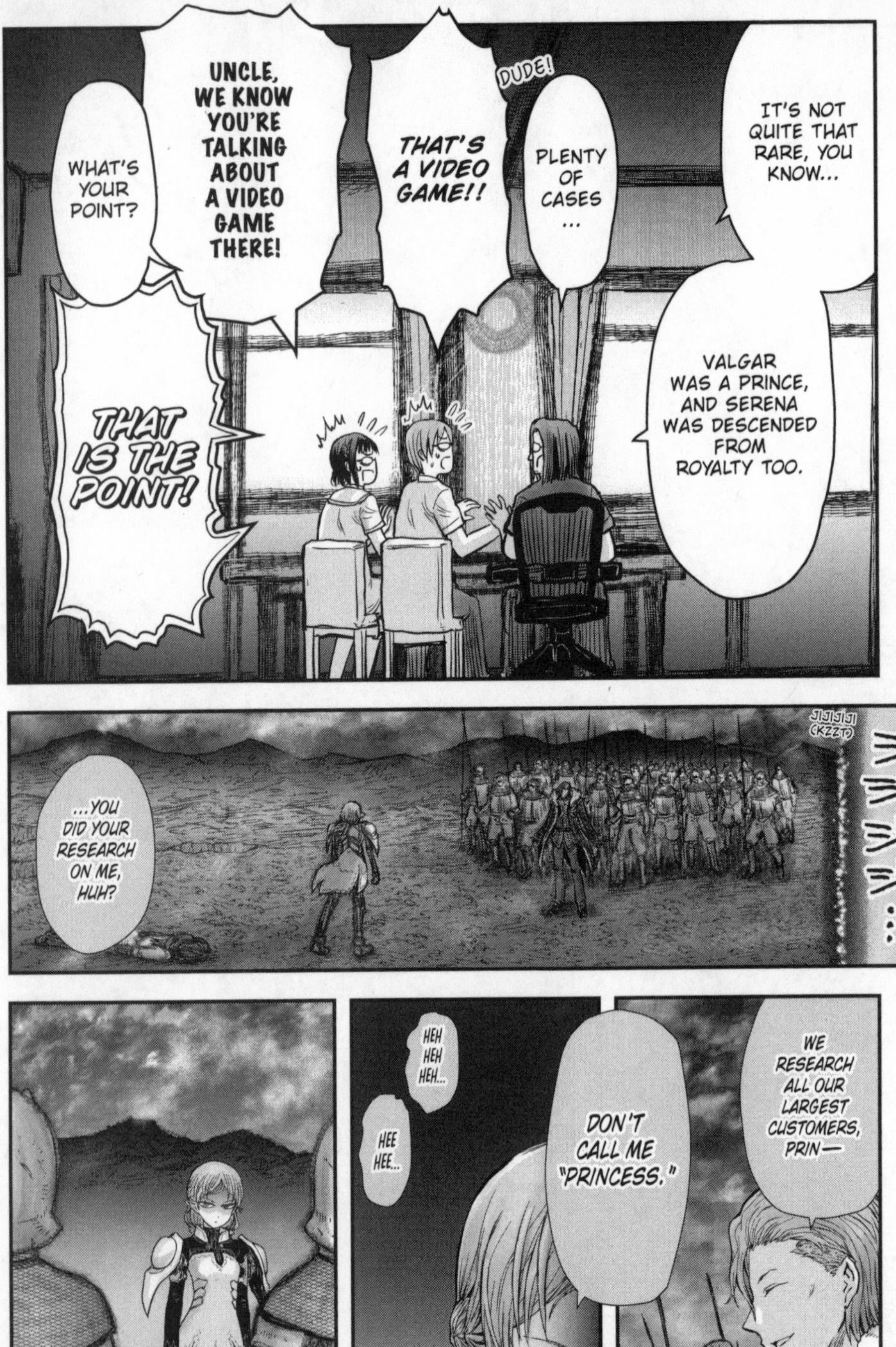
IT'S NOT QUITE THAT RARE, YOU KNOW...
PLENTY OF CASES ...
VALGAR WAS A PRINCE, AND SERENA WAS DESCENDED FROM ROYALTY TOO.
DUDE!
THAT'S A VIDEO GAME!!
UNCLE, WE KNOW YOU'RE TALKING ABOUT A VIDEO GAME THERE!
WHAT'S YOUR POINT?
THAT IS THE POINT!
JIJIJIJI (KZZT)
...YOU DID YOUR RESEARCH ON ME, HUH?
WE RESEARCH ALL OUR LARGEST CUSTOMERS, PRIN—
DON'T CALL ME "PRINCESS."
HEH HEH HEH...
HEE HEE...

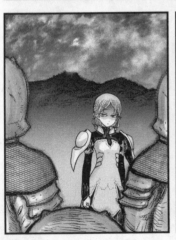

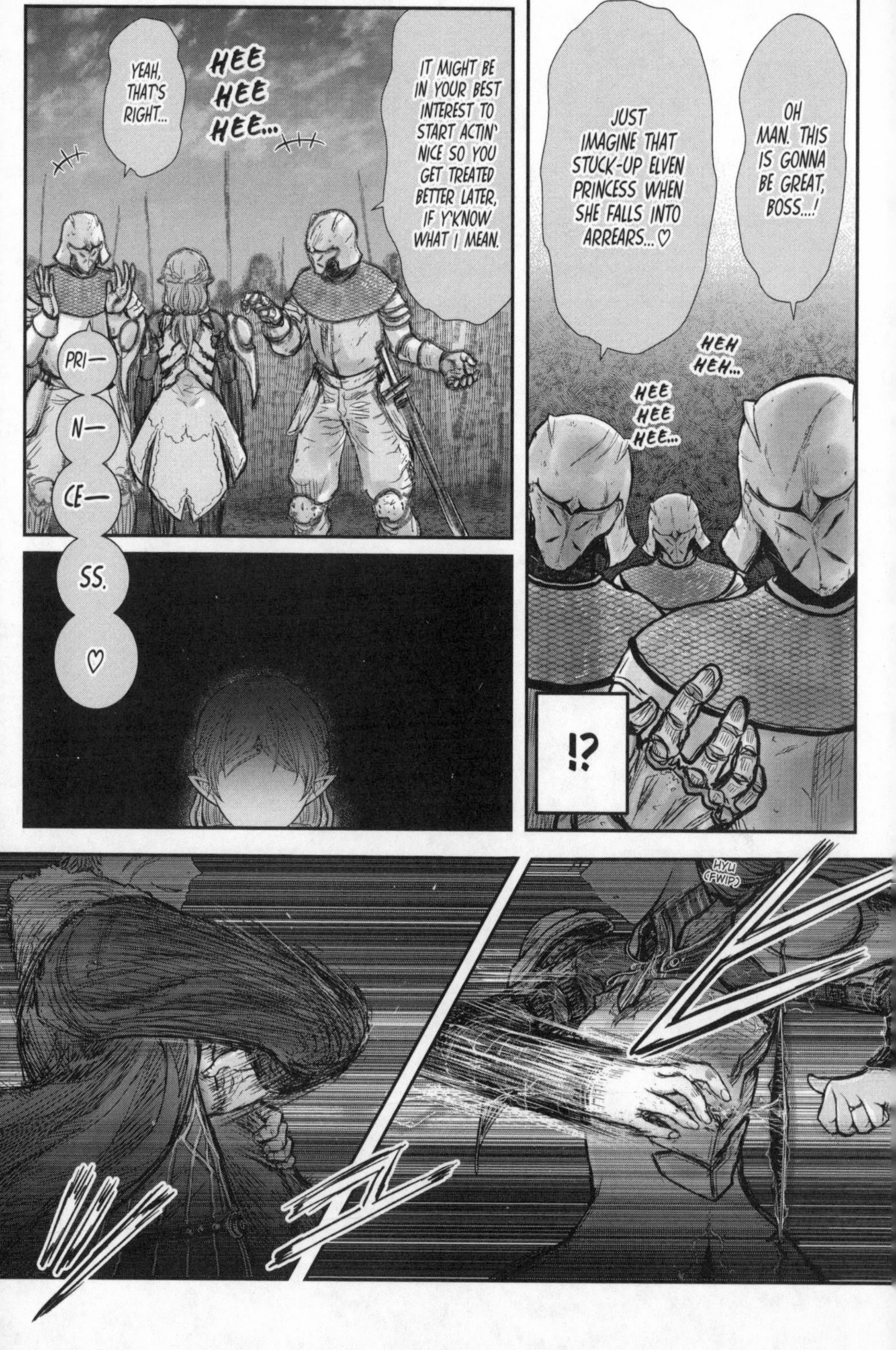
OH MAN. THIS IS GONNA BE GREAT, BOSS...!
JUST IMAGINE THAT STUCK-UP ELVEN PRINCESS WHEN SHE FALLS INTO ARREARS...♡
HEH HEH...
HEE HEE HEE...
!?
IT MIGHT BE IN YOUR BEST INTEREST TO START ACTIN' NICE SO YOU GET TREATED BETTER LATER, IF Y'KNOW WHAT I MEAN.
HEE HEE HEE...
YEAH, THAT'S RIGHT...
PRI—
N—
CE—
SS.
♡
HYU (FWIP)

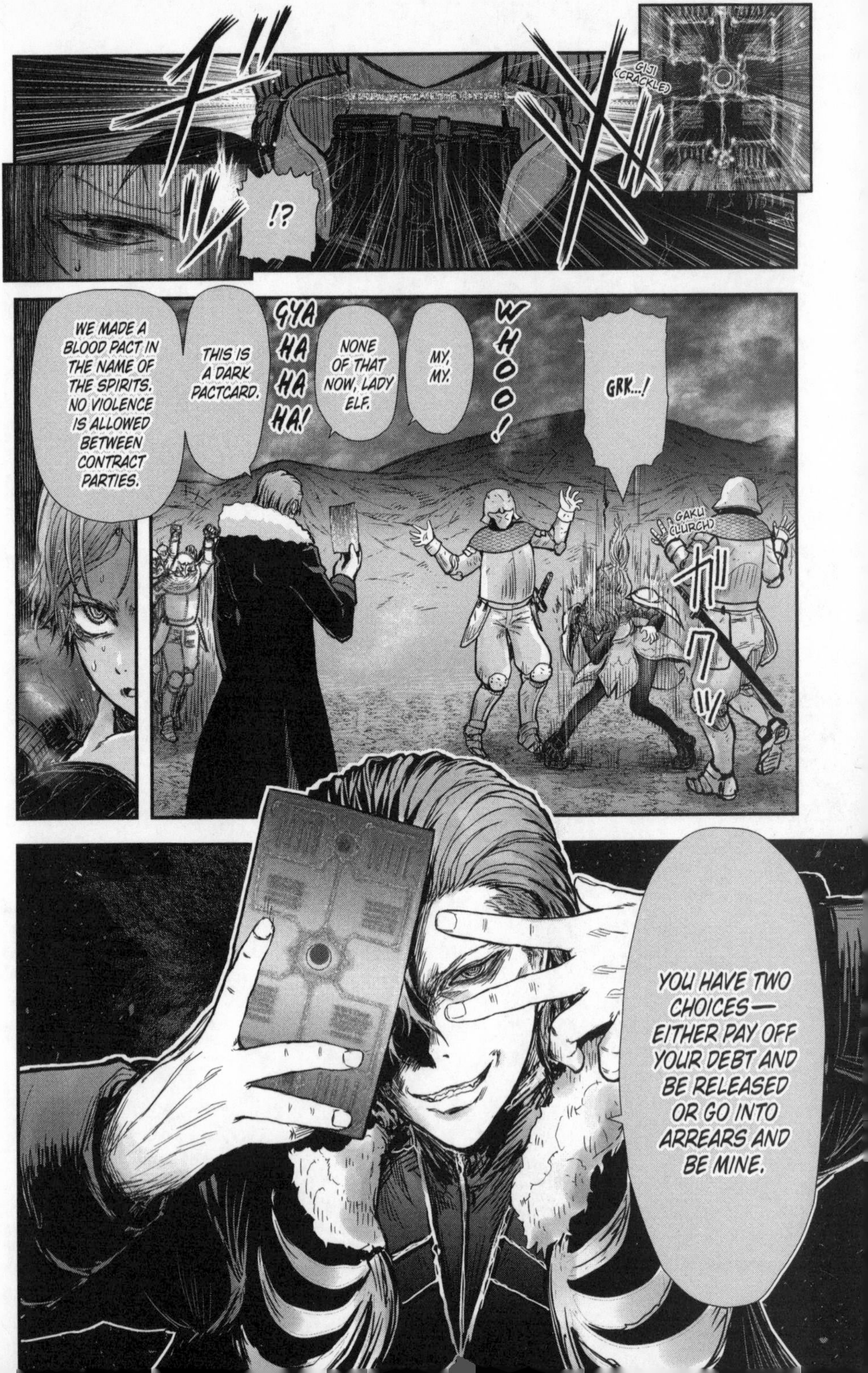
GIJI (CRACKLE)
!?
GRK...!
GAKU (LURCH)
WHOOO!
MY, MY.
NONE OF THAT NOW, LADY ELF.
GYA HA HA HA HA!
THIS IS A DARK PACTCARD.
WE MADE A BLOOD PACT IN THE NAME OF THE SPIRITS. NO VIOLENCE IS ALLOWED BETWEEN CONTRACT PARTIES.
YOU HAVE TWO CHOICES— EITHER PAY OFF YOUR DEBT AND BE RELEASED OR GO INTO ARREARS AND BE MINE.

HEE... HEE... HEE

HA HA...

WHOO?!

HEH HEH HEH...

YOU WERE A BIT CARELESS IN OFFERING YOURSELF UP FOR COLLATERAL ...!

A MARITAL CONNECTION TO ELVEN ROYALTY IS SURE TO OPEN NEW DOORS FOR THE COMPANY ...!

ZA

ZA

ZA

ZA

ZA (STEP)

ZA (STEP)

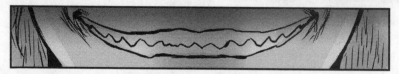

HYU (FWISH)

PAKIN (SNAP)

THE NAME HAGEN REGFALGEN WILL BECOME KNOWN THROUGH-OUT—

KURO-CHELGID SWORD STYLE SECRET: RIOL-RAN. MANIFEST.

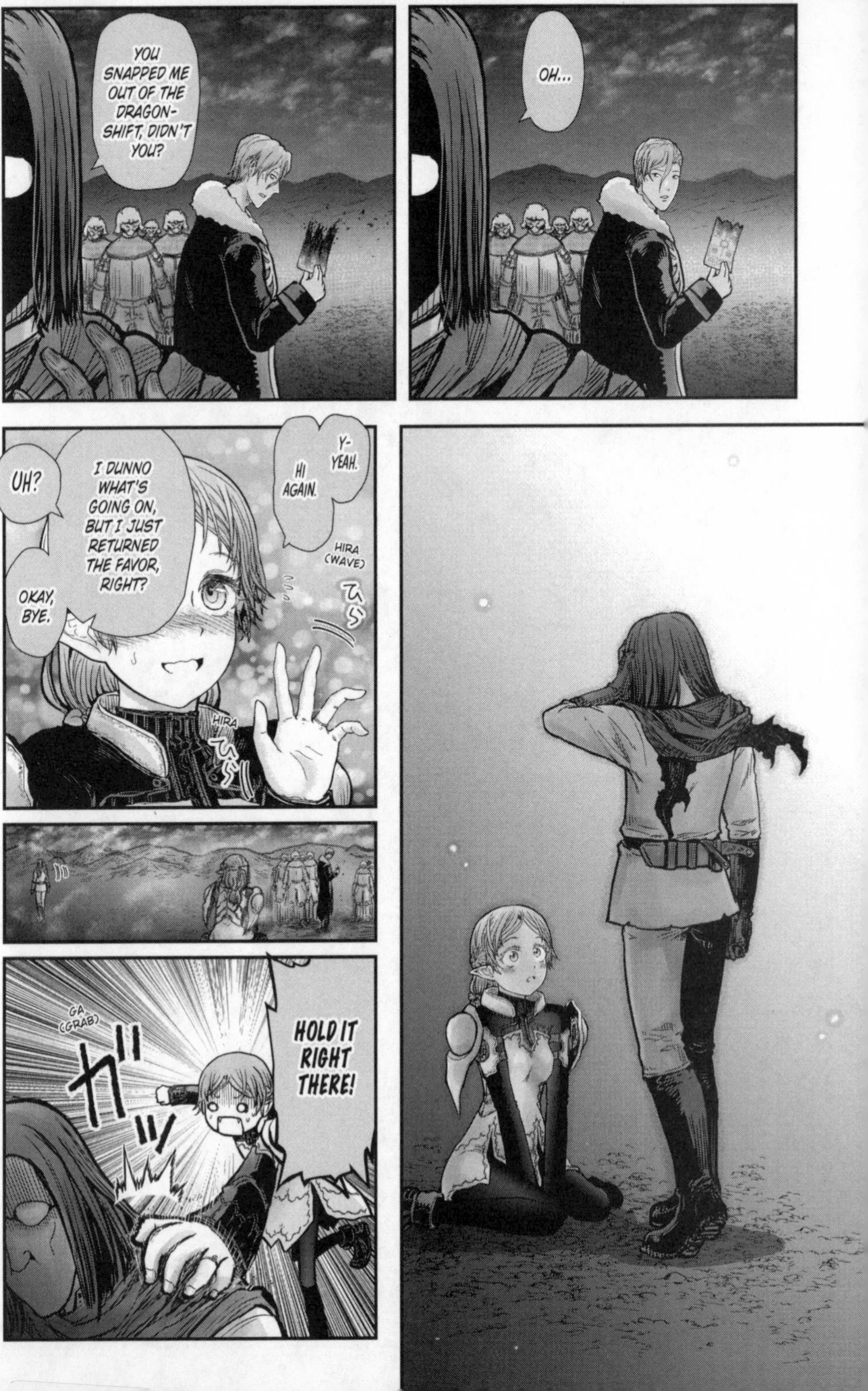
OH...
YOU SNAPPED ME OUT OF THE DRAGON-SHIFT, DIDN'T YOU?
Y-YEAH.
HI AGAIN.
HIRA (WAVE)
ひら
I DUNNO WHAT'S GOING ON, BUT I JUST RETURNED THE FAVOR, RIGHT?
UH?
OKAY, BYE.
HIRA
ひら
HOLD IT RIGHT THERE!
GA (GRAB)
ガッ

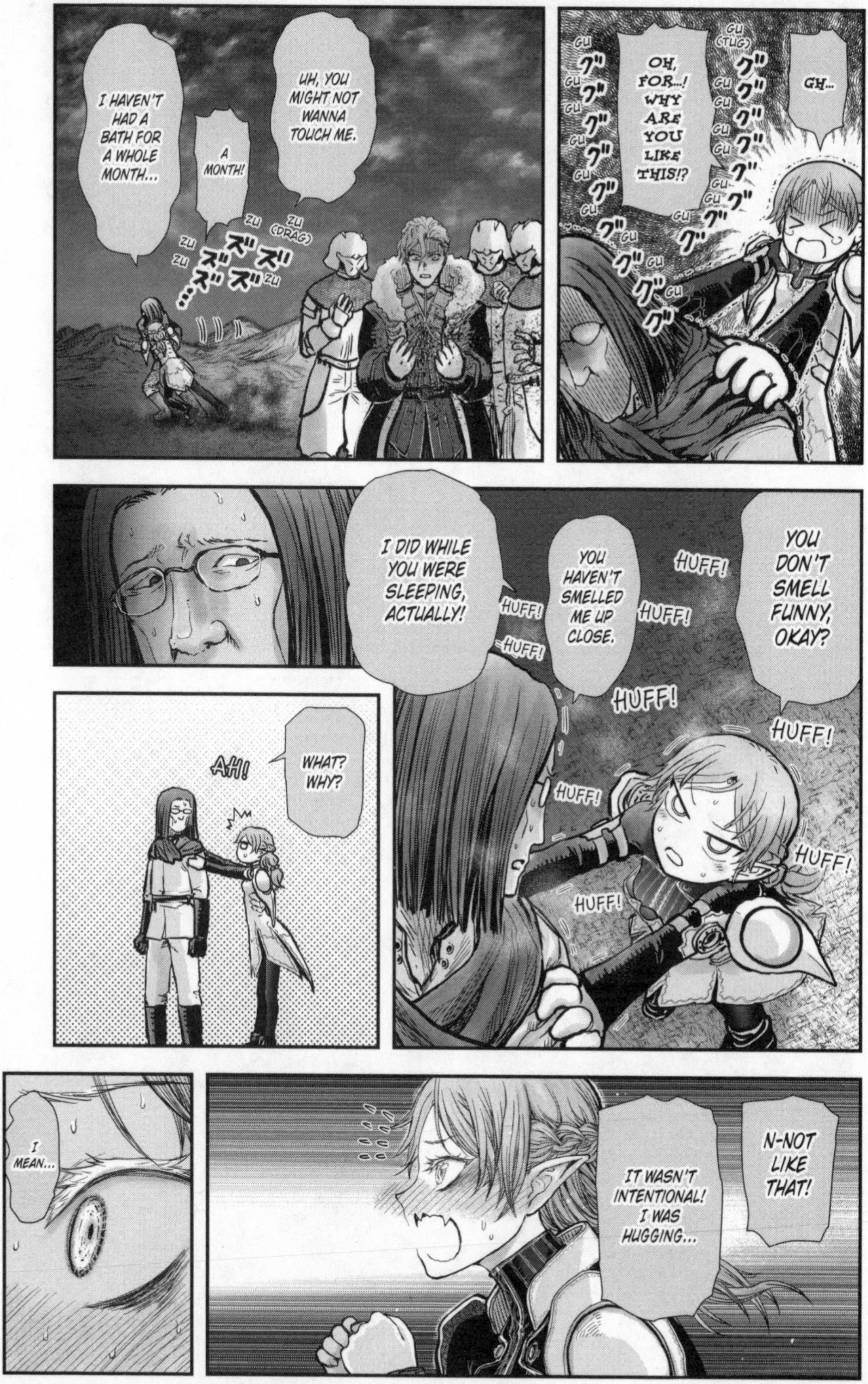
GH...
GU (TUG)
グググググググ
GU GU GU GU GU GU GU GU GU GU GU GU GU GU GU GU
OH, FOR...! WHY ARE YOU LIKE THIS!?
UH, YOU MIGHT NOT WANNA TOUCH ME.
ZU (DRAG)
ズズズズ...
ZU ZU ZU
A MONTH!
I HAVEN'T HAD A BATH FOR A WHOLE MONTH...
YOU DON'T SMELL FUNNY, OKAY?
HUFF! HUFF! HUFF! HUFF! HUFF! HUFF!
YOU HAVEN'T SMELLED ME UP CLOSE.
HUFF! HUFF! HUFF!
I DID WHILE YOU WERE SLEEPING, ACTUALLY!
WHAT? WHY?
AH!
N-NOT LIKE THAT!
IT WASN'T INTENTIONAL! I WAS HUGGING...
I MEAN...

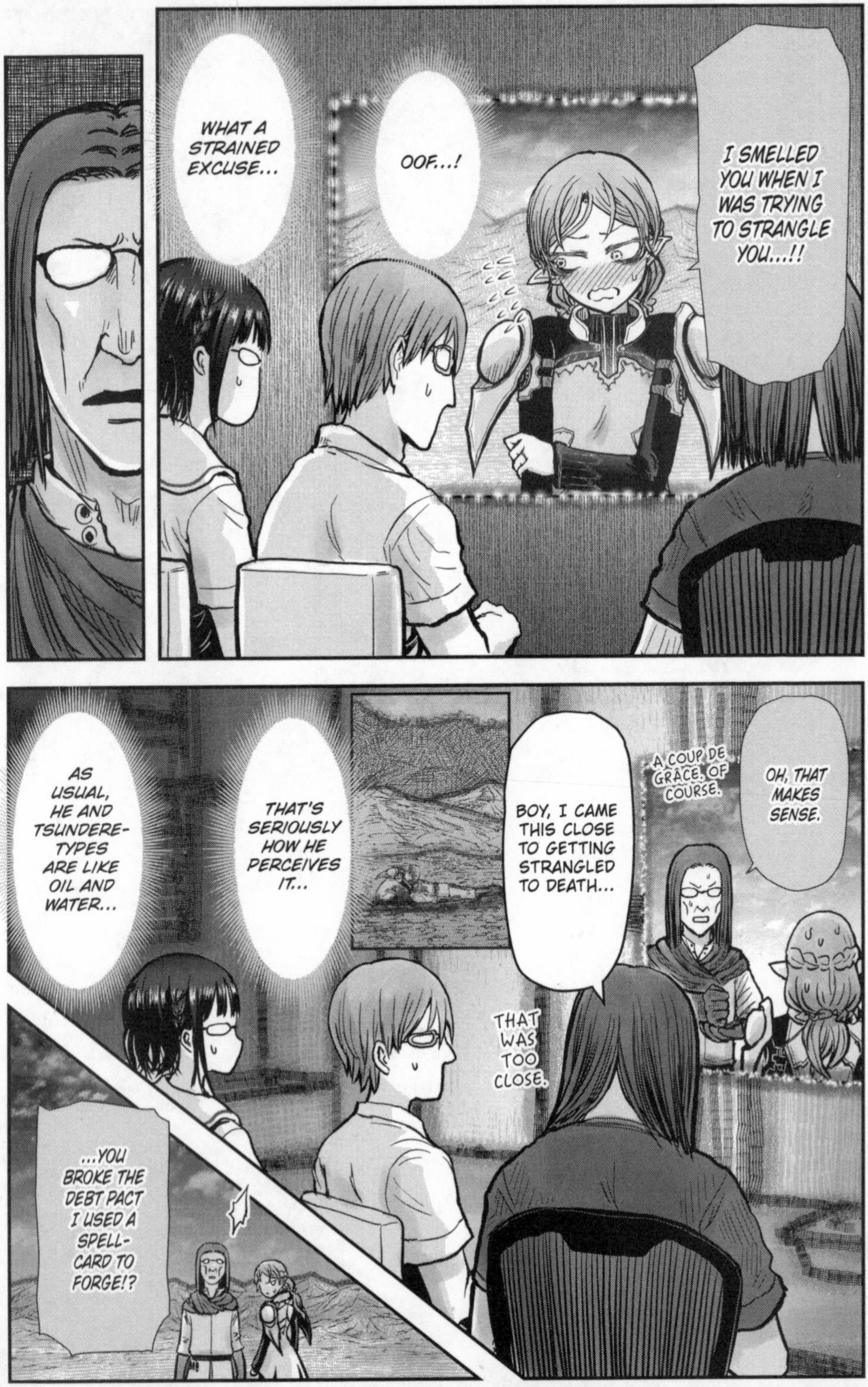
I SMELLED YOU WHEN I WAS TRYING TO STRANGLE YOU...!!
OOF...!
WHAT A STRAINED EXCUSE...
OH, THAT MAKES SENSE.
A COUP DE GRACE, OF COURSE.
BOY, I CAME THIS CLOSE TO GETTING STRANGLED TO DEATH...
THAT WAS TOO CLOSE.
THAT'S SERIOUSLY HOW HE PERCEIVES IT...
AS USUAL, HE AND TSUNDERE-TYPES ARE LIKE OIL AND WATER...
...YOU BROKE THE DEBT PACT I USED A SPELL-CARD TO FORGE!?

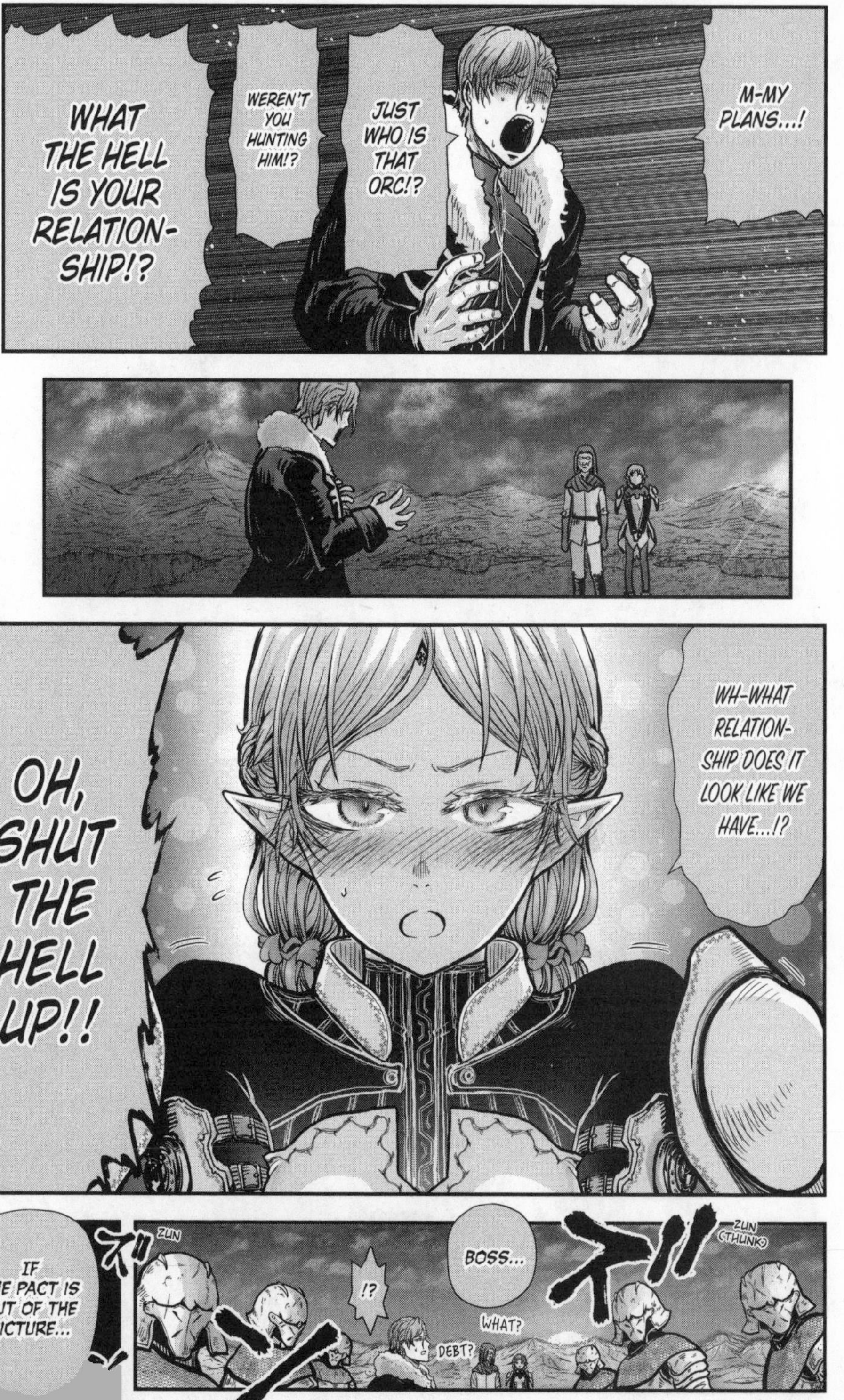
M-MY PLANS...!
JUST WHO IS THAT ORC!?
WEREN'T YOU HUNTING HIM!?
WHAT THE HELL IS YOUR RELATION-SHIP!?
WH-WHAT RELATION-SHIP DOES IT LOOK LIKE WE HAVE...!?
OH, SHUT THE HELL UP!!
ZUN (THUNK)
BOSS...
!?
WHAT?
DEBT?
ZUN
IF THE PACT IS OUT OF THE PICTURE...

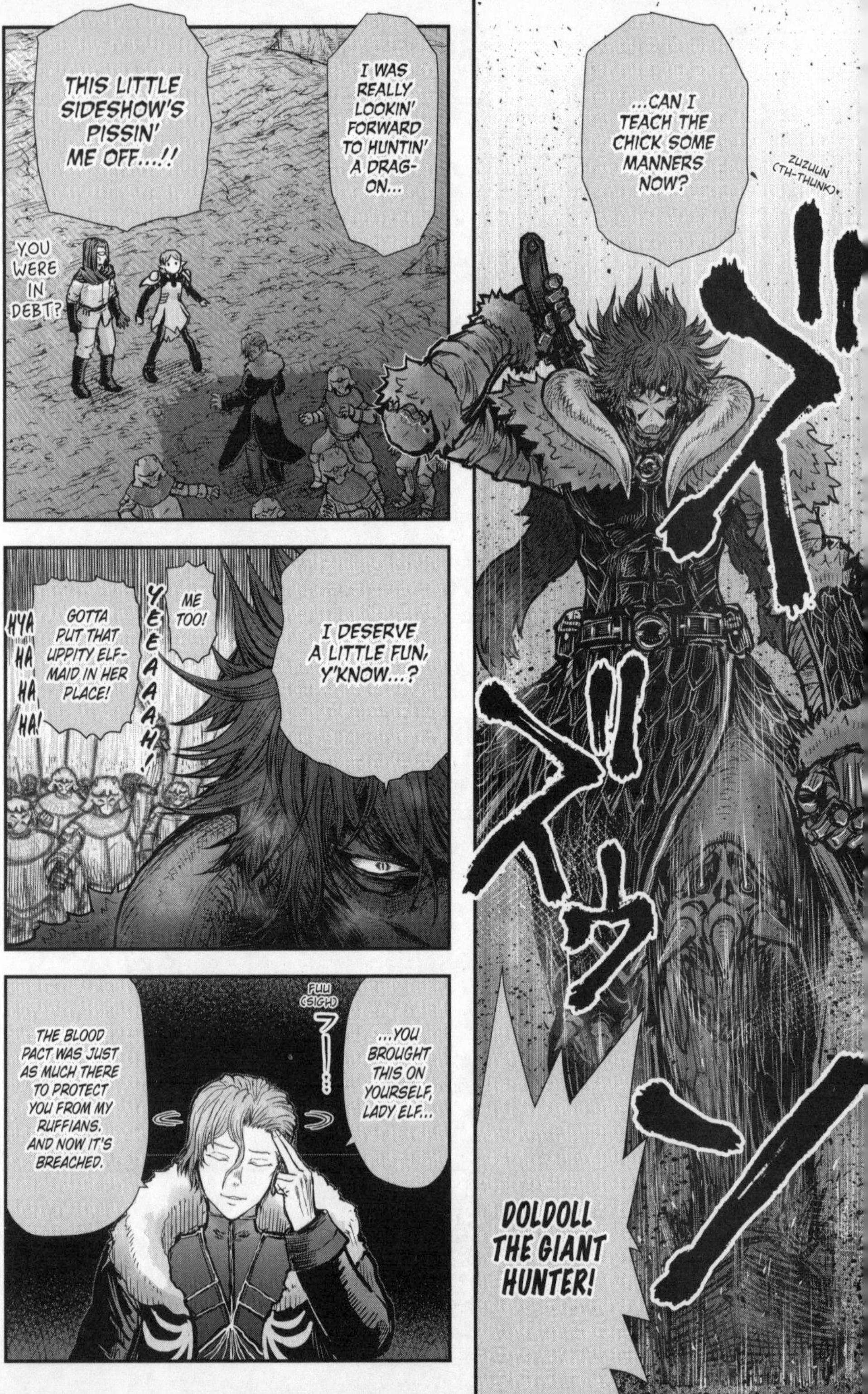
...CAN I TEACH THE CHICK SOME MANNERS NOW?
ZUZUUN (TH-THUNK)
DOLDOLL THE GIANT HUNTER!
I WAS REALLY LOOKIN' FORWARD TO HUNTIN' A DRAG-ON...
THIS LITTLE SIDESHOW'S PISSIN' ME OFF...!!
YOU WERE IN DEBT?
I DESERVE A LITTLE FUN, Y'KNOW...?
YEEAAAAH!
ME TOO!
GOTTA PUT THAT UPPITY ELF-MAID IN HER PLACE!
HYA HA HA HA HA!
FUU (SIGH)
...YOU BROUGHT THIS ON YOURSELF, LADY ELF...
THE BLOOD PACT WAS JUST AS MUCH THERE TO PROTECT YOU FROM MY RUFFIANS. AND NOW IT'S BREACHED.

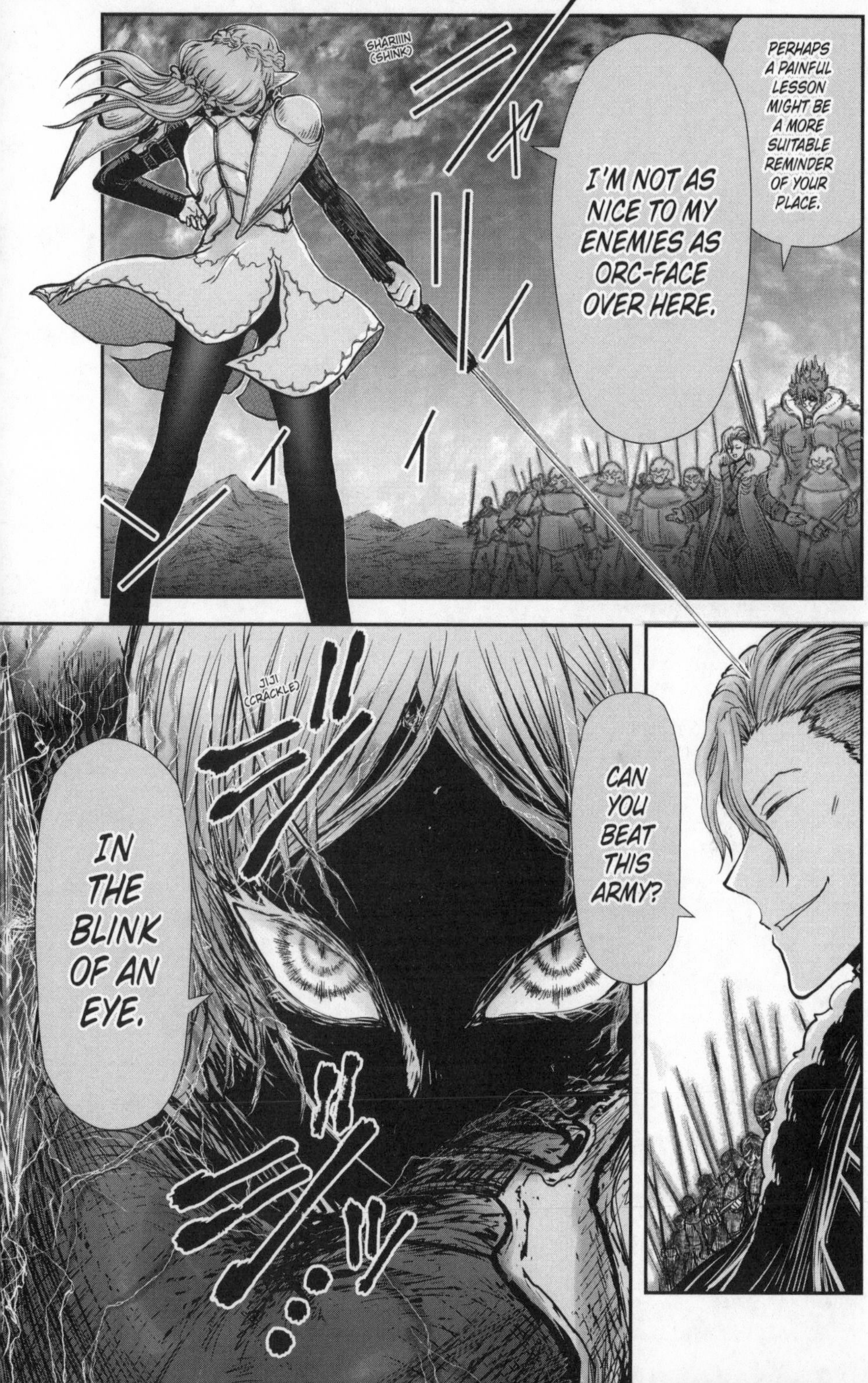
PERHAPS A PAINFUL LESSON MIGHT BE A MORE SUITABLE REMINDER OF YOUR PLACE.
I'M NOT AS NICE TO MY ENEMIES AS ORC-FACE OVER HERE.
SHARIIIN (SHINK)
CAN YOU BEAT THIS ARMY?
JIJI (CRACKLE)
IN THE BLINK OF AN EYE.

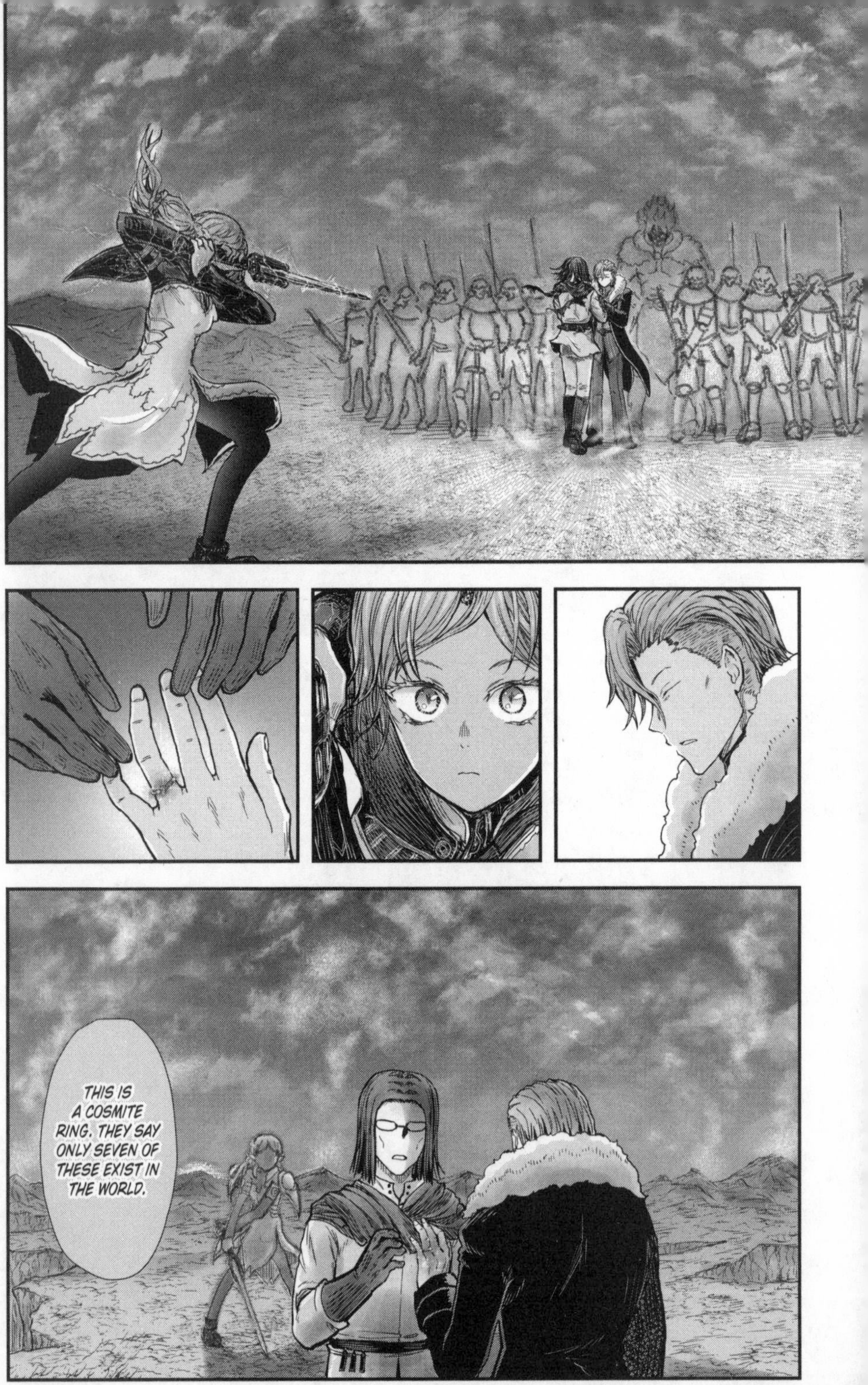
THIS IS A COSMITE RING. THEY SAY ONLY SEVEN OF THESE EXIST IN THE WORLD.

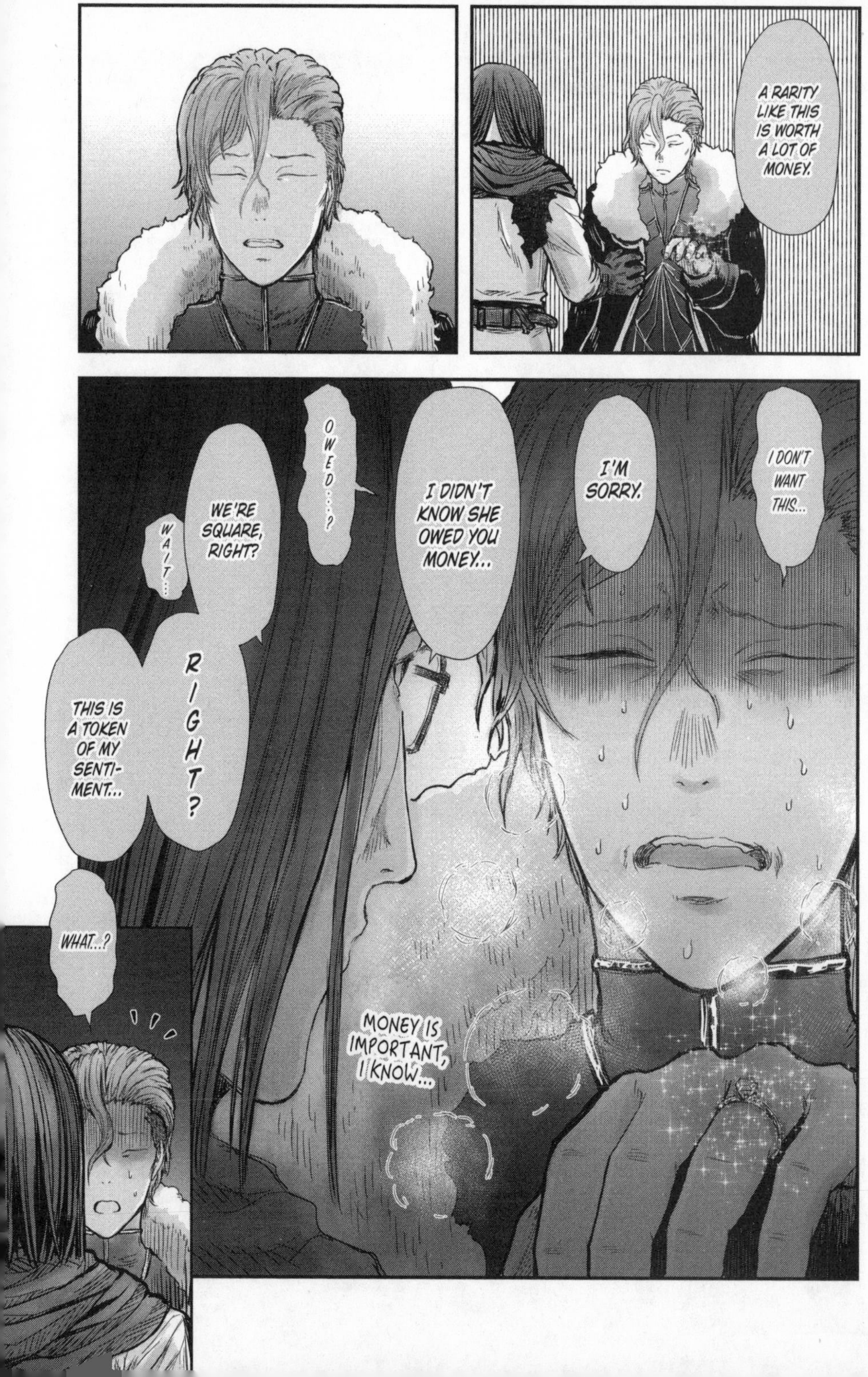
A RARITY LIKE THIS IS WORTH A LOT OF MONEY.
I DON'T WANT THIS...
I'M SORRY.
I DIDN'T KNOW SHE OWED YOU MONEY...
OWED...?
WE'RE SQUARE, RIGHT?
WAIT...
RIGHT?
THIS IS A TOKEN OF MY SENTIMENT...
MONEY IS IMPORTANT, I KNOW...
WHAT...?

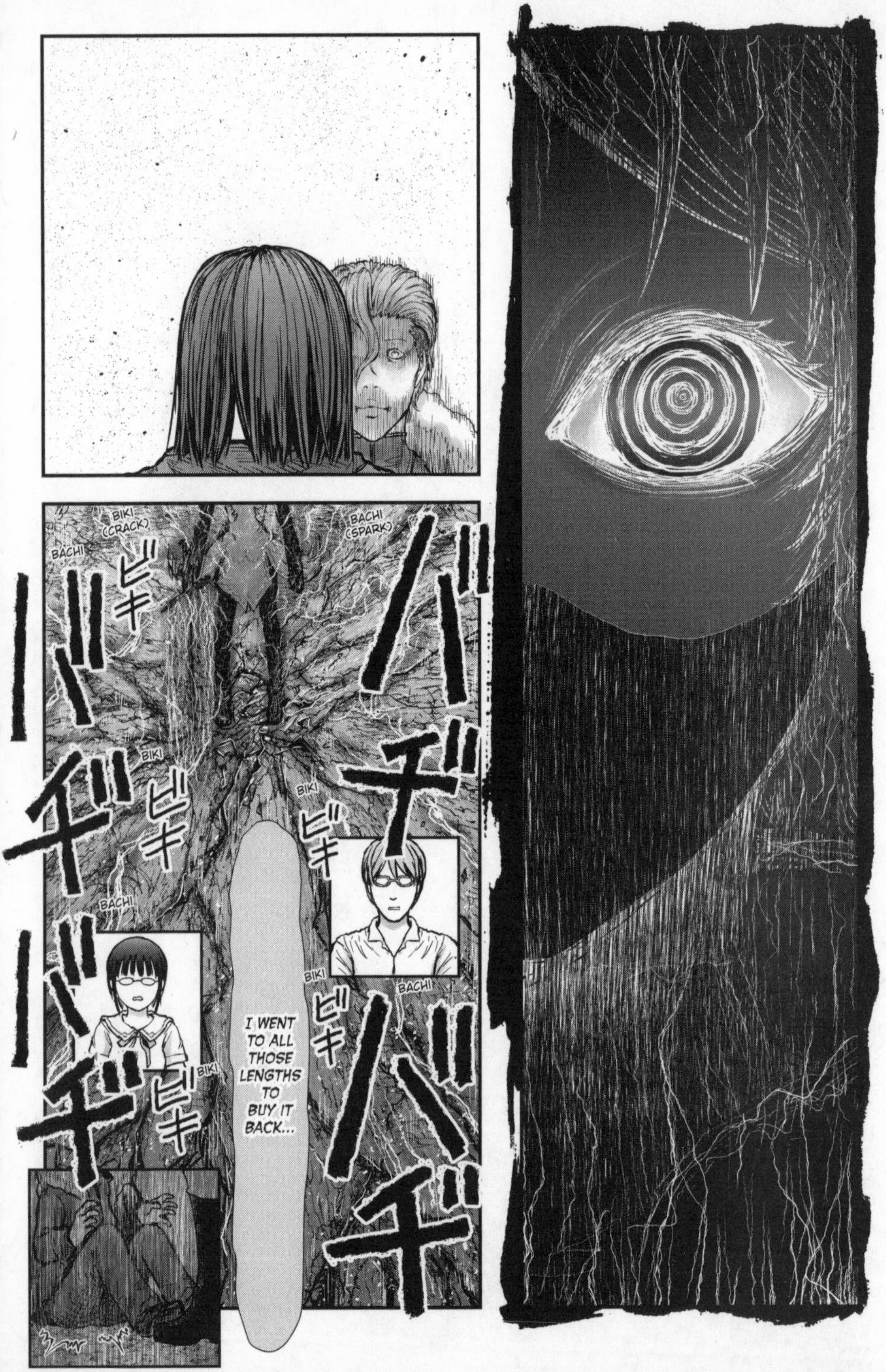
BACHI (SPARK)
バチ
BIKI (CRACK)
ビキ
BACHI
バチ
BIKI
ビキ
BIKI
ビキ
BACHI
BACHI
BIKI
ビキ
バチ
I WENT TO ALL THOSE LENGTHS TO BUY IT BACK...
BIKI
ビキ
バチ

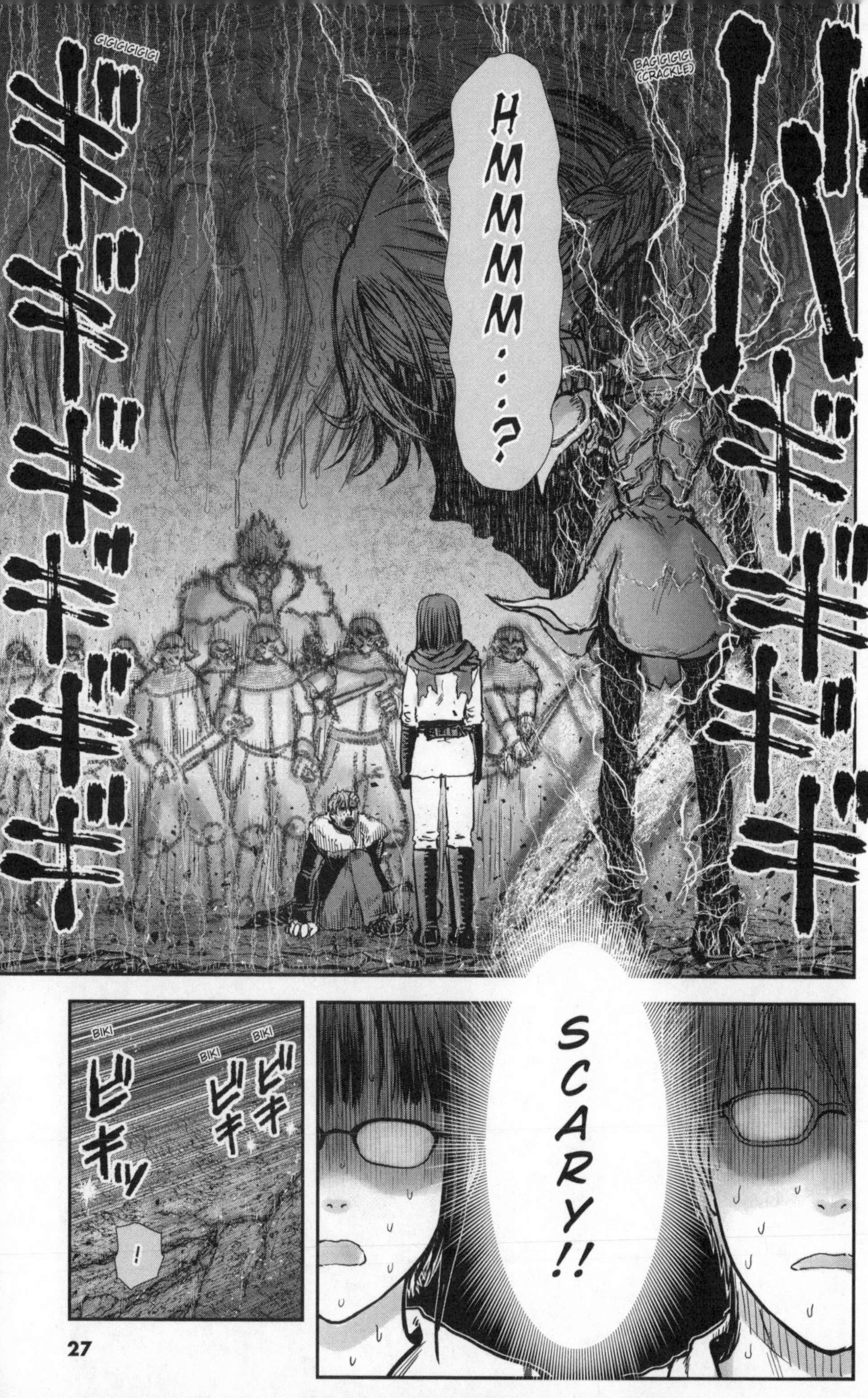

BAGIGIGIGI (CRACKLE)
HMMMM...?
GIGIGIGIGI
SCARY!!
BIKI
BIKI
BIKI
!

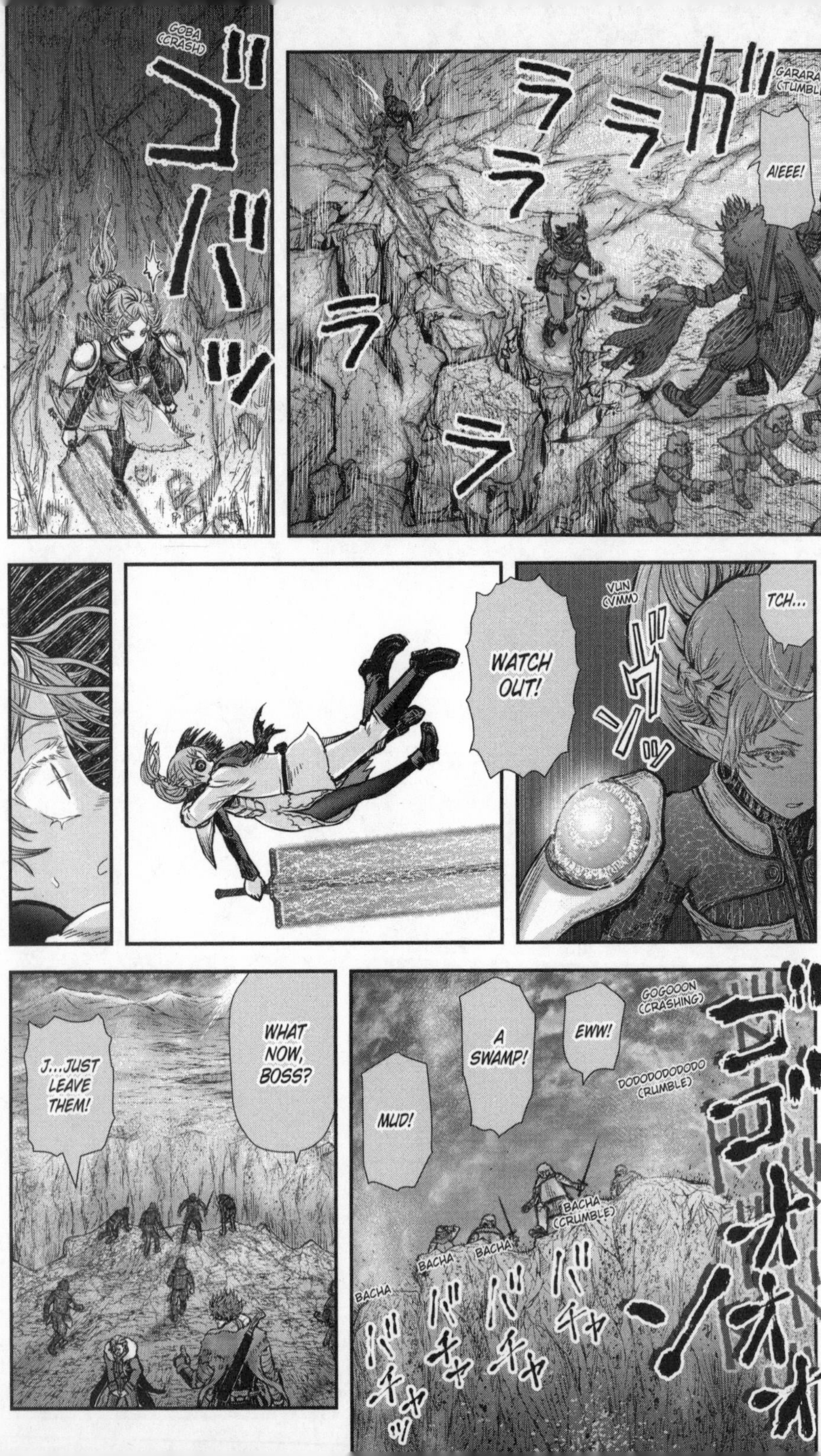

GARARARA (TUMBLE)
AIEEE!
GOBA (CRASH)
TCH...
VUN (VMM)
WATCH OUT!
GOGOOON (CRASHING)
EWW!
DODODODODODO (RUMBLE)
A SWAMP!
MUD!
BACHA (CRUMBLE)
BACHA
BACHA
BACHA
WHAT NOW, BOSS?
J...JUST LEAVE THEM!

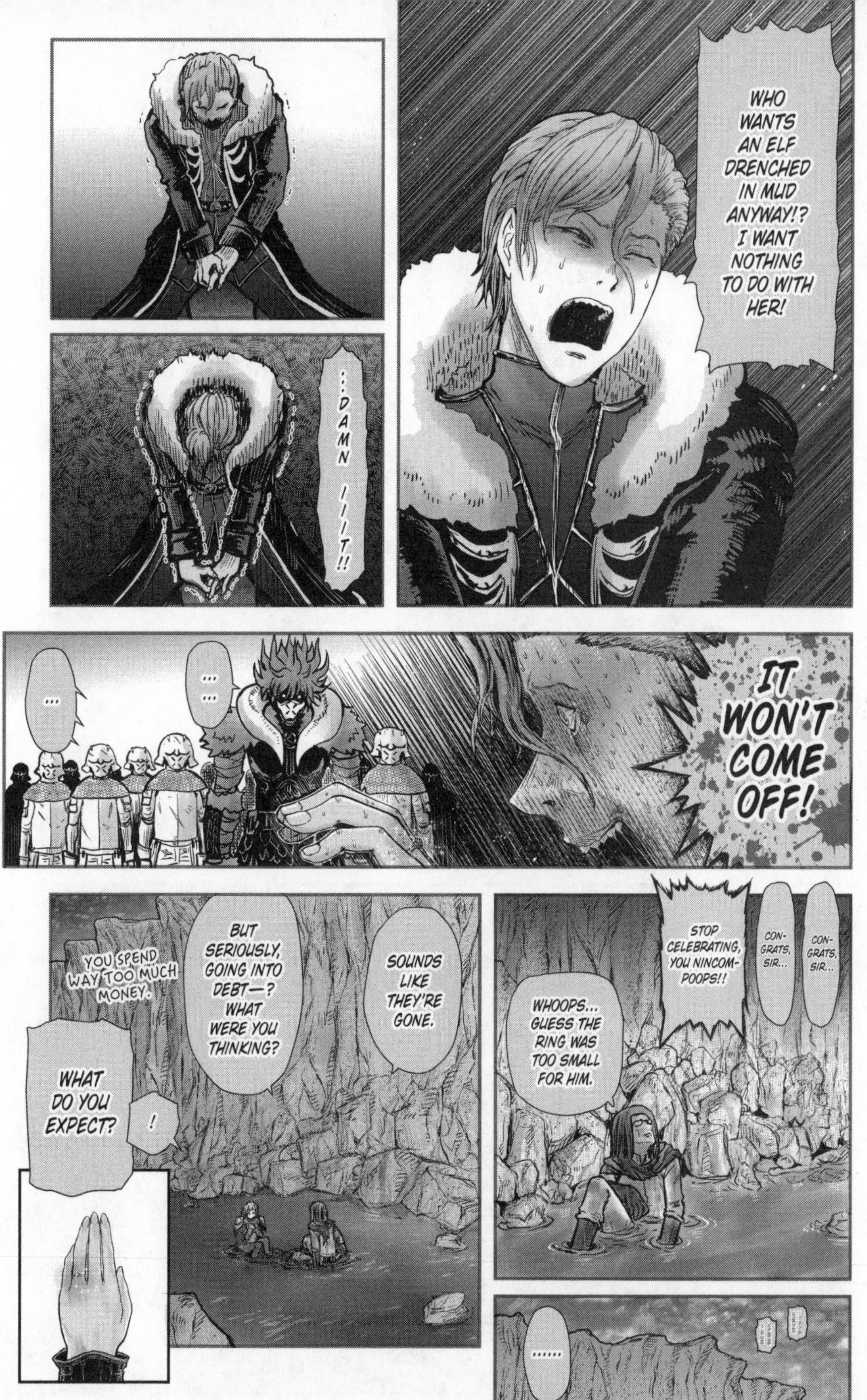
WHO WANTS AN ELF DRENCHED IN MUD ANYWAY!? I WANT NOTHING TO DO WITH HER!
...DAMN IIIT!!
IT WON'T COME OFF!
... ...
...
CON-GRATS, SIR...
CON-GRATS, SIR...
STOP CELEBRATING, YOU NINCOM-POOPS!!
WHOOPS... GUESS THE RING WAS TOO SMALL FOR HIM.
......
SOUNDS LIKE THEY'RE GONE.
BUT SERIOUSLY, GOING INTO DEBT—? WHAT WERE YOU THINKING?
YOU SPEND WAY TOO MUCH MONEY.
WHAT DO YOU EXPECT?
!

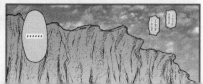

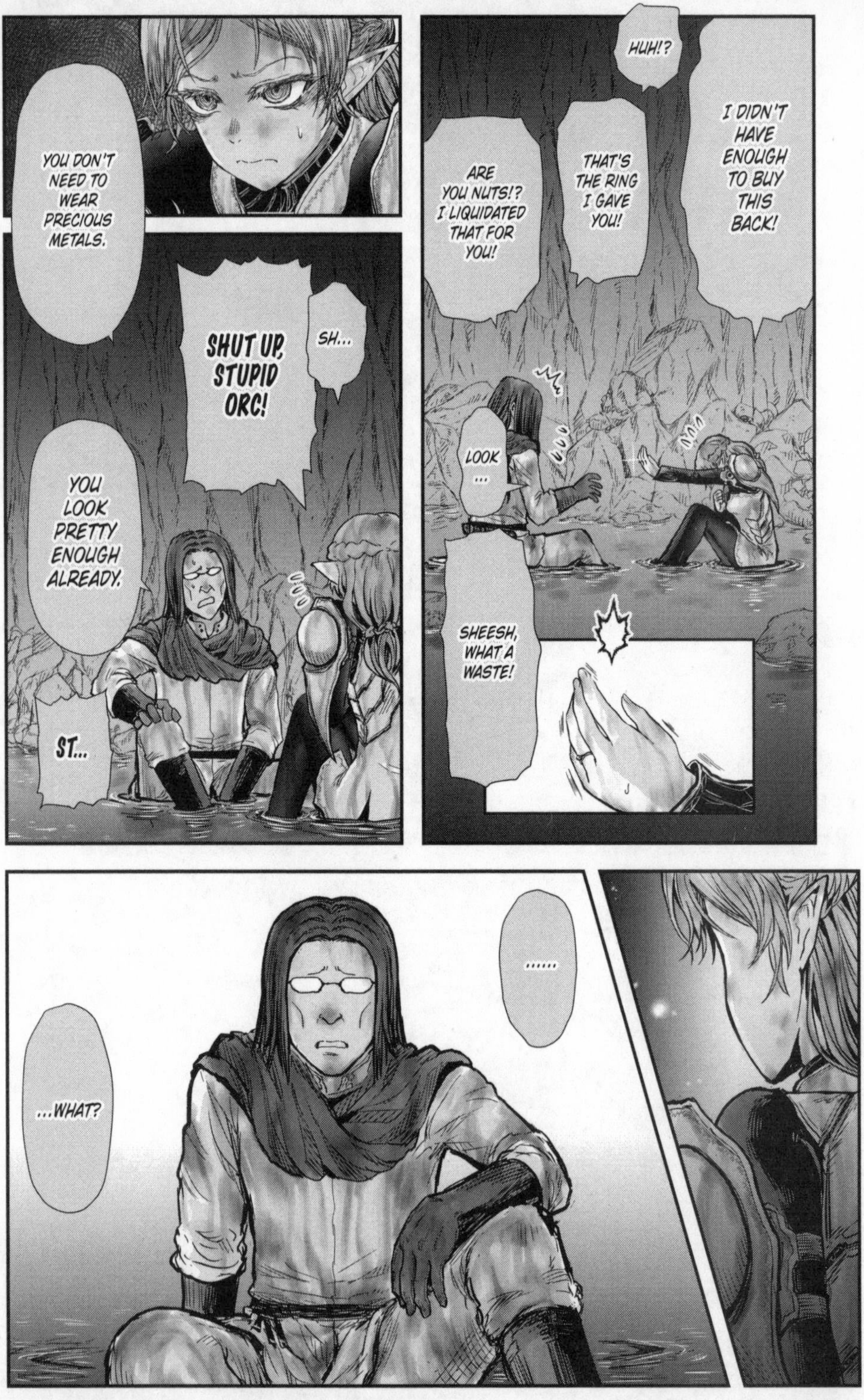
I DIDN'T HAVE ENOUGH TO BUY THIS BACK!
HUH!?
THAT'S THE RING I GAVE YOU!
ARE YOU NUTS!? I LIQUIDATED THAT FOR YOU!
LOOK ...
SHEESH, WHAT A WASTE!
YOU DON'T NEED TO WEAR PRECIOUS METALS.
SH...
SHUT UP, STUPID ORC!
YOU LOOK PRETTY ENOUGH ALREADY.
ST...
......
...WHAT?

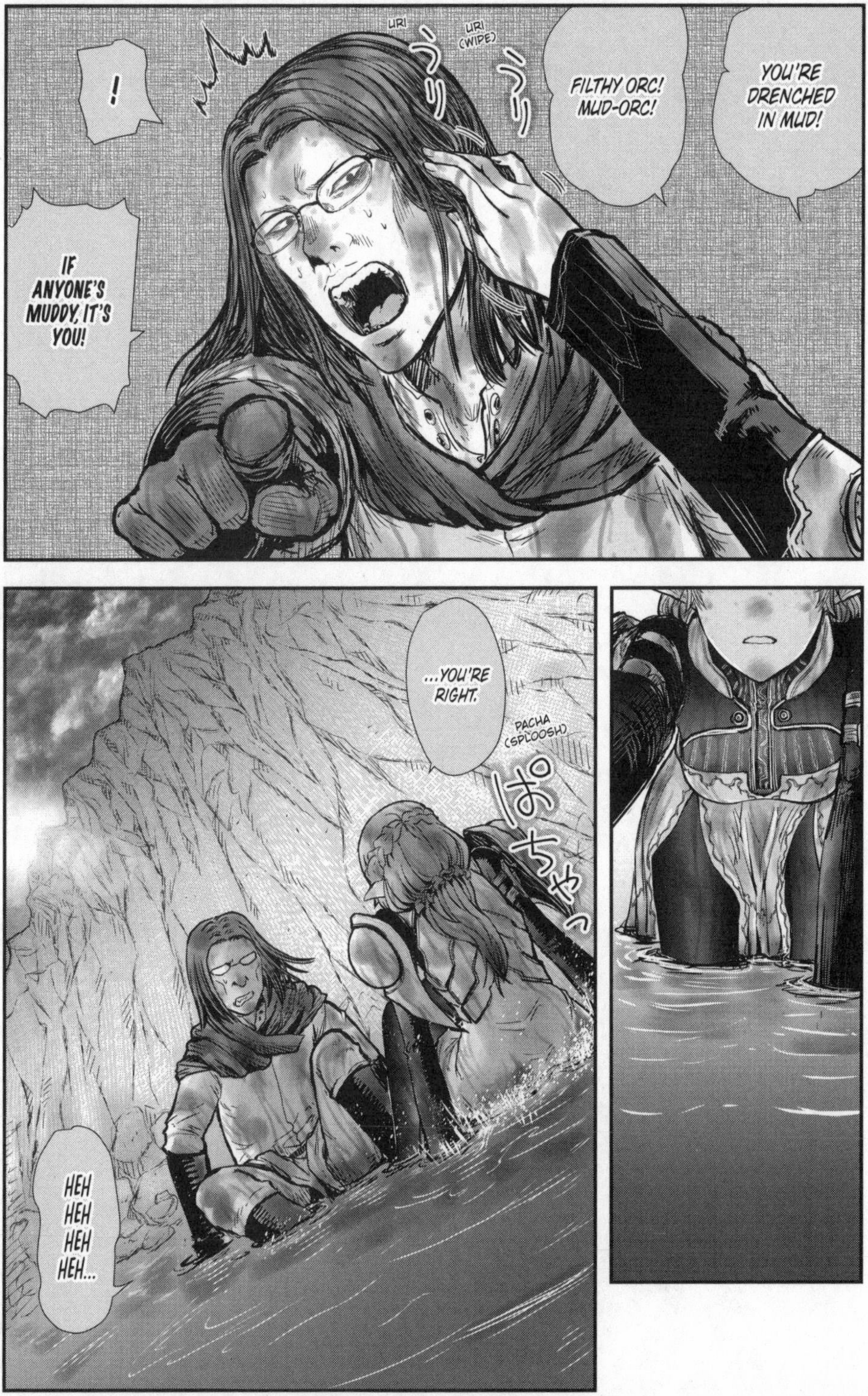
YOU'RE DRENCHED IN MUD!
FILTHY ORC! MUD-ORC!
URI URI (WIPE)
!
IF ANYONE'S MUDDY, IT'S YOU!
...YOU'RE RIGHT.
PACHA (SPLOOSH)
ぱちゃっ
HEH HEH HEH HEH...

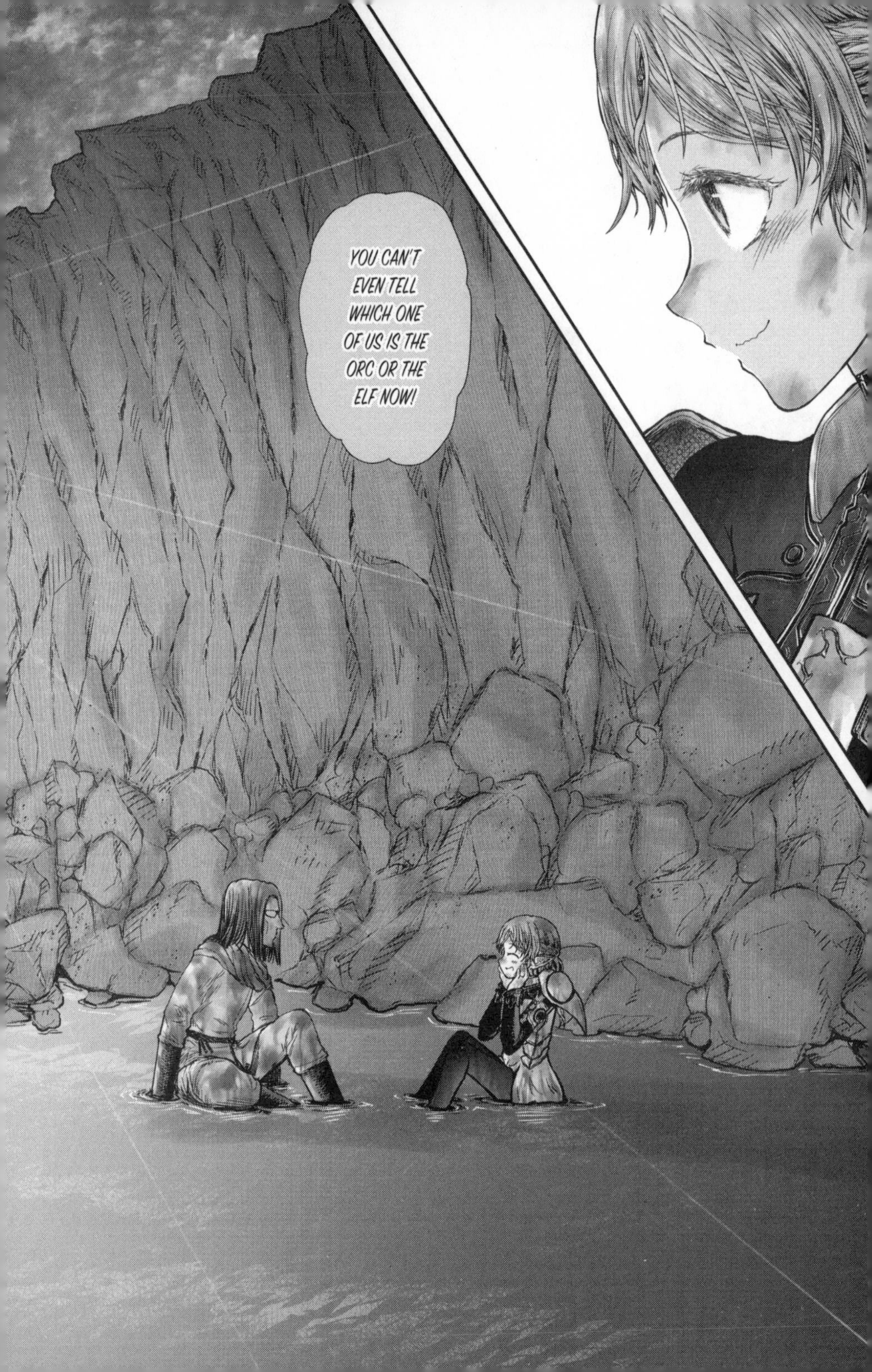
YOU CAN'T EVEN TELL WHICH ONE OF US IS THE ORC OR THE ELF NOW!

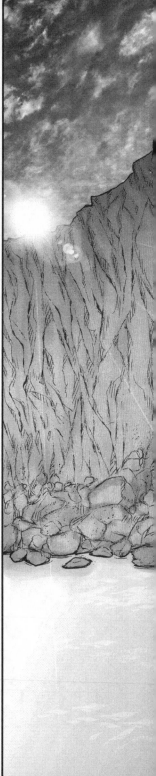

...I'VE HAD ENOUGH OF BEING DIRTY.

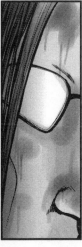

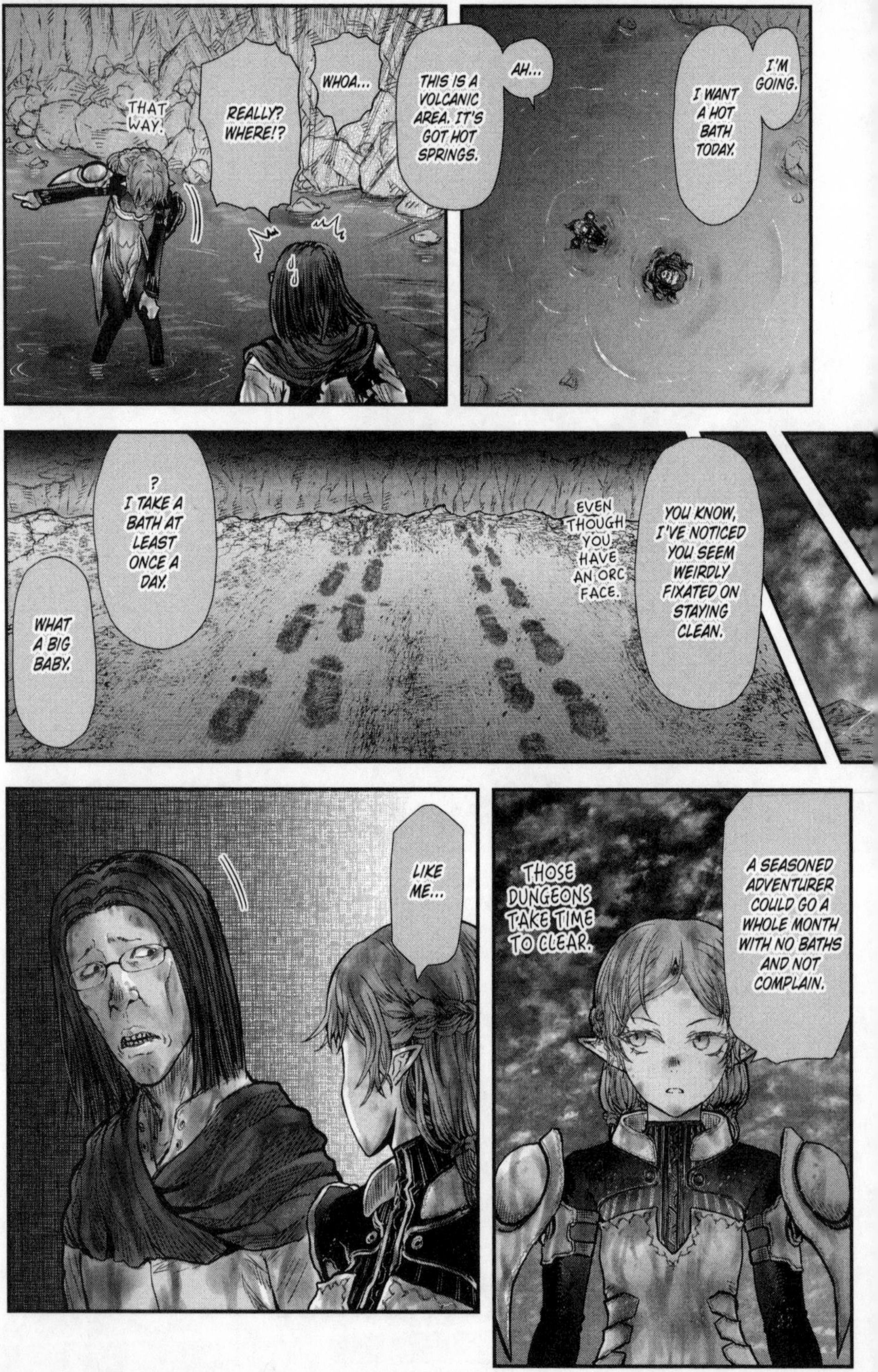
I'M GOING.
I WANT A HOT BATH TODAY.
AH...
THIS IS A VOLCANIC AREA. IT'S GOT HOT SPRINGS.
WHOA...
REALLY? WHERE!?
THAT WAY.
YOU KNOW, I'VE NOTICED YOU SEEM WEIRDLY FIXATED ON STAYING CLEAN.
EVEN THOUGH YOU HAVE AN ORC FACE.
? I TAKE A BATH AT LEAST ONCE A DAY.
WHAT A BIG BABY.
A SEASONED ADVENTURER COULD GO A WHOLE MONTH WITH NO BATHS AND NOT COMPLAIN.
THOSE DUNGEONS TAKE TIME TO CLEAR.
LIKE ME...

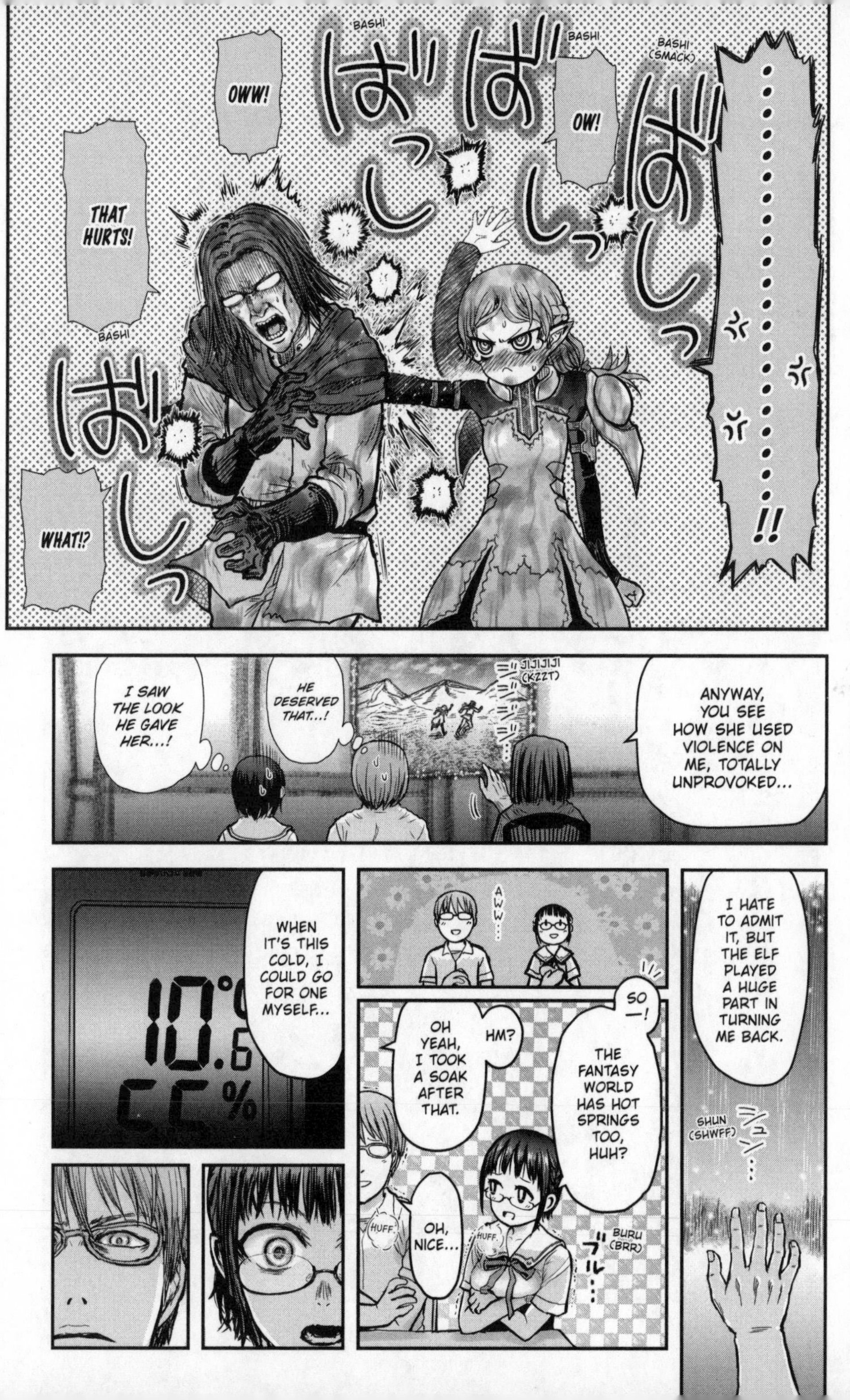
……………!!
BASHI (SMACK)
ばしっ
OW!
BASHI
ばしっ
OWW!
BASHI
ばしっ
THAT HURTS!
WHAT!?
ANYWAY, YOU SEE HOW SHE USED VIOLENCE ON ME, TOTALLY UNPROVOKED...
JIJIJIJI (KZZT)
HE DESERVED THAT...!
I SAW THE LOOK HE GAVE HER...!
I HATE TO ADMIT IT, BUT THE ELF PLAYED A HUGE PART IN TURNING ME BACK.
SHUN (SHWFF)
シュン…
AWW...
SO—!
THE FANTASY WORLD HAS HOT SPRINGS TOO, HUH?
HM?
OH YEAH, I TOOK A SOAK AFTER THAT.
OH, NICE...
HUFF.
HUFF.
BURU (BRR)
ブル…
WHEN IT'S THIS COLD, I COULD GO FOR ONE MYSELF...

IT'S 10°C IN AUGUST!?
IT'S WAY TOO COLD!
ゴオオオオオ
GOOOOOOOOOOO (HUMMM)
UNCLE, TURN OFF THE AC SPELL FOR A WHILE!
オオオオ
SURE.
ヒャ〜〜〜…
HIYAAA (CHILL)
ガタガタ
GATAGATA (SHIVER)
ガタガタ
GATAGATA
ガタガタ
GATAGATA
ガタガタ
GATAGATA

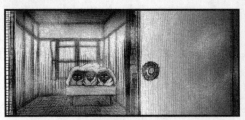

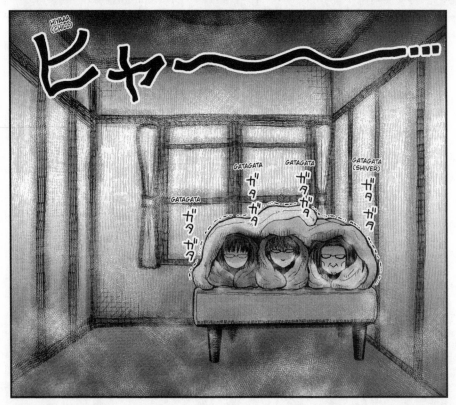

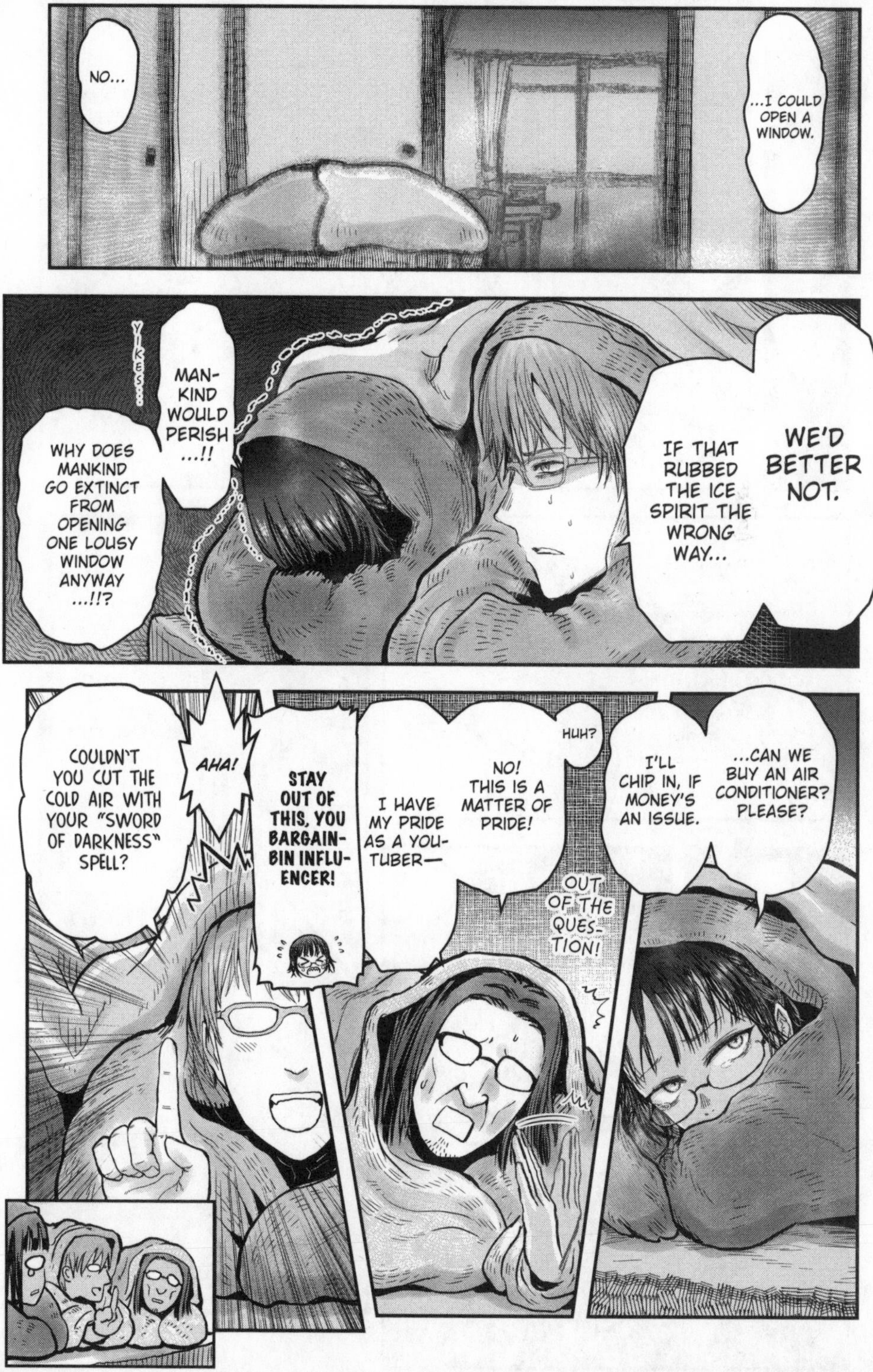

...I COULD OPEN A WINDOW.
NO...
WE'D BETTER NOT.
IF THAT RUBBED THE ICE SPIRIT THE WRONG WAY...
MAN-KIND WOULD PERISH ...!!
YIKES...
WHY DOES MANKIND GO EXTINCT FROM OPENING ONE LOUSY WINDOW ANYWAY ...!!?
...CAN WE BUY AN AIR CONDITIONER? PLEASE?
I'LL CHIP IN, IF MONEY'S AN ISSUE.
HUH?
NO! THIS IS A MATTER OF PRIDE!
OUT OF THE QUES-TION!
I HAVE MY PRIDE AS A YOU-TUBER—
STAY OUT OF THIS, YOU BARGAIN-BIN INFLU-ENCER!
AHA!
COULDN'T YOU CUT THE COLD AIR WITH YOUR "SWORD OF DARKNESS" SPELL?

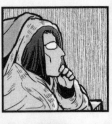

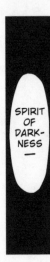

DOESN'T IT CUT INVISIBLE FORCES?
HM?
OH, I DON'T THINK IT WORKS LIKE THAT...
WHAT IF WE JUST DROP THE MAGIC AND BUY AN AC UNIT ALREADY?
TAKAFUMI, GIVE ME YOUR CELL.
?
SPIRIT OF DARKNESS —
BECOME A BLADE AND REVEAL THY FORM.
VUN (VMM)
!
SHU (FWIP)
?
?
LOOK.

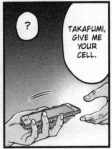

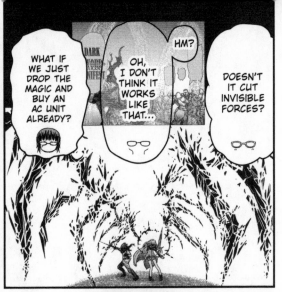

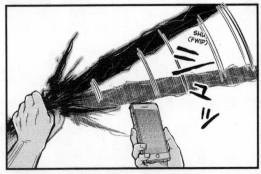

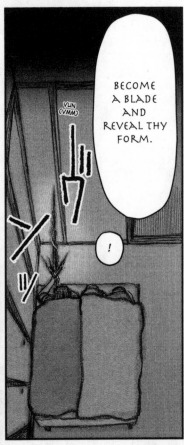

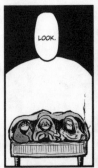

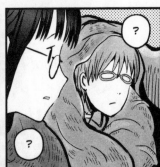

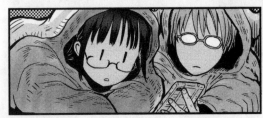

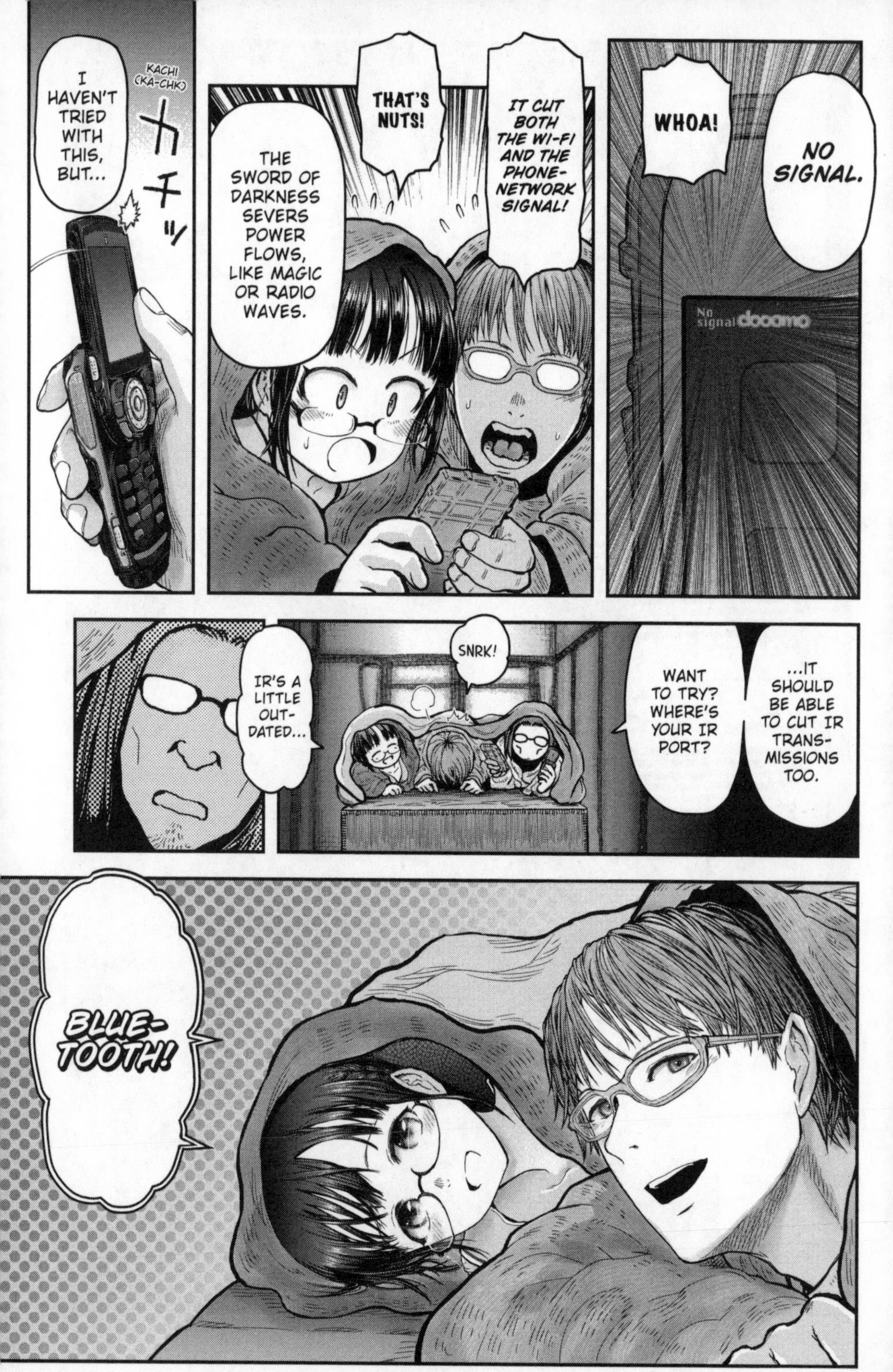
NO SIGNAL.
WHOA!
No signal docomo
IT CUT BOTH THE WI-FI AND THE PHONE-NETWORK SIGNAL!
THAT'S NUTS!
THE SWORD OF DARKNESS SEVERS POWER FLOWS, LIKE MAGIC OR RADIO WAVES.
カチッ
KACHI (KA-CHK)
I HAVEN'T TRIED WITH THIS, BUT...
...IT SHOULD BE ABLE TO CUT IR TRANSMISSIONS TOO.
WANT TO TRY? WHERE'S YOUR IR PORT?
SNRK!
IR'S A LITTLE OUT-DATED...
BLUE-TOOTH!

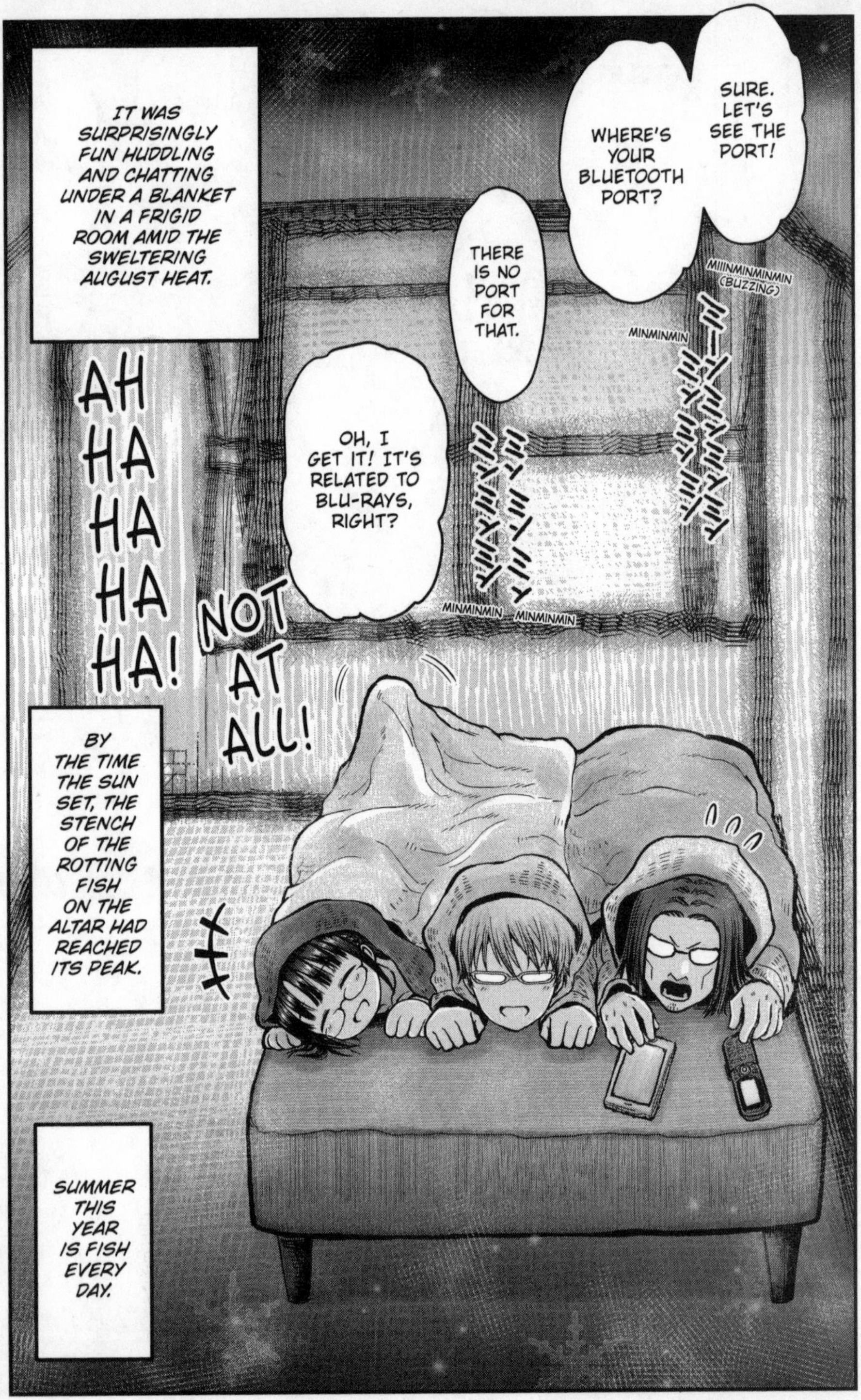
SURE. LET'S SEE THE PORT!
WHERE'S YOUR BLUETOOTH PORT?
MIIINMINMINMIN (BUZZING)
IT WAS SURPRISINGLY FUN HUDDLING AND CHATTING UNDER A BLANKET IN A FRIGID ROOM AMID THE SWELTERING AUGUST HEAT.
THERE IS NO PORT FOR THAT.
MINMINMIN
OH, I GET IT! IT'S RELATED TO BLU-RAYS, RIGHT?
MINMINMIN
MINMINMIN
AH HA HA HA HA HA!
NOT AT ALL!
BY THE TIME THE SUN SET, THE STENCH OF THE ROTTING FISH ON THE ALTAR HAD REACHED ITS PEAK.
SUMMER THIS YEAR IS FISH EVERY DAY.

Infrared (IR) Transmissions and Bluetooth

Bluetooth is a technology widely used in laptops and smartphones. IR, conversely, utilizes light. In addition to being used for TV remotes, IR was adopted for cellular phones in pre-smartphone days via a standard called IrDA.
Fun fact: The name "Bluetooth" comes from a king of Denmark named Harald "Bluetooth" Gormsson.

TIPS

UNCLE from ANOTHER WORLD

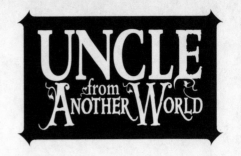

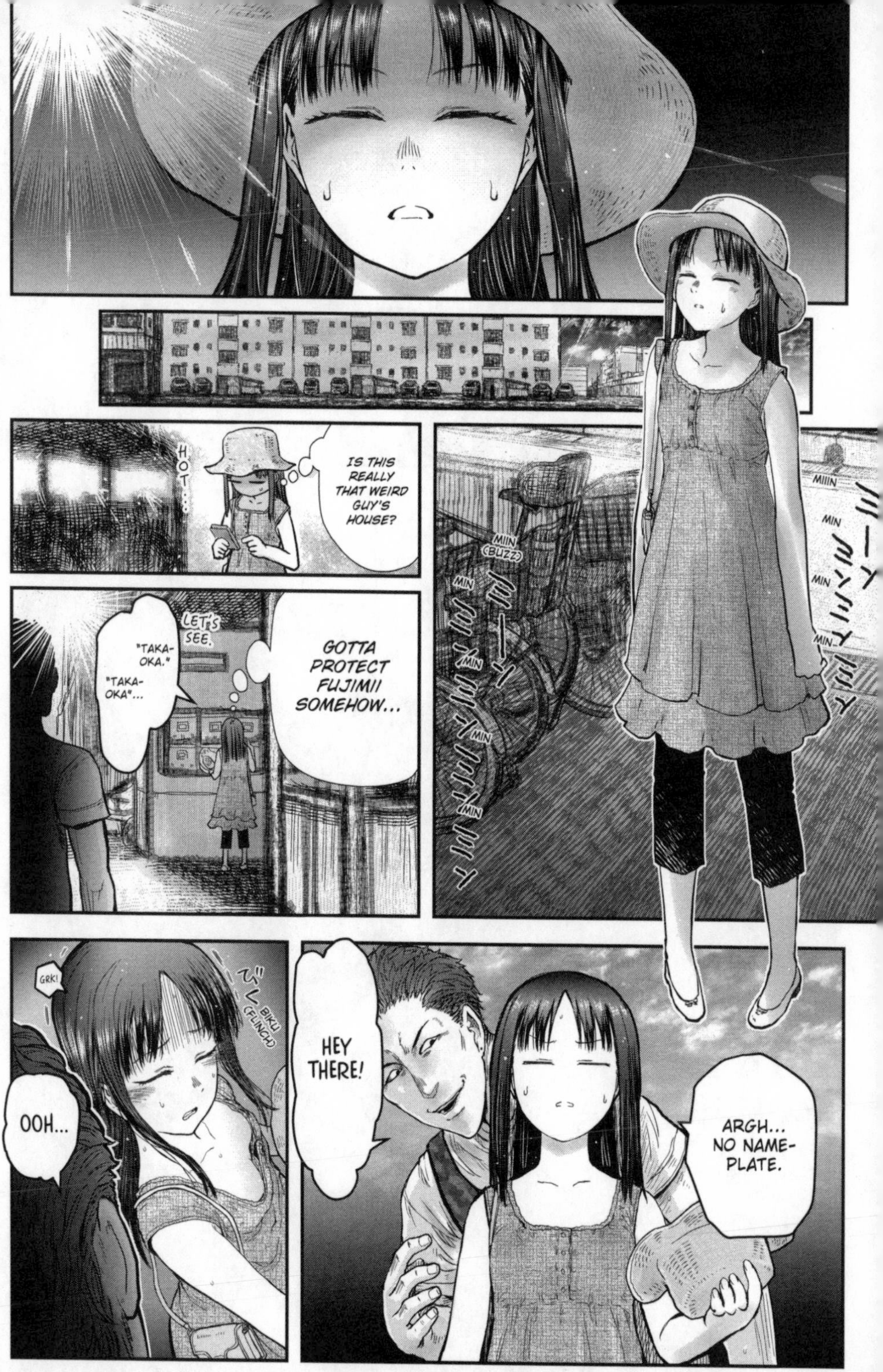
MIIN
MIN
MIN
MIN
MIIN (BUZZ)
MIN
MIN
MIN
MIN
HOT...
IS THIS REALLY THAT WEIRD GUY'S HOUSE?
GOTTA PROTECT FUJIMII SOMEHOW...
LET'S SEE.
"TAKA-OKA."
"TAKA-OKA"...
ARGH... NO NAME-PLATE.
HEY THERE!
BIKU (FLINCH)
GRK!
OOH...

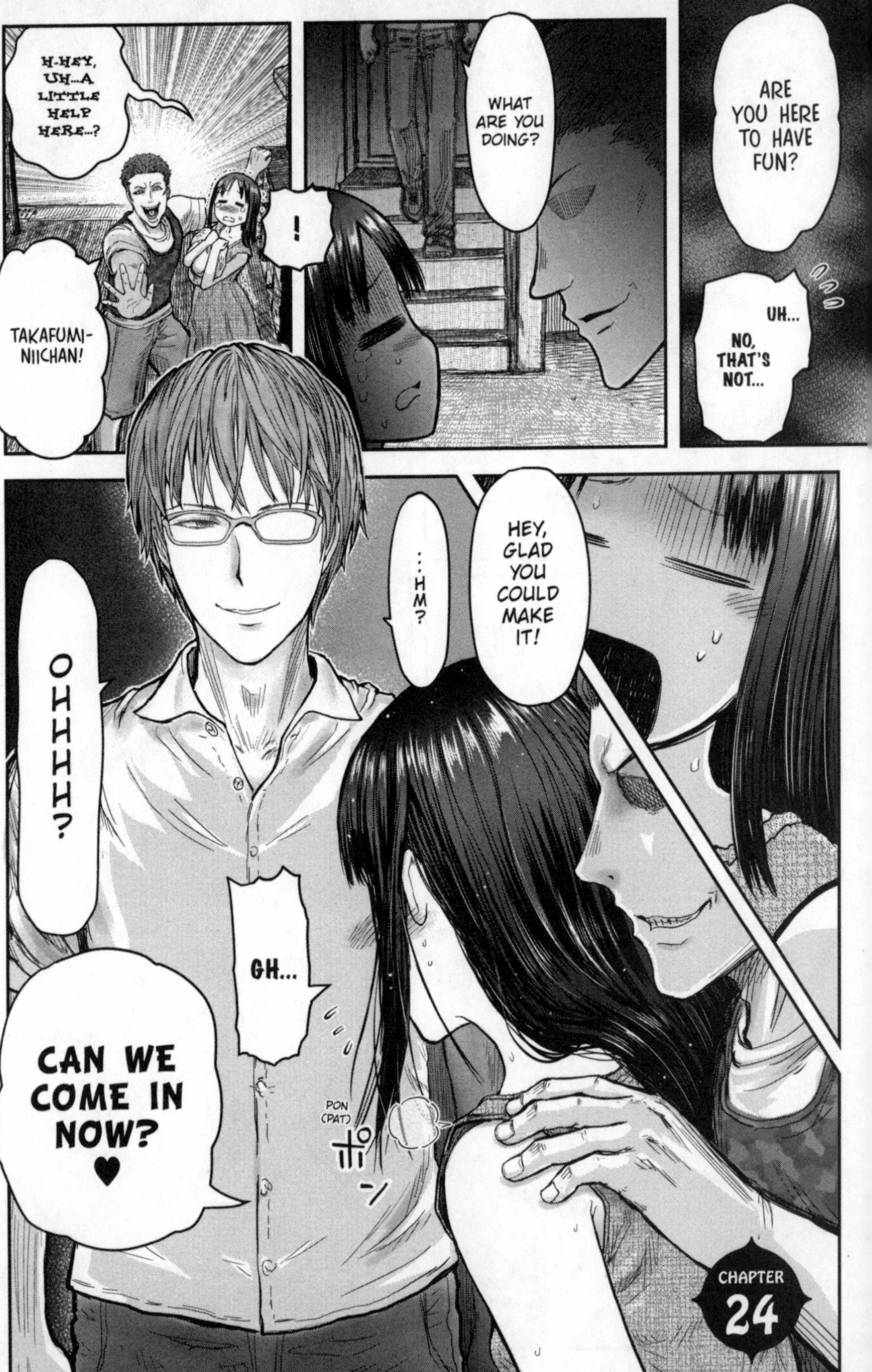

ARE YOU HERE TO HAVE FUN?
UH...
NO, THAT'S NOT...
WHAT ARE YOU DOING?
!
H-HEY, UH...A LITTLE HELP HERE...?
TAKAFUMI-NIICHAN!
HEY, GLAD YOU COULD MAKE IT!
...HM?
OHHHHH?
GH...
PON (PAT)
CAN WE COME IN NOW? ♥
CHAPTER 24

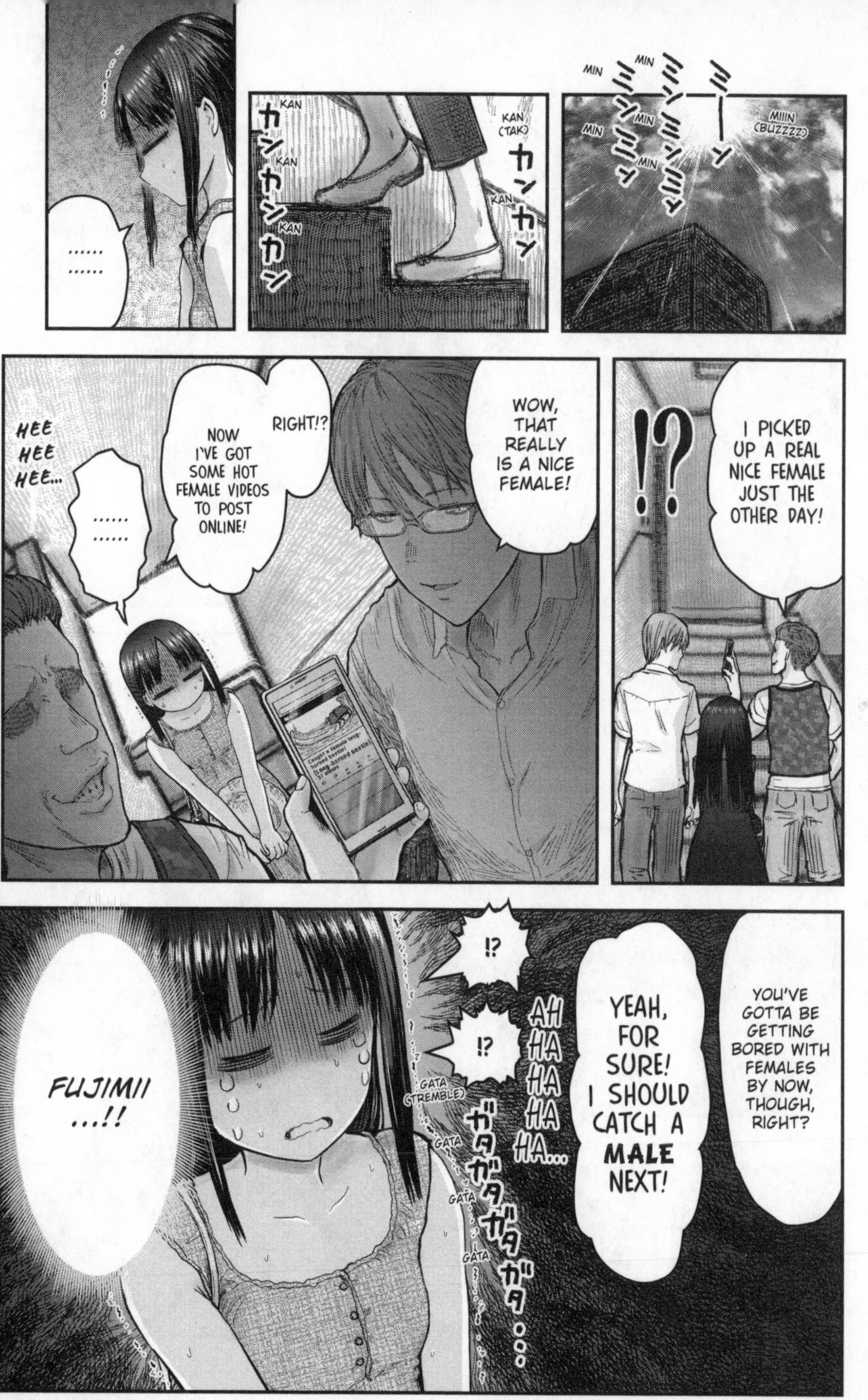

MIN
MIN
ミーン
MIN
ミンミンミー
MIN
MIN
MIIN (BUZZZZ)
KAN
KAN (TAK)
カンカン
KAN
KAN
KAN
カンカンカン
......
......
!?
I PICKED UP A REAL NICE FEMALE JUST THE OTHER DAY!
WOW, THAT REALLY IS A NICE FEMALE!
RIGHT!?
NOW I'VE GOT SOME HOT FEMALE VIDEOS TO POST ONLINE!
HEE HEE HEE...
......
......
YOU'VE GOTTA BE GETTING BORED WITH FEMALES BY NOW, THOUGH, RIGHT?
YEAH, FOR SURE! I SHOULD CATCH A **MALE** NEXT!
AH HA HA HA HA HA...
!?
!?
GATA (TREMBLE)
GATA
GATA
GATA
ガタガタガタガタ...
FUJIMI...!!

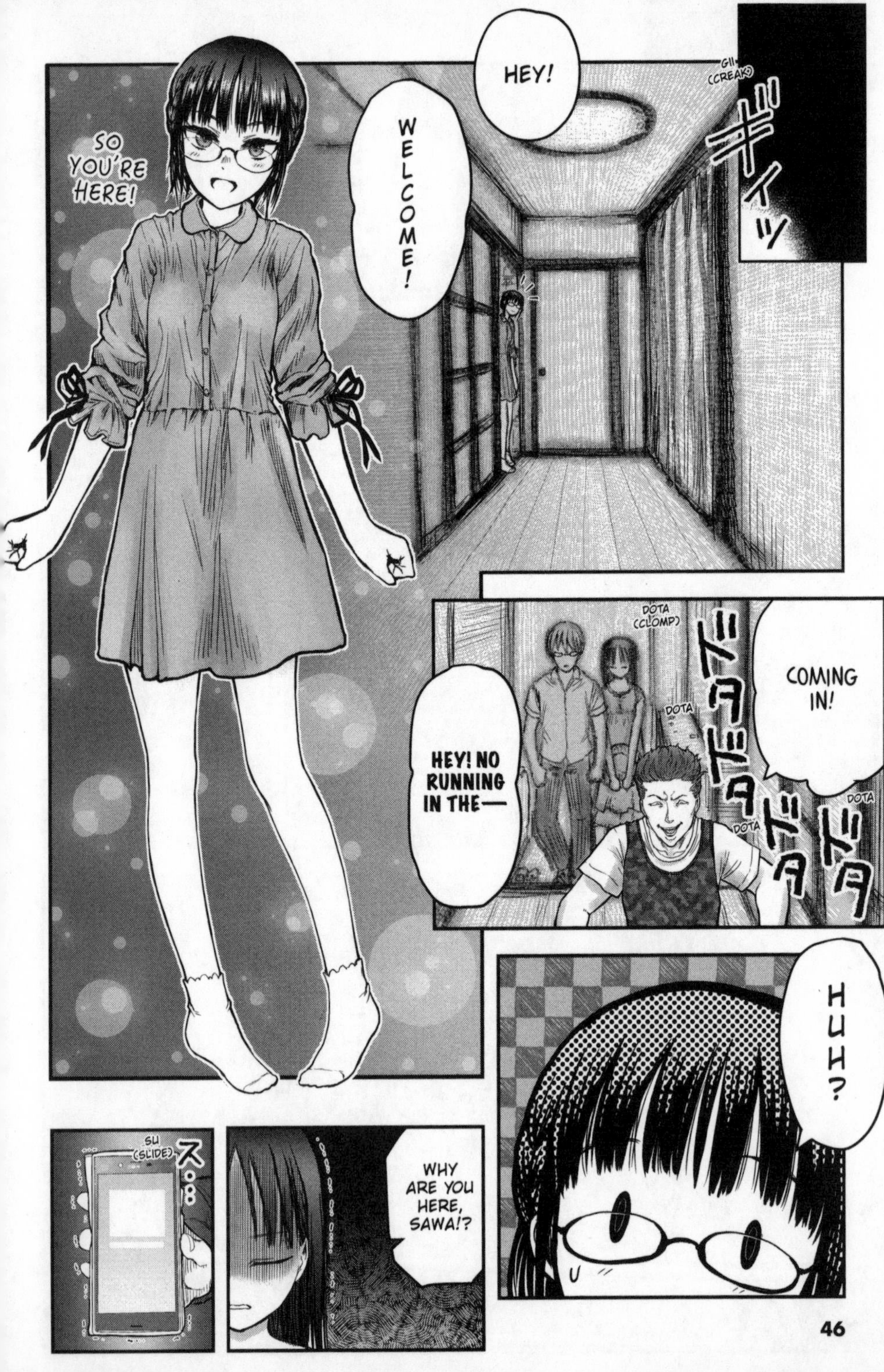
HEY!
GII (CREAK)
ギイッ
WELCOME!
DOTA (CLOMP)
DOTA
DOTA
DOTA
ドタドタドタドタ
COMING IN!
HEY! NO RUNNING IN THE—
HUH?
SO YOU'RE HERE!
WHY ARE YOU HERE, SAWA!?
SU (SLIDE)
ス…

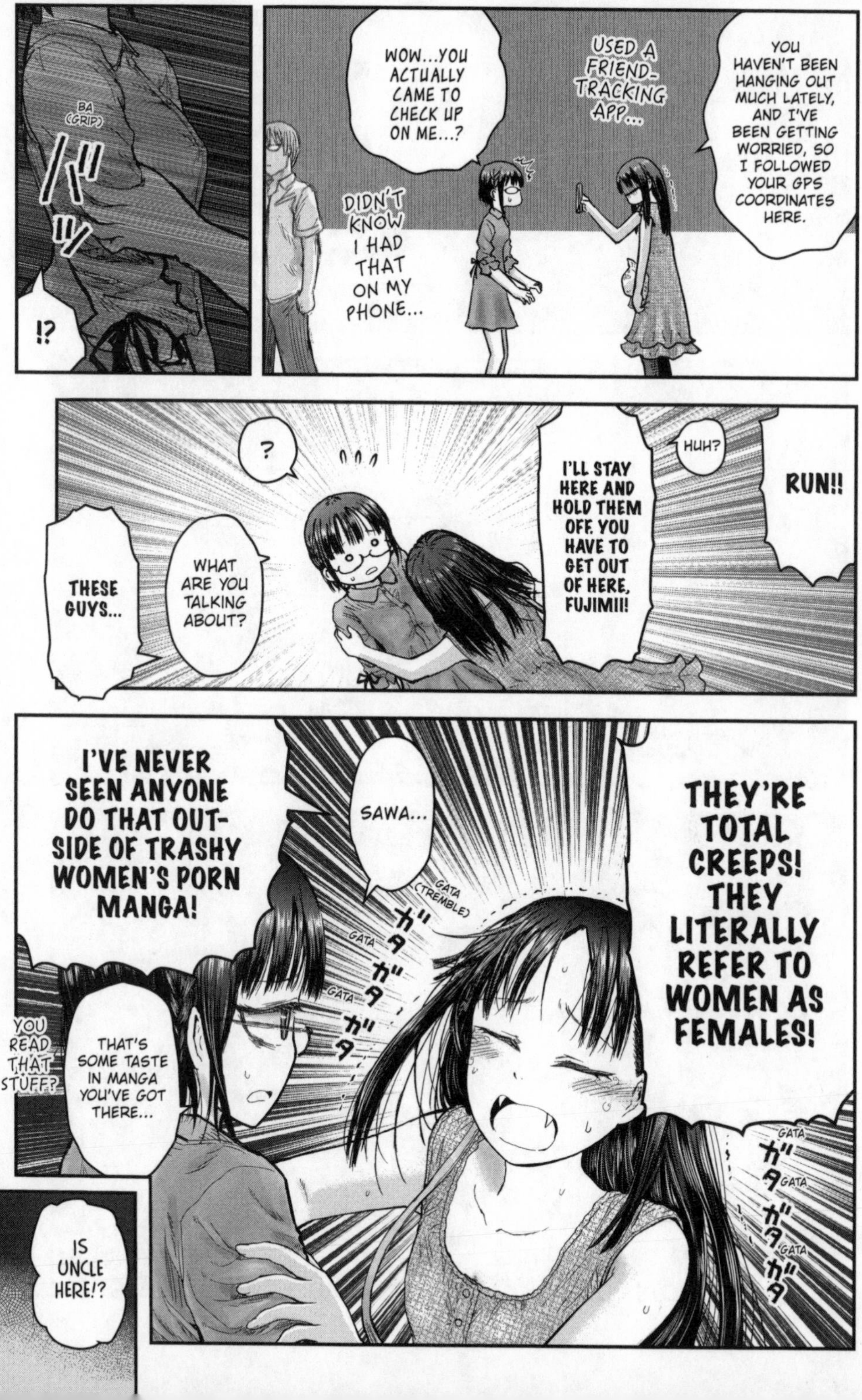
YOU HAVEN'T BEEN HANGING OUT MUCH LATELY, AND I'VE BEEN GETTING WORRIED, SO I FOLLOWED YOUR GPS COORDINATES HERE.
USED A FRIEND-TRACKING APP...
WOW...YOU ACTUALLY CAME TO CHECK UP ON ME...?
DIDN'T KNOW I HAD THAT ON MY PHONE...
BA (GRIP)
バ
ッ
!?
RUN!!
HUH?
I'LL STAY HERE AND HOLD THEM OFF. YOU HAVE TO GET OUT OF HERE, FUJIMI!!
?
WHAT ARE YOU TALKING ABOUT?
THESE GUYS...
THEY'RE TOTAL CREEPS! THEY LITERALLY REFER TO WOMEN AS FEMALES!
GATA
ガタ
GATA
ガタ
GATA
ガタ
I'VE NEVER SEEN ANYONE DO THAT OUT-SIDE OF TRASHY WOMEN'S PORN MANGA!
SAWA...
GATA (TREMBLE)
ガタ
GATA
ガタ
GATA
ガタ
THAT'S SOME TASTE IN MANGA YOU'VE GOT THERE...
YOU READ THAT STUFF?
IS UNCLE HERE!?

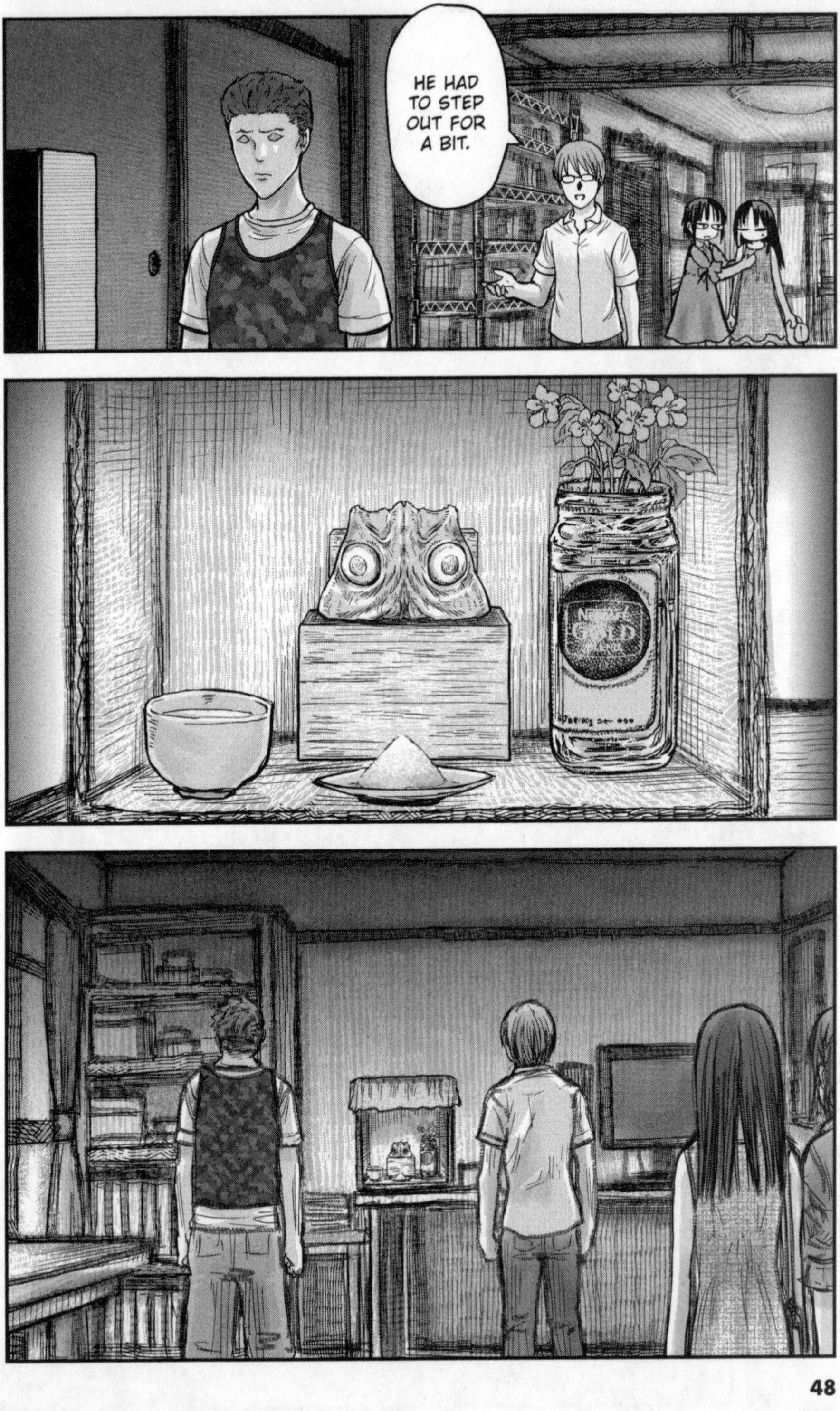
HE HAD TO STEP OUT FOR A BIT.

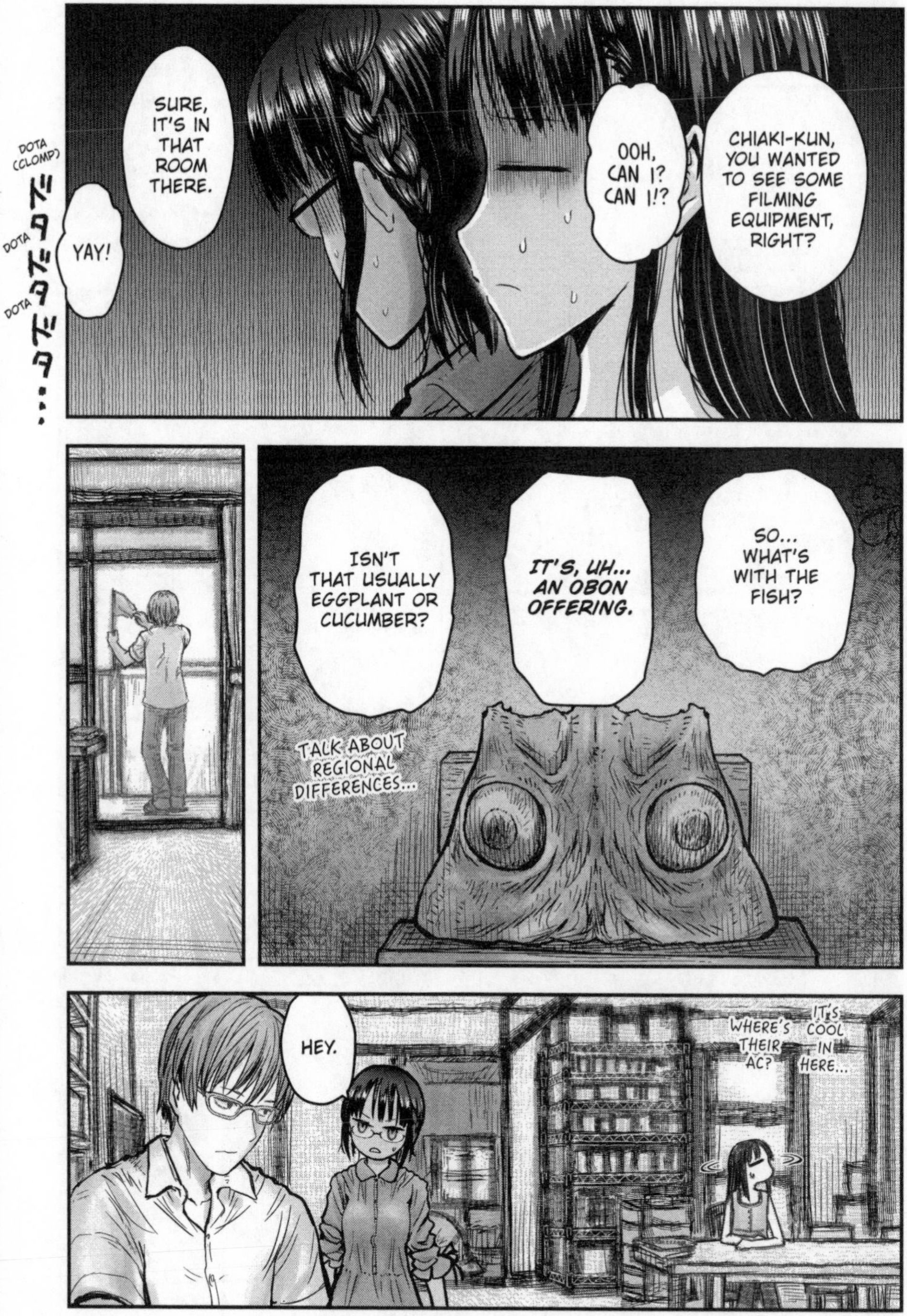
CHIAKI-KUN, YOU WANTED TO SEE SOME FILMING EQUIPMENT, RIGHT?
OOH, CAN I? CAN I!?
SURE, IT'S IN THAT ROOM THERE.
YAY!
DOTA (CLOMP)
DOTA
DOTA
SO... WHAT'S WITH THE FISH?
IT'S, UH... AN OBON OFFERING.
ISN'T THAT USUALLY EGGPLANT OR CUCUMBER?
TALK ABOUT REGIONAL DIFFERENCES...
IT'S COOL IN HERE...
WHERE'S THEIR AC?
HEY.

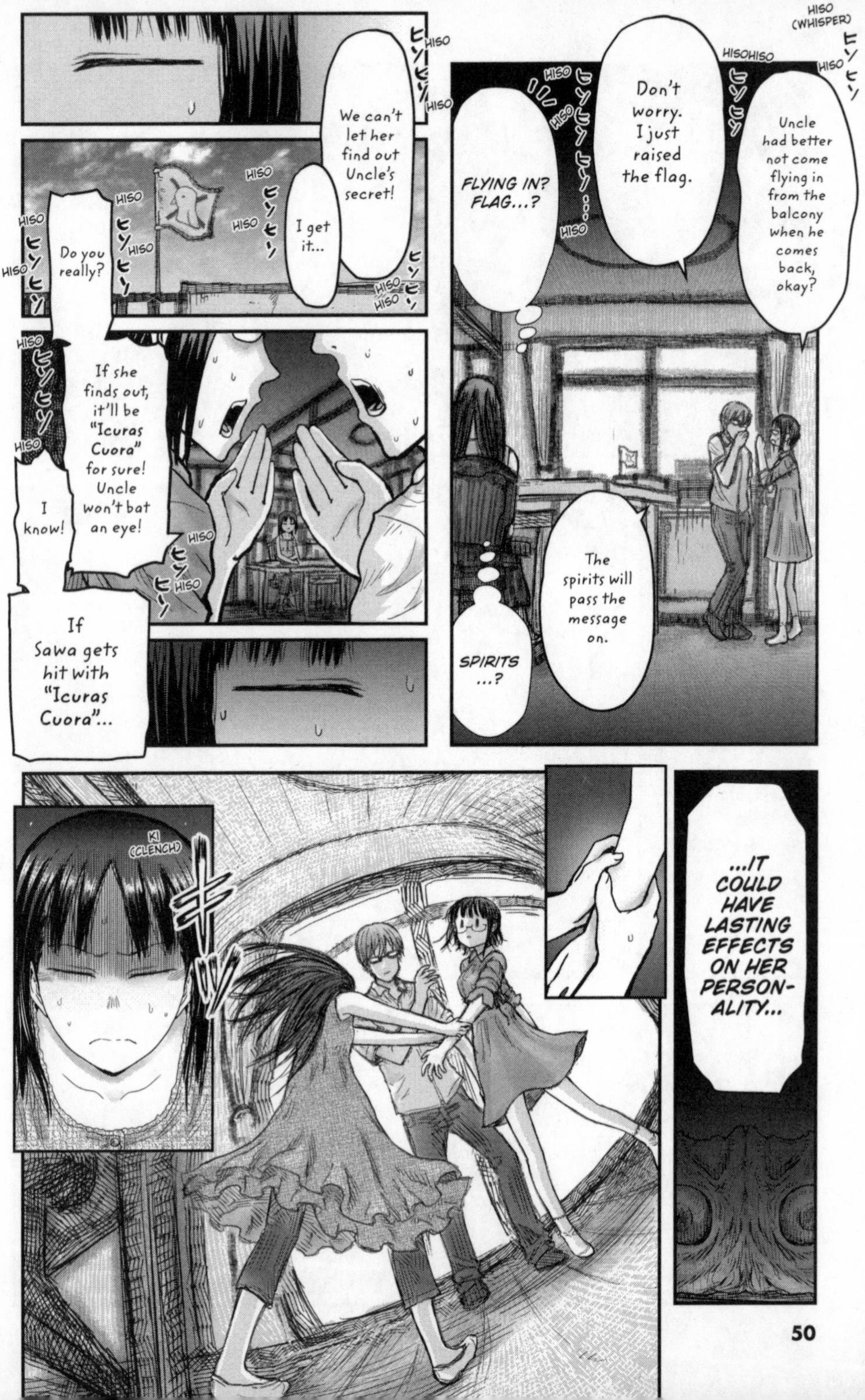
HISO (WHISPER)
HISOHISO
ヒソヒソ
Uncle had better not come flying in from the balcony when he comes back, okay?
Don't worry. I just raised the flag.
FLYING IN? FLAG...?
The spirits will pass the message on.
SPIRITS ...?
HISO
We can't let her find out Uncle's secret!
I get it...
Do you really?
If she finds out, it'll be "Icuras Cuora" for sure! Uncle won't bat an eye!
I know!
If Sawa gets hit with "Icuras Cuora"...
...IT COULD HAVE LASTING EFFECTS ON HER PERSONALITY...
KI (CLENCH)

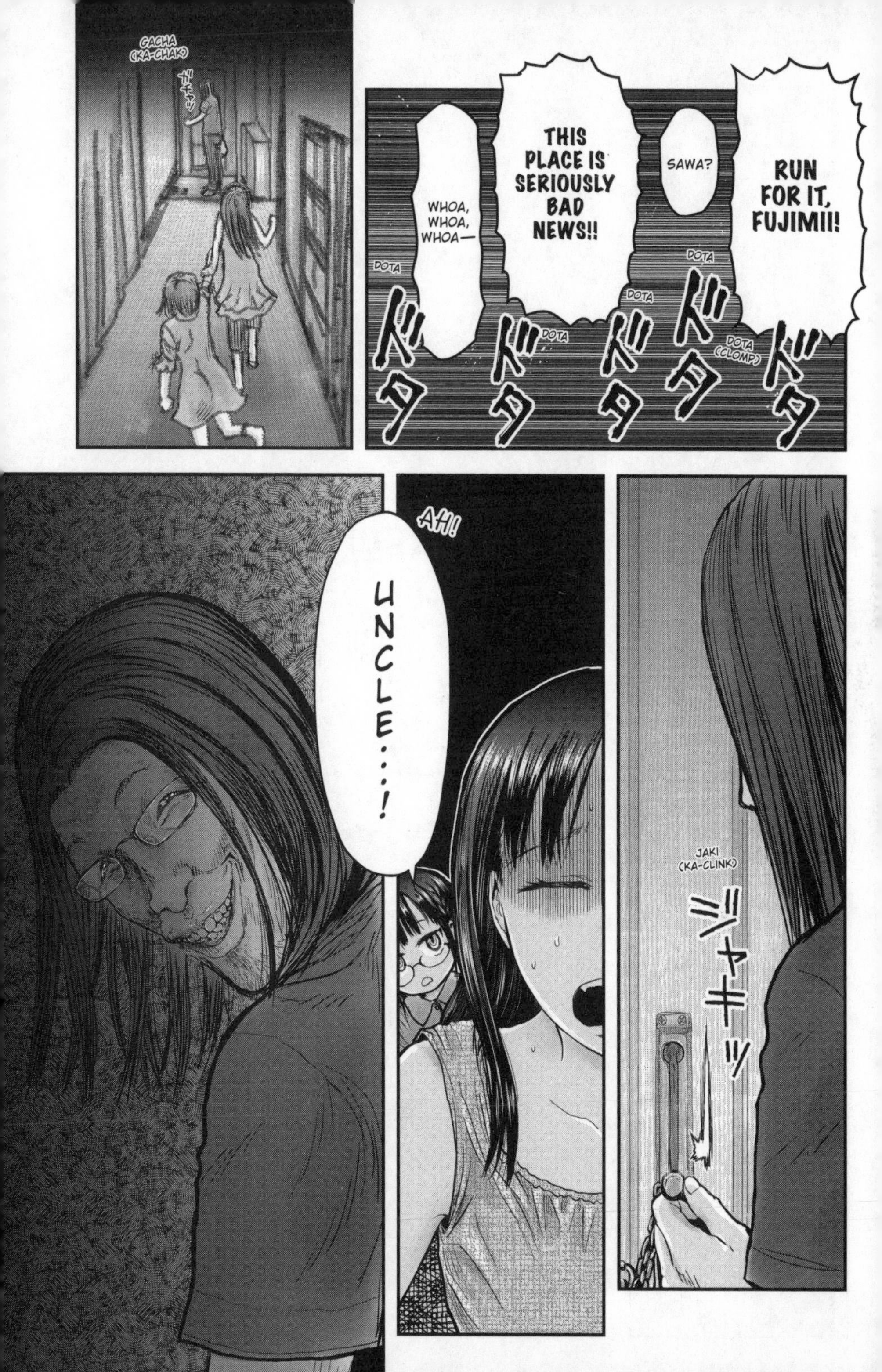
RUN FOR IT, FUJIMI!!
SAWA?
THIS PLACE IS SERIOUSLY BAD NEWS!!
WHOA, WHOA, WHOA—
DOTA (CLOMP)
DOTA
DOTA
DOTA
DOTA
ドタドタドタドタドタ
GACHA (KA-CHAK)
ガチャッ
JAKI (KA-CLINK)
ジャキッ
AH!
UNCLE...!

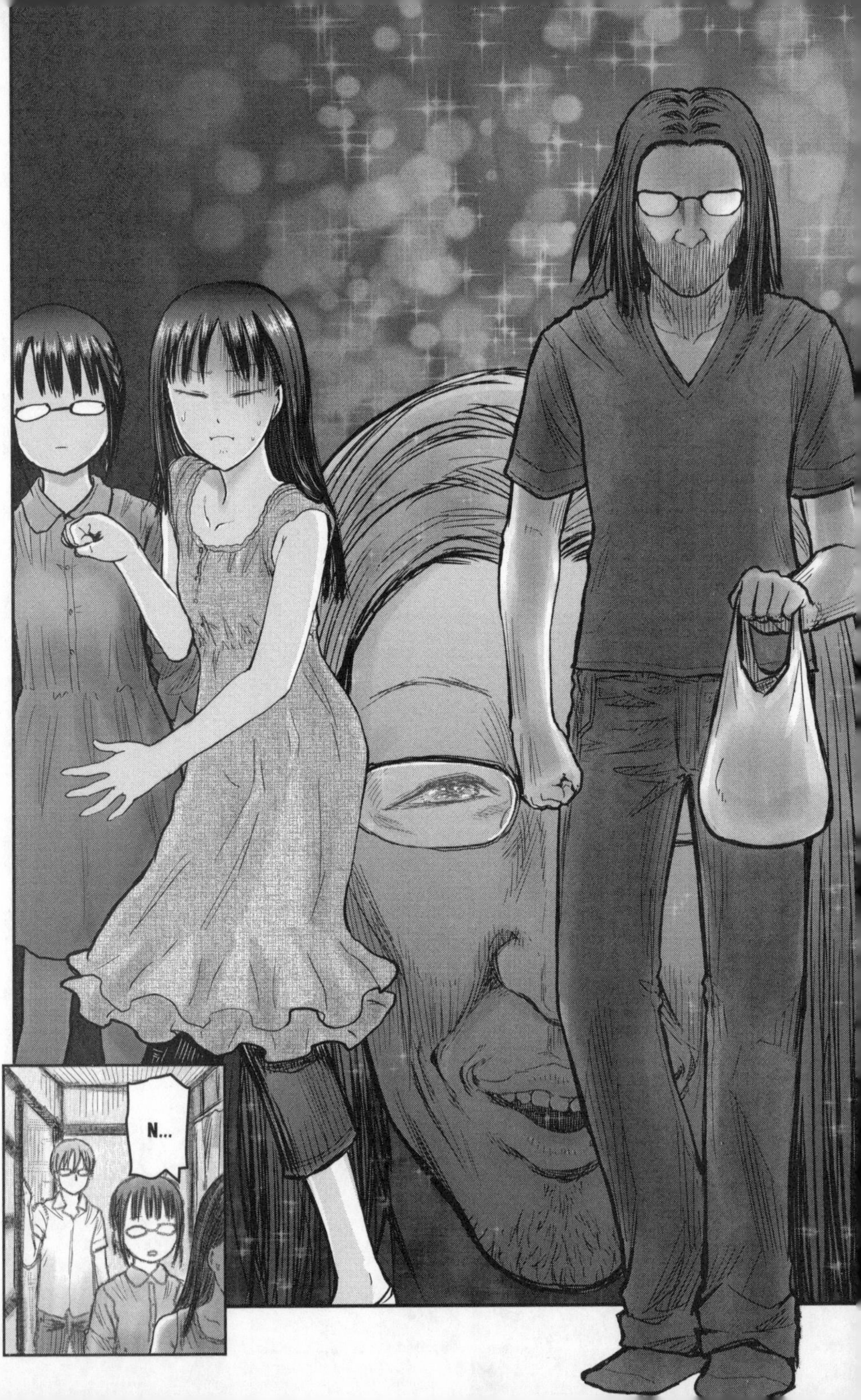
N...

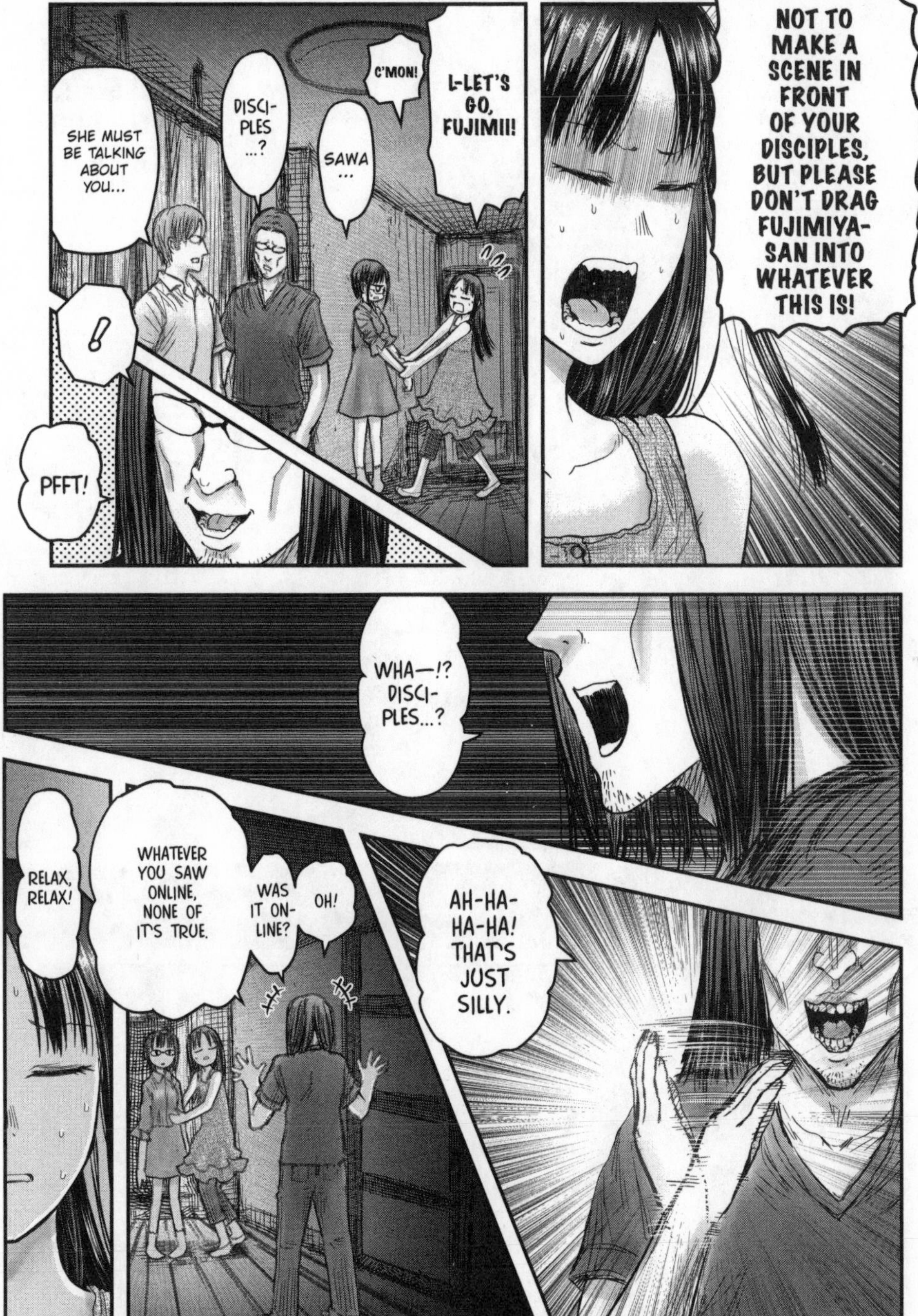
NOT TO MAKE A SCENE IN FRONT OF YOUR DISCIPLES, BUT PLEASE DON'T DRAG FUJIMIYA-SAN INTO WHATEVER THIS IS!
L-LET'S GO, FUJIMII!
C'MON!
SAWA ...
DISCI-PLES ...?
SHE MUST BE TALKING ABOUT YOU...
!
PFFT!
WHA—!? DISCI-PLES...?
AH-HA-HA-HA! THAT'S JUST SILLY.
OH!
WAS IT ON-LINE?
WHATEVER YOU SAW ONLINE, NONE OF IT'S TRUE.
RELAX, RELAX!

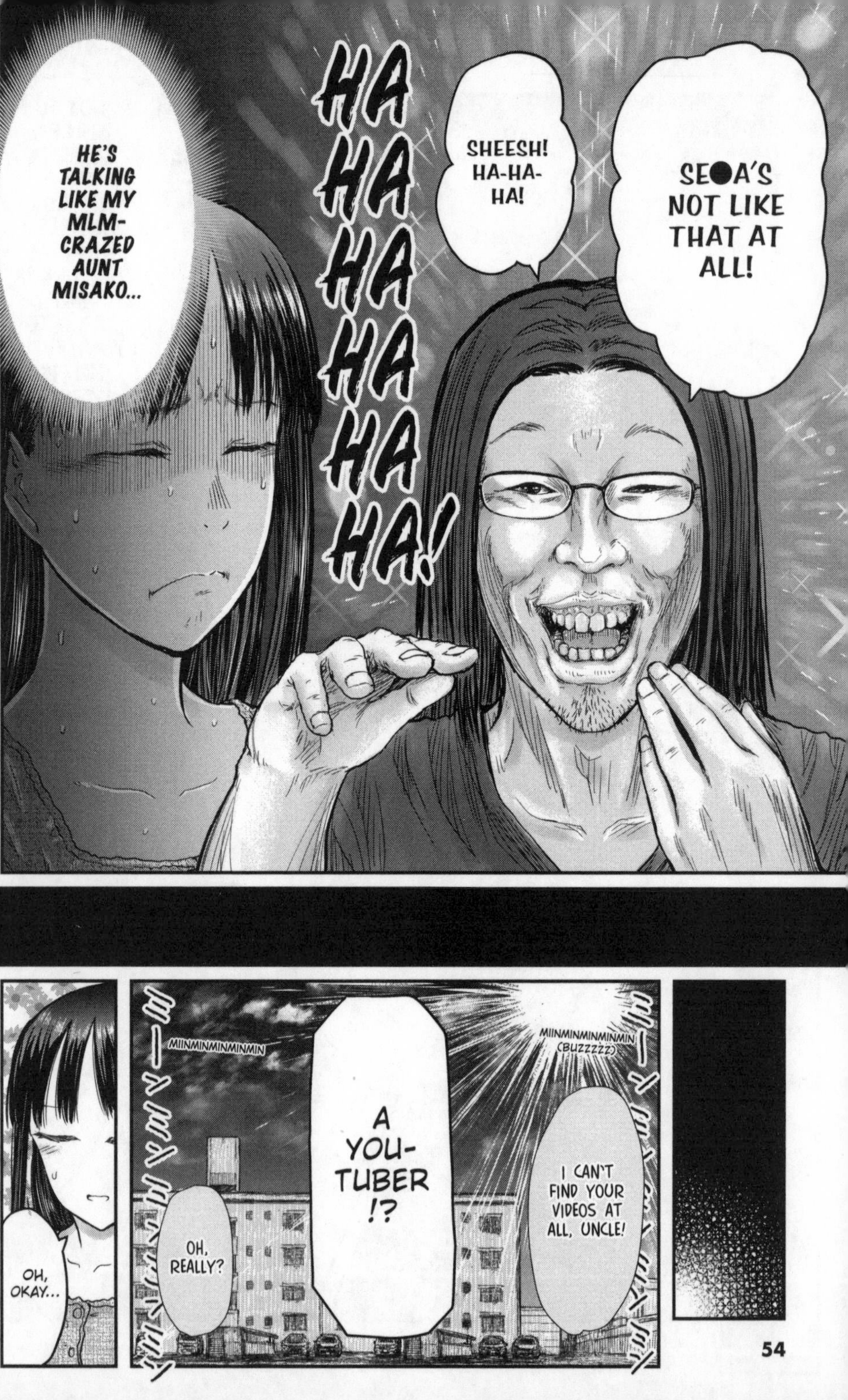
SE●A'S NOT LIKE THAT AT ALL!
SHEESH! HA-HA-HA!
HA HA HA HA HA HA HA!
HE'S TALKING LIKE MY MLM-CRAZED AUNT MISAKO...
MIINMINMINMINMIN (BUZZZZZ)
I CAN'T FIND YOUR VIDEOS AT ALL, UNCLE!
A YOU-TUBER !?
OH, REALLY?
MIINMINMINMINMIN
OH, OKAY...

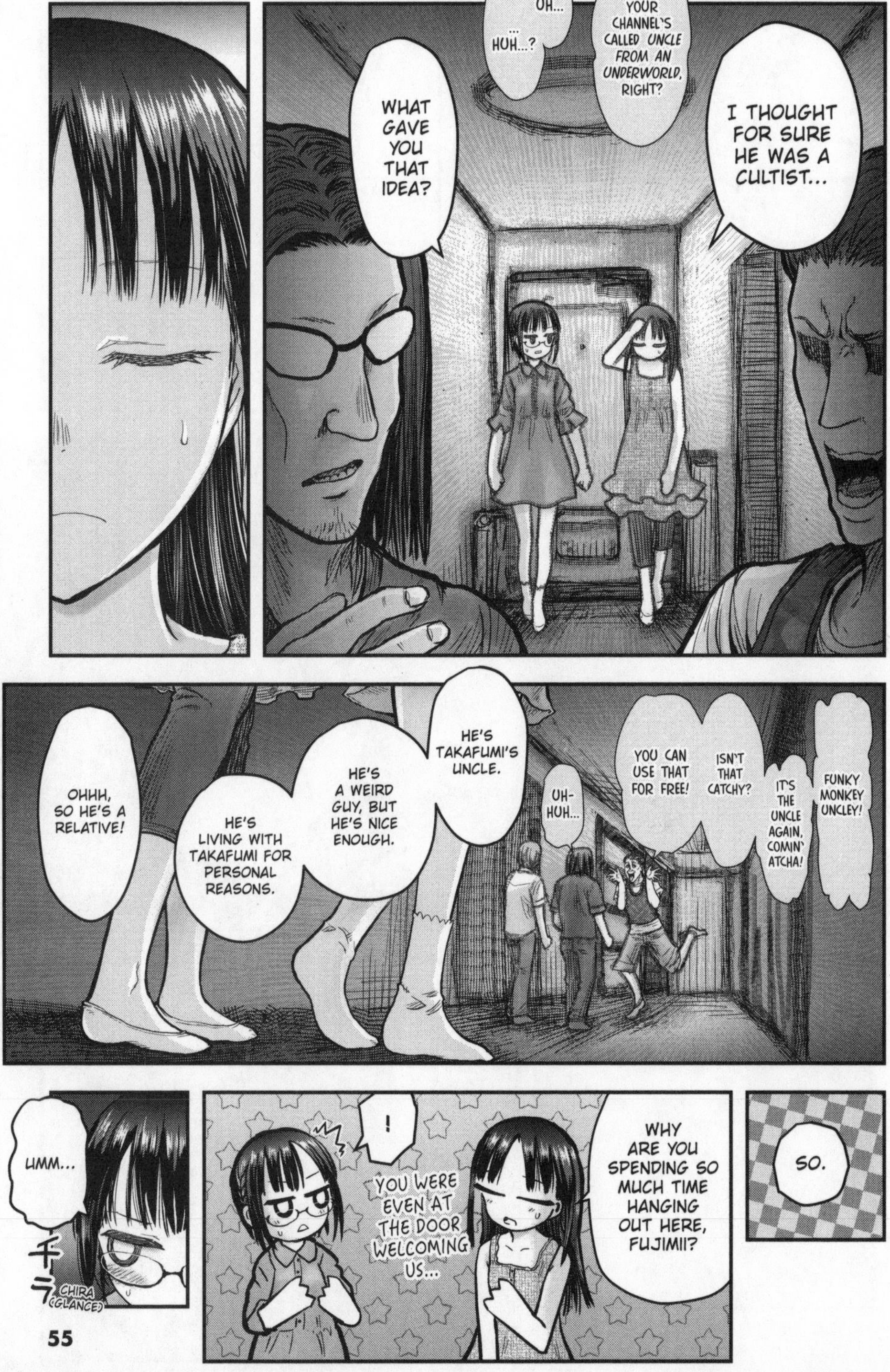
I THOUGHT FOR SURE HE WAS A CULTIST...
YOUR CHANNEL'S CALLED UNCLE FROM AN UNDERWORLD, RIGHT?
UH... ...HUH...?
WHAT GAVE YOU THAT IDEA?
FUNKY MONKEY UNCLEY!
IT'S THE UNCLE AGAIN, COMIN' ATCHA!
ISN'T THAT CATCHY?
YOU CAN USE THAT FOR FREE!
UH-HUH...
HE'S TAKAFUMI'S UNCLE.
HE'S A WEIRD GUY, BUT HE'S NICE ENOUGH.
HE'S LIVING WITH TAKAFUMI FOR PERSONAL REASONS.
OHHH, SO HE'S A RELATIVE!
SO.
WHY ARE YOU SPENDING SO MUCH TIME HANGING OUT HERE, FUJIMII?
!
YOU WERE EVEN AT THE DOOR WELCOMING US...
UMM...
チラ
CHIRA (GLANCE)

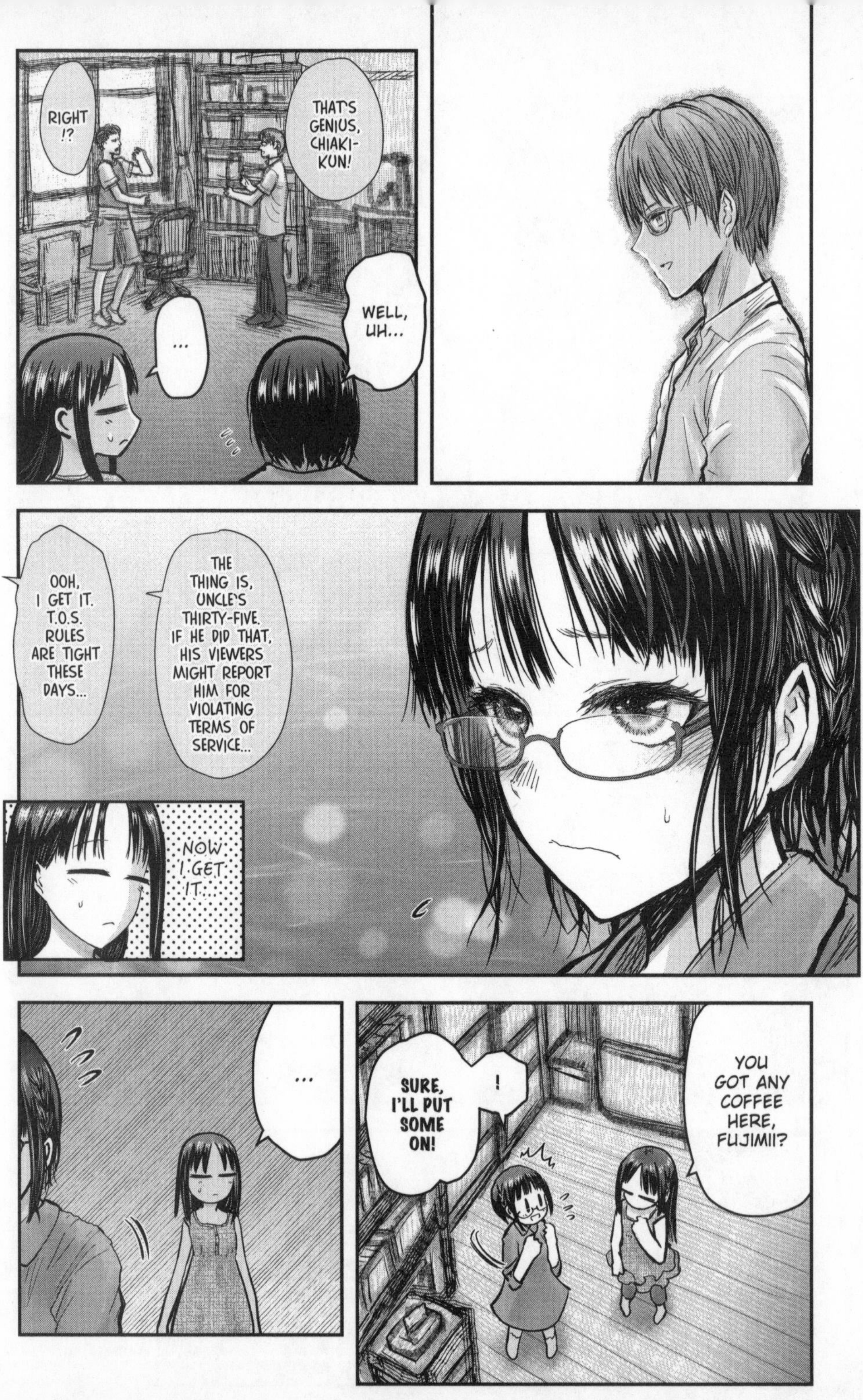
THAT'S GENIUS, CHIAKI-KUN!
RIGHT!?
WELL, UH...
...
THE THING IS, UNCLE'S THIRTY-FIVE. IF HE DID THAT, HIS VIEWERS MIGHT REPORT HIM FOR VIOLATING TERMS OF SERVICE...
OOH, I GET IT. T.O.S. RULES ARE TIGHT THESE DAYS...
NOW I GET IT...
YOU GOT ANY COFFEE HERE, FUJIMII?
!
SURE, I'LL PUT SOME ON!
...

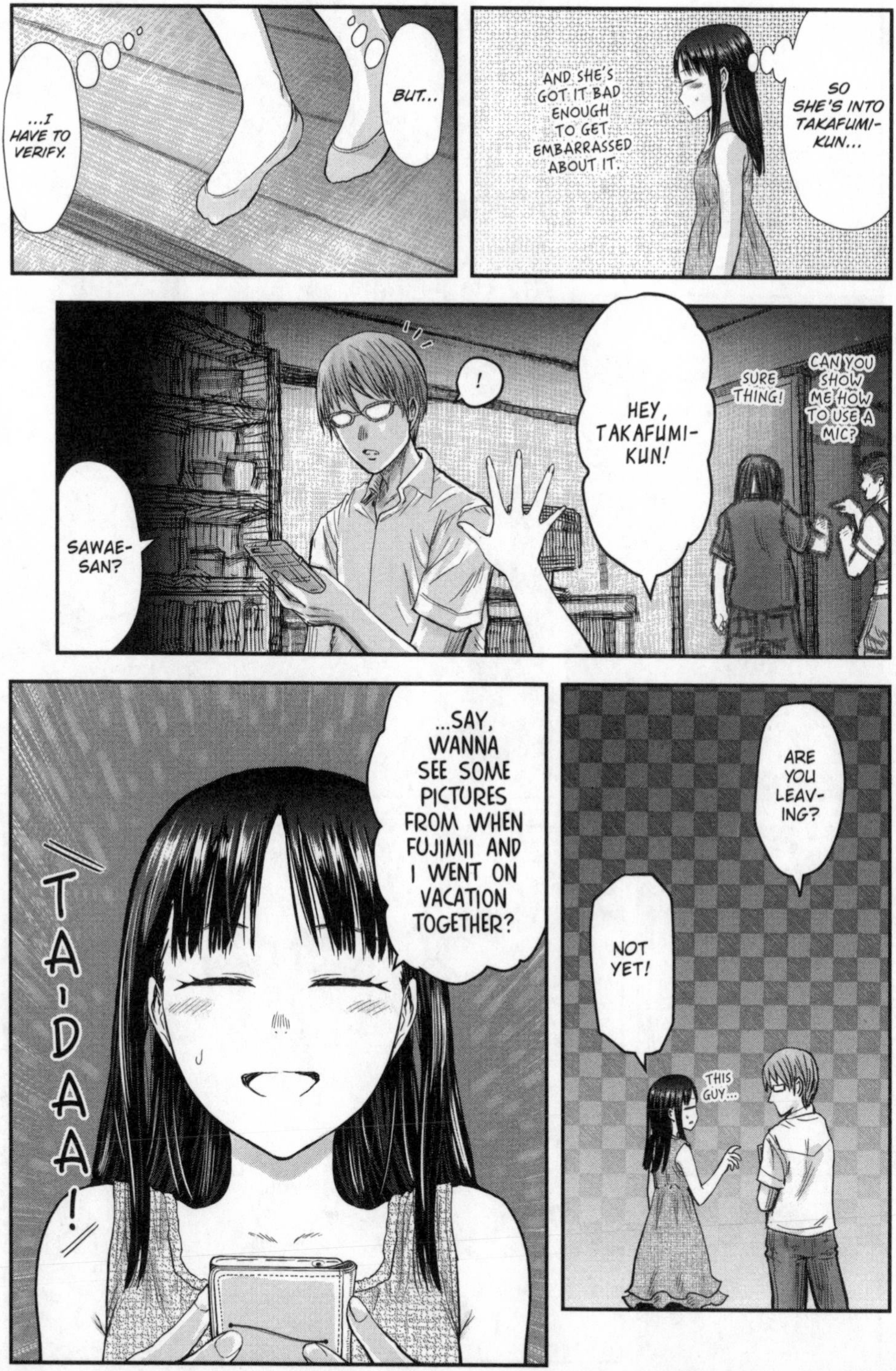
SO SHE'S INTO TAKAFUMI-KUN...
AND SHE'S GOT IT BAD ENOUGH TO GET EMBARRASSED ABOUT IT.
BUT...
...I HAVE TO VERIFY.
CAN YOU SHOW ME HOW TO USE A MIC?
SURE THING!
HEY, TAKAFUMI-KUN!
!
SAWAE-SAN?
ARE YOU LEAVING?
NOT YET!
THIS GUY...
...SAY, WANNA SEE SOME PICTURES FROM WHEN FUJIMII AND I WENT ON VACATION TOGETHER?
TA-DAA!

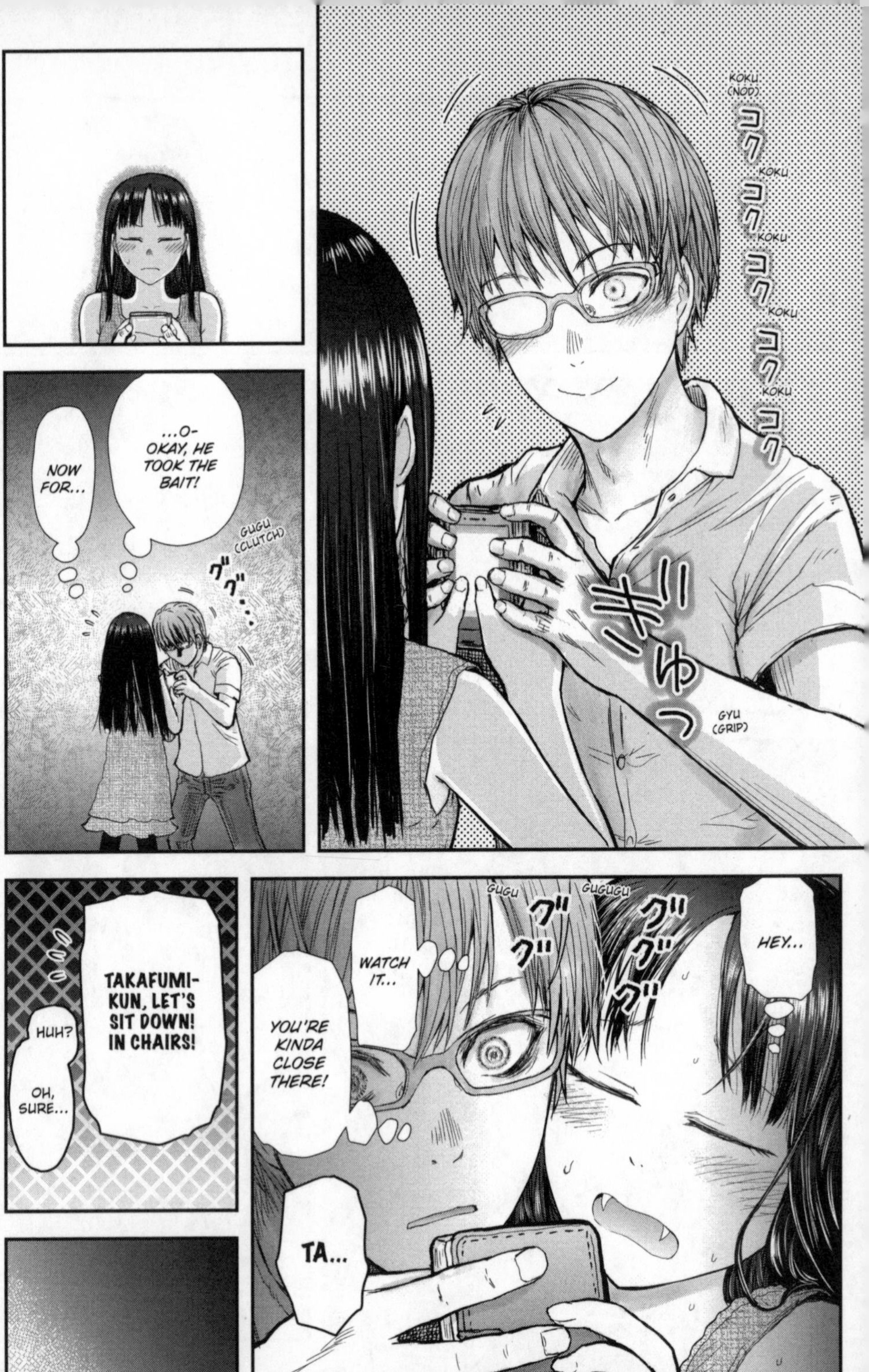
KOKU (NOD)
KOKU
KOKU
KOKU
KOKU
GYU (GRIP)
...O-OKAY, HE TOOK THE BAIT!
NOW FOR...
GUGU (CLUTCH)
HEY...
GUGUGU
GUGU
WATCH IT...
YOU'RE KINDA CLOSE THERE!
TA...
TAKAFUMI-KUN, LET'S SIT DOWN! IN CHAIRS!
HUH?
OH, SURE...

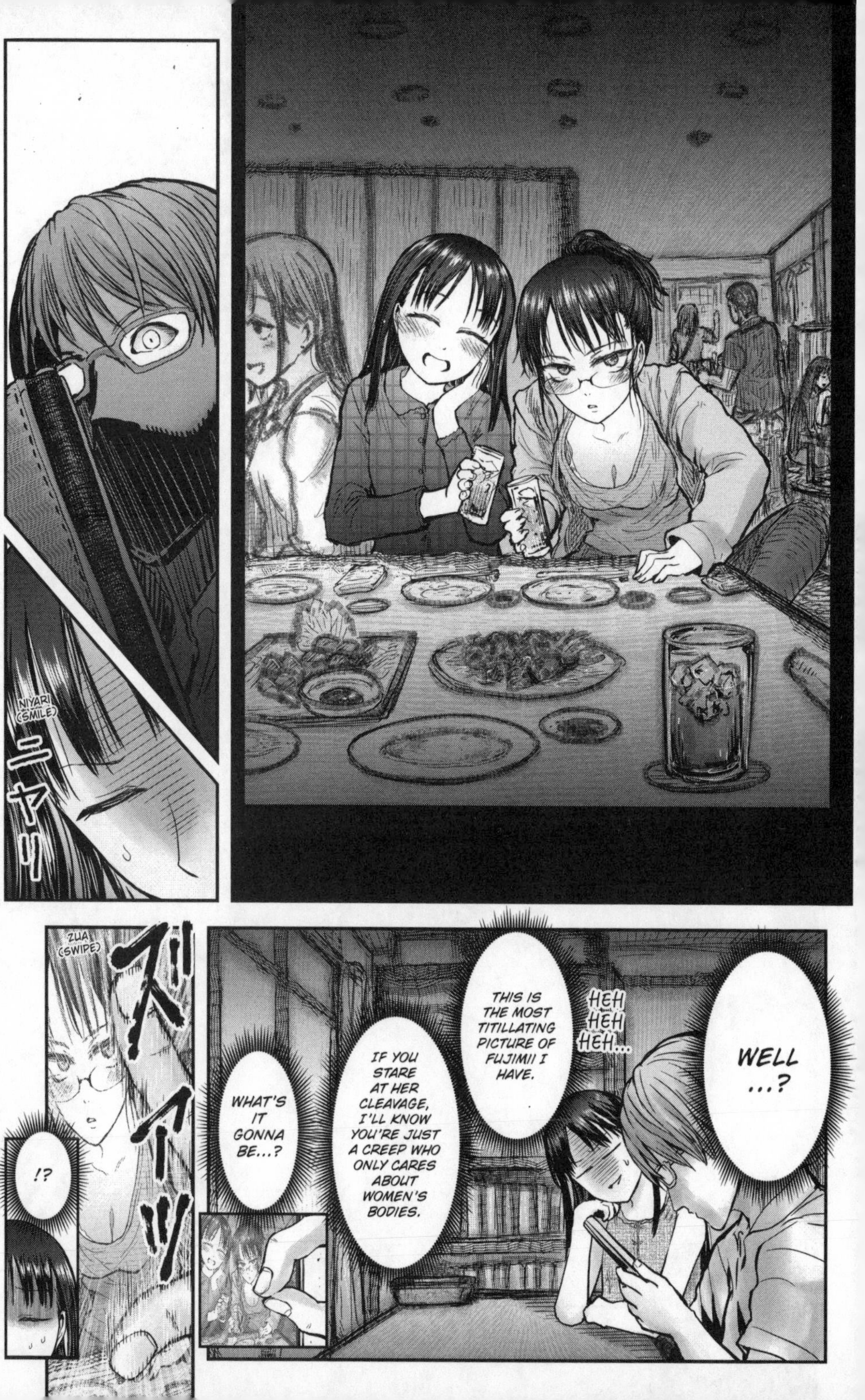
NIYARI (SMILE)
ニヤリ
WELL ...?
HEH HEH HEH...
THIS IS THE MOST TITILLATING PICTURE OF FUJIMII I HAVE.
IF YOU STARE AT HER CLEAVAGE, I'LL KNOW YOU'RE JUST A CREEP WHO ONLY CARES ABOUT WOMEN'S BODIES.
WHAT'S IT GONNA BE...?
ZUA (SWIPE)
!?

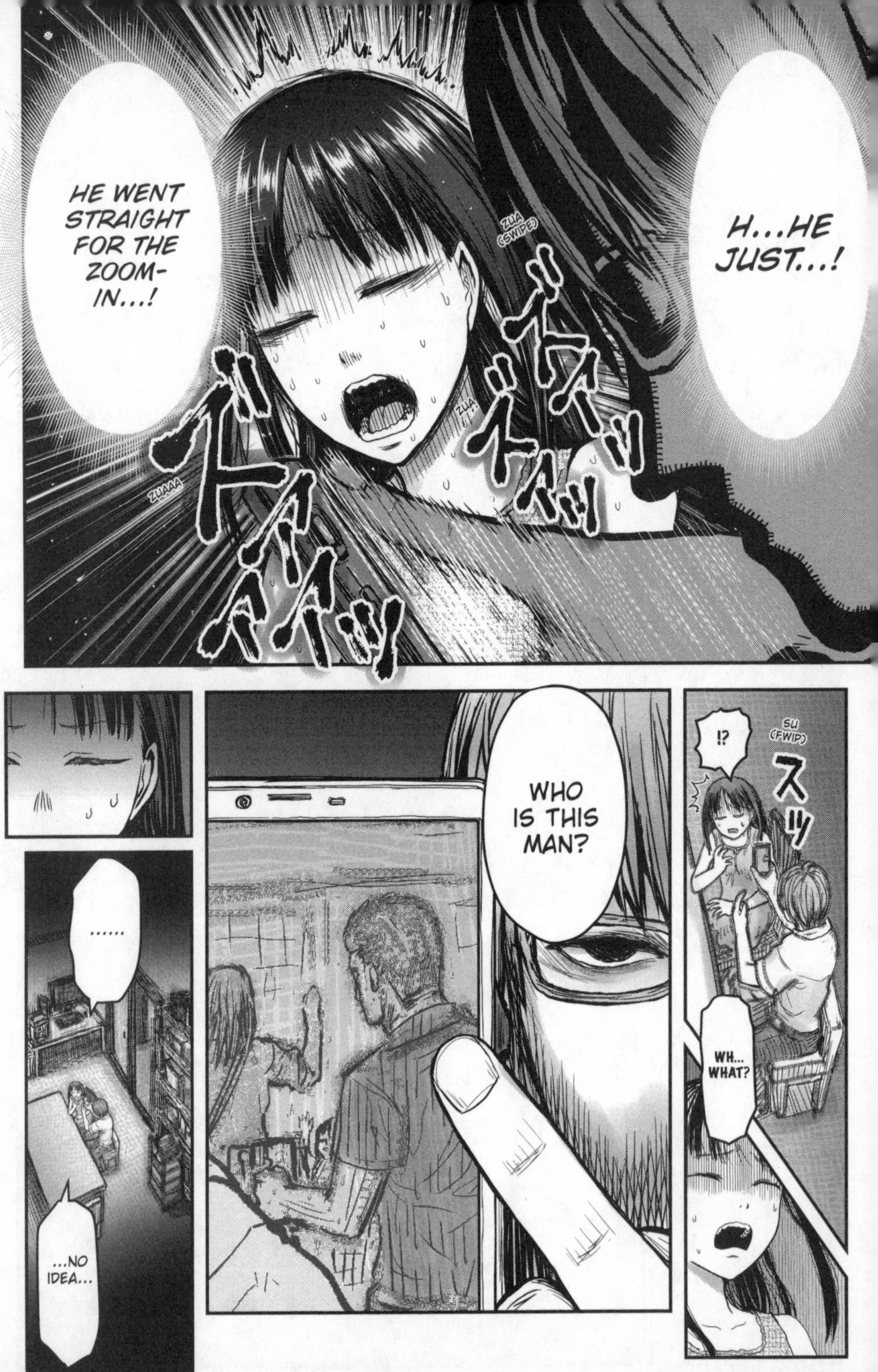
H...HE JUST...!
HE WENT STRAIGHT FOR THE ZOOM-IN...!
ZUA (SWIPE)
ZUA
ZUAAA
SU (FWIP)
スッ
!?
WH... WHAT?
WHO IS THIS MAN?
......
...NO IDEA...

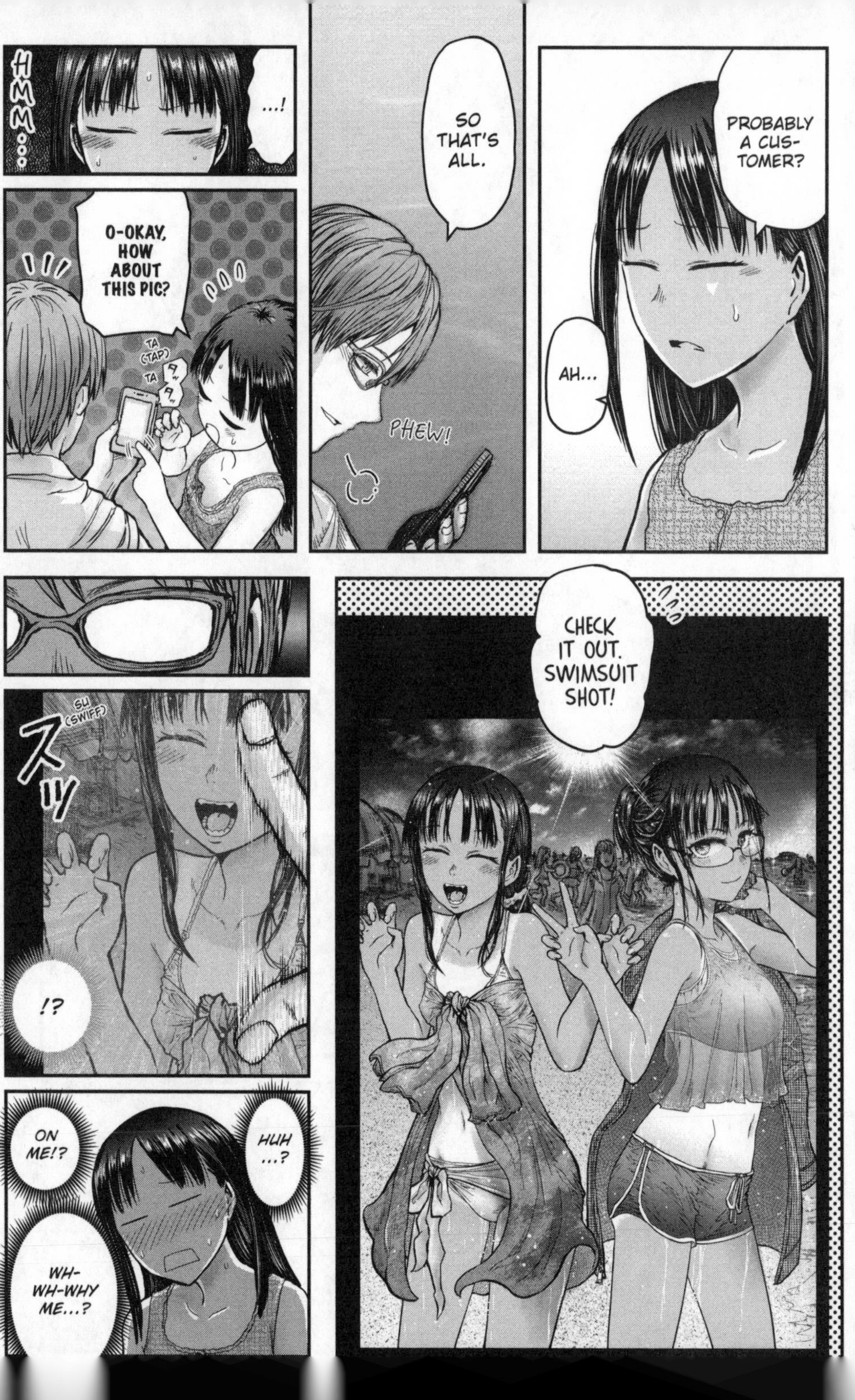
PROBABLY A CUS-TOMER?
AH...
SO THAT'S ALL.
PHEW!
...!
HMM...
O-OKAY, HOW ABOUT THIS PIC?
TA (TAP) TA
CHECK IT OUT. SWIMSUIT SHOT!
SU (SWIFF)
!?
HUH ...?
ON ME!?
WH-WH-WHY ME...?

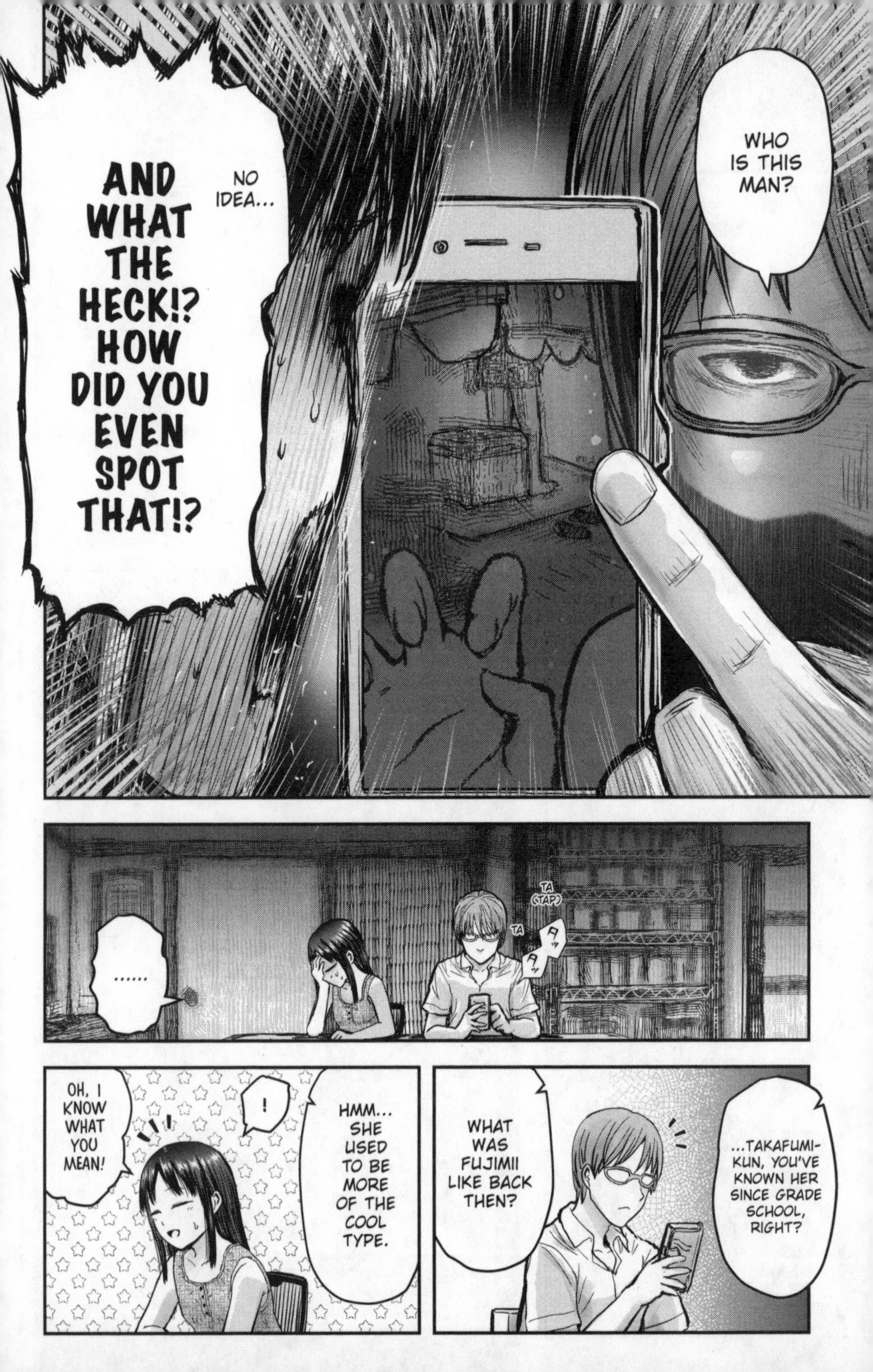
WHO IS THIS MAN?
NO IDEA...
AND WHAT THE HECK!? HOW DID YOU EVEN SPOT THAT!?
TA (TAP)
タッ
TA
タッ
......
...TAKAFUMI-KUN, YOU'VE KNOWN HER SINCE GRADE SCHOOL, RIGHT?
WHAT WAS FUJIMII LIKE BACK THEN?
HMM... SHE USED TO BE MORE OF THE COOL TYPE.
!
OH, I KNOW WHAT YOU MEAN!

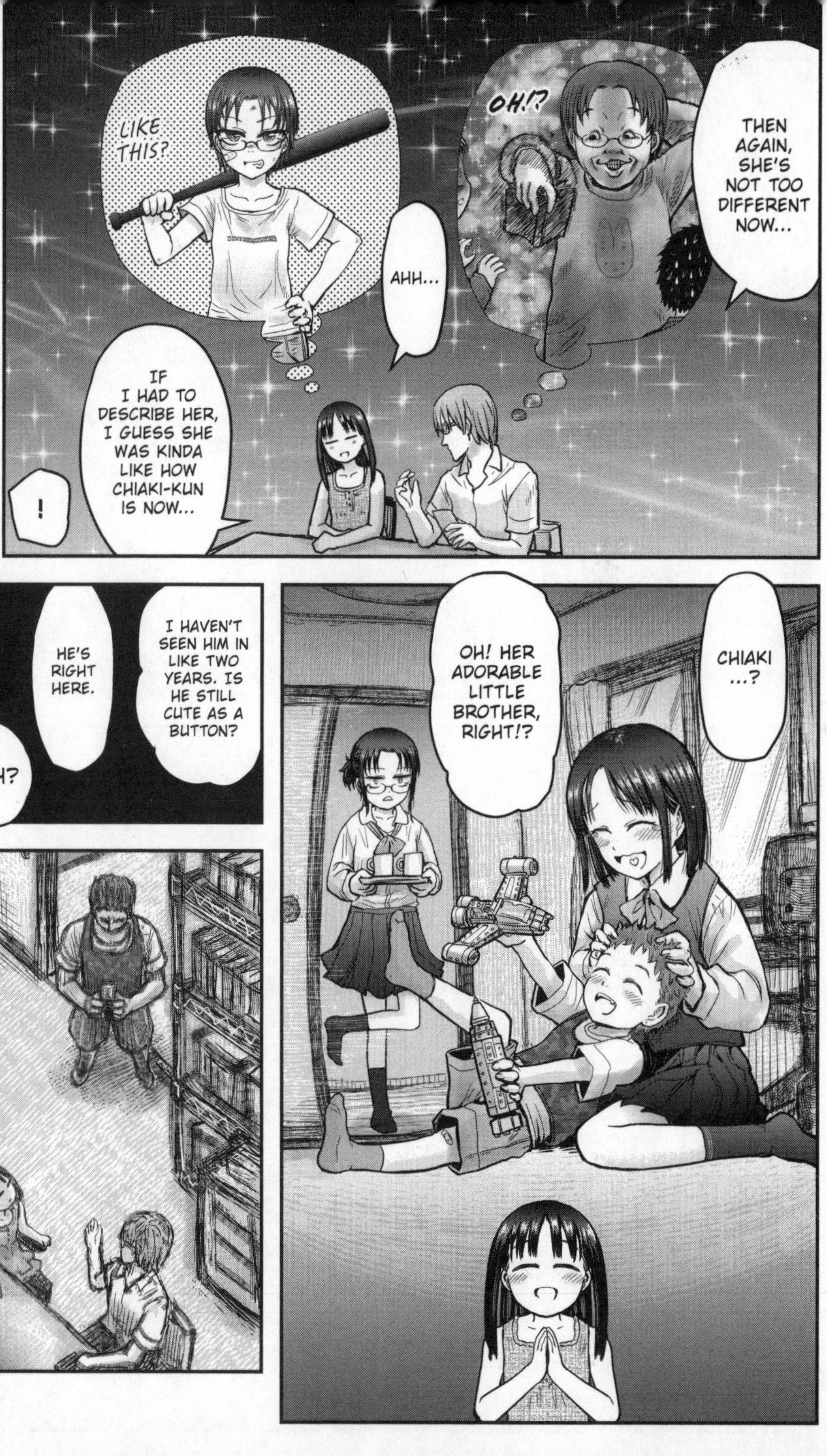
THEN AGAIN, SHE'S NOT TOO DIFFERENT NOW...
OH!?
LIKE THIS?
AHH...
IF I HAD TO DESCRIBE HER, I GUESS SHE WAS KINDA LIKE HOW CHIAKI-KUN IS NOW...
!
CHIAKI ...?
OH! HER ADORABLE LITTLE BROTHER, RIGHT!?
I HAVEN'T SEEN HIM IN LIKE TWO YEARS. IS HE STILL CUTE AS A BUTTON?
HE'S RIGHT HERE.
HUH?

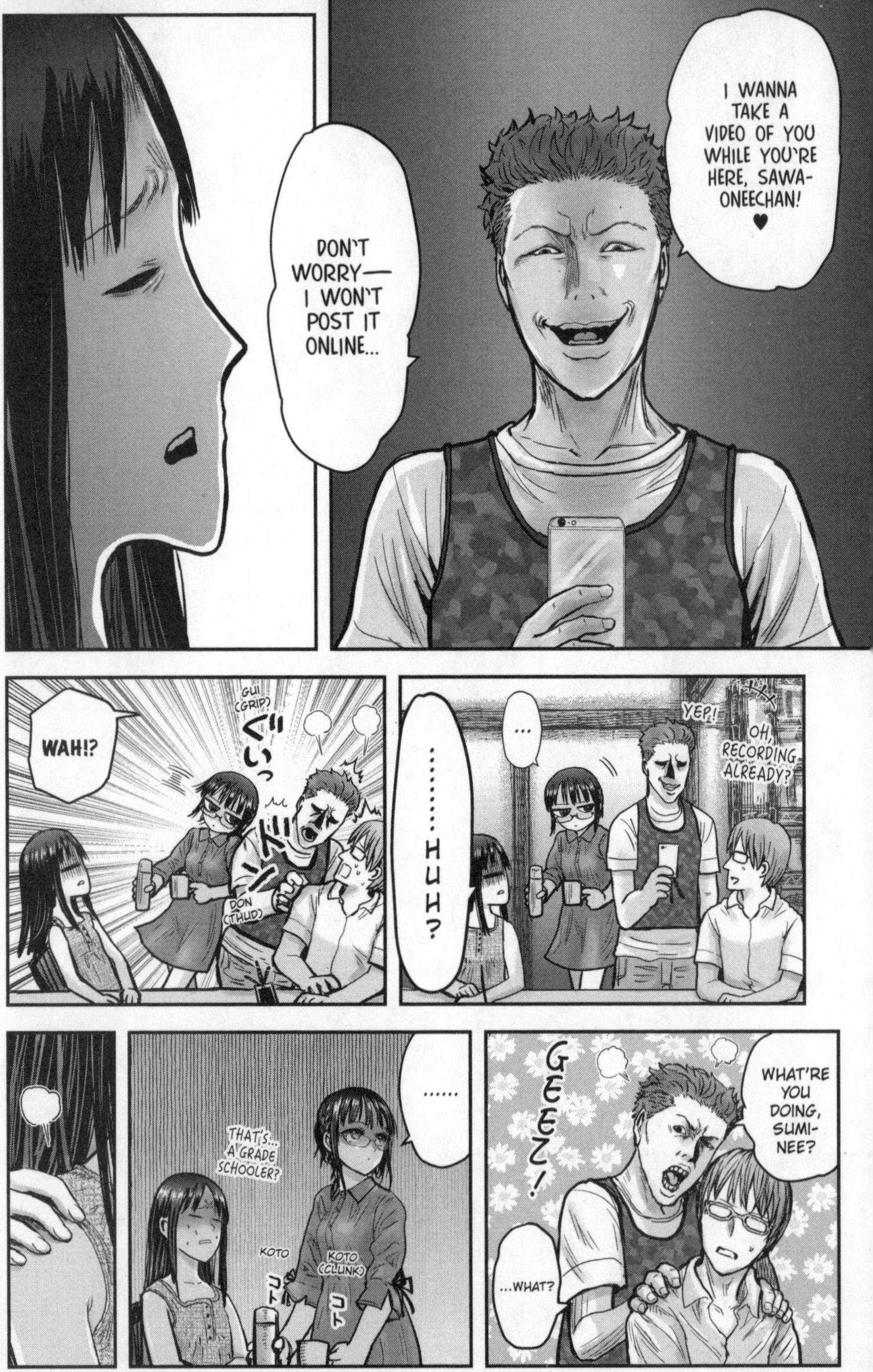
I WANNA TAKE A VIDEO OF YOU WHILE YOU'RE HERE, SAWA-ONEECHAN! ♥
DON'T WORRY— I WON'T POST IT ONLINE...
YEP!
OH, RECORDING ALREADY?
...
......HUH?
GUI (GRIP)
ぐいっ
WAH!?
DON (THUD)
WHAT'RE YOU DOING, SUMI-NEE?
GEEZ!
...WHAT?
......
THAT'S... A GRADE SCHOOLER?
KOTO (CLUNK)
コト
KOTO
コト

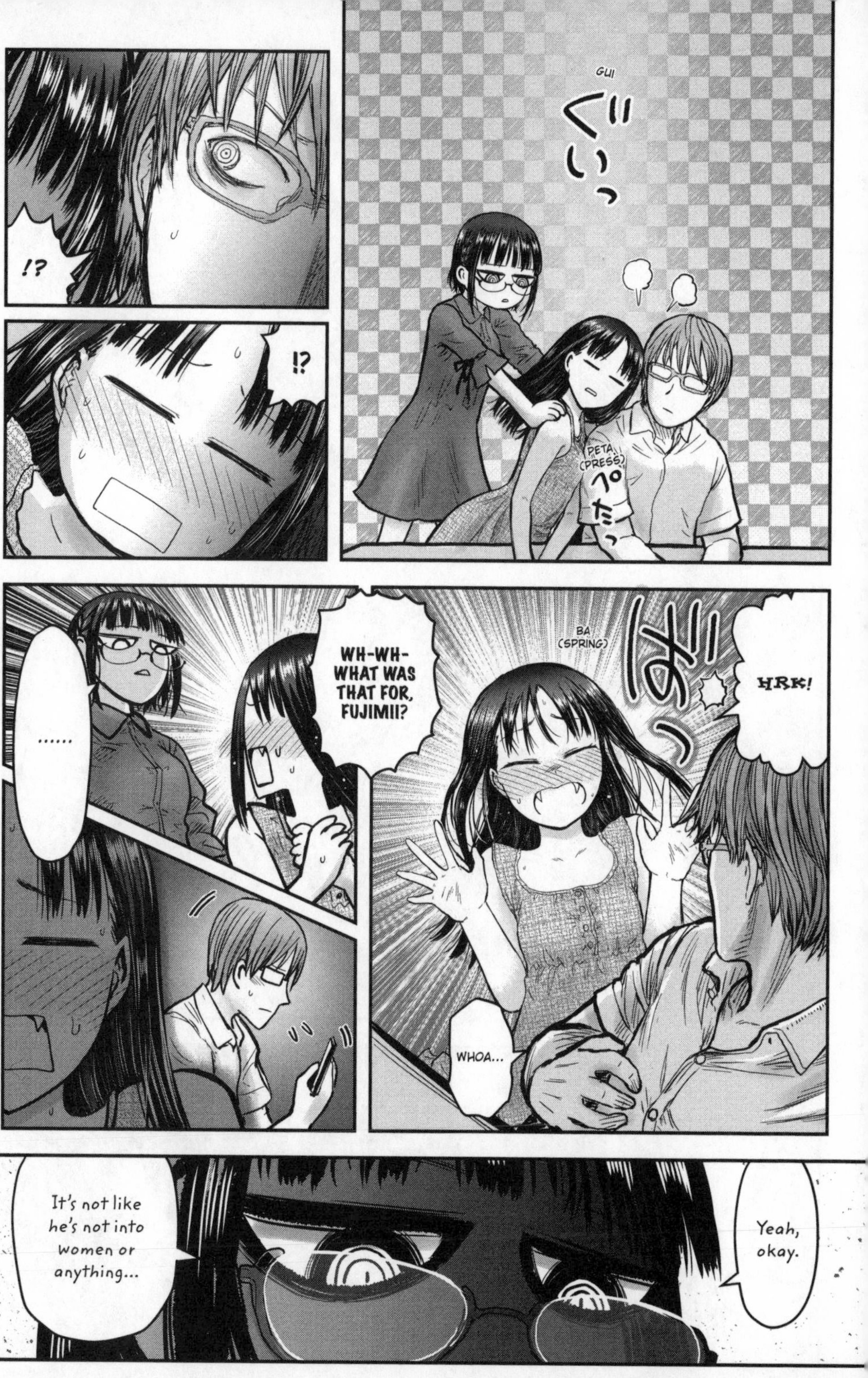
GUI
ぐいっ
PETA (PRESS)
ぺたっ
!?
!?
HRK!
BA (SPRING)
ばっ
WHOA...
WH-WH-WHAT WAS THAT FOR, FUJIMI!?
......
Yeah, okay.
It's not like he's not into women or anything...

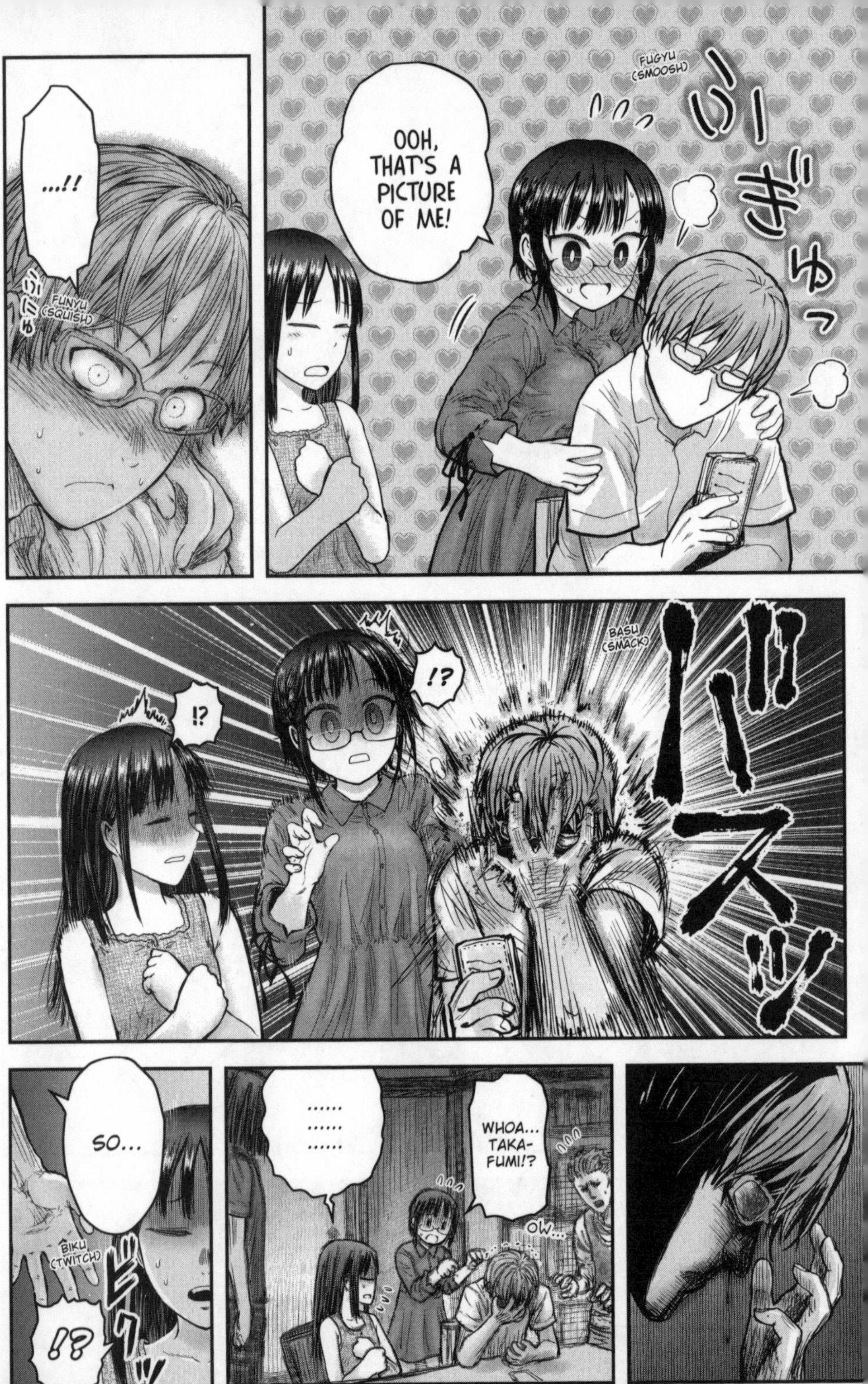
FUGYU (SMOOSH)
OOH, THAT'S A PICTURE OF ME!
...!!
FUNYU (SQUISH)
BASU (SMACK)
!?
!?
WHOA... TAKA-FUMI!?
OW...
......
......
......
SO...
BIKU (TWITCH)
!?

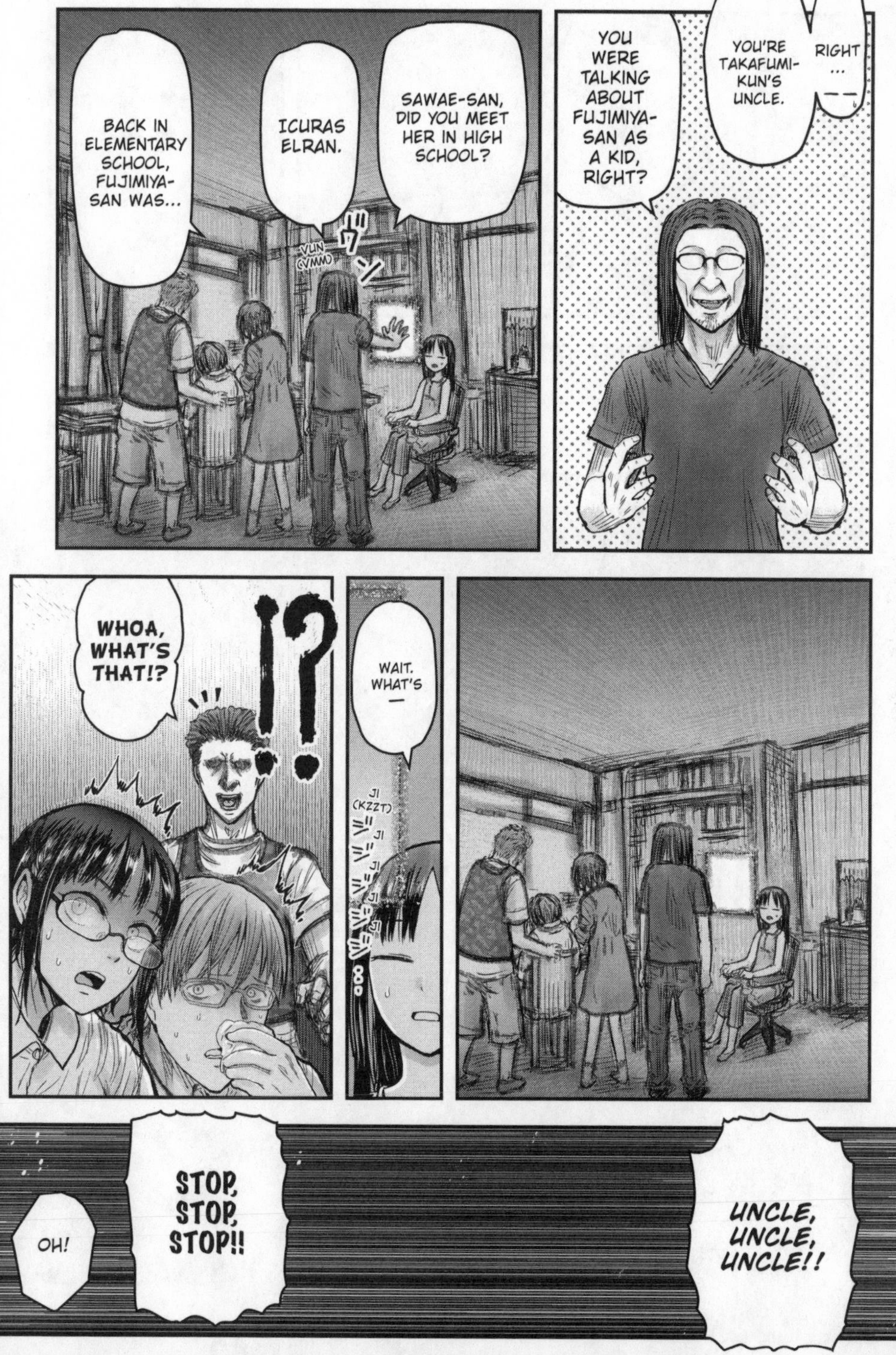
RIGHT ... ——
YOU'RE TAKAFUMI-KUN'S UNCLE.
YOU WERE TALKING ABOUT FUJIMIYA-SAN AS A KID, RIGHT?
SAWAE-SAN, DID YOU MEET HER IN HIGH SCHOOL?
VUN (VMM)
ICURAS ELRAN.
BACK IN ELEMENTARY SCHOOL, FUJIMIYA-SAN WAS...
WAIT. WHAT'S —
JI (KZZT) JI JI JI JI
WHOA, WHAT'S THAT!?
!?
UNCLE, UNCLE, UNCLE!!
STOP, STOP, STOP!!
OH!

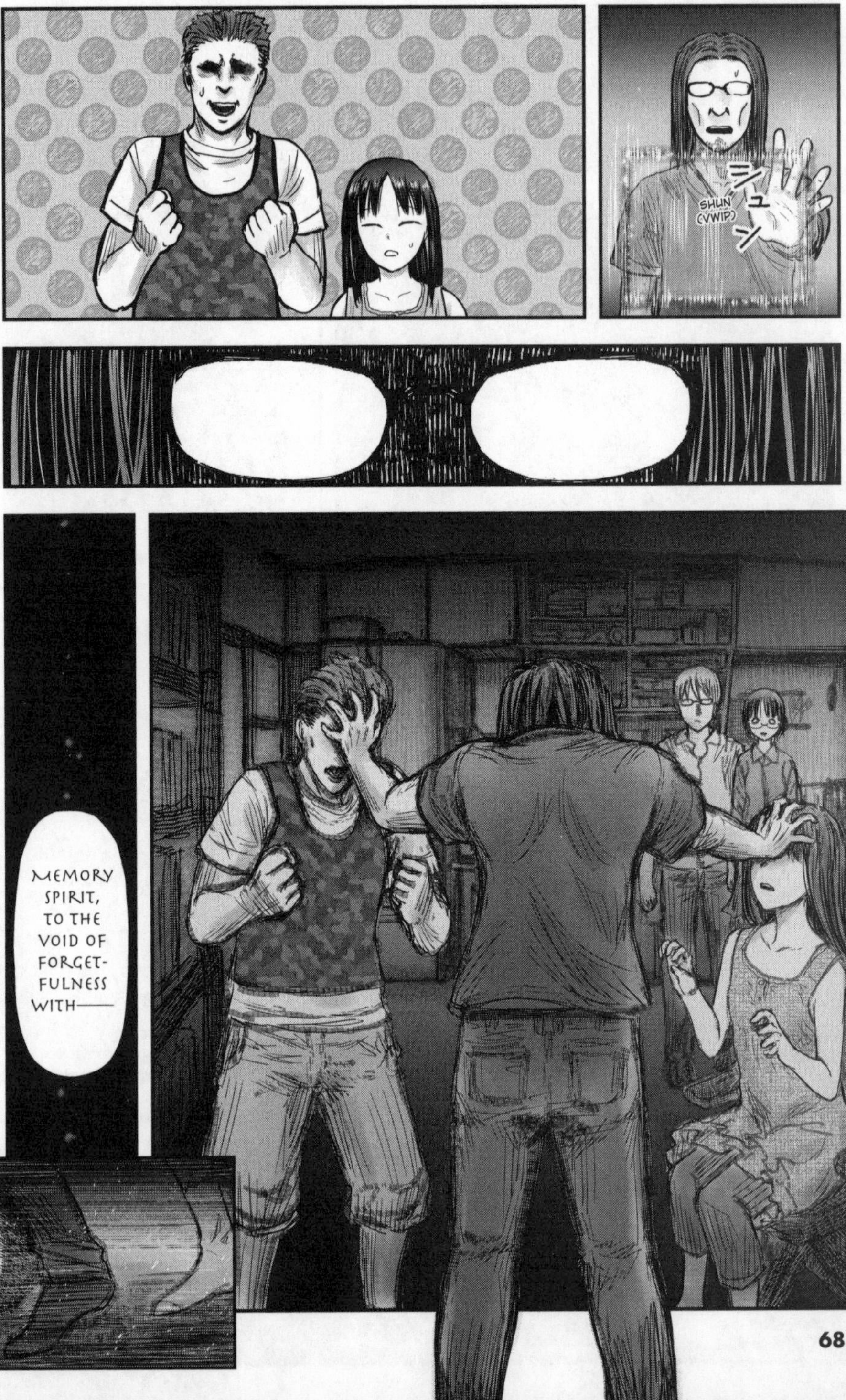
シュン
SHUN (VWIP)
MEMORY SPIRIT, TO THE VOID OF FORGET-FULNESS WITH——

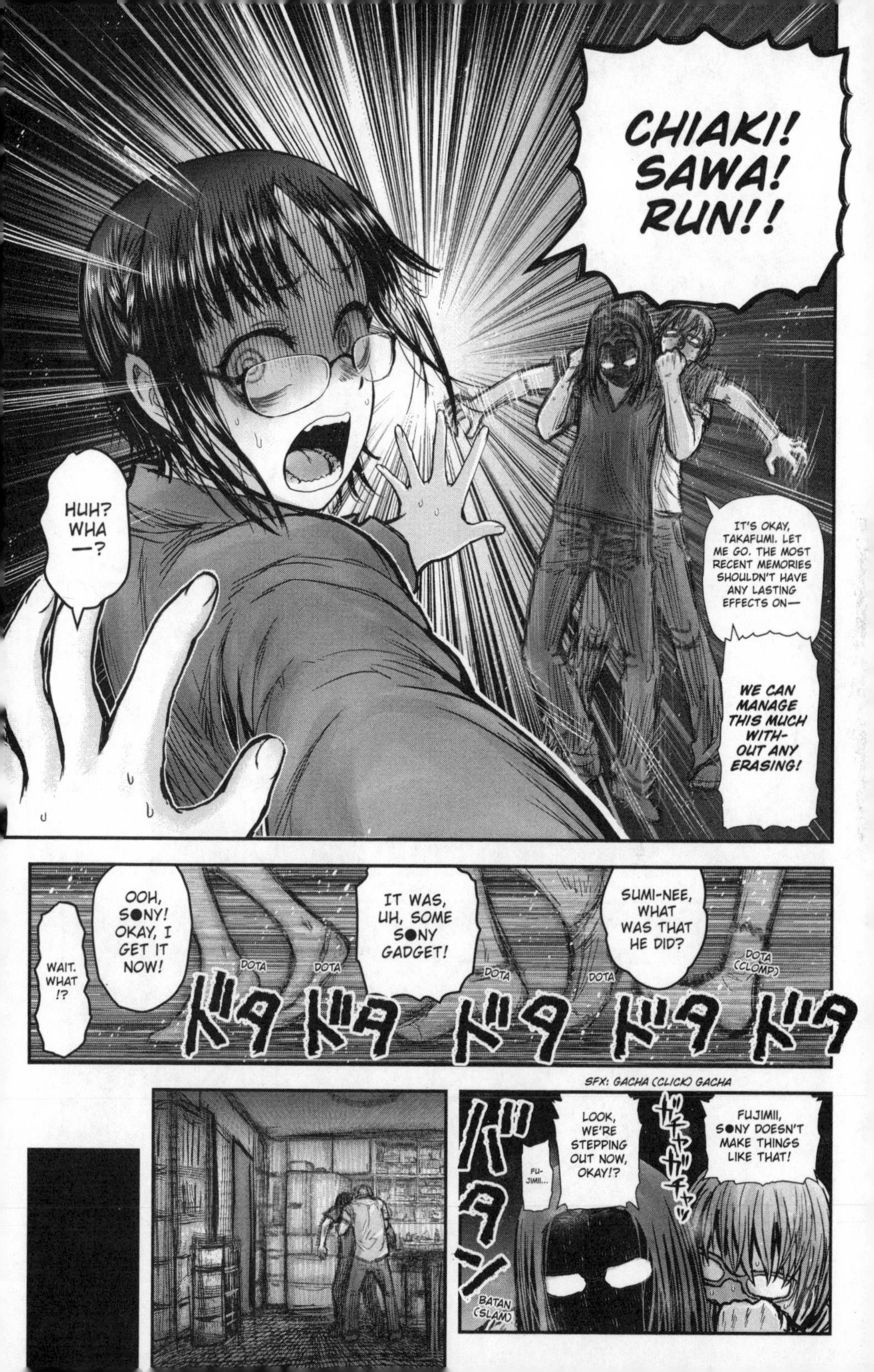
CHIAKI! SAWA! RUN!!
IT'S OKAY, TAKAFUMI. LET ME GO. THE MOST RECENT MEMORIES SHOULDN'T HAVE ANY LASTING EFFECTS ON—
WE CAN MANAGE THIS MUCH WITHOUT ANY ERASING!
HUH? WHA—?
SUMI-NEE, WHAT WAS THAT HE DID?
IT WAS, UH, SOME S●NY GADGET!
OOH, S●NY! OKAY, I GET IT NOW!
WAIT. WHAT!?
DOTA (CLOMP)
DOTA
DOTA
DOTA
DOTA
ドタドタドタドタドタ
SFX: GACHA (CLICK) GACHA
FUJIMII, S●NY DOESN'T MAKE THINGS LIKE THAT!
ガチャガチャ
LOOK, WE'RE STEPPING OUT NOW, OKAY!?
FU-JIMII...
バタン
BATAN (SLAM)

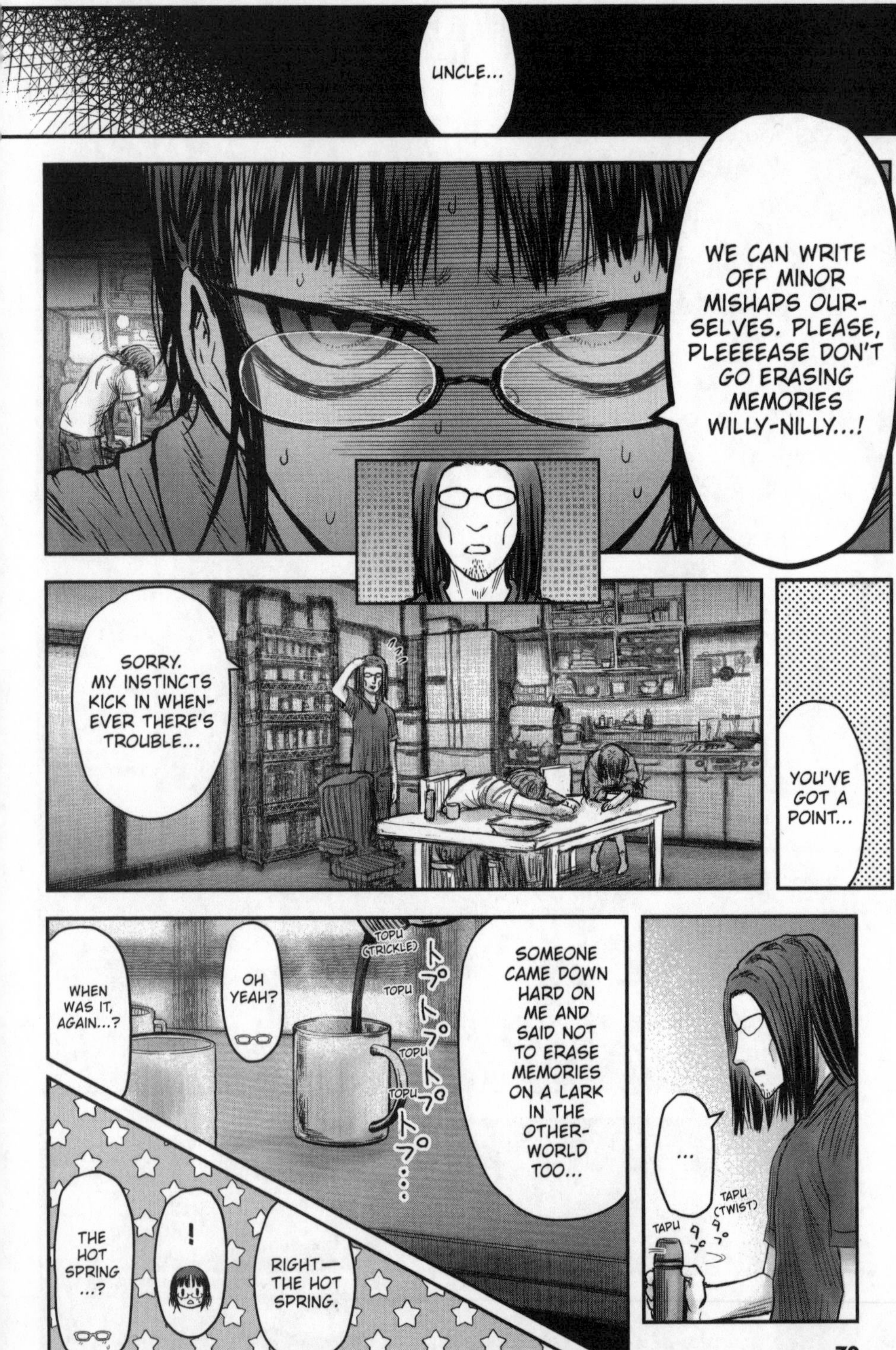
UNCLE...
WE CAN WRITE OFF MINOR MISHAPS OURSELVES. PLEASE, PLEEEEASE DON'T GO ERASING MEMORIES WILLY-NILLY...!
YOU'VE GOT A POINT...
SORRY. MY INSTINCTS KICK IN WHENEVER THERE'S TROUBLE...
...
TAPU (TWIST)
TAPU
SOMEONE CAME DOWN HARD ON ME AND SAID NOT TO ERASE MEMORIES ON A LARK IN THE OTHERWORLD TOO...
TOPU (TRICKLE)
TOPU
TOPU
TOPU
OH YEAH?
WHEN WAS IT, AGAIN...?
RIGHT— THE HOT SPRING.
!
THE HOT SPRING ...?

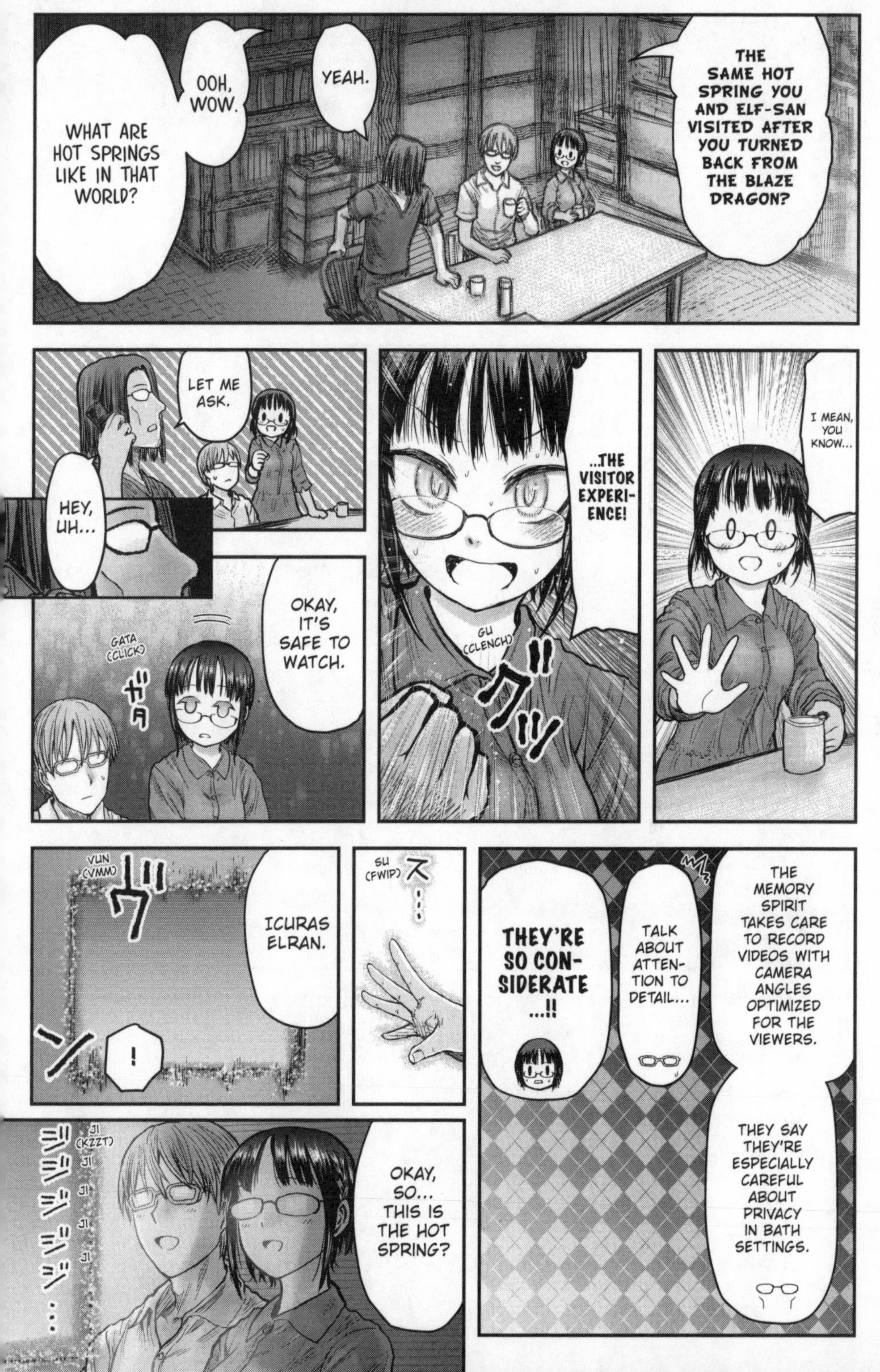
THE SAME HOT SPRING YOU AND ELF-SAN VISITED AFTER YOU TURNED BACK FROM THE BLAZE DRAGON?
YEAH.
OOH, WOW.
WHAT ARE HOT SPRINGS LIKE IN THAT WORLD?
I MEAN, YOU KNOW...
...THE VISITOR EXPERIENCE!
GU (CLENCH)
グッ
LET ME ASK.
HEY, UH...
OKAY, IT'S SAFE TO WATCH.
GATA (CLICK)
ガタ
THE MEMORY SPIRIT TAKES CARE TO RECORD VIDEOS WITH CAMERA ANGLES OPTIMIZED FOR THE VIEWERS.
TALK ABOUT ATTENTION TO DETAIL...
THEY'RE SO CON-SIDERATE ...!!
THEY SAY THEY'RE ESPECIALLY CAREFUL ABOUT PRIVACY IN BATH SETTINGS.
SU (FWIP)
ス…
ICURAS ELRAN.
VUN (VMM)
ヴン
!
OKAY, SO... THIS IS THE HOT SPRING?
JI (KZZT) JI JI JI JI
ジジジジ…

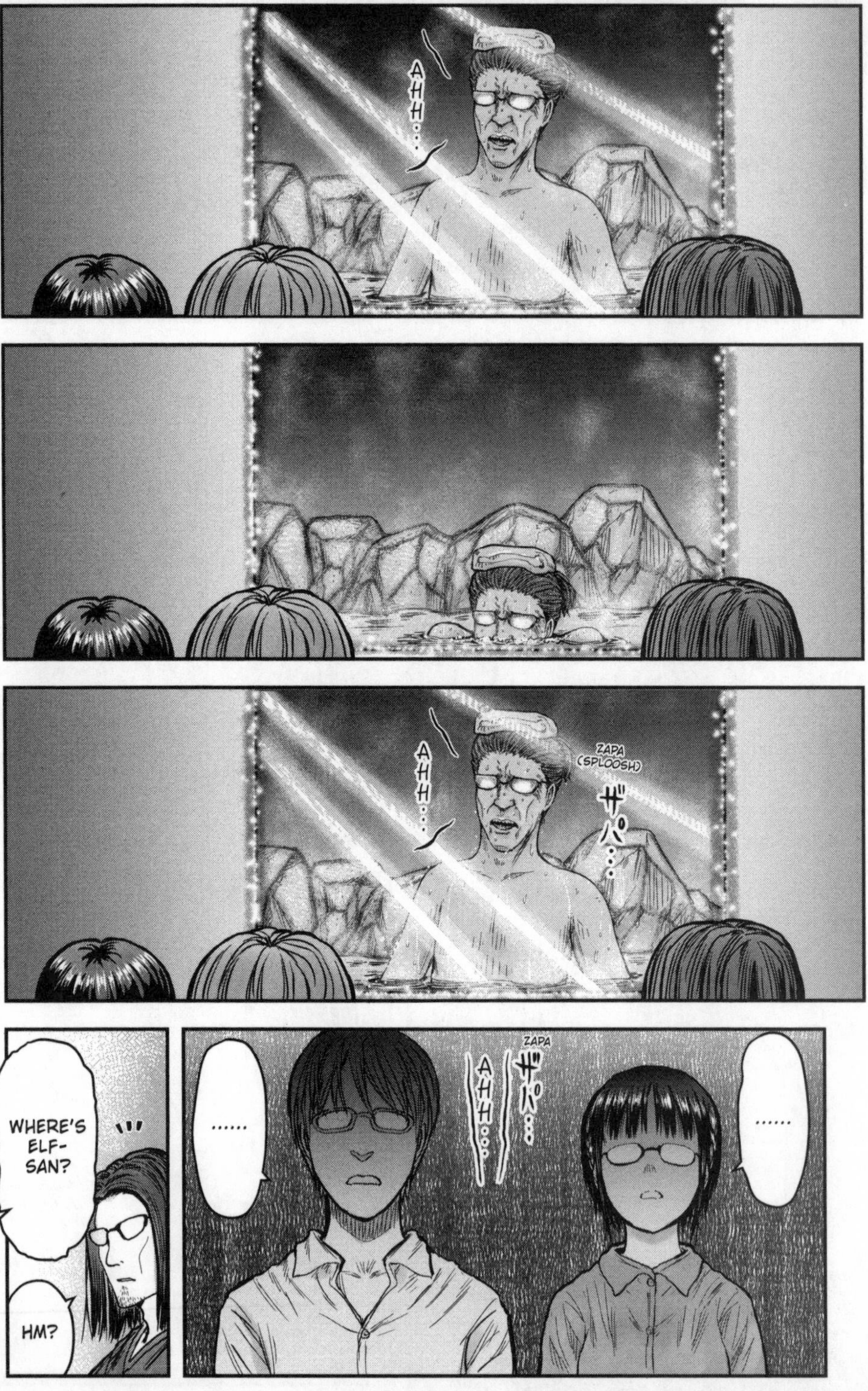
AHH...
ZAPA (SPLOOSH)
ザパ...
AHH...
......
ZAPA
ザパ...
AHH...
......
WHERE'S ELF-SAN?
HM?

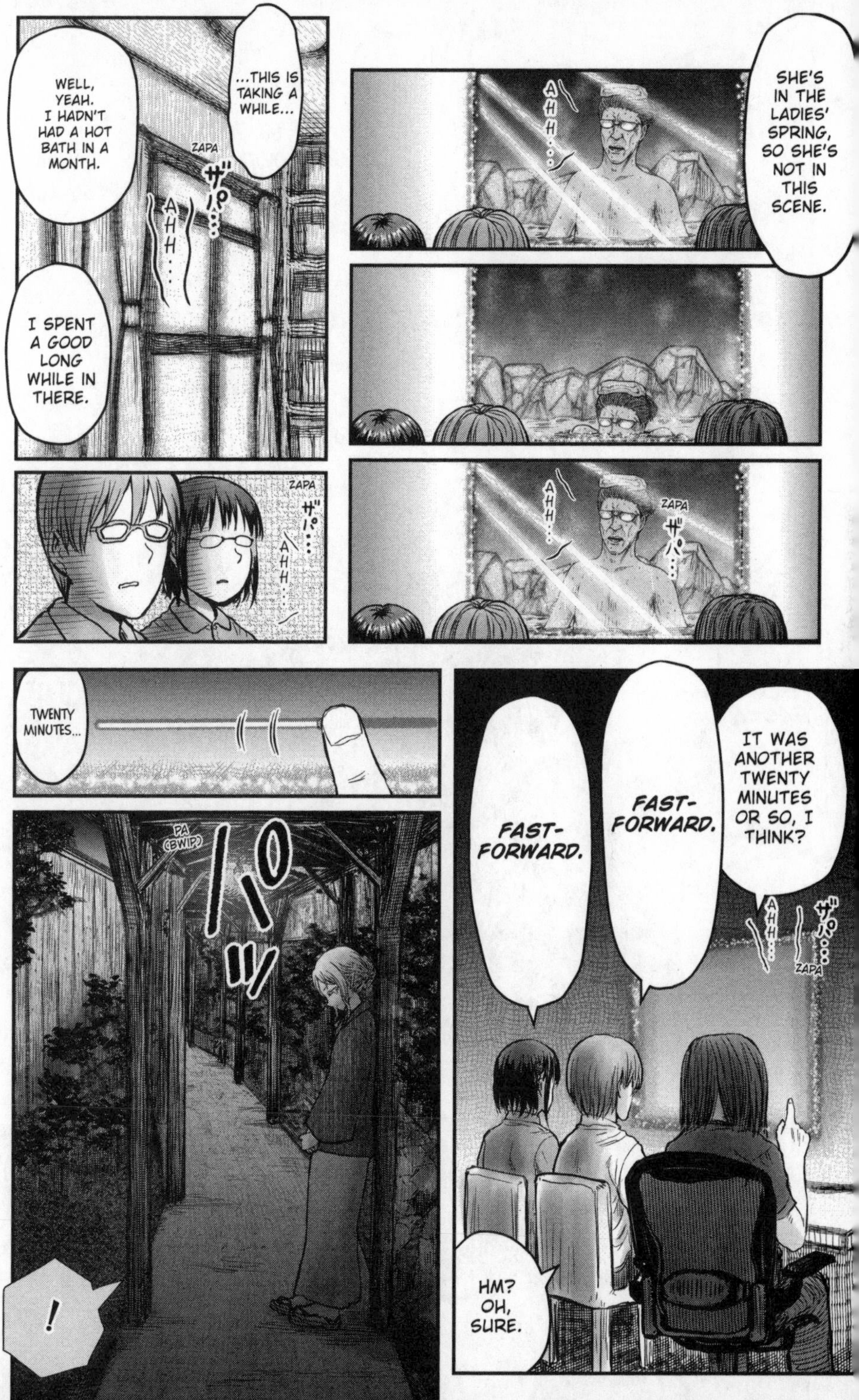
AHH...
SHE'S IN THE LADIES' SPRING, SO SHE'S NOT IN THIS SCENE.
AHH...
ザパ…
ZAPA
...THIS IS TAKING A WHILE...
WELL, YEAH. I HADN'T HAD A HOT BATH IN A MONTH.
ザパ…
ZAPA
AHH...
I SPENT A GOOD LONG WHILE IN THERE.
ザパ…
ZAPA
AHH...
IT WAS ANOTHER TWENTY MINUTES OR SO, I THINK?
FAST-FORWARD.
FAST-FORWARD.
ザパ…
ZAPA
AHH...
HM? OH, SURE.
TWENTY MINUTES...
パッ
PA (BWIP)
!

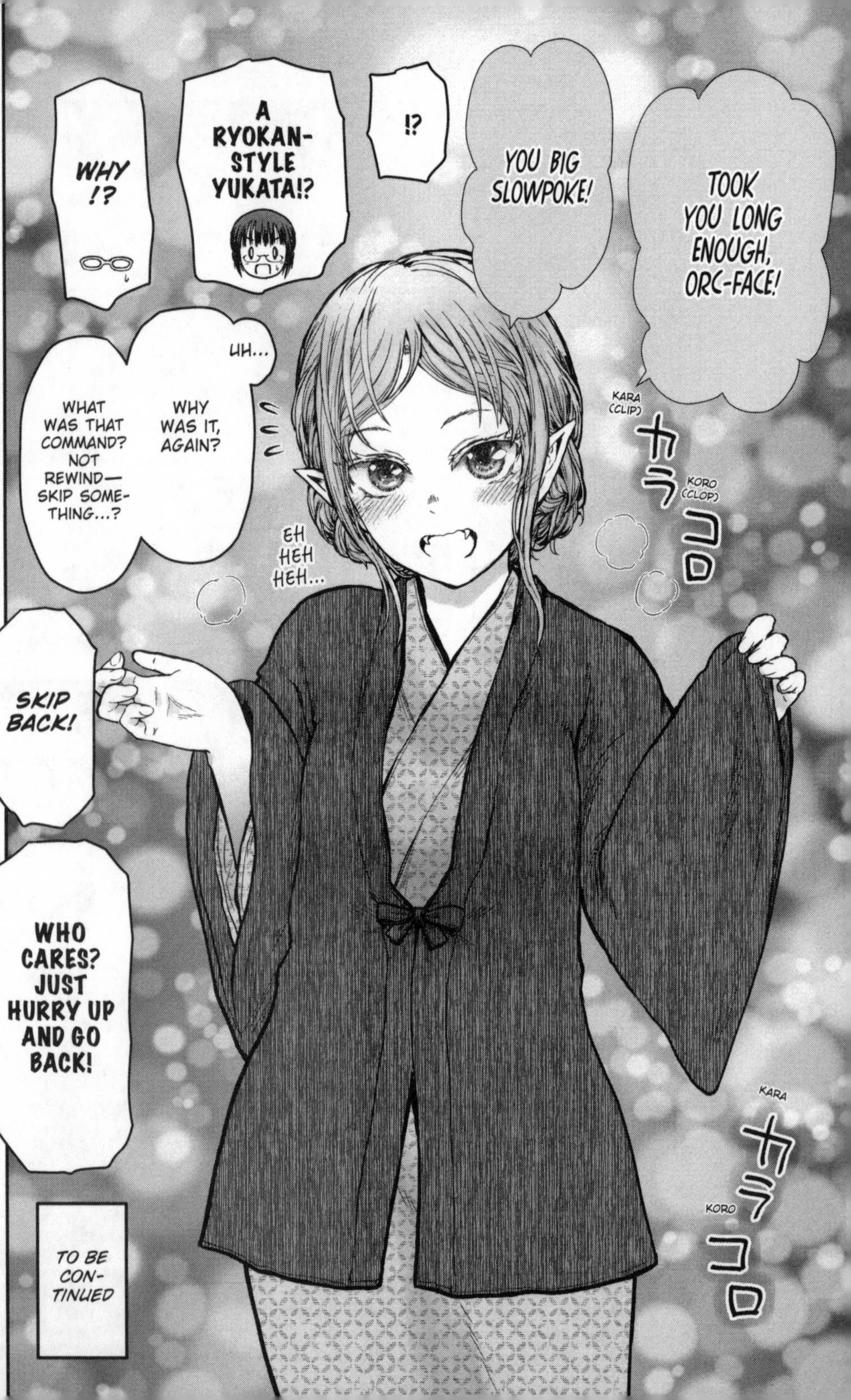
TOOK YOU LONG ENOUGH, ORC-FACE!
YOU BIG SLOWPOKE!
!?
A RYOKAN-STYLE YUKATA!?
WHY !?
KARA (CLIP) カラ
KORO (CLOP) コロ
EH HEH HEH...
UH...
WHY WAS IT, AGAIN?
WHAT WAS THAT COMMAND? NOT REWIND—SKIP SOMETHING...?
SKIP BACK!
WHO CARES? JUST HURRY UP AND GO BACK!
KARA カラ
KORO コロ
TO BE CONTINUED

Average Height of a Male Fourth Grader

Approx. 134 cm (4 feet, 4.75 inches)

Chiaki Fujimiya's height: 171 cm (5 feet, 7.3 inches) (Still growing)

TIPS

UNCLE from ANOTHER WORLD

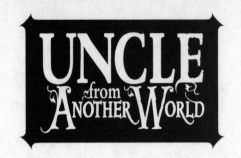

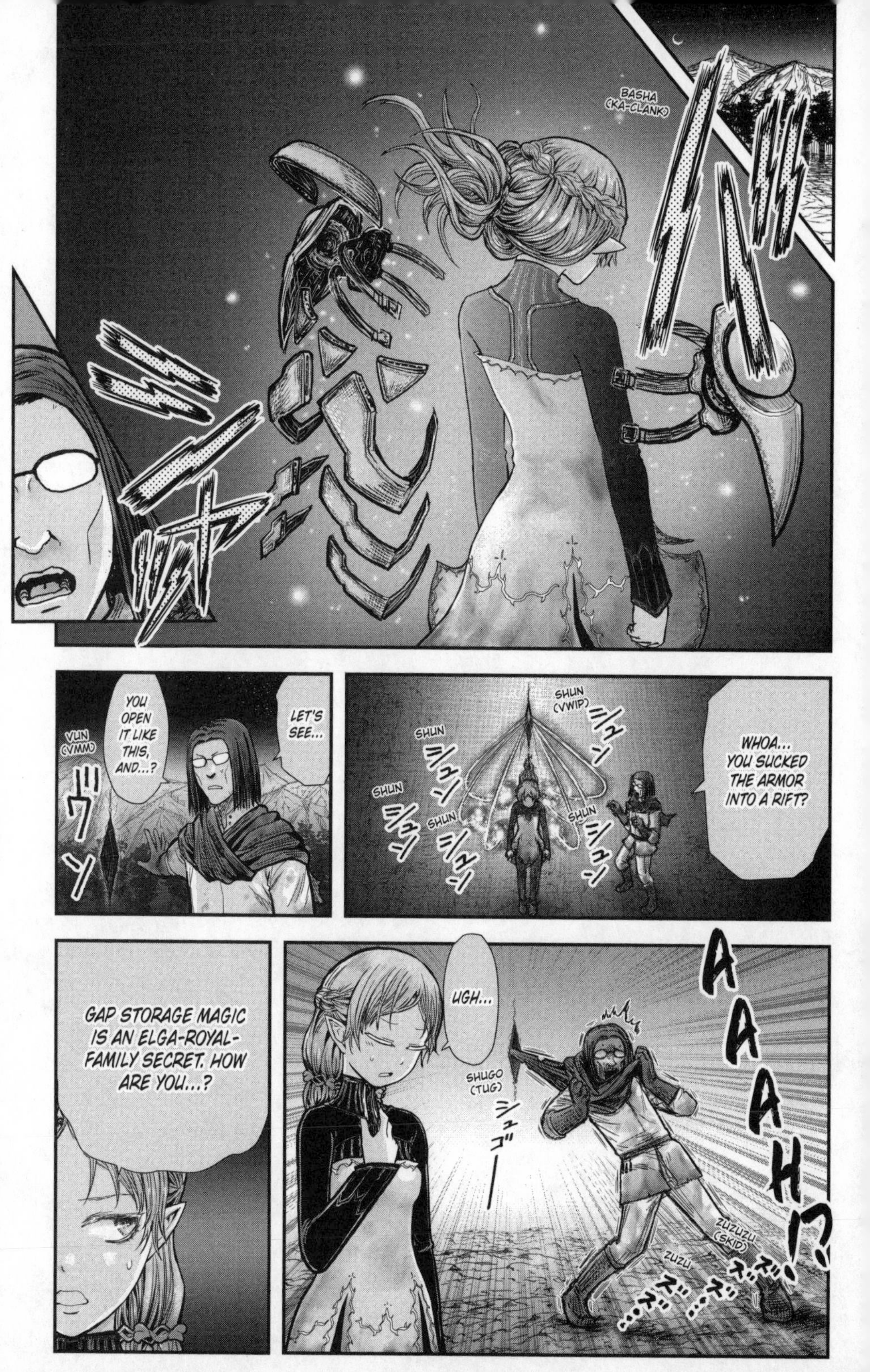

BASHA (KA-CLANK)
SHUN (VWIP)
SHUN
SHUN
SHUN
SHUN
WHOA... YOU SUCKED THE ARMOR INTO A RIFT?
LET'S SEE...
YOU OPEN IT LIKE THIS, AND...?
VUN (VMM)
AAAAH!?
UGH...
SHUGO (TUG)
ZUZUZU (SKID)
ZUZU
GAP STORAGE MAGIC IS AN ELGA-ROYAL-FAMILY SECRET. HOW ARE YOU...?

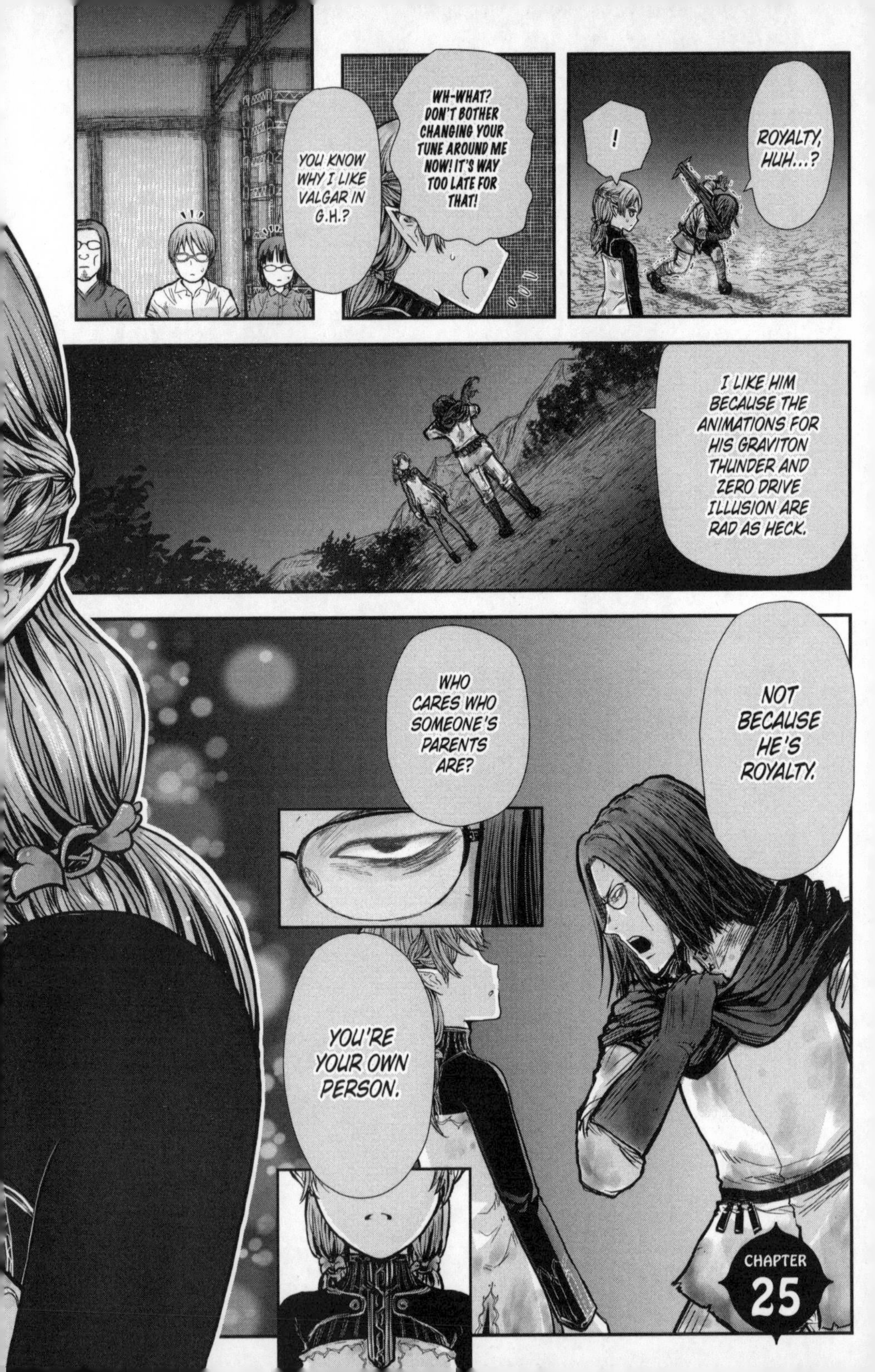
ROYALTY, HUH...?
!
WH-WHAT? DON'T BOTHER CHANGING YOUR TUNE AROUND ME NOW! IT'S WAY TOO LATE FOR THAT!
YOU KNOW WHY I LIKE VALGAR IN G.H.?
I LIKE HIM BECAUSE THE ANIMATIONS FOR HIS GRAVITON THUNDER AND ZERO DRIVE ILLUSION ARE RAD AS HECK.
NOT BECAUSE HE'S ROYALTY.
WHO CARES WHO SOMEONE'S PARENTS ARE?
YOU'RE YOUR OWN PERSON.
CHAPTER 25

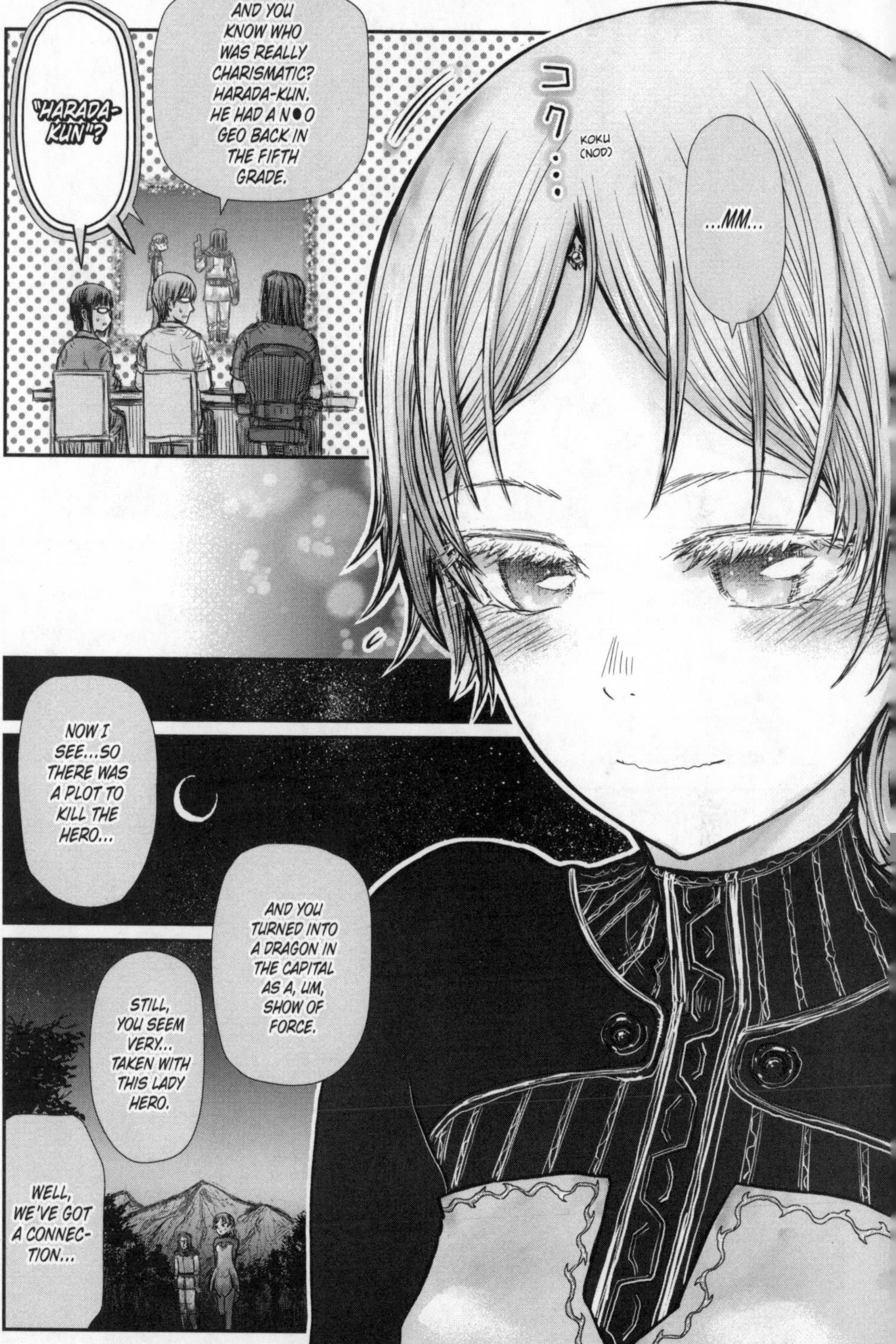
コク…
KOKU (NOD)
...MM...
AND YOU KNOW WHO WAS REALLY CHARISMATIC? HARADA-KUN. HE HAD A N●O GEO BACK IN THE FIFTH GRADE.
"HARADA-KUN"?
NOW I SEE...SO THERE WAS A PLOT TO KILL THE HERO...
AND YOU TURNED INTO A DRAGON IN THE CAPITAL AS A, UM, SHOW OF FORCE.
STILL, YOU SEEM VERY... TAKEN WITH THIS LADY HERO.
WELL, WE'VE GOT A CONNECTION...

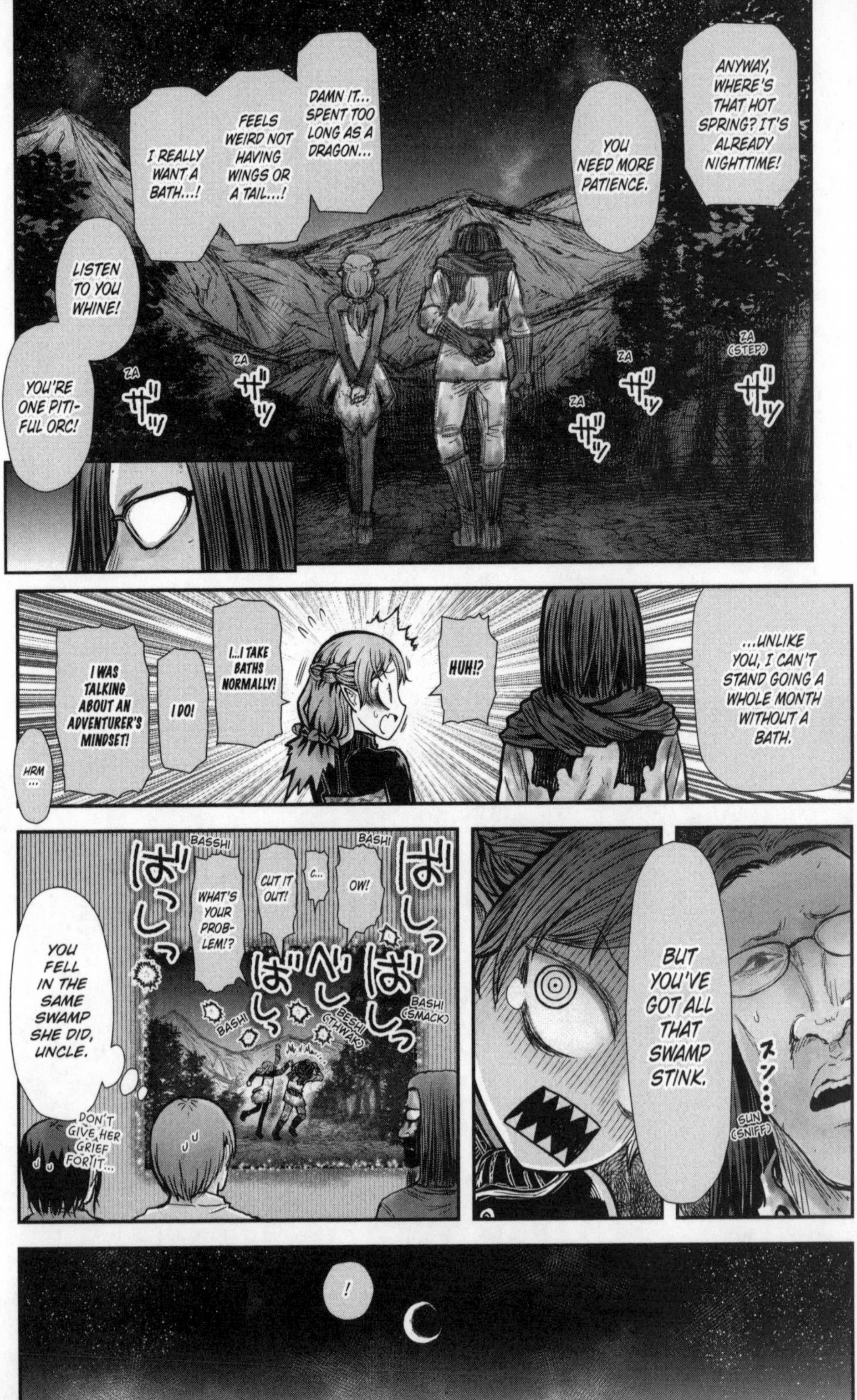
ANYWAY, WHERE'S THAT HOT SPRING? IT'S ALREADY NIGHTTIME!
YOU NEED MORE PATIENCE.
DAMN IT... SPENT TOO LONG AS A DRAGON...
FEELS WEIRD NOT HAVING WINGS OR A TAIL...!
I REALLY WANT A BATH...!
ZA (STEP)
ZA
ZA
ZA
ZA
LISTEN TO YOU WHINE!
YOU'RE ONE PITI-FUL ORC!
...UNLIKE YOU, I CAN'T STAND GOING A WHOLE MONTH WITHOUT A BATH.
HUH!?
I...I TAKE BATHS NORMALLY!
I DO!
I WAS TALKING ABOUT AN ADVENTURER'S MINDSET!
HRM...
SUN (SNIFF)
BUT YOU'VE GOT ALL THAT SWAMP STINK.
BASHI
OW!
C...
CUT IT OUT!
WHAT'S YOUR PROB-LEM!?
BASSHI
BASHI (SMACK)
BESHI (THWAK)
BASHI
YOU FELL IN THE SAME SWAMP SHE DID, UNCLE.
DON'T GIVE HER GRIEF FOR IT...
!

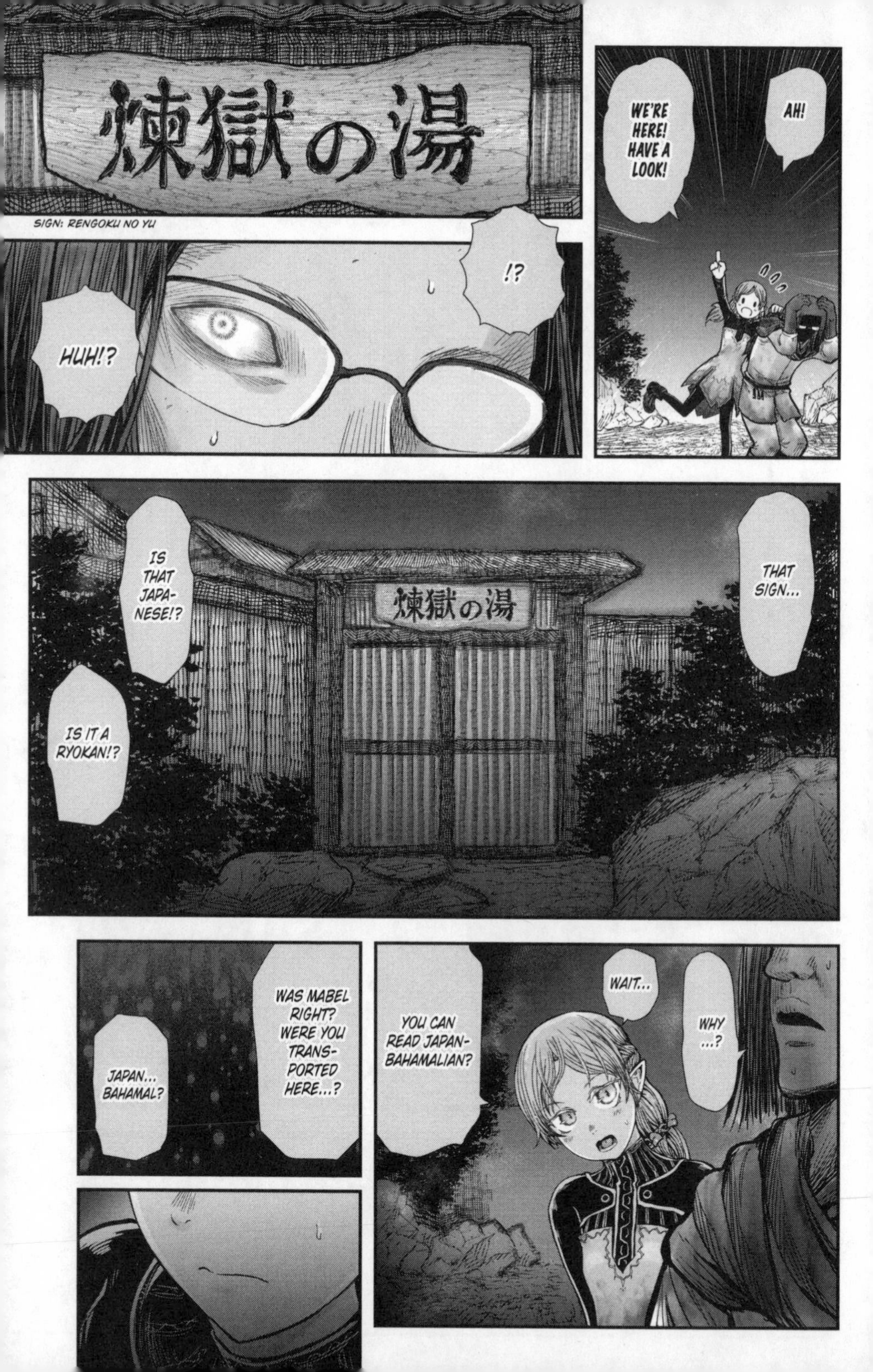
AH!
WE'RE HERE! HAVE A LOOK!
煉獄の湯
SIGN: RENGOKU NO YU
!?
HUH!?
THAT SIGN...
IS THAT JAPA-NESE!?
IS IT A RYOKAN!?
WAIT...
WHY ...?
YOU CAN READ JAPAN-BAHAMALIAN?
WAS MABEL RIGHT? WERE YOU TRANS-PORTED HERE...?
JAPAN... BAHAMAL?

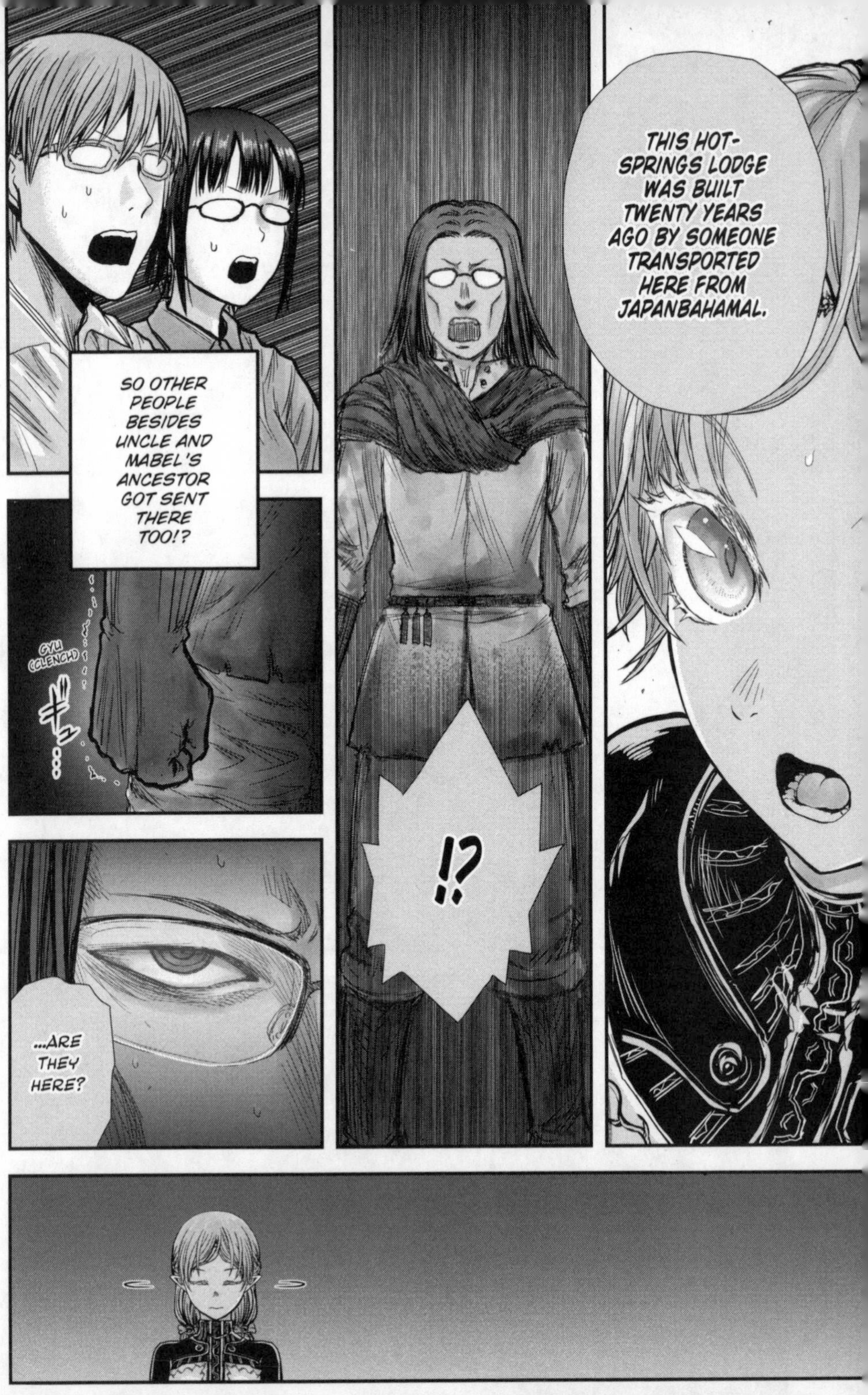
THIS HOT-SPRINGS LODGE WAS BUILT TWENTY YEARS AGO BY SOMEONE TRANSPORTED HERE FROM JAPANBAHAMAL.
!?
SO OTHER PEOPLE BESIDES UNCLE AND MABEL'S ANCESTOR GOT SENT THERE TOO!?
GYU (CLENCH)
...ARE THEY HERE?

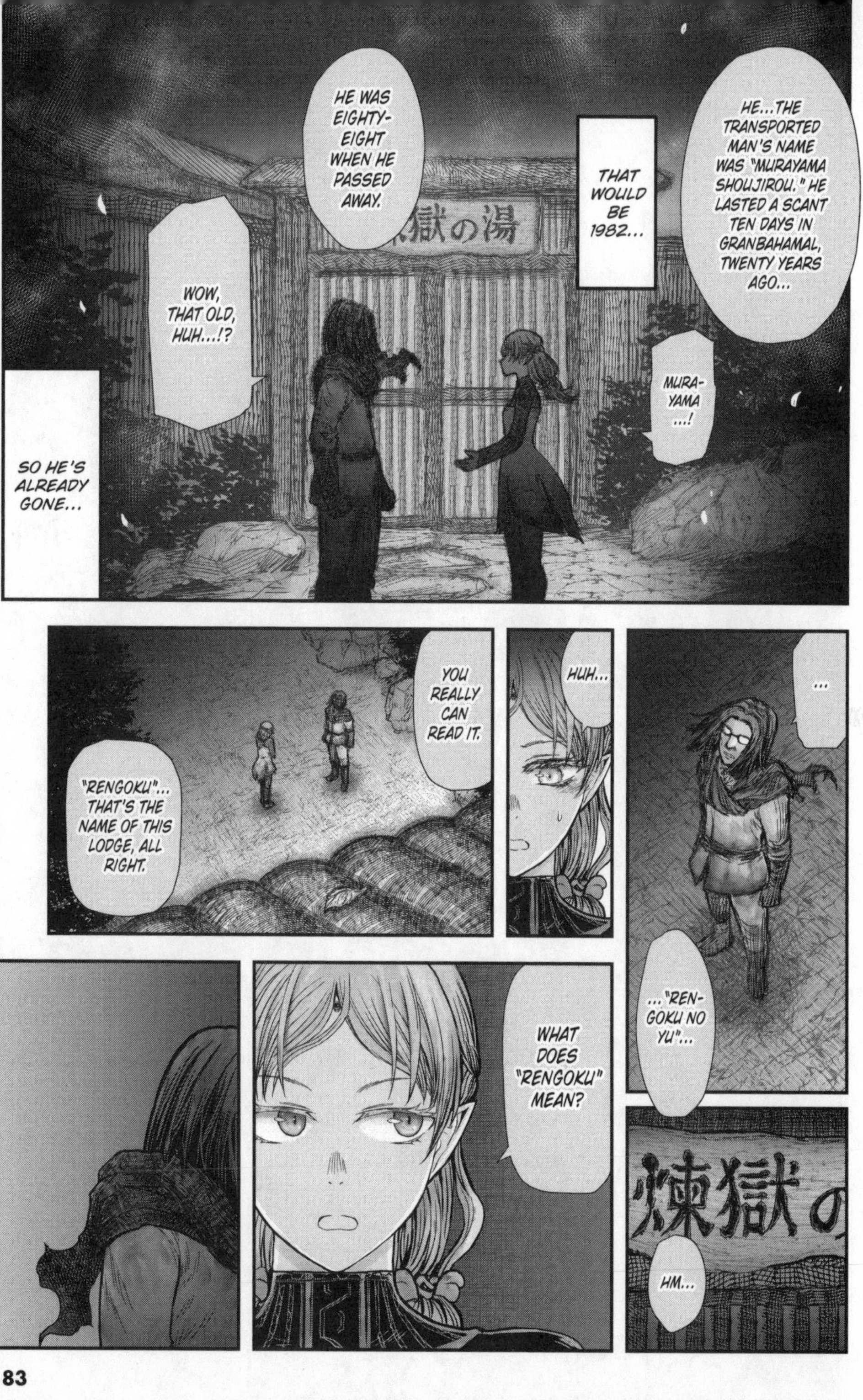
HE...THE TRANSPORTED MAN'S NAME WAS "MURAYAMA SHOUJIROU." HE LASTED A SCANT TEN DAYS IN GRANBAHAMAL, TWENTY YEARS AGO...
THAT WOULD BE 1982...
HE WAS EIGHTY-EIGHT WHEN HE PASSED AWAY.
MURA-YAMA ...!
WOW, THAT OLD, HUH...!?
SO HE'S ALREADY GONE...
...
..."REN-GOKU NO YU"...
HUH...
YOU REALLY CAN READ IT.
"RENGOKU"... THAT'S THE NAME OF THIS LODGE, ALL RIGHT.
WHAT DOES "RENGOKU" MEAN?
HM...

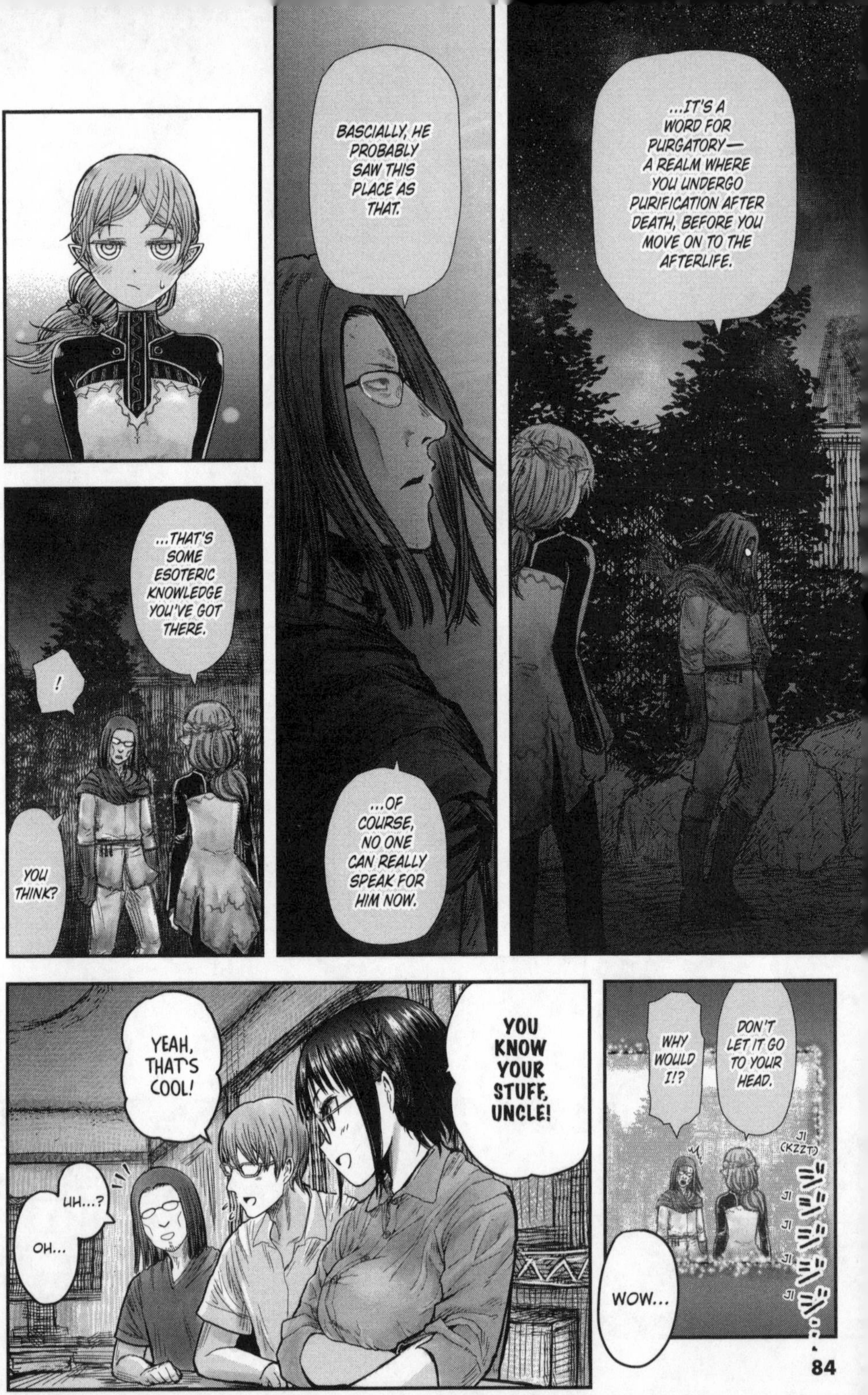
...IT'S A WORD FOR PURGATORY— A REALM WHERE YOU UNDERGO PURIFICATION AFTER DEATH, BEFORE YOU MOVE ON TO THE AFTERLIFE.
BASCIALLY, HE PROBABLY SAW THIS PLACE AS THAT.
...OF COURSE, NO ONE CAN REALLY SPEAK FOR HIM NOW.
...THAT'S SOME ESOTERIC KNOWLEDGE YOU'VE GOT THERE.
!
YOU THINK?
DON'T LET IT GO TO YOUR HEAD.
WHY WOULD I!?
JI (KZZT)
JI
JI
JI
JI
WOW...
YOU KNOW YOUR STUFF, UNCLE!
YEAH, THAT'S COOL!
UH...?
OH...

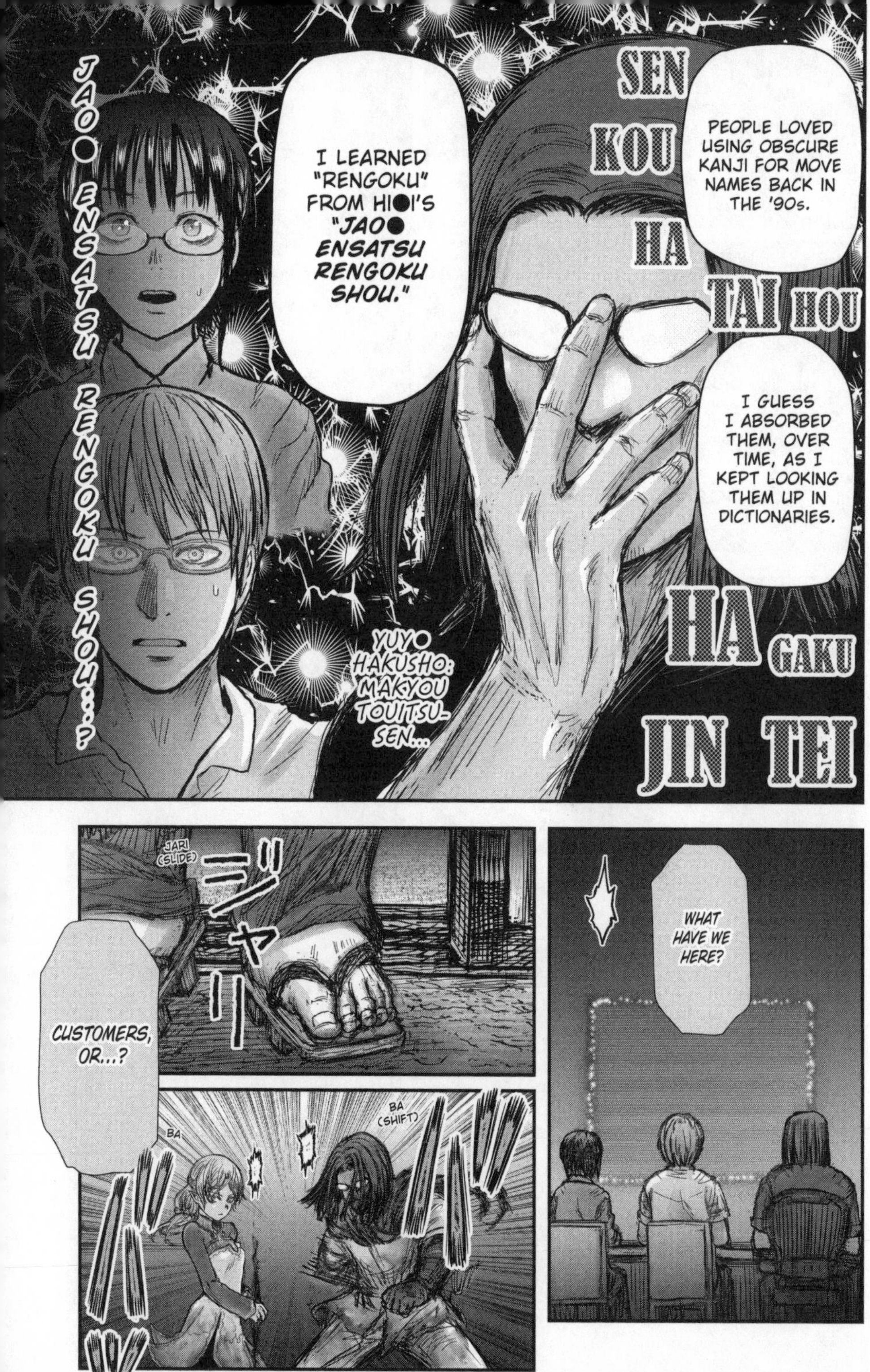
PEOPLE LOVED USING OBSCURE KANJI FOR MOVE NAMES BACK IN THE '90s.
I GUESS I ABSORBED THEM, OVER TIME, AS I KEPT LOOKING THEM UP IN DICTIONARIES.
SEN KOU HA TAI HOU HA GAKU JIN TEI
I LEARNED "RENGOKU" FROM HI●I'S "JAO● ENSATSU RENGOKU SHOU."
YUYO HAKUSHO: MAKYOU TOUITSU-SEN...
JAO● ENSATSU RENGOKU SHOU...?
WHAT HAVE WE HERE?
JARI (SLIDE)
CUSTOMERS, OR...?
BA (SHIFT)
BA

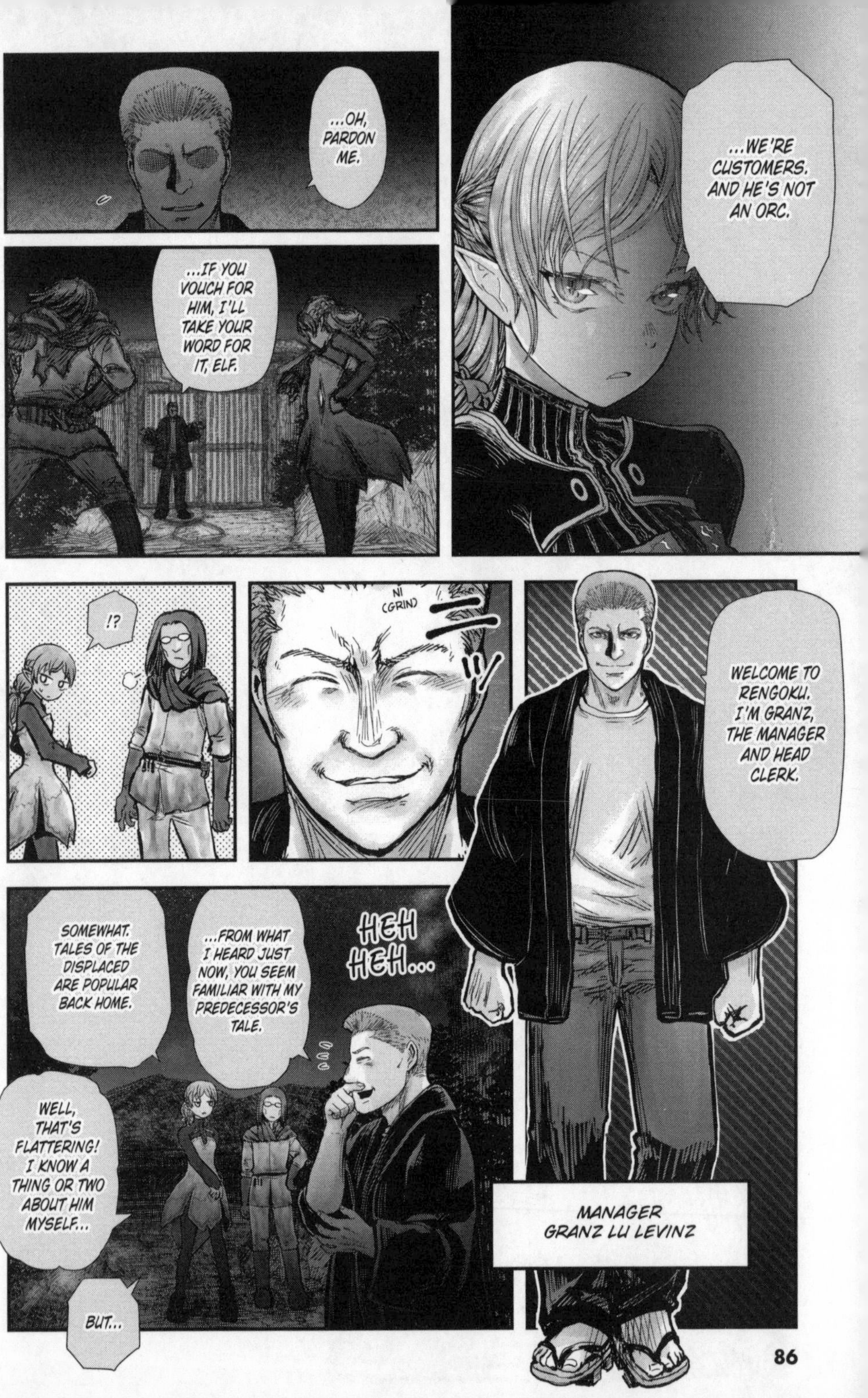
...WE'RE CUSTOMERS. AND HE'S NOT AN ORC.
...OH, PARDON ME.
...IF YOU VOUCH FOR HIM, I'LL TAKE YOUR WORD FOR IT, ELF.
WELCOME TO RENGOKU. I'M GRANZ, THE MANAGER AND HEAD CLERK.
MANAGER GRANZ LU LEVINZ
NI (GRIN)
!?
HEH HEH...
...FROM WHAT I HEARD JUST NOW, YOU SEEM FAMILIAR WITH MY PREDECESSOR'S TALE.
SOMEWHAT. TALES OF THE DISPLACED ARE POPULAR BACK HOME.
WELL, THAT'S FLATTERING! I KNOW A THING OR TWO ABOUT HIM MYSELF...
BUT...

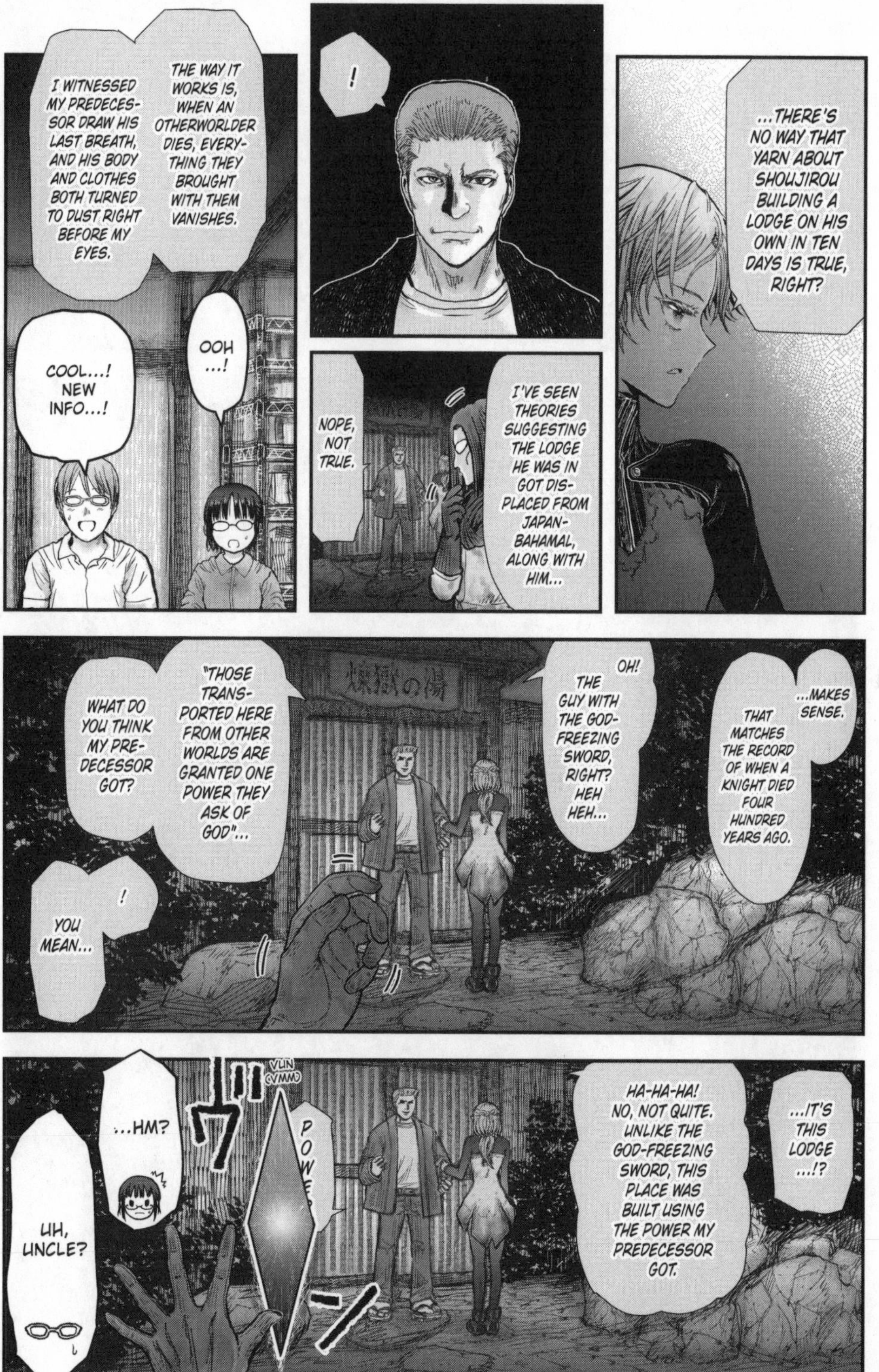
...THERE'S NO WAY THAT YARN ABOUT SHOUJIROU BUILDING A LODGE ON HIS OWN IN TEN DAYS IS TRUE, RIGHT?
!
I'VE SEEN THEORIES SUGGESTING THE LODGE HE WAS IN GOT DISPLACED FROM JAPAN-BAHAMAL, ALONG WITH HIM...
NOPE, NOT TRUE.
THE WAY IT WORKS IS, WHEN AN OTHERWORLDER DIES, EVERYTHING THEY BROUGHT WITH THEM VANISHES.
I WITNESSED MY PREDECESSOR DRAW HIS LAST BREATH, AND HIS BODY AND CLOTHES BOTH TURNED TO DUST RIGHT BEFORE MY EYES.
OOH ...!
COOL...! NEW INFO...!
...MAKES SENSE.
THAT MATCHES THE RECORD OF WHEN A KNIGHT DIED FOUR HUNDRED YEARS AGO.
OH! THE GUY WITH THE GOD-FREEZING SWORD, RIGHT? HEH HEH...
煉獄の湯
"THOSE TRANSPORTED HERE FROM OTHER WORLDS ARE GRANTED ONE POWER THEY ASK OF GOD"...
WHAT DO YOU THINK MY PREDECESSOR GOT?
!
YOU MEAN...
...IT'S THIS LODGE ...!?
HA-HA-HA! NO, NOT QUITE. UNLIKE THE GOD-FREEZING SWORD, THIS PLACE WAS BUILT USING THE POWER MY PREDECESSOR GOT.
POWE
VUN (VMM)
...HM?
UH, UNCLE?

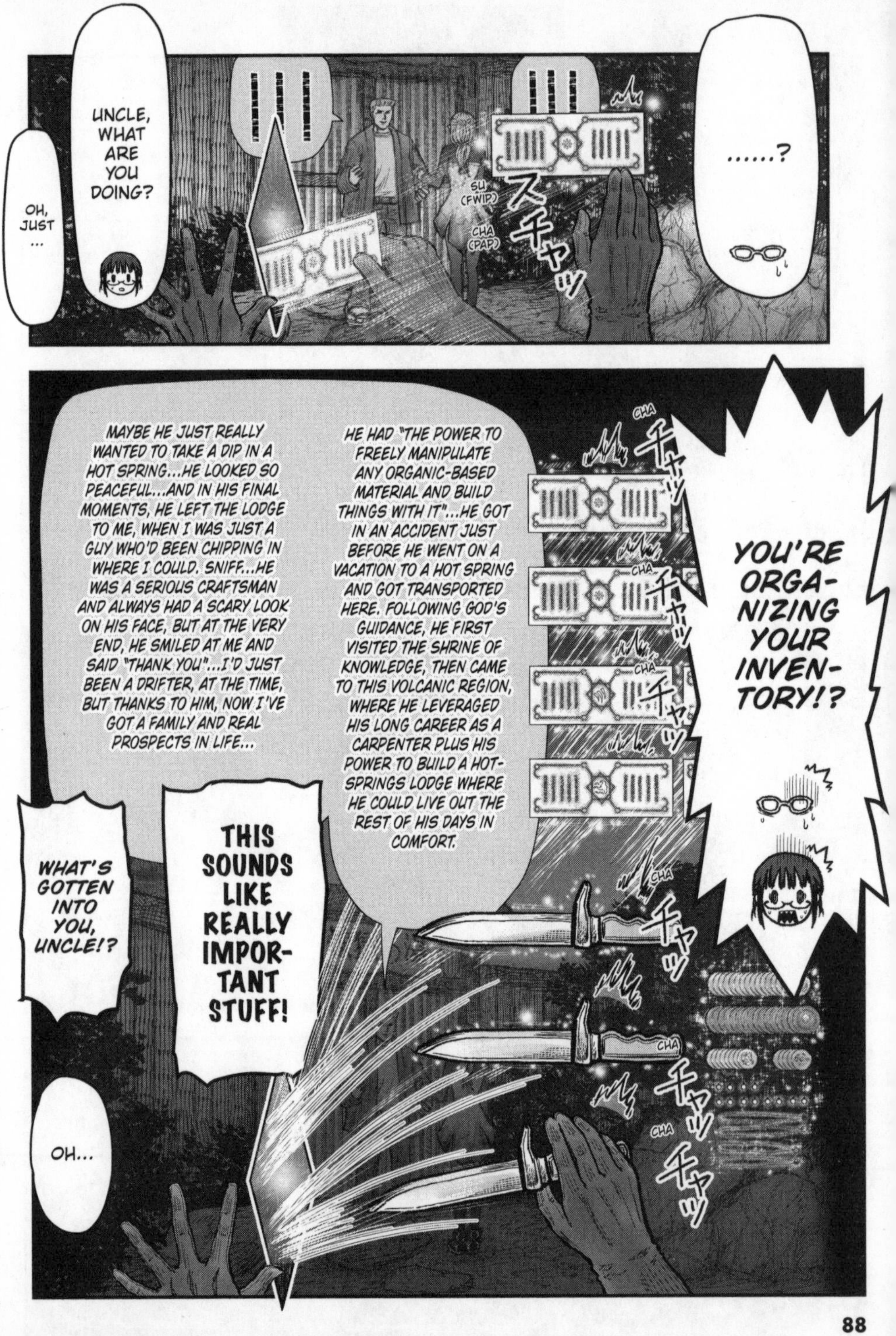
......?
SU (FWIP)
CHA (PAP)
UNCLE, WHAT ARE YOU DOING?
OH, JUST ...
YOU'RE ORGANIZING YOUR INVENTORY!?
CHA
CHA
CHA
HE HAD "THE POWER TO FREELY MANIPULATE ANY ORGANIC-BASED MATERIAL AND BUILD THINGS WITH IT"...HE GOT IN AN ACCIDENT JUST BEFORE HE WENT ON A VACATION TO A HOT SPRING AND GOT TRANSPORTED HERE. FOLLOWING GOD'S GUIDANCE, HE FIRST VISITED THE SHRINE OF KNOWLEDGE, THEN CAME TO THIS VOLCANIC REGION, WHERE HE LEVERAGED HIS LONG CAREER AS A CARPENTER PLUS HIS POWER TO BUILD A HOT-SPRINGS LODGE WHERE HE COULD LIVE OUT THE REST OF HIS DAYS IN COMFORT.
MAYBE HE JUST REALLY WANTED TO TAKE A DIP IN A HOT SPRING...HE LOOKED SO PEACEFUL...AND IN HIS FINAL MOMENTS, HE LEFT THE LODGE TO ME, WHEN I WAS JUST A GUY WHO'D BEEN CHIPPING IN WHERE I COULD. SNIFF...HE WAS A SERIOUS CRAFTSMAN AND ALWAYS HAD A SCARY LOOK ON HIS FACE, BUT AT THE VERY END, HE SMILED AT ME AND SAID "THANK YOU"...I'D JUST BEEN A DRIFTER, AT THE TIME, BUT THANKS TO HIM, NOW I'VE GOT A FAMILY AND REAL PROSPECTS IN LIFE...
CHA
CHA
CHA
THIS SOUNDS LIKE REALLY IMPORTANT STUFF!
WHAT'S GOTTEN INTO YOU, UNCLE!?
OH...

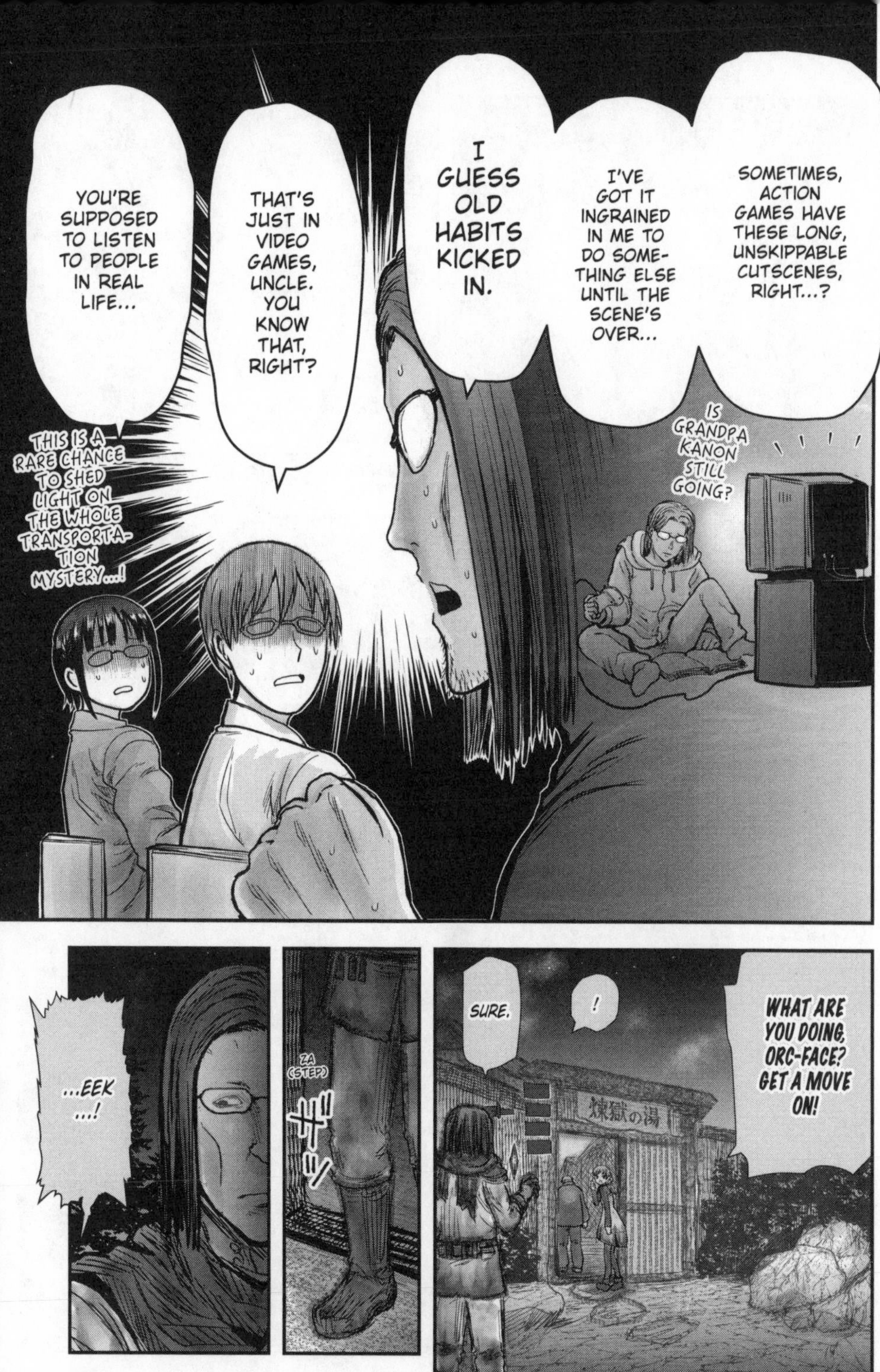
SOMETIMES, ACTION GAMES HAVE THESE LONG, UNSKIPPABLE CUTSCENES, RIGHT...?
I'VE GOT IT INGRAINED IN ME TO DO SOME-THING ELSE UNTIL THE SCENE'S OVER...
I GUESS OLD HABITS KICKED IN.
IS GRANDPA KANON STILL GOING?
THAT'S JUST IN VIDEO GAMES, UNCLE. YOU KNOW THAT, RIGHT?
YOU'RE SUPPOSED TO LISTEN TO PEOPLE IN REAL LIFE...
THIS IS A RARE CHANCE TO SHED LIGHT ON THE WHOLE TRANSPORTA-TION MYSTERY...!
WHAT ARE YOU DOING, ORC-FACE? GET A MOVE ON!
!
SURE.
煉獄の湯
ZA (STEP)
ザッ
...EEK ...!

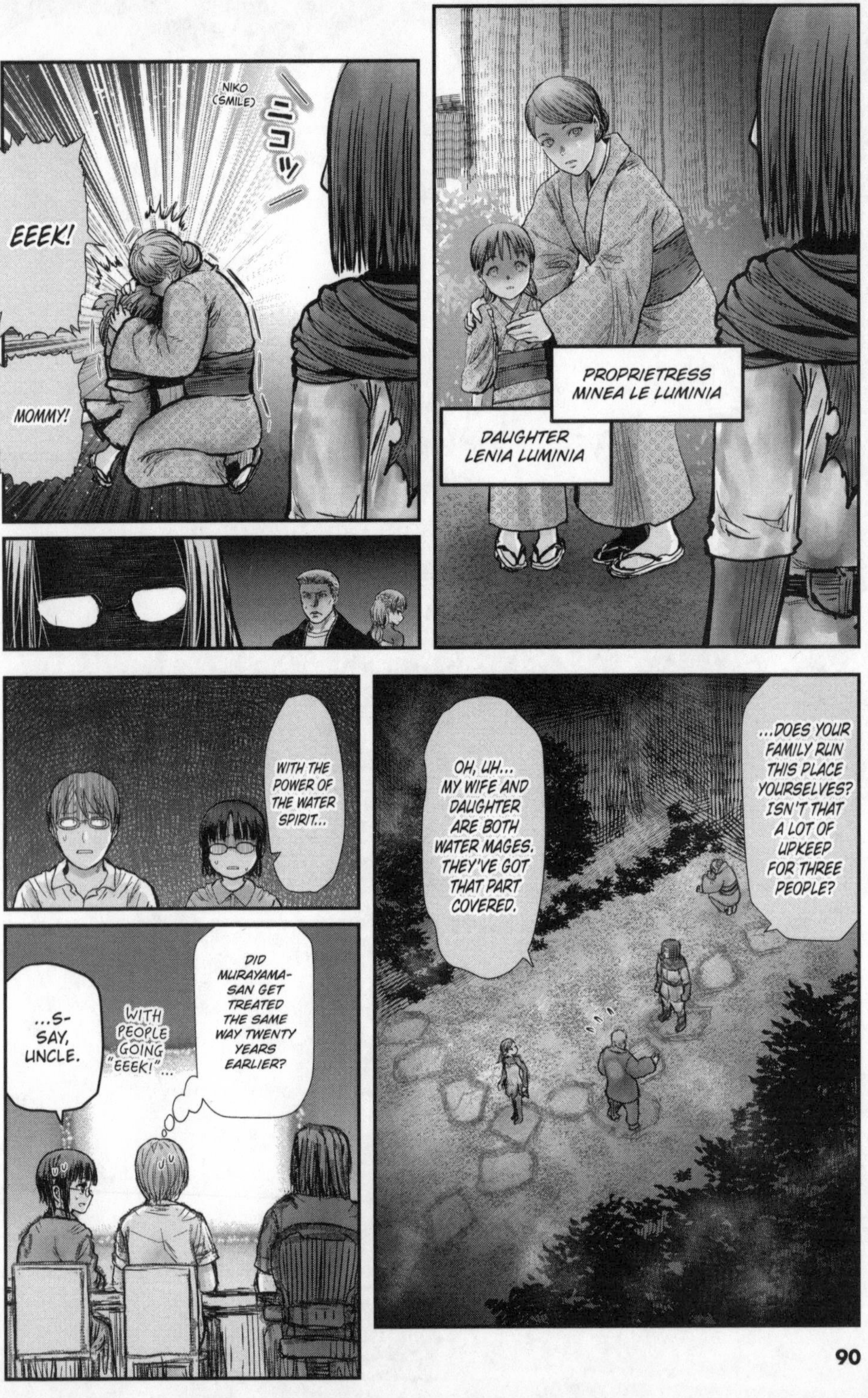

PROPRIETRESS MINEA LE LUMINIA
DAUGHTER LENIA LUMINIA
ニコッ
NIKO (SMILE)
EEEK!
MOMMY!
...DOES YOUR FAMILY RUN THIS PLACE YOURSELVES? ISN'T THAT A LOT OF UPKEEP FOR THREE PEOPLE?
OH, UH... MY WIFE AND DAUGHTER ARE BOTH WATER MAGES. THEY'VE GOT THAT PART COVERED.
WITH THE POWER OF THE WATER SPIRIT...
DID MURAYAMA-SAN GET TREATED THE SAME WAY TWENTY YEARS EARLIER?
WITH PEOPLE GOING "EEEK!"...
...S-SAY, UNCLE.

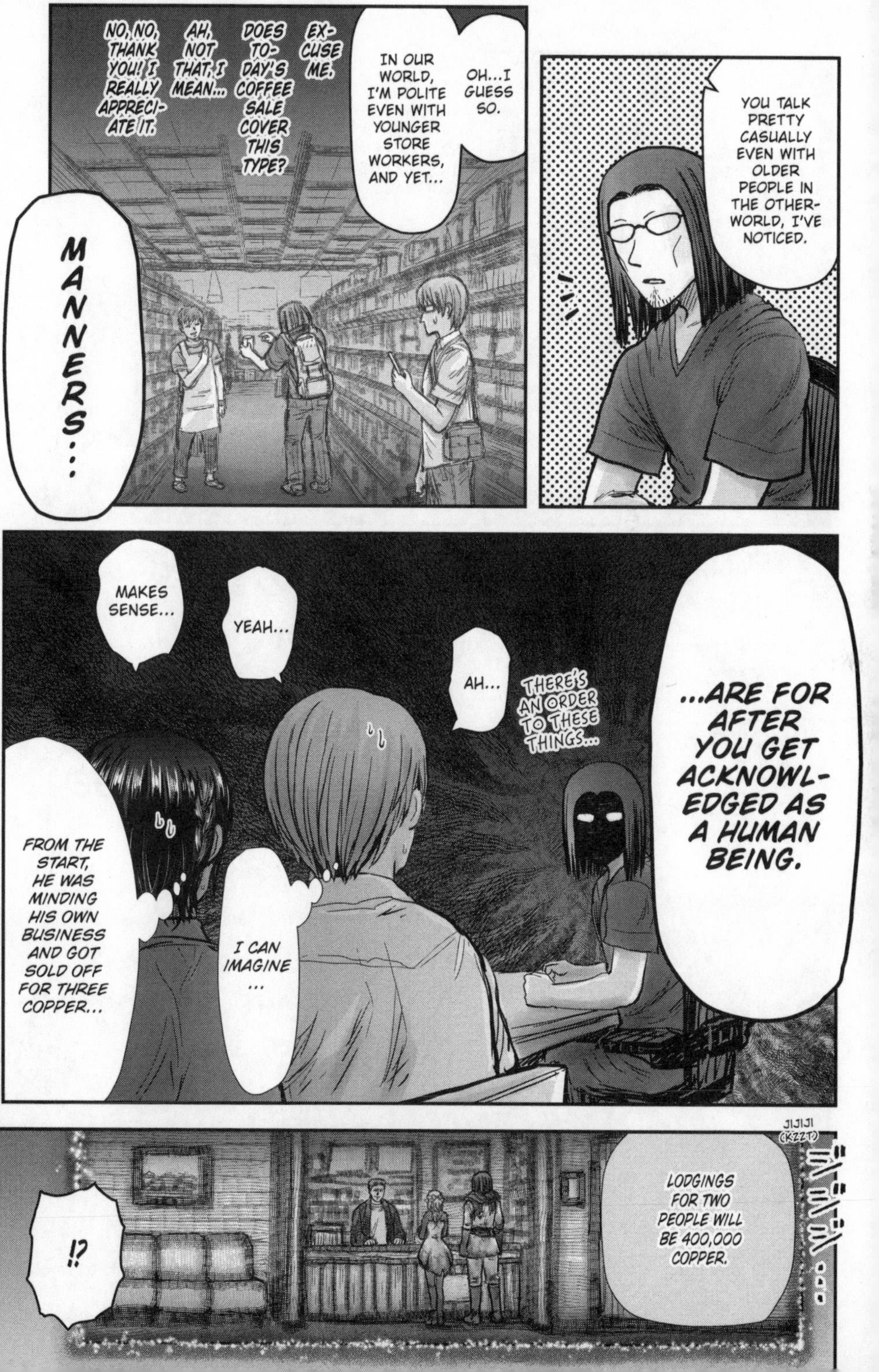
YOU TALK PRETTY CASUALLY EVEN WITH OLDER PEOPLE IN THE OTHER-WORLD, I'VE NOTICED.
OH...I GUESS SO.
IN OUR WORLD, I'M POLITE EVEN WITH YOUNGER STORE WORKERS, AND YET...
EX-CUSE ME.
DOES TO-DAY'S COFFEE SALE COVER THIS TYPE?
AH, NOT THAT. I MEAN...
NO, NO, THANK YOU! I REALLY APPRECI-ATE IT.
MANNERS...
...ARE FOR AFTER YOU GET ACKNOWL-EDGED AS A HUMAN BEING.
THERE'S AN ORDER TO THESE THINGS...
AH...
YEAH...
MAKES SENSE...
I CAN IMAGINE...
FROM THE START, HE WAS MINDING HIS OWN BUSINESS AND GOT SOLD OFF FOR THREE COPPER...
JIJIJI (KZZT)
LODGINGS FOR TWO PEOPLE WILL BE 400,000 COPPER.
!?

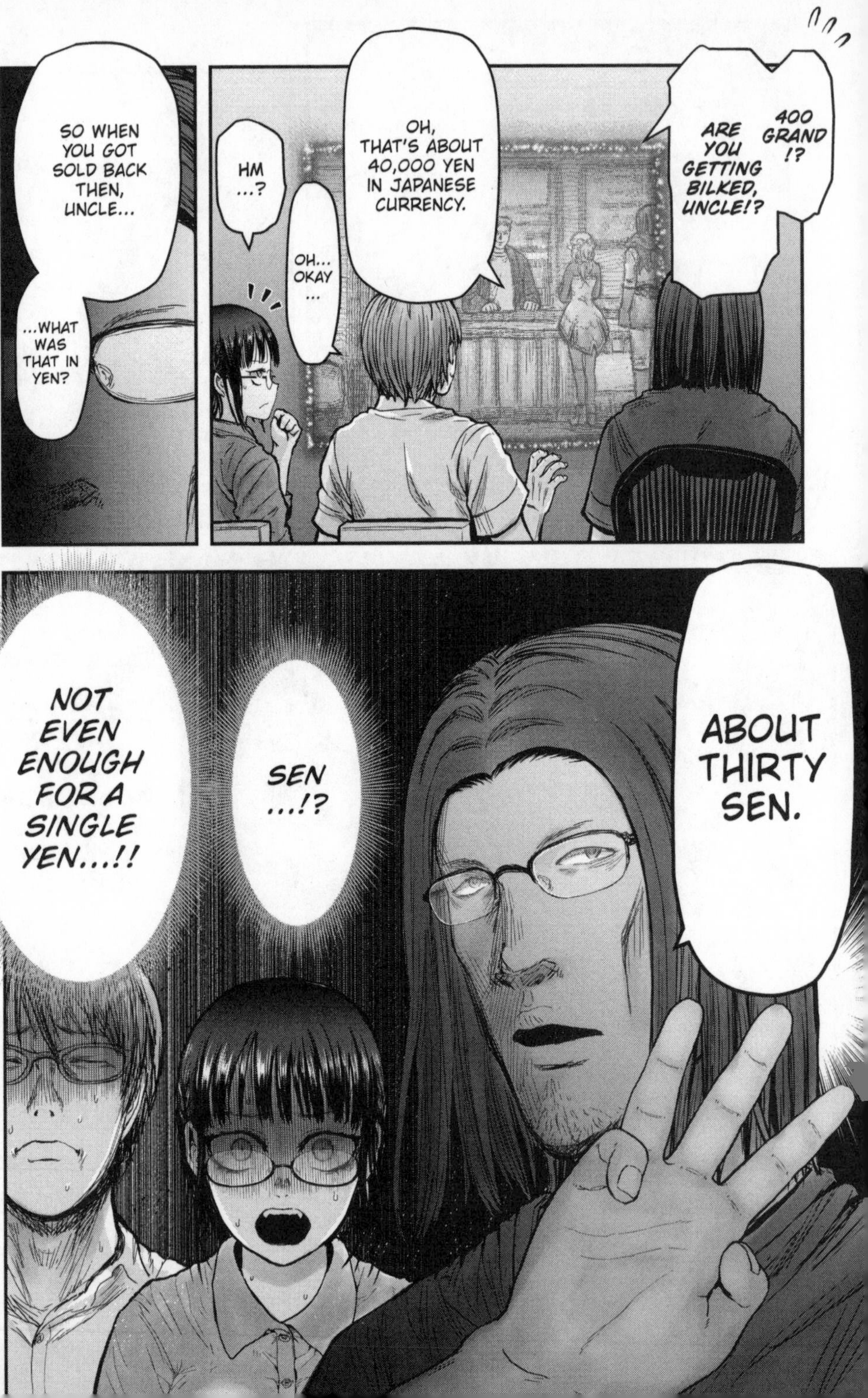
400 GRAND!?
ARE YOU GETTING BILKED, UNCLE!?
OH, THAT'S ABOUT 40,000 YEN IN JAPANESE CURRENCY.
HM...?
OH... OKAY...
SO WHEN YOU GOT SOLD BACK THEN, UNCLE...
...WHAT WAS THAT IN YEN?
ABOUT THIRTY SEN.
SEN...!?
NOT EVEN ENOUGH FOR A SINGLE YEN...!!

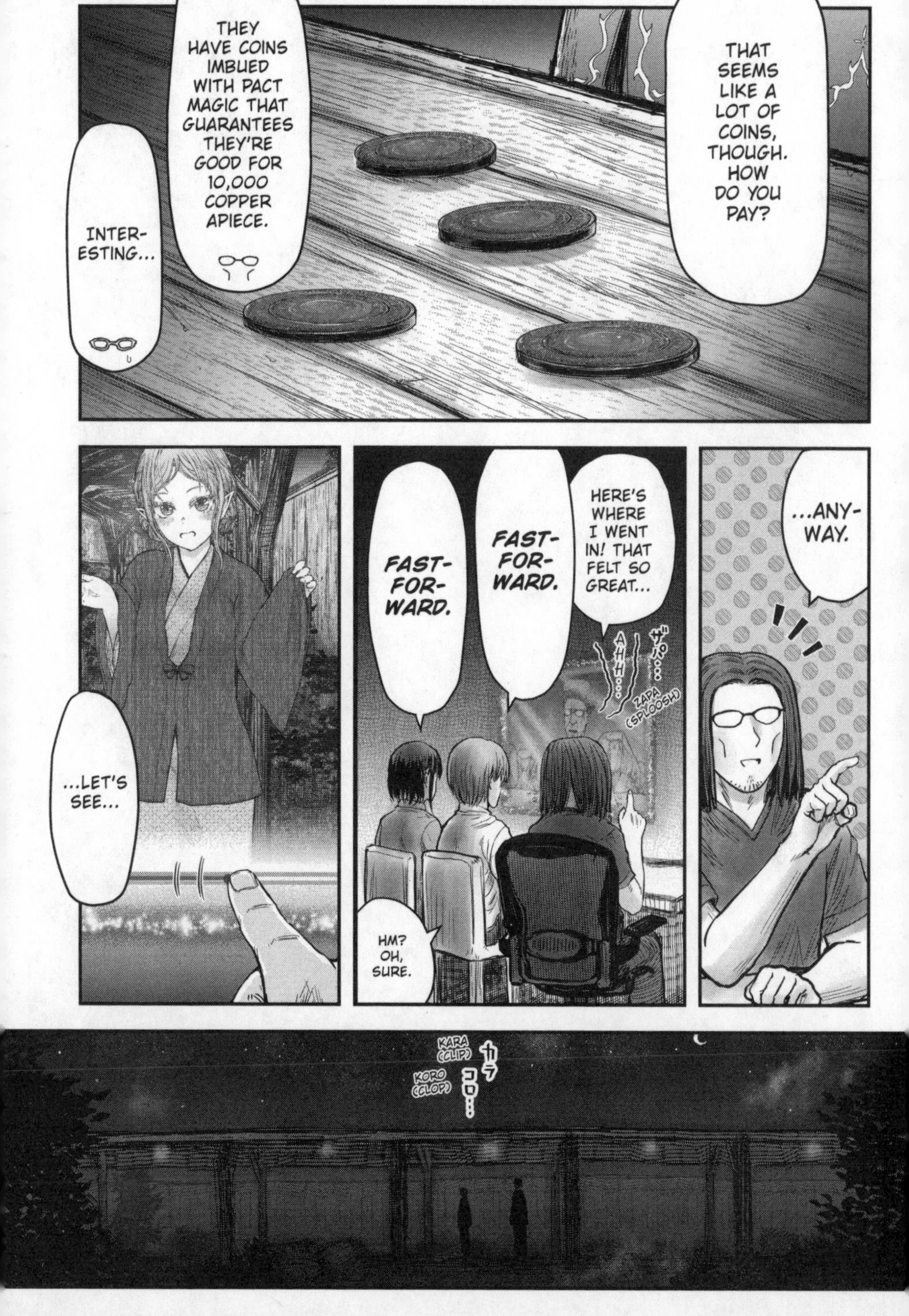
THAT SEEMS LIKE A LOT OF COINS, THOUGH. HOW DO YOU PAY?
THEY HAVE COINS IMBUED WITH PACT MAGIC THAT GUARANTEES THEY'RE GOOD FOR 10,000 COPPER APIECE.
INTER-ESTING...
...ANY-WAY.
HERE'S WHERE I WENT IN! THAT FELT SO GREAT...
AHHH...
ZAPA (SPLOOSH)
FAST-FOR-WARD.
FAST-FOR-WARD.
HM? OH, SURE.
...LET'S SEE...
KARA (CLIP)
KORO (CLOP)

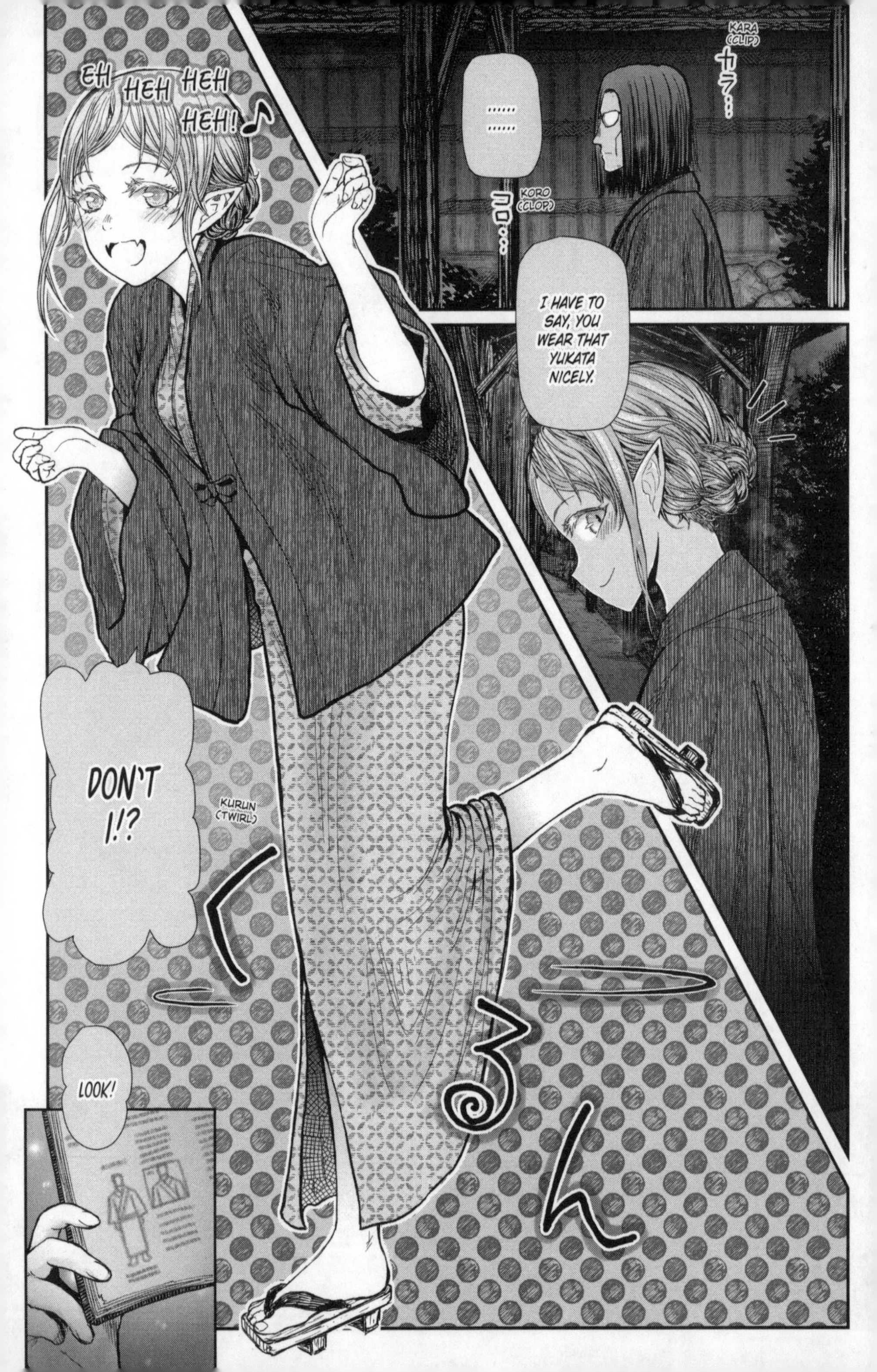
KARA (CLIP)
カラ…
……
……
KORO (CLOP)
コロ…
I HAVE TO SAY, YOU WEAR THAT YUKATA NICELY.
EH HEH HEH HEH!♪
DON'T I!?
KURUN (TWIRL)
LOOK!

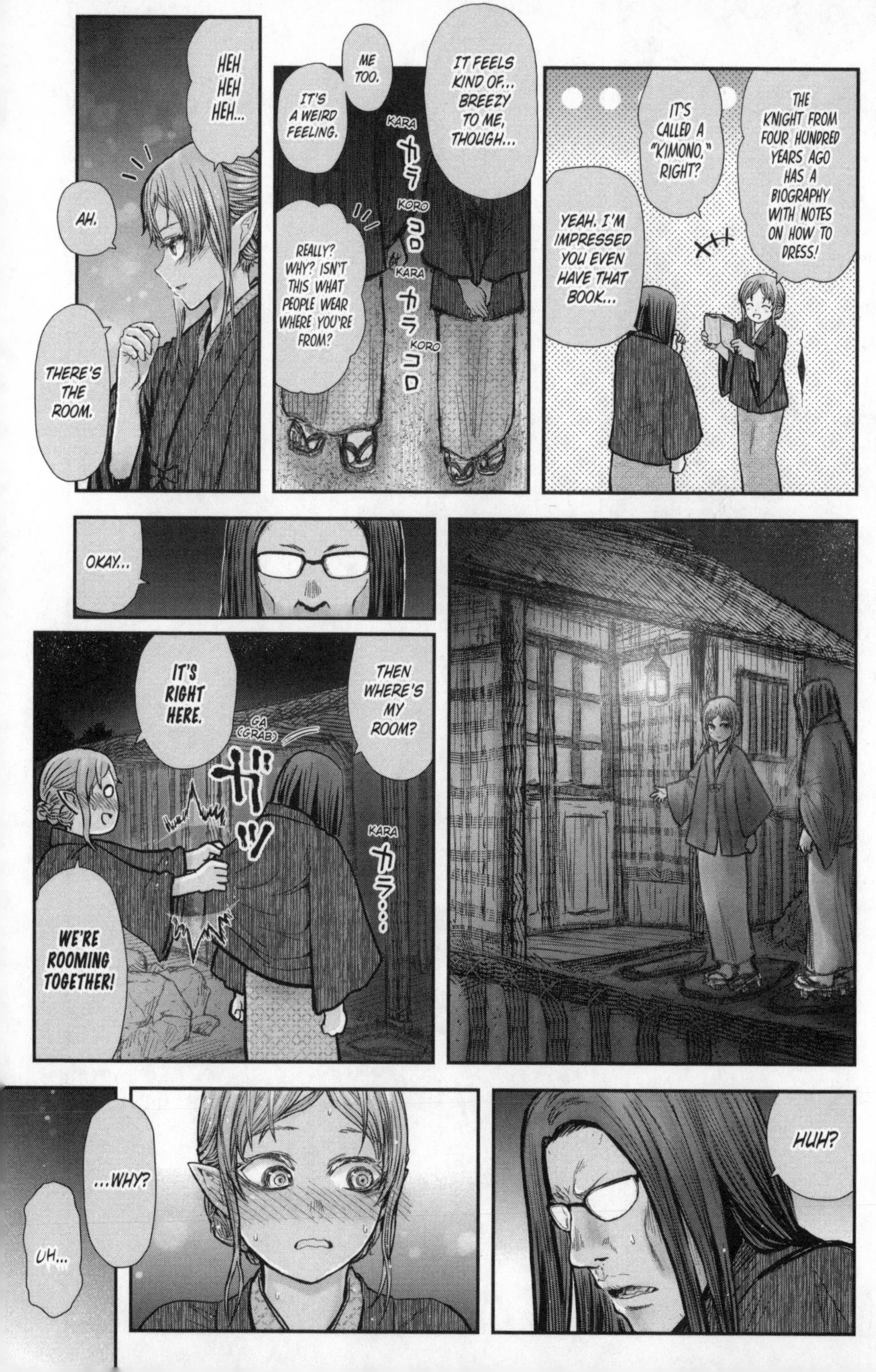
THE KNIGHT FROM FOUR HUNDRED YEARS AGO HAS A BIOGRAPHY WITH NOTES ON HOW TO DRESS!
IT'S CALLED A "KIMONO," RIGHT?
YEAH. I'M IMPRESSED YOU EVEN HAVE THAT BOOK...
IT FEELS KIND OF... BREEZY TO ME, THOUGH...
ME TOO.
IT'S A WEIRD FEELING.
KARA カラ
KORO コロ
KARA カラ
KORO コロ
REALLY? WHY? ISN'T THIS WHAT PEOPLE WEAR WHERE YOU'RE FROM?
HEH HEH HEH...
AH.
THERE'S THE ROOM.
OKAY...
THEN WHERE'S MY ROOM?
IT'S RIGHT HERE.
GA (GRAB) ガッ
KARA カラ...
WE'RE ROOMING TOGETHER!
HUH?
...WHY?
UH...

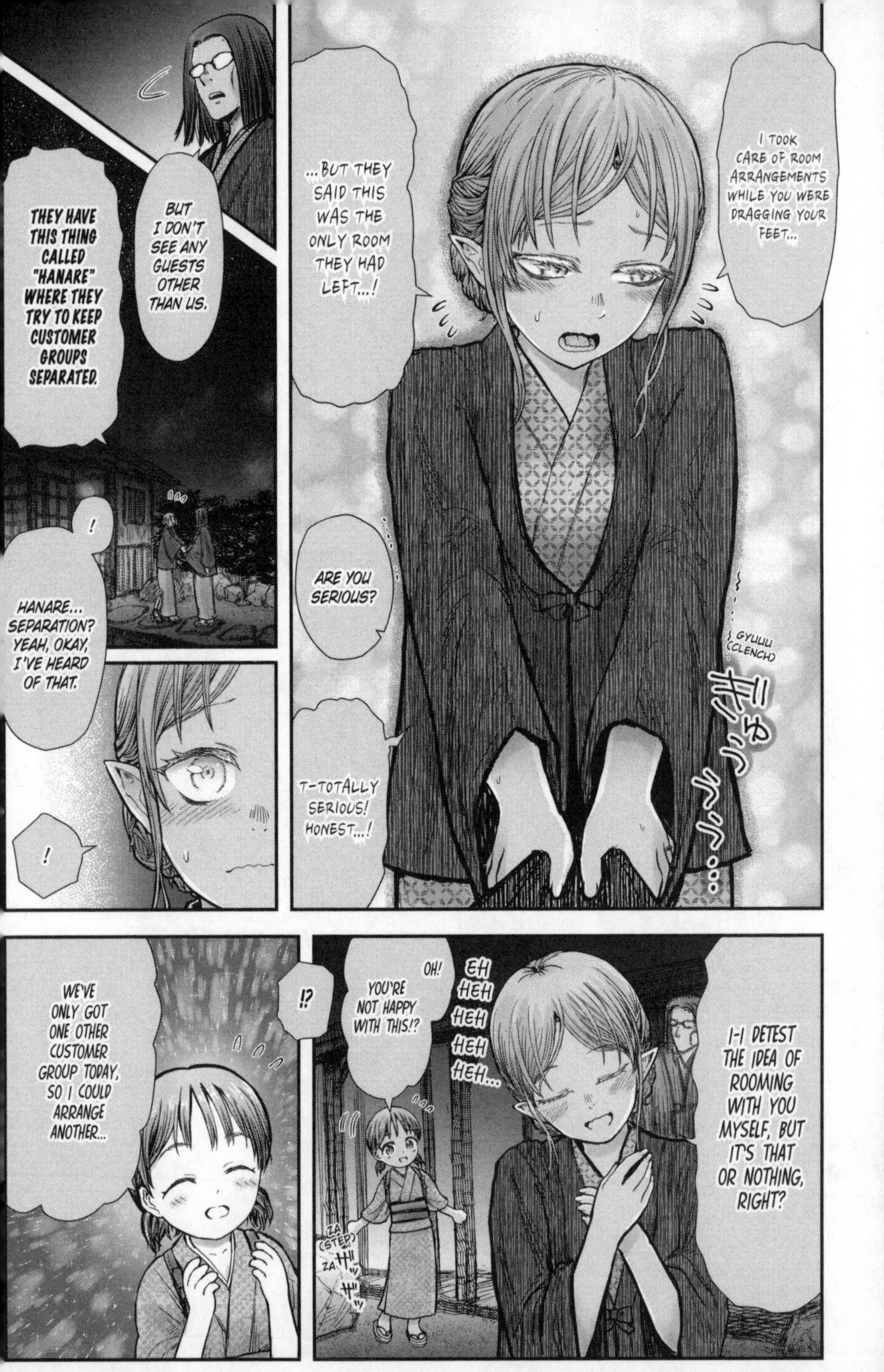
I TOOK CARE OF ROOM ARRANGEMENTS WHILE YOU WERE DRAGGING YOUR FEET...
...BUT THEY SAID THIS WAS THE ONLY ROOM THEY HAD LEFT...!
ARE YOU SERIOUS?
T-TOTALLY SERIOUS! HONEST...!
GYUUU (CLENCH)
BUT I DON'T SEE ANY GUESTS OTHER THAN US.
THEY HAVE THIS THING CALLED "HANARE" WHERE THEY TRY TO KEEP CUSTOMER GROUPS SEPARATED.
!
HANARE... SEPARATION? YEAH, OKAY, I'VE HEARD OF THAT.
!
I-I DETEST THE IDEA OF ROOMING WITH YOU MYSELF, BUT IT'S THAT OR NOTHING, RIGHT?
EH HEH HEH HEH HEH...
OH!
YOU'RE NOT HAPPY WITH THIS!?
ZA (STEP) ZA
!?
WE'VE ONLY GOT ONE OTHER CUSTOMER GROUP TODAY, SO I COULD ARRANGE ANOTHER...

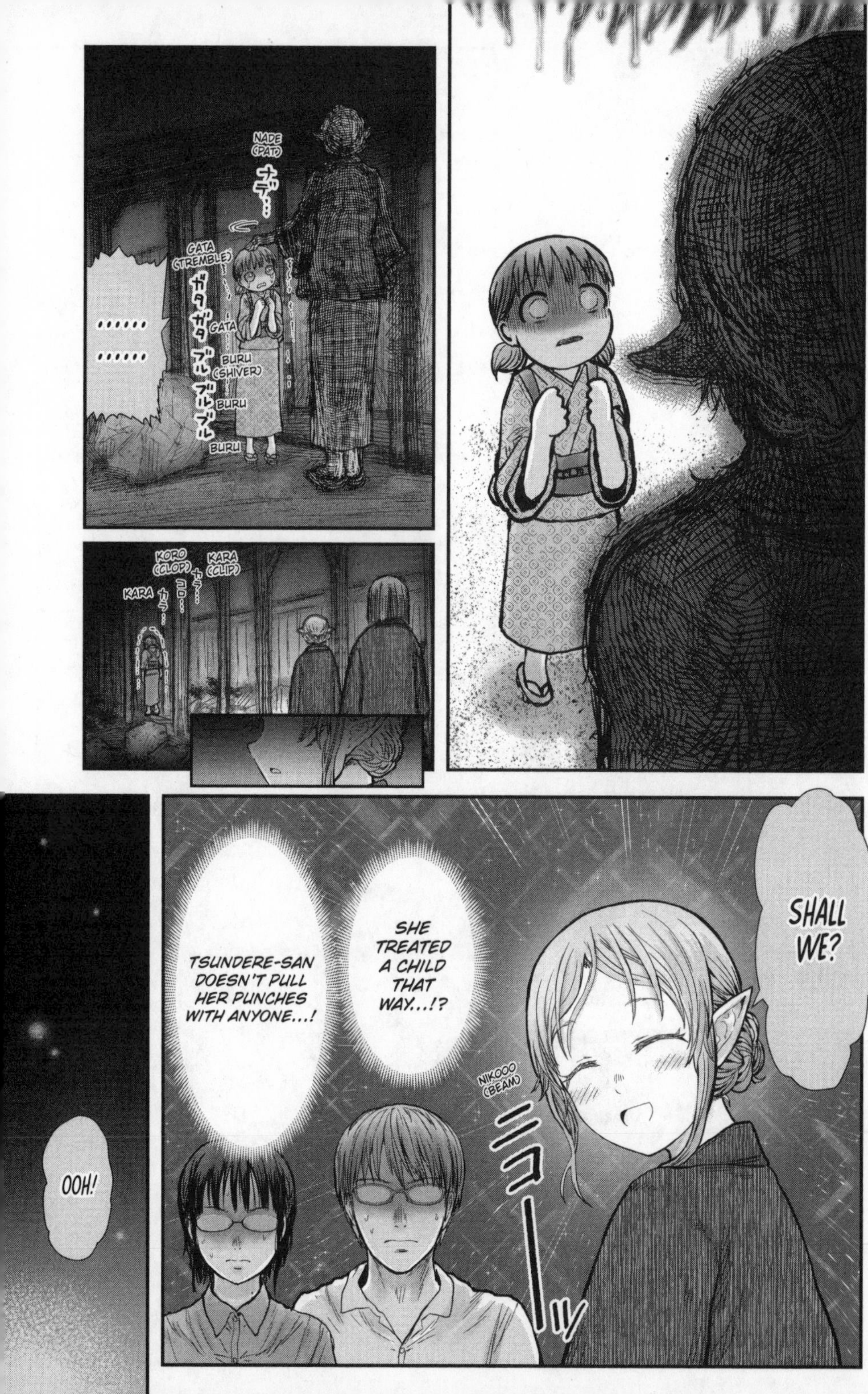
NADE (PAT)
ナデ…
GATA (TREMBLE)
ガタガタ
GATA
BURU (SHIVER)
ブルブル
BURU
BURU
......
......
KORO (CLOP)
コロ…
KARA (CLIP)
カラ…
KARA
カラ…
SHALL WE?
NIKOOO (BEAM)
ニコーーッ
SHE TREATED A CHILD THAT WAY...!?
TSUNDERE-SAN DOESN'T PULL HER PUNCHES WITH ANYONE...!
OOH!

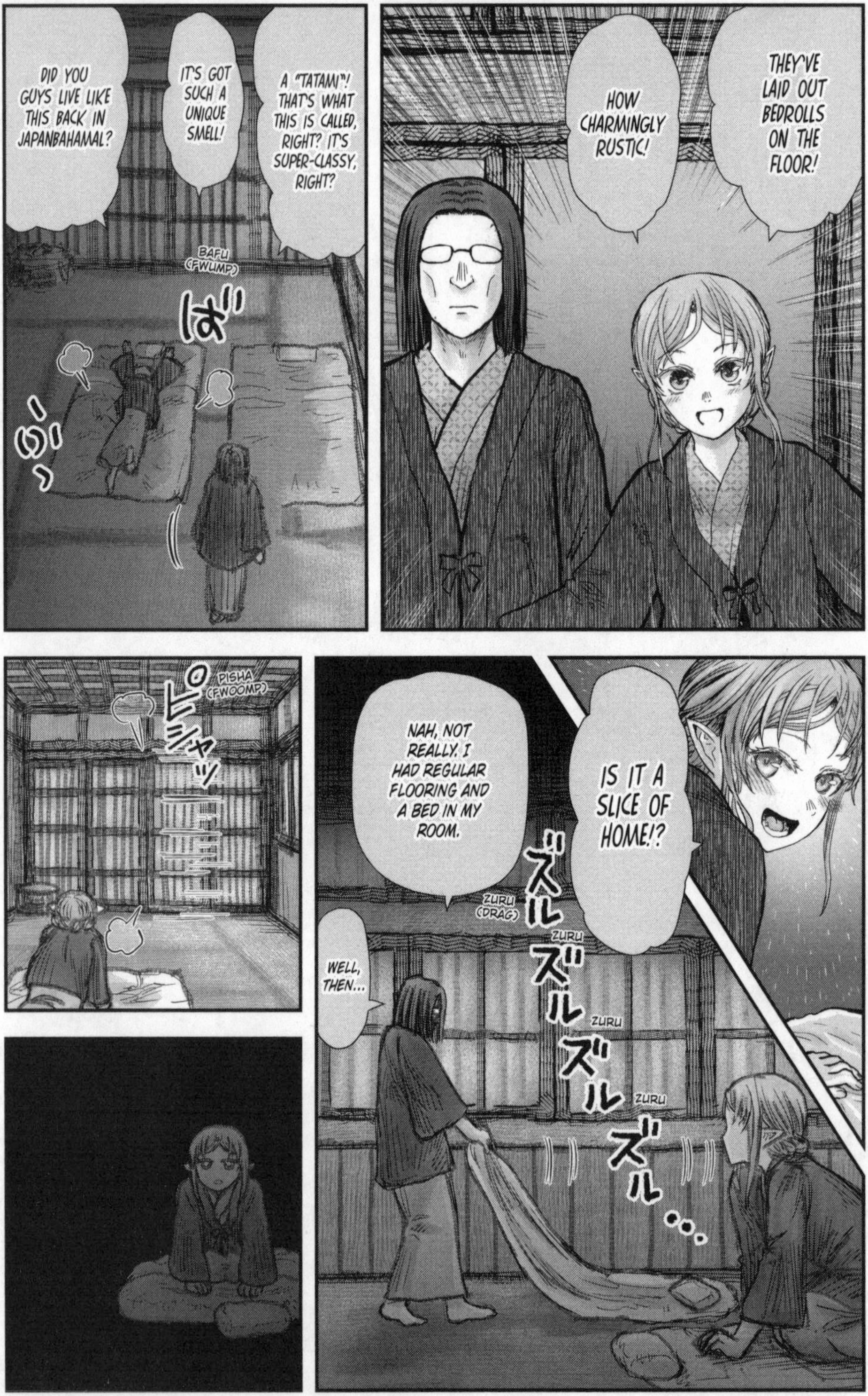
THEY'VE LAID OUT BEDROLLS ON THE FLOOR!
HOW CHARMINGLY RUSTIC!
A "TATAMI"! THAT'S WHAT THIS IS CALLED, RIGHT? IT'S SUPER-CLASSY, RIGHT?
IT'S GOT SUCH A UNIQUE SMELL!
DID YOU GUYS LIVE LIKE THIS BACK IN JAPANBAHAMAL?
BAFU (FWUMP)
IS IT A SLICE OF HOME!?
NAH, NOT REALLY. I HAD REGULAR FLOORING AND A BED IN MY ROOM.
ZURU (DRAG)
WELL, THEN...
ZURU
ZURU
ZURU
PISHA (FWOOMP)

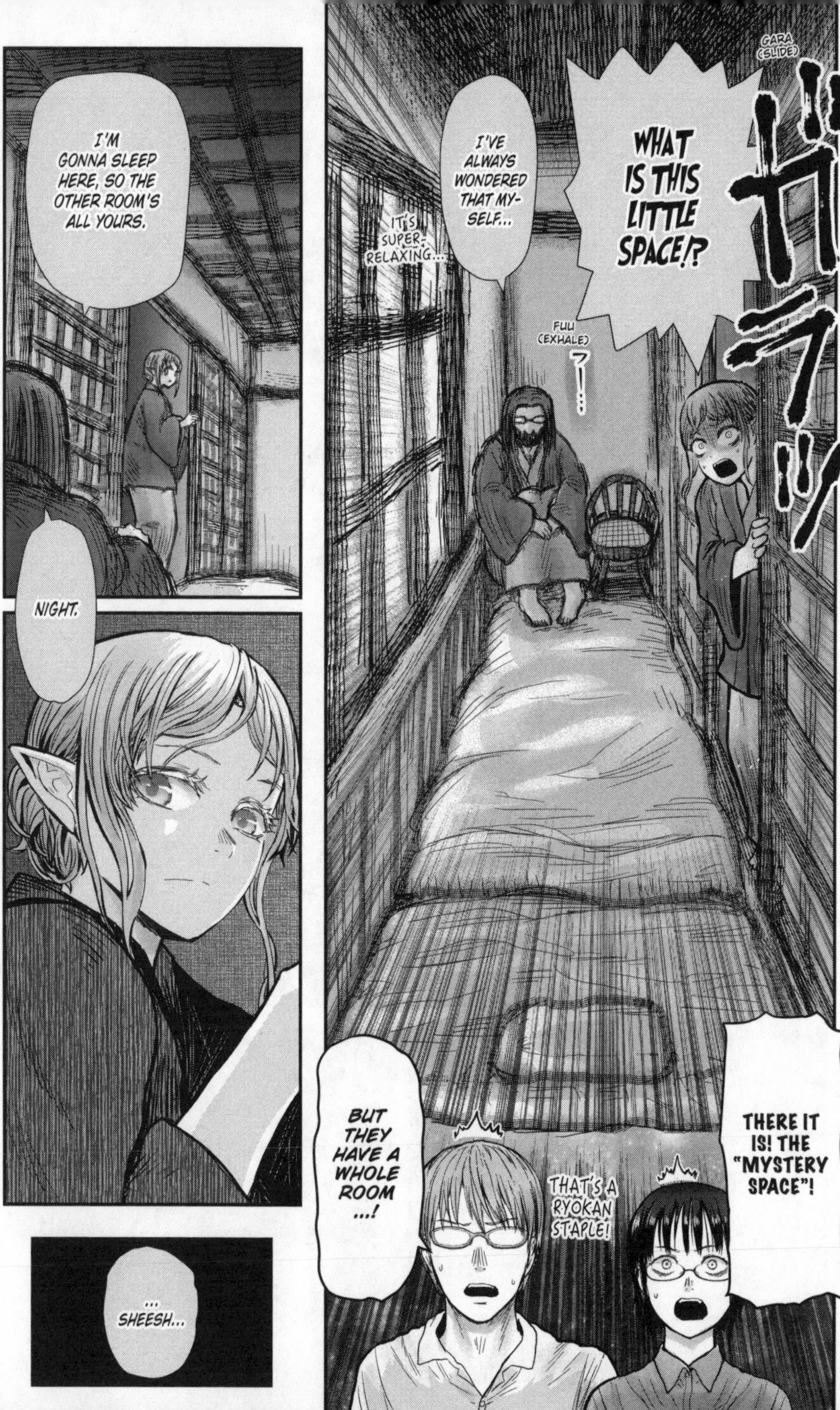
GARA (SLIDE)
ガラッ
WHAT IS THIS LITTLE SPACE!?
I'VE ALWAYS WONDERED THAT MY-SELF...
IT'S SUPER-RELAXING...
FUU (EXHALE)
フー…
THERE IT IS! THE "MYSTERY SPACE"!
THAT'S A RYOKAN STAPLE!
BUT THEY HAVE A WHOLE ROOM...!
I'M GONNA SLEEP HERE, SO THE OTHER ROOM'S ALL YOURS.
NIGHT.
... SHEESH...

STUPID ORC...

I SPENT A WHOLE MONTH LOOKING FOR HIM...

HWAGH!?

ARE YOU TIRED?

NOSHI (CLEAN)

BIKU (FLINCH)

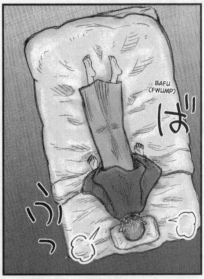

BAFU (FWUMP)

100

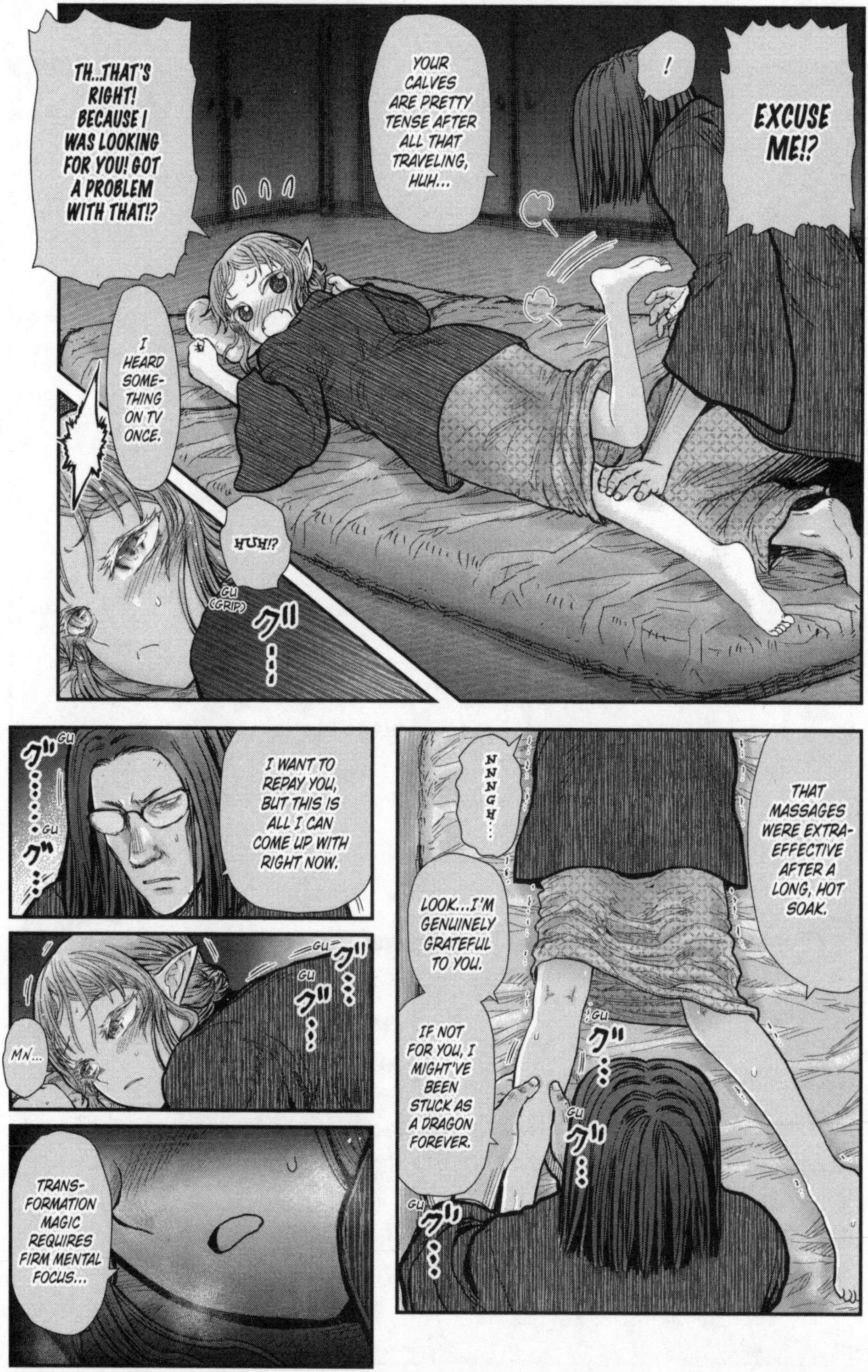
!
EXCUSE ME!?
YOUR CALVES ARE PRETTY TENSE AFTER ALL THAT TRAVELING, HUH...
TH...THAT'S RIGHT! BECAUSE I WAS LOOKING FOR YOU! GOT A PROBLEM WITH THAT!?
I HEARD SOMETHING ON TV ONCE.
HUH!?
GU (GRIP)
THAT MASSAGES WERE EXTRA-EFFECTIVE AFTER A LONG, HOT SOAK.
NNNGH...
LOOK...I'M GENUINELY GRATEFUL TO YOU.
IF NOT FOR YOU, I MIGHT'VE BEEN STUCK AS A DRAGON FOREVER.
GU
GU
GU
I WANT TO REPAY YOU, BUT THIS IS ALL I CAN COME UP WITH RIGHT NOW.
GU
GU
GU
GU
MN...
TRANS-FORMATION MAGIC REQUIRES FIRM MENTAL FOCUS...

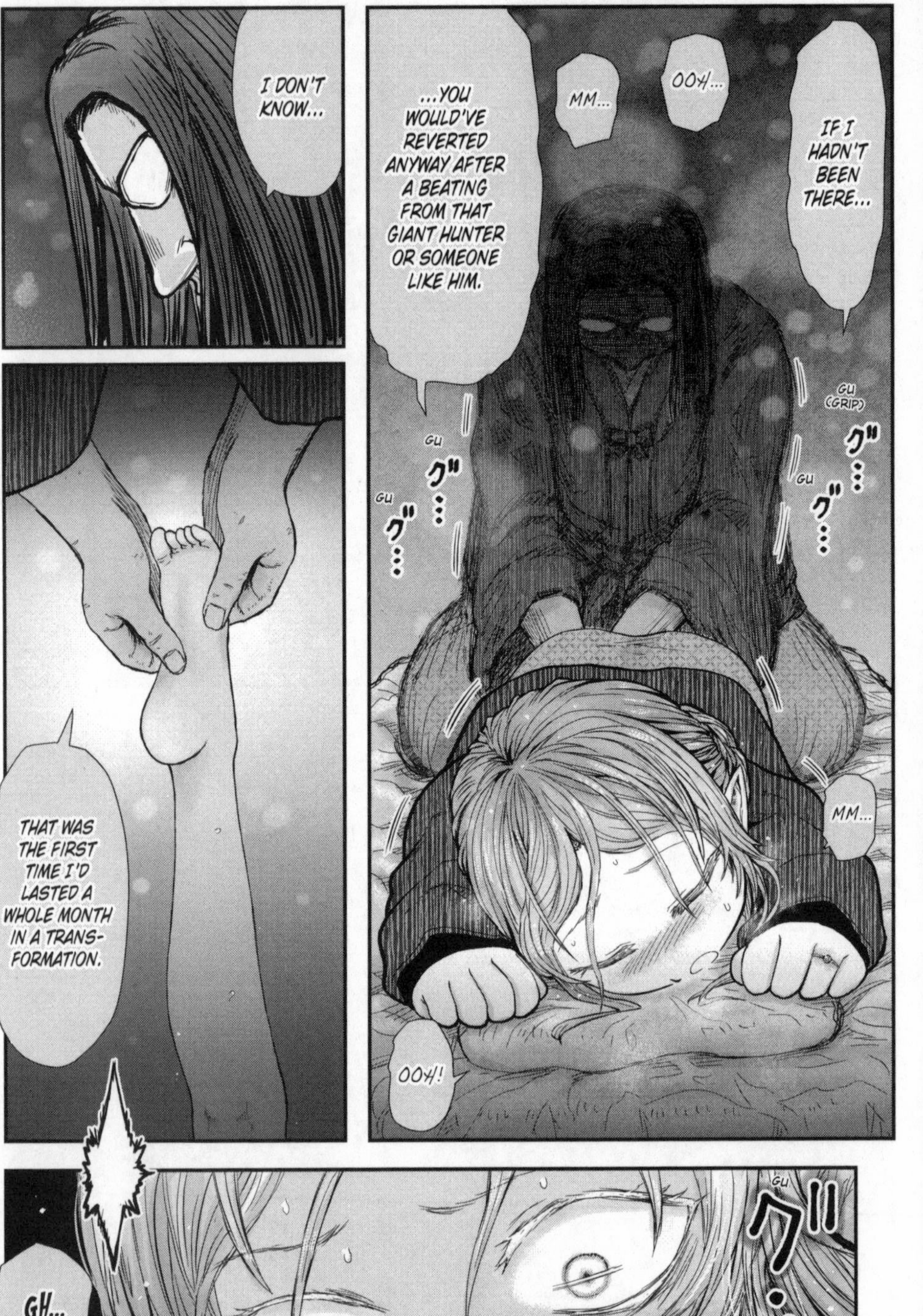
IF I HADN'T BEEN THERE...
OOH...
MM...
...YOU WOULD'VE REVERTED ANYWAY AFTER A BEATING FROM THAT GIANT HUNTER OR SOMEONE LIKE HIM.
GU (GRIP)
グ...
GU
グ...
MM...
GU
グ...
GU
グ...
OOH!
I DON'T KNOW...
THAT WAS THE FIRST TIME I'D LASTED A WHOLE MONTH IN A TRANS-FORMATION.
GU
グ....
GH...

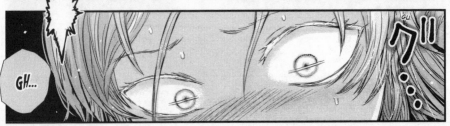

NRGH!?
GU GU GU
GU GU GU
GU GU
I'M NOT SURE I'D HAVE TURNED BACK WITHOUT THE WARM HEART'S LIGHT YOU GAVE ME—
OW...
THAT HURTS!
OW, OW, OW, OW, OW!
GU GU
GU
WHAT THE HECK!? WHAT ARE YOU DOING!?
BIKU (TWITCH)
Y... YOU'RE HURTING ME.
KAKU (JERK)
KAKU KAKU
FURU (TREMBLE) FURU
GYU (CLENCH)
GU GU GU
GU GU GU GU
AH...
BECHI (SMACK)
OW...
WHY WON'T YOU STOP...?
GU GU GU GU GU GU GU GU GU GU GU GU GU GU

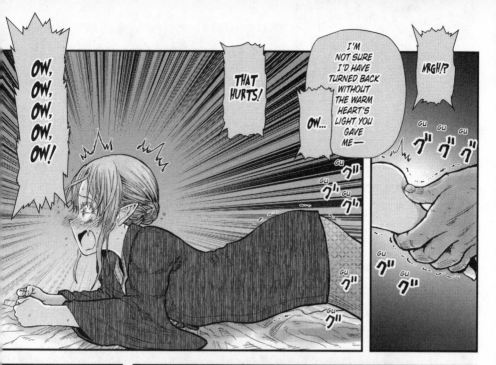

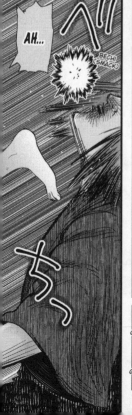

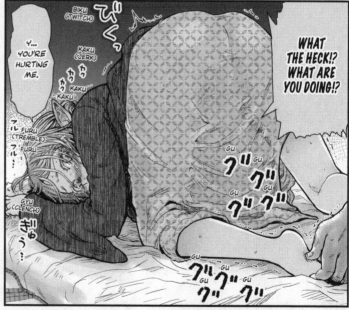

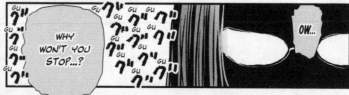

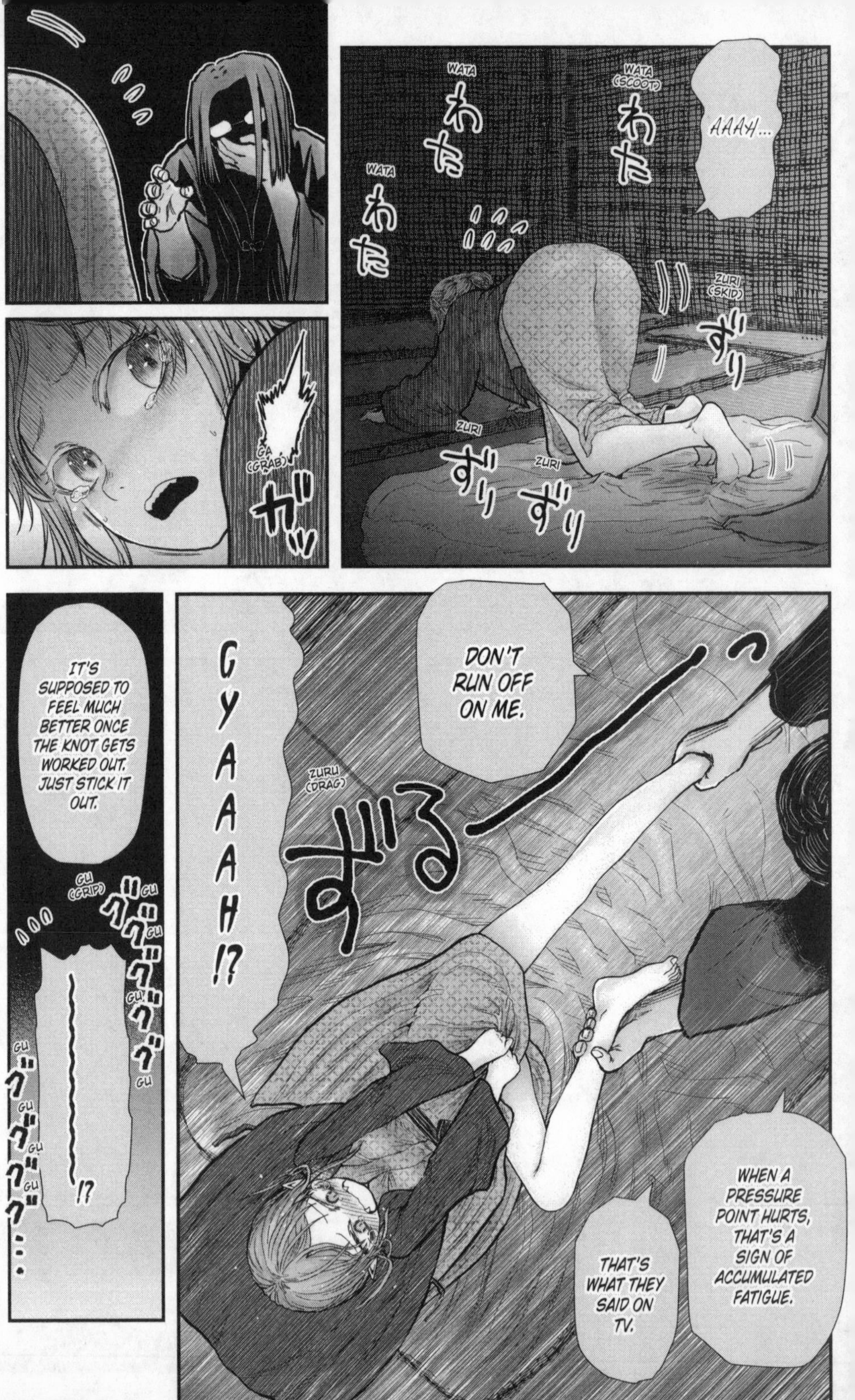
AAAH...
WATA (SCOOT)
わた
WATA
わた
ZURI (SKID)
ずり
ZURI
ずり
ZURI
ずり
GA (GRAB)
DON'T RUN OFF ON ME.
ZURU (DRAG)
ずる
GYAAAAH!?
WHEN A PRESSURE POINT HURTS, THAT'S A SIGN OF ACCUMULATED FATIGUE.
THAT'S WHAT THEY SAID ON TV.
IT'S SUPPOSED TO FEEL MUCH BETTER ONCE THE KNOT GETS WORKED OUT. JUST STICK IT OUT.
GU (GRIP)
GU
GU
GU
GU
GU
GU
——!?

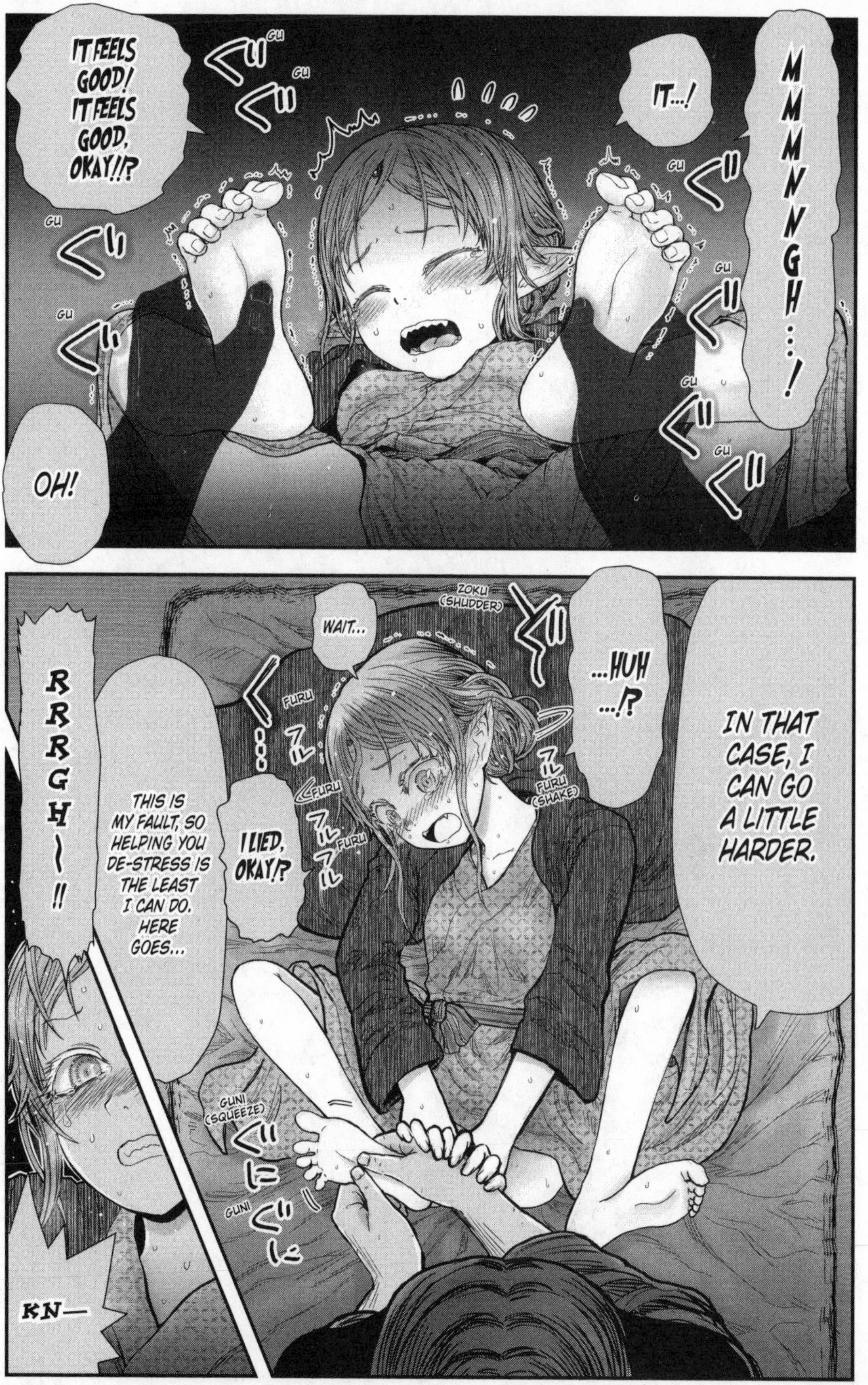
MMMNNGH...!
GU
IT...!
IT FEELS GOOD! IT FEELS GOOD, OKAY!!?
GU
OH!
IN THAT CASE, I CAN GO A LITTLE HARDER.
...HUH ...!?
ZOKU (SHUDDER)
FURU (SHAKE)
WAIT...
FURU
I LIED, OKAY!?
THIS IS MY FAULT, SO HELPING YOU DE-STRESS IS THE LEAST I CAN DO. HERE GOES...
RRRGH~!!
GUNI (SQUEEZE)
GUNI
KN—

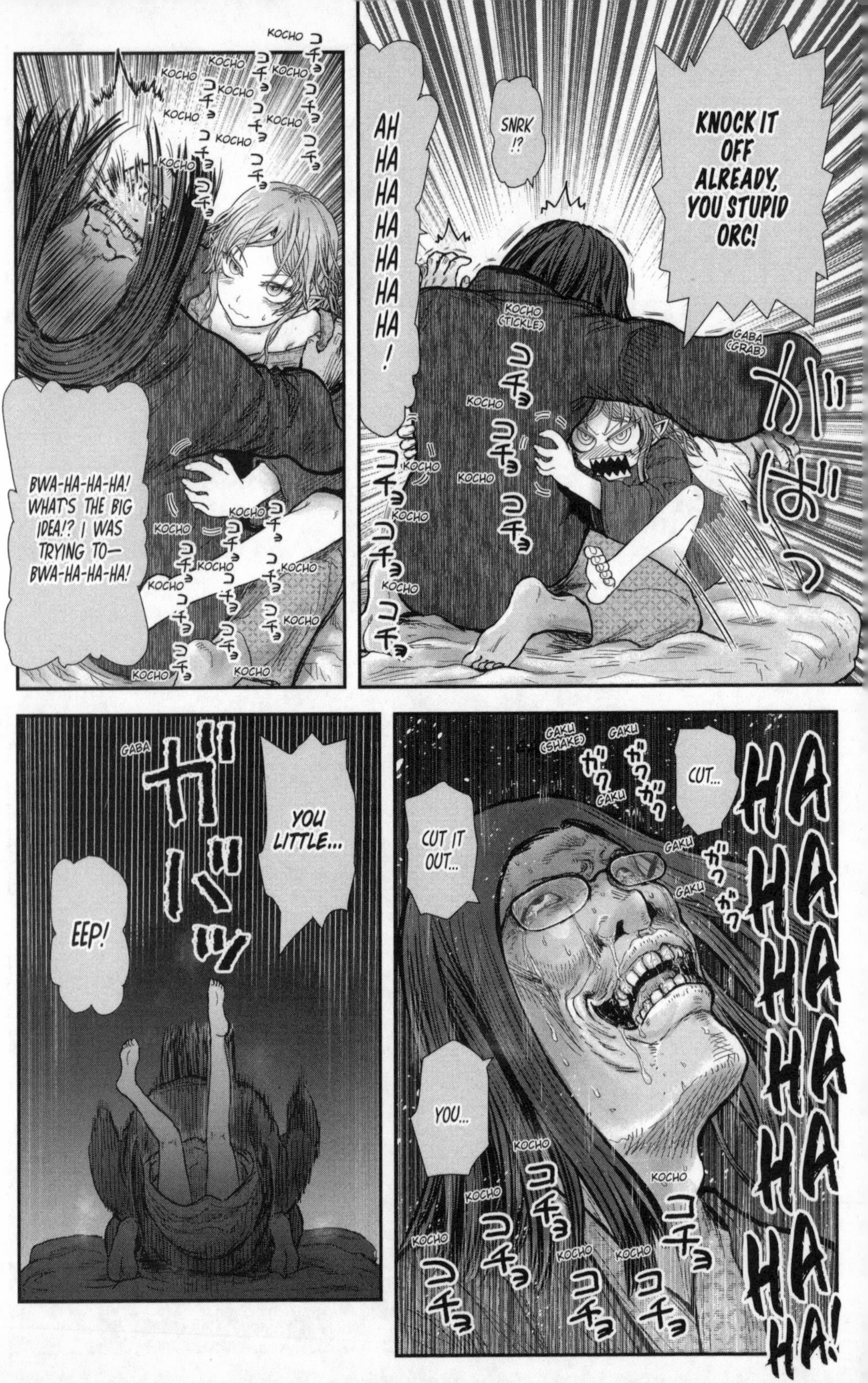
KNOCK IT OFF ALREADY, YOU STUPID ORC!
SNRK !?
AH HA HA HA HA HA HA HA!
GABA (GRAB)
KOCHO (TICKLE)
KOCHO
KOCHO
KOCHO
KOCHO
KOCHO
KOCHO
KOCHO
KOCHO
KOCHO
KOCHO
KOCHO
KOCHO
KOCHO
BWA-HA-HA-HA! WHAT'S THE BIG IDEA!? I WAS TRYING TO— BWA-HA-HA-HA!
KOCHO
KOCHO
KOCHO
KOCHO
KOCHO
KOCHO
KOCHO
KOCHO
HA HA HA HA HA HA HA
HA HA HA HA HA HA HA!
GAKU (SHAKE)
GAKU
GAKU
GAKU
GAKU
CUT...
CUT IT OUT...
YOU...
KOCHO
KOCHO
KOCHO
KOCHO
KOCHO
KOCHO
YOU LITTLE...
GABA
EEP!

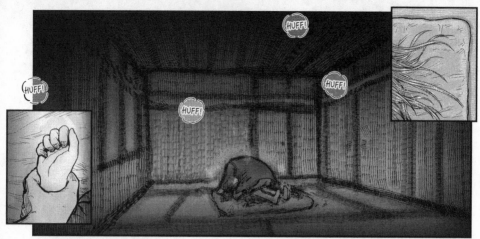

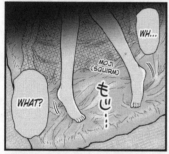

ORC-FACE...?

YOU'RE HEAVY.

GET OFF.

HUFF!

...

HUFF!

HUFF!

......?

WH...

WHAT?

MOJI
(SQUIRM)

もじ…

AH...

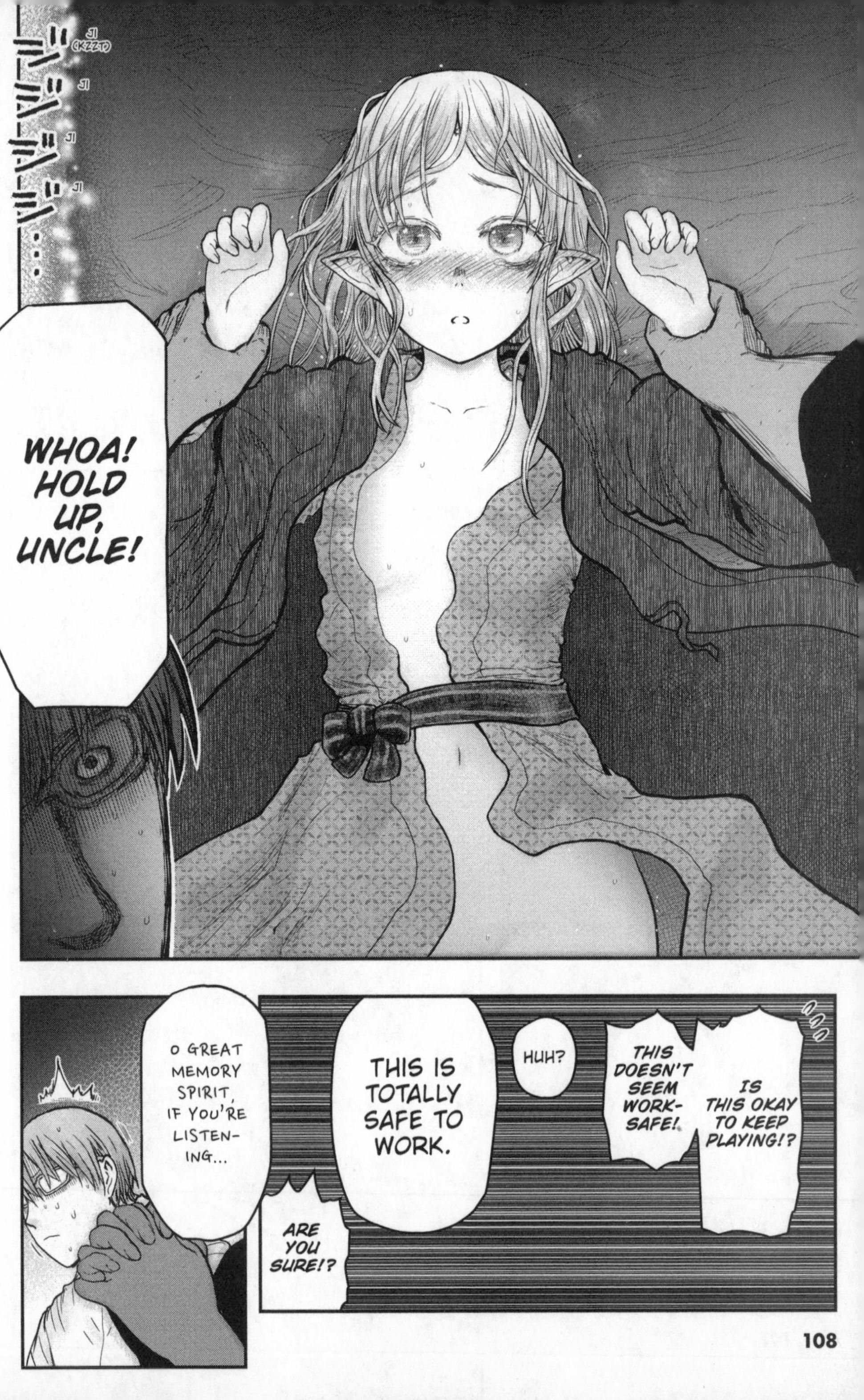
JI
CKZZT
JI
JI
JI
WHOA! HOLD UP, UNCLE!
IS THIS OKAY TO KEEP PLAYING!?
THIS DOESN'T SEEM WORK-SAFE!
HUH?
THIS IS TOTALLY SAFE TO WORK.
ARE YOU SURE!?
O GREAT MEMORY SPIRIT, IF YOU'RE LISTEN-ING...

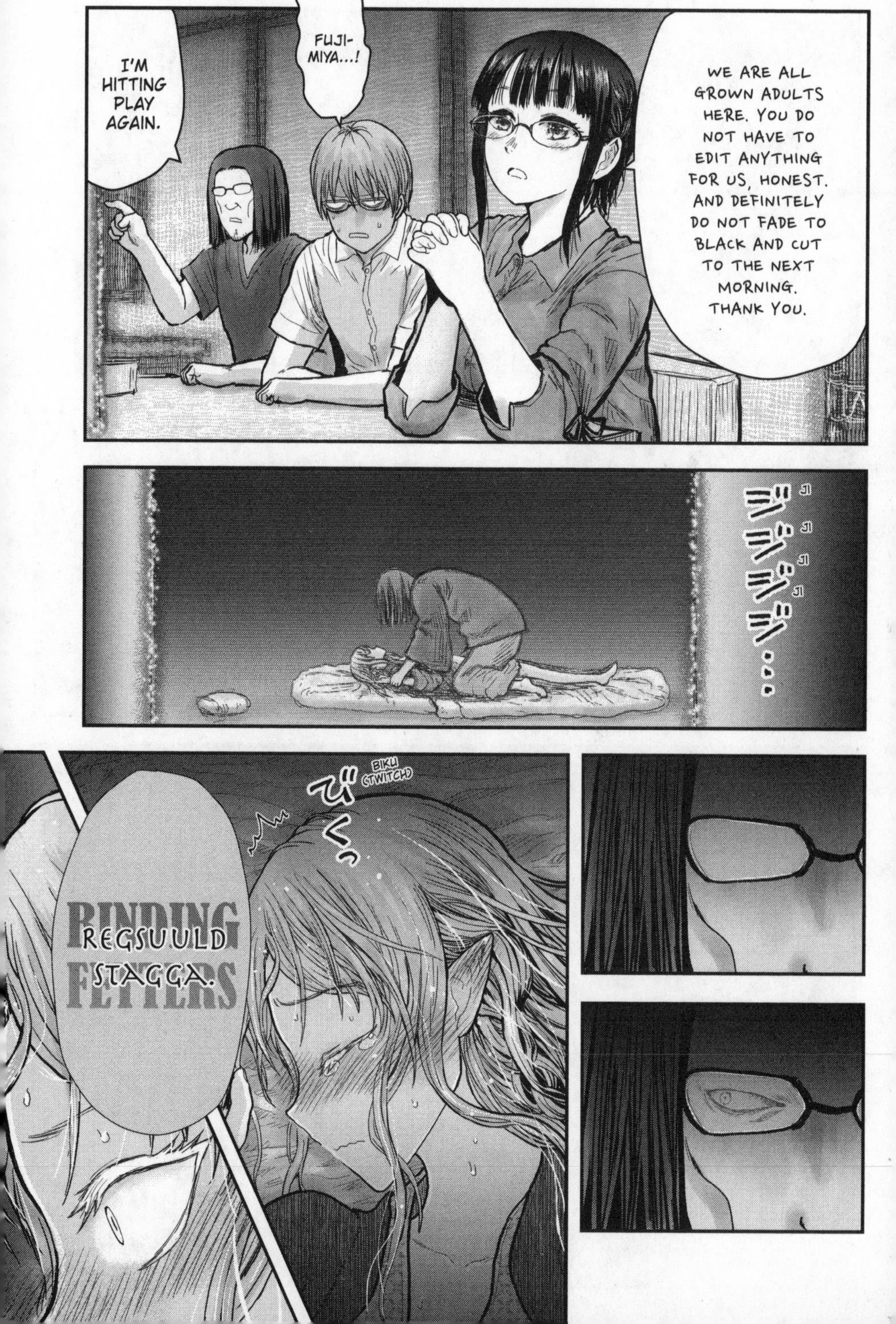
WE ARE ALL GROWN ADULTS HERE. YOU DO NOT HAVE TO EDIT ANYTHING FOR US, HONEST. AND DEFINITELY DO NOT FADE TO BLACK AND CUT TO THE NEXT MORNING. THANK YOU.
FUJI-MIYA...!
I'M HITTING PLAY AGAIN.
ジジジジ…
JI JI JI JI
びくっ
BIKU (TWITCH)
BINDING FETTERS
REGSUULD STAGGA.

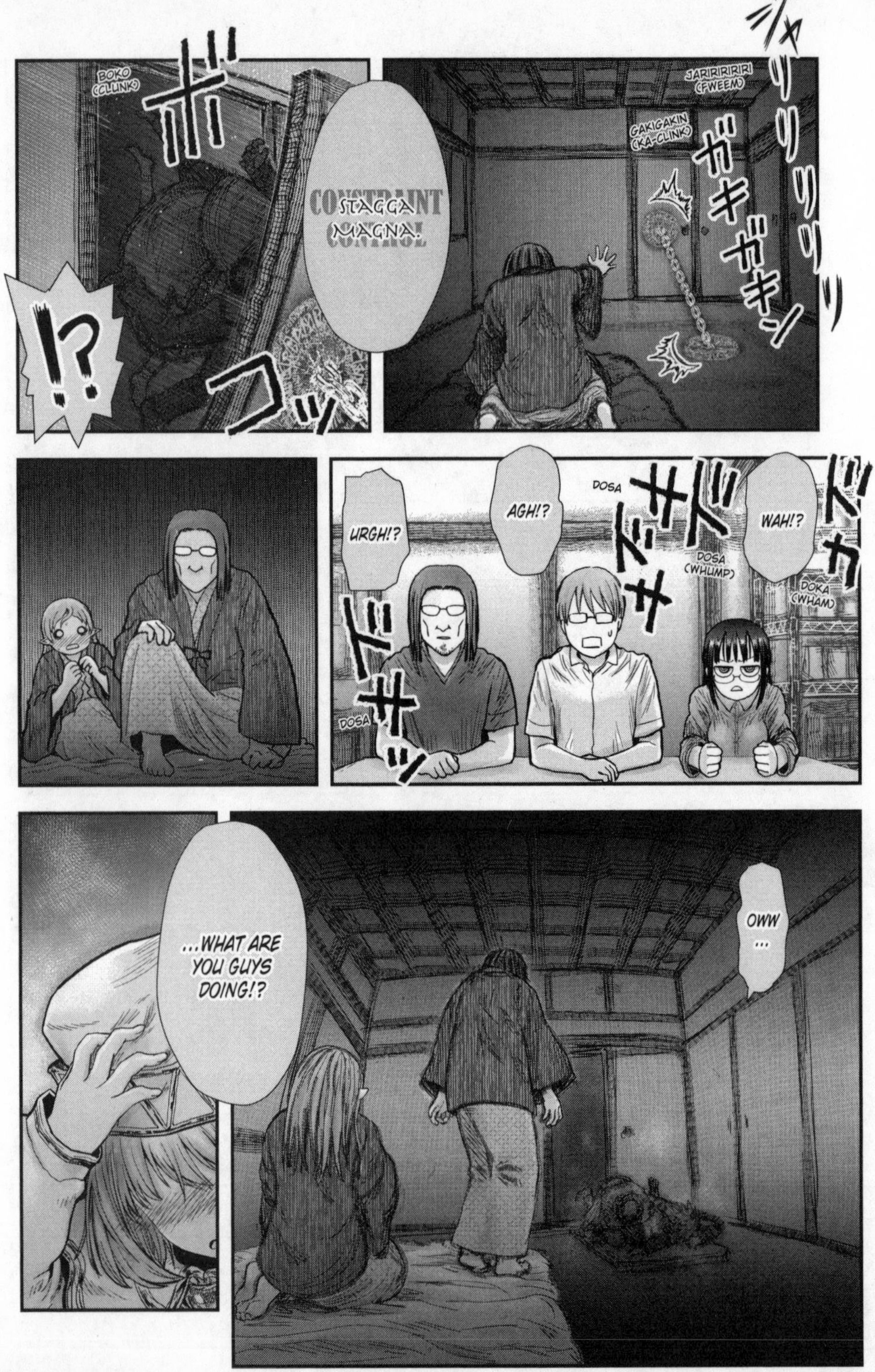
ジャリリリリリッ
JARIRIRIRIRI (FWEEM)
ガキガキン
GAKIGAKIN (KA-CLINK)
BOKO (CLUNK)
CONSTRAINT CONTROL
STAGGA MAGNA.
!?
WAH!?
DOKA (WHAM)
DOSA (WHUMP)
AGH!?
DOSA
URGH!?
DOSA
OWW...
...WHAT ARE YOU GUYS DOING!?

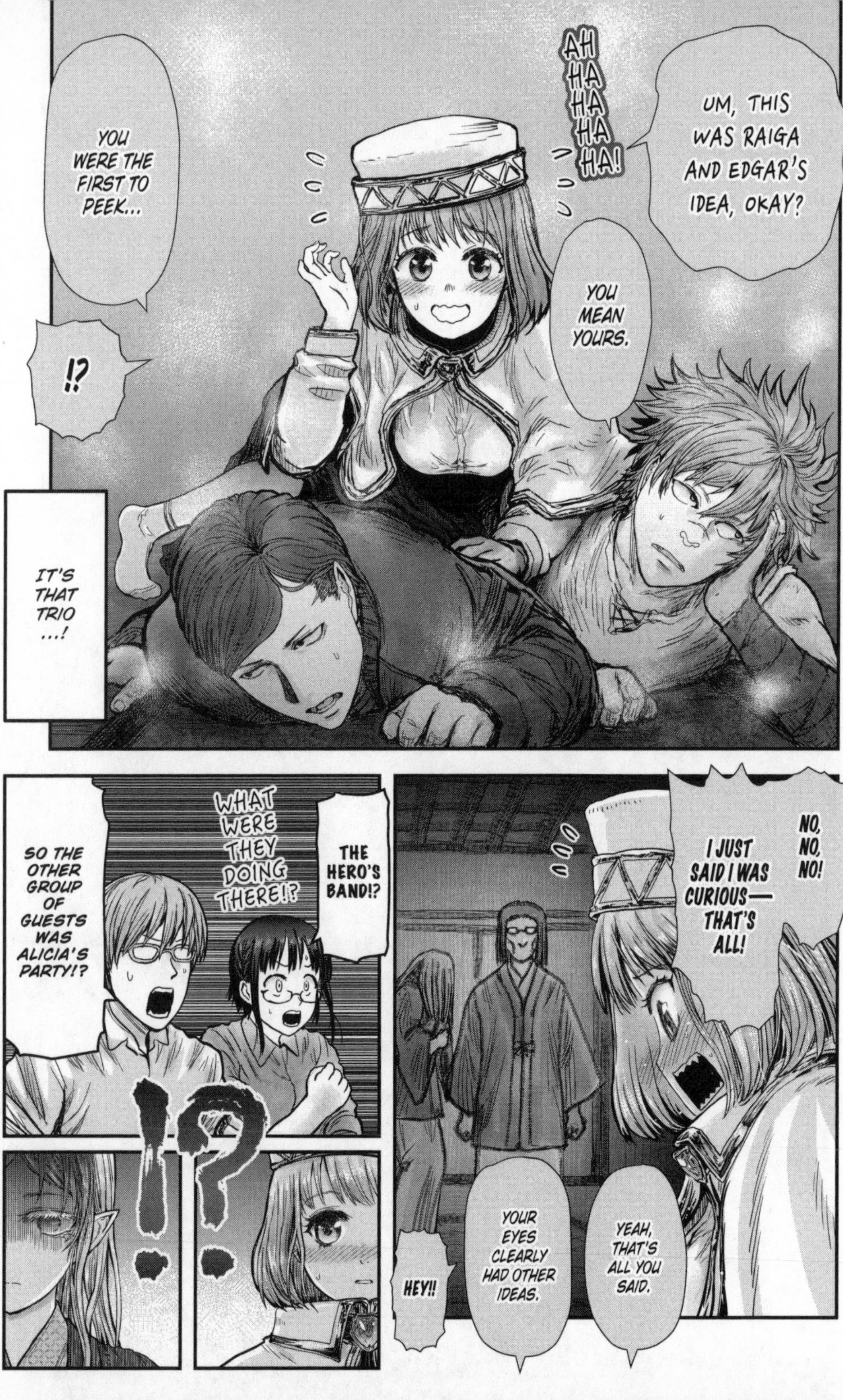
UM, THIS WAS RAIGA AND EDGAR'S IDEA, OKAY?
AH HA HA HA HA HA!
YOU MEAN YOURS.
YOU WERE THE FIRST TO PEEK...
!?
IT'S THAT TRIO ...!
NO, NO, NO!
I JUST SAID I WAS CURIOUS—THAT'S ALL!
YEAH, THAT'S ALL YOU SAID.
YOUR EYES CLEARLY HAD OTHER IDEAS.
HEY!!
THE HERO'S BAND!?
WHAT WERE THEY DOING THERE!?
SO THE OTHER GROUP OF GUESTS WAS ALICIA'S PARTY!?
!?
!!

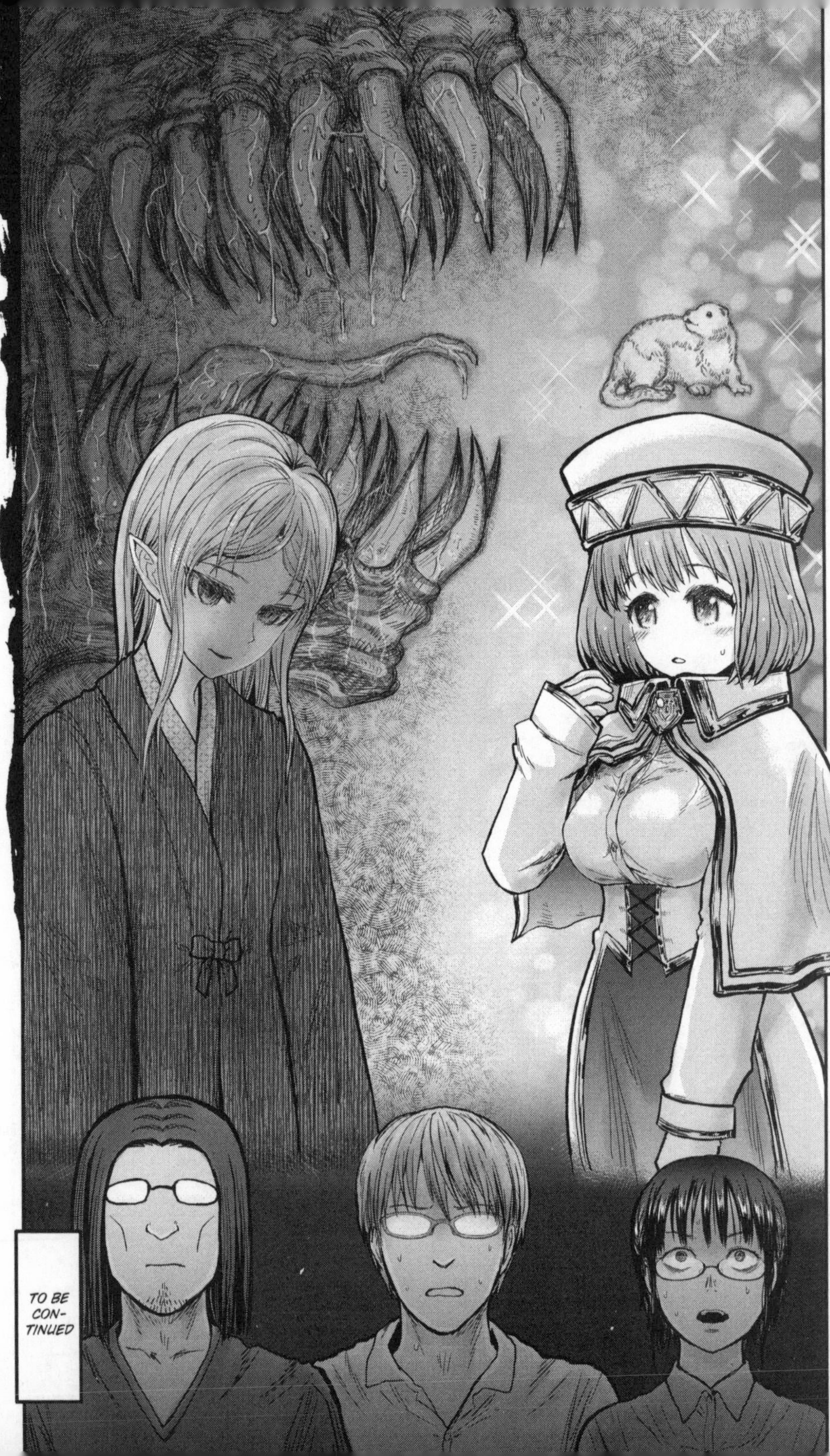
TO BE CON-TINUED

Rengoku (Purgatory)

A place people inhabit when their mortal life ends, before they reach heaven.
Rengoku sounds like a Buddhist term, but it's actually from Catholicism.

TIPS

UNCLE from ANOTHER WORLD

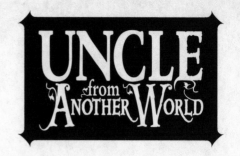

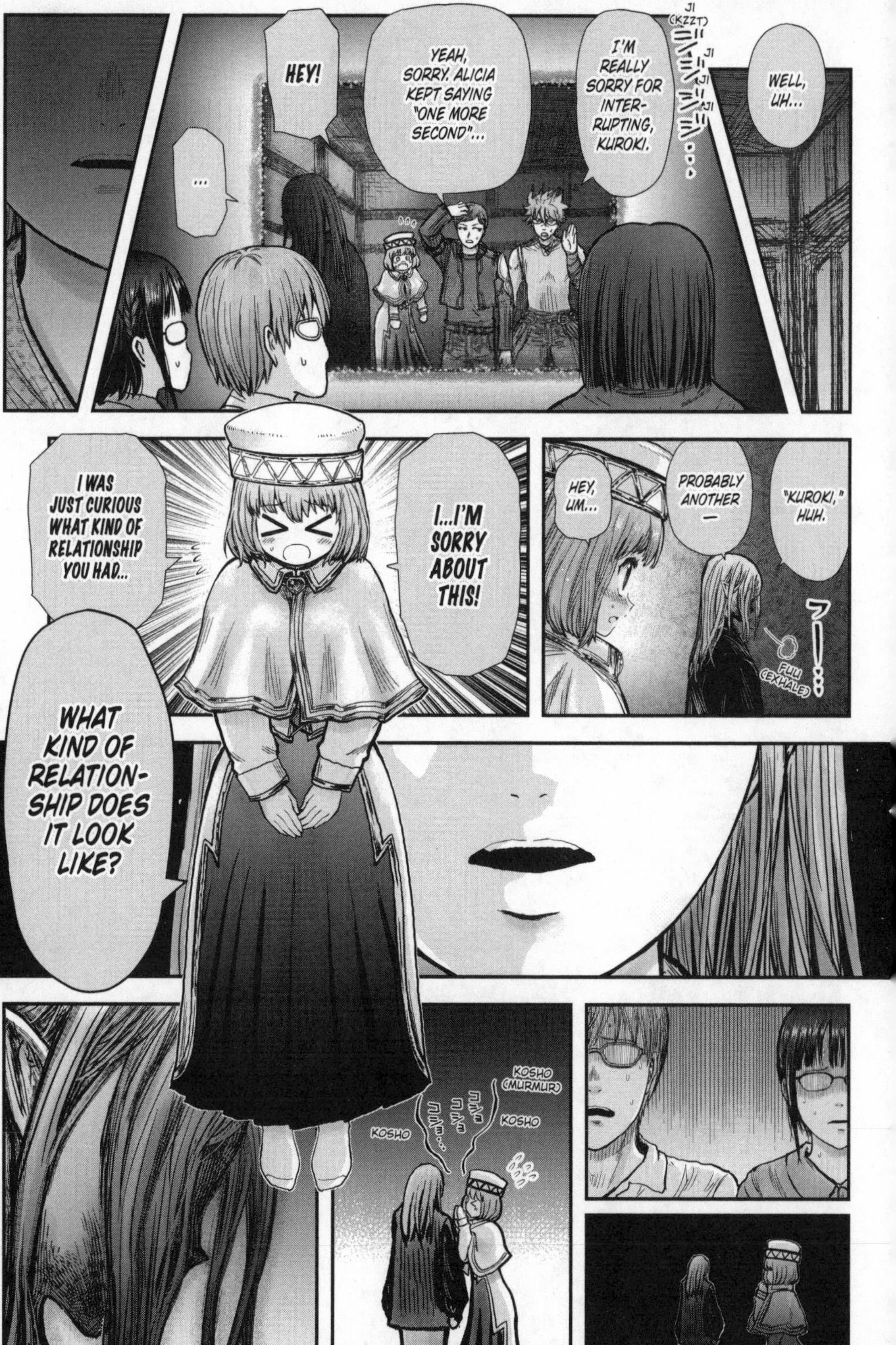
WELL, UH...
JI (KZZT) JI JI JI
I'M REALLY SORRY FOR INTER-RUPTING, KUROKI.
YEAH, SORRY. ALICIA KEPT SAYING "ONE MORE SECOND"...
HEY!
...
"KUROKI," HUH.
PROBABLY ANOTHER—
HEY, UM...
FUU (EXHALE)
I...I'M SORRY ABOUT THIS!
I WAS JUST CURIOUS WHAT KIND OF RELATIONSHIP YOU HAD...
WHAT KIND OF RELATION-SHIP DOES IT LOOK LIKE?
KOSHO (MURMUR)
KOSHO
KOSHO

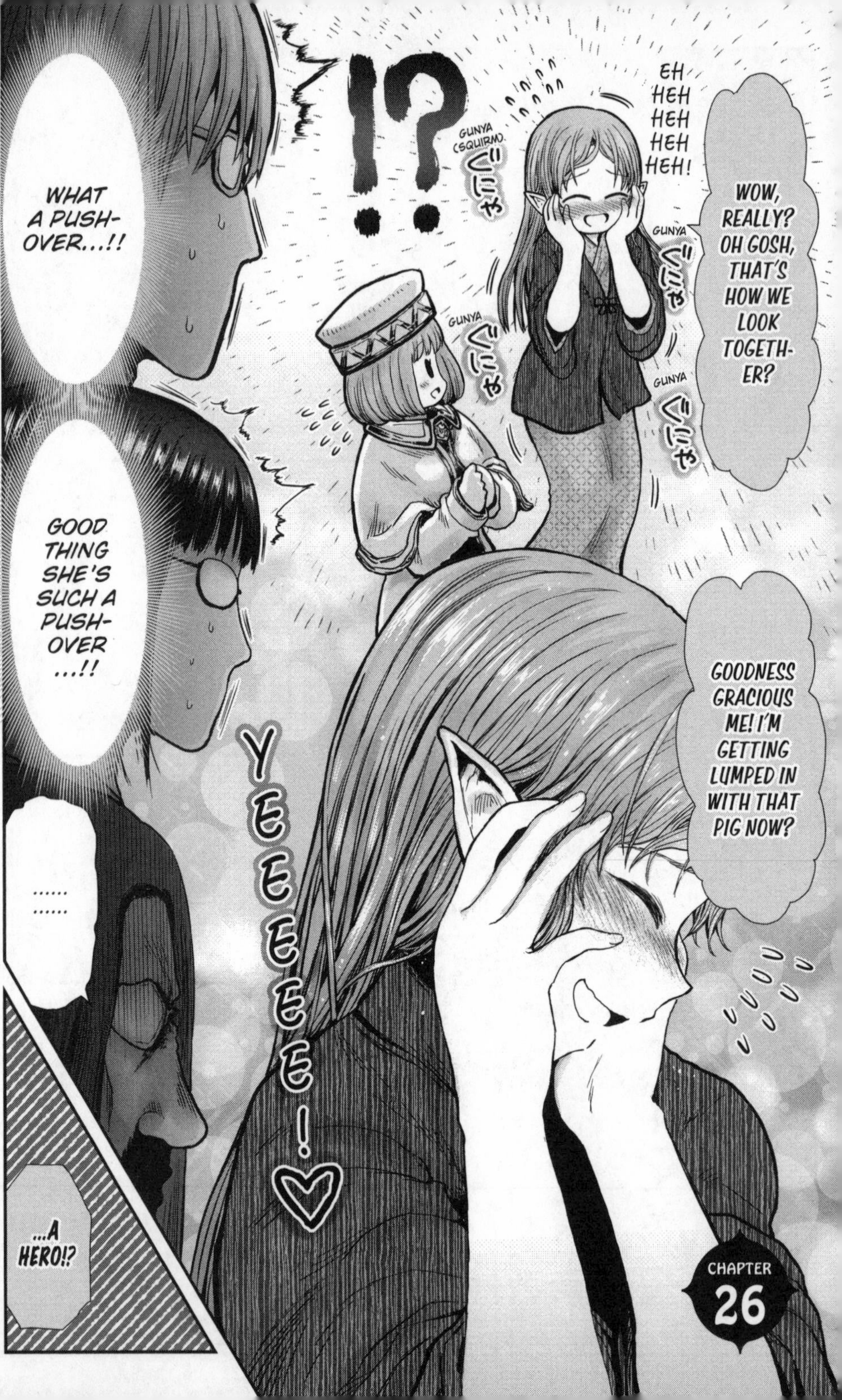

WOW, REALLY? OH GOSH, THAT'S HOW WE LOOK TOGETHER?
EH HEH HEH HEH HEH!
GUNYA
GUNYA
GUNYA
GUNYA (SQUIRM)
!?
WHAT A PUSH-OVER...!!
GOODNESS GRACIOUS ME! I'M GETTING LUMPED IN WITH THAT PIG NOW?
YEEEEEE!
GOOD THING SHE'S SUCH A PUSH-OVER...!!
......
......
...A HERO!?
CHAPTER 26

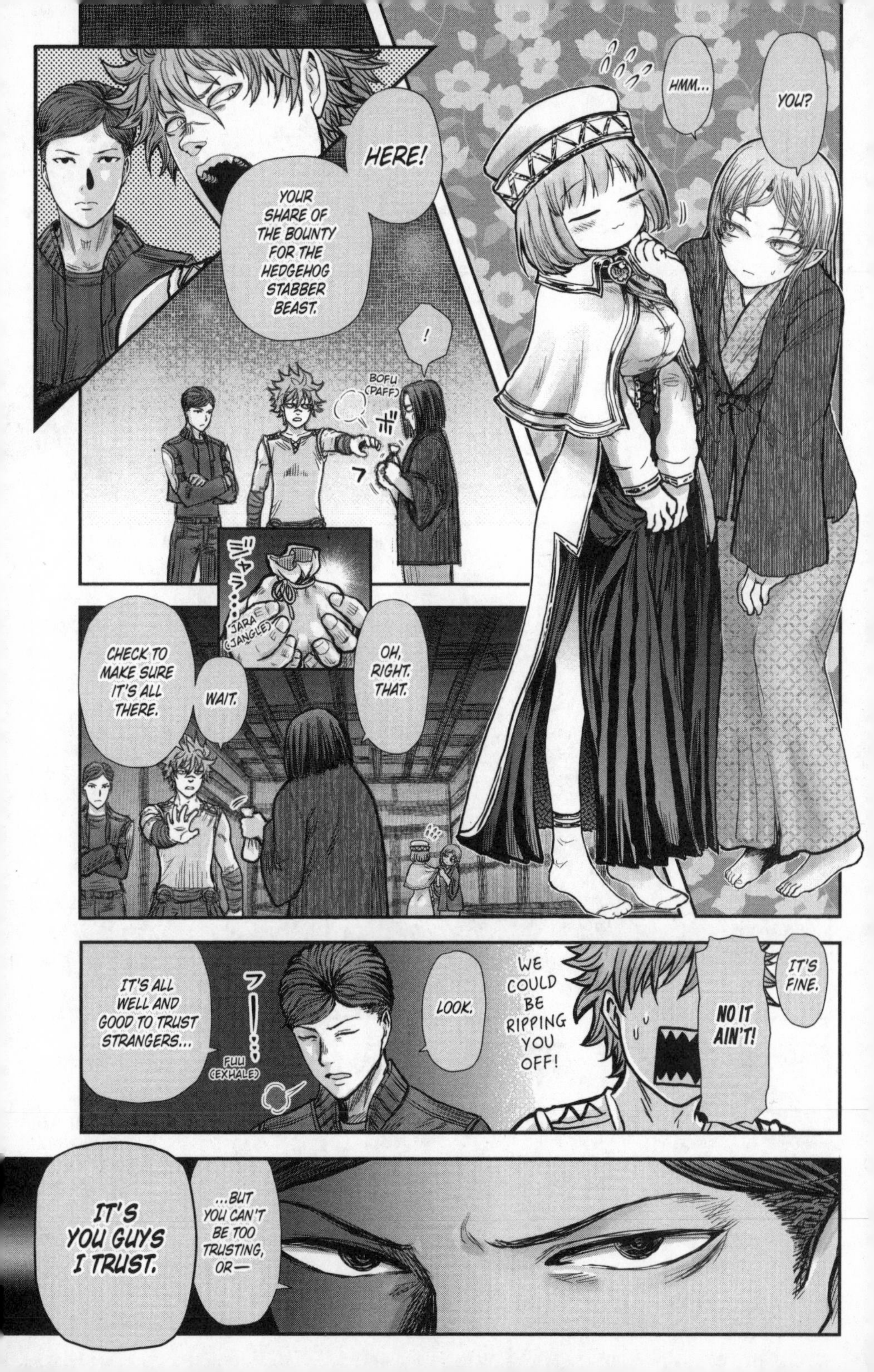
YOU?
HMM...
HERE!
YOUR SHARE OF THE BOUNTY FOR THE HEDGEHOG STABBER BEAST.
!
BOFU (PAFF)
JARA (JANGLE)
OH, RIGHT. THAT.
WAIT.
CHECK TO MAKE SURE IT'S ALL THERE.
IT'S FINE.
NO IT AIN'T!
WE COULD BE RIPPING YOU OFF!
LOOK.
FUU (EXHALE)
IT'S ALL WELL AND GOOD TO TRUST STRANGERS...
...BUT YOU CAN'T BE TOO TRUSTING, OR—
IT'S YOU GUYS I TRUST.

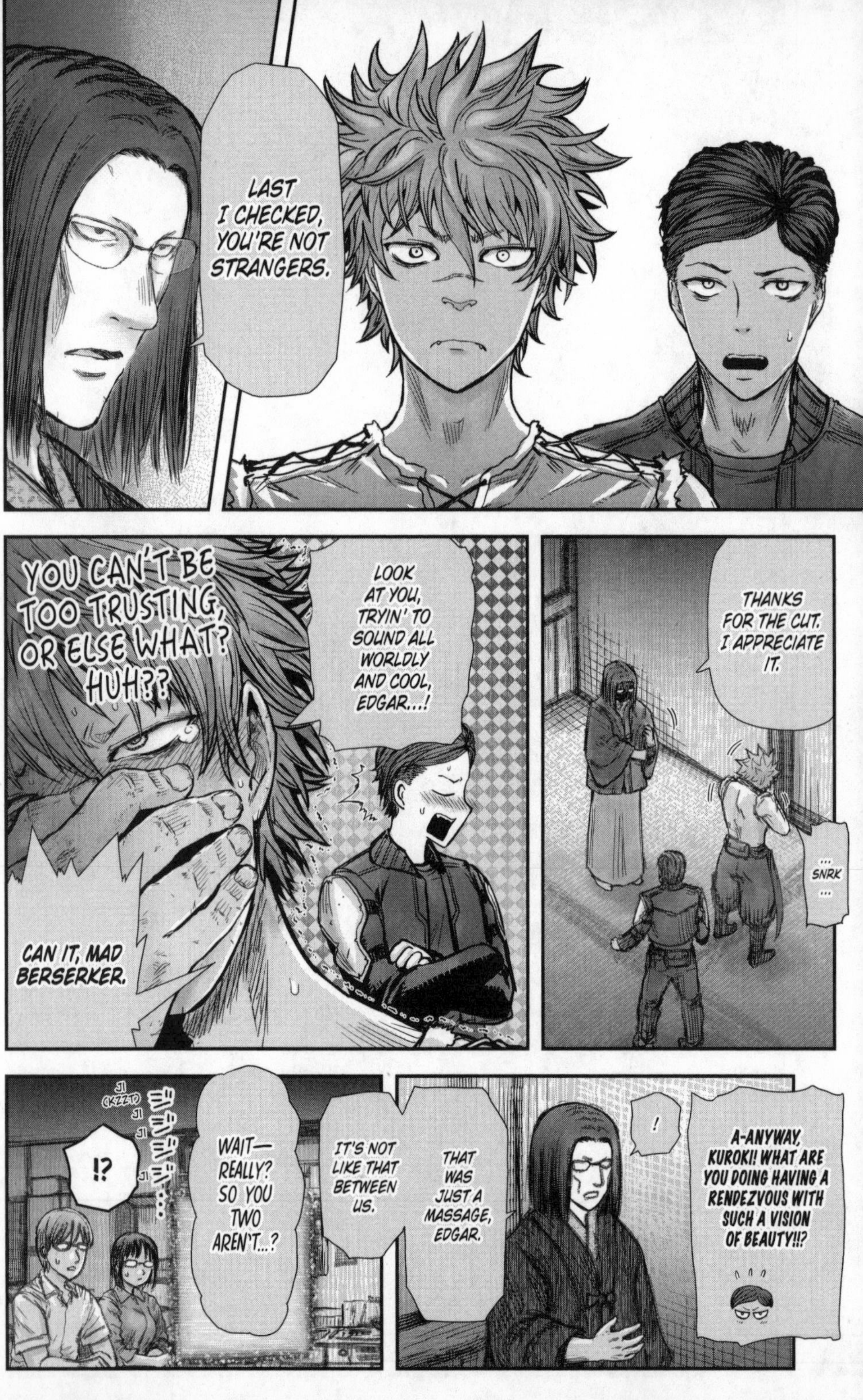
LAST I CHECKED, YOU'RE NOT STRANGERS.
THANKS FOR THE CUT. I APPRECIATE IT.
...SNRK...
LOOK AT YOU, TRYIN' TO SOUND ALL WORLDLY AND COOL, EDGAR...!
YOU CAN'T BE TOO TRUSTING, OR ELSE WHAT? HUH??
CAN IT, MAD BERSERKER.
A-ANYWAY, KUROKI! WHAT ARE YOU DOING HAVING A RENDEZVOUS WITH SUCH A VISION OF BEAUTY!!?
!
THAT WAS JUST A MASSAGE, EDGAR.
IT'S NOT LIKE THAT BETWEEN US.
WAIT— REALLY? SO YOU TWO AREN'T...?
!?
JI (CKZZT) JI JI JI

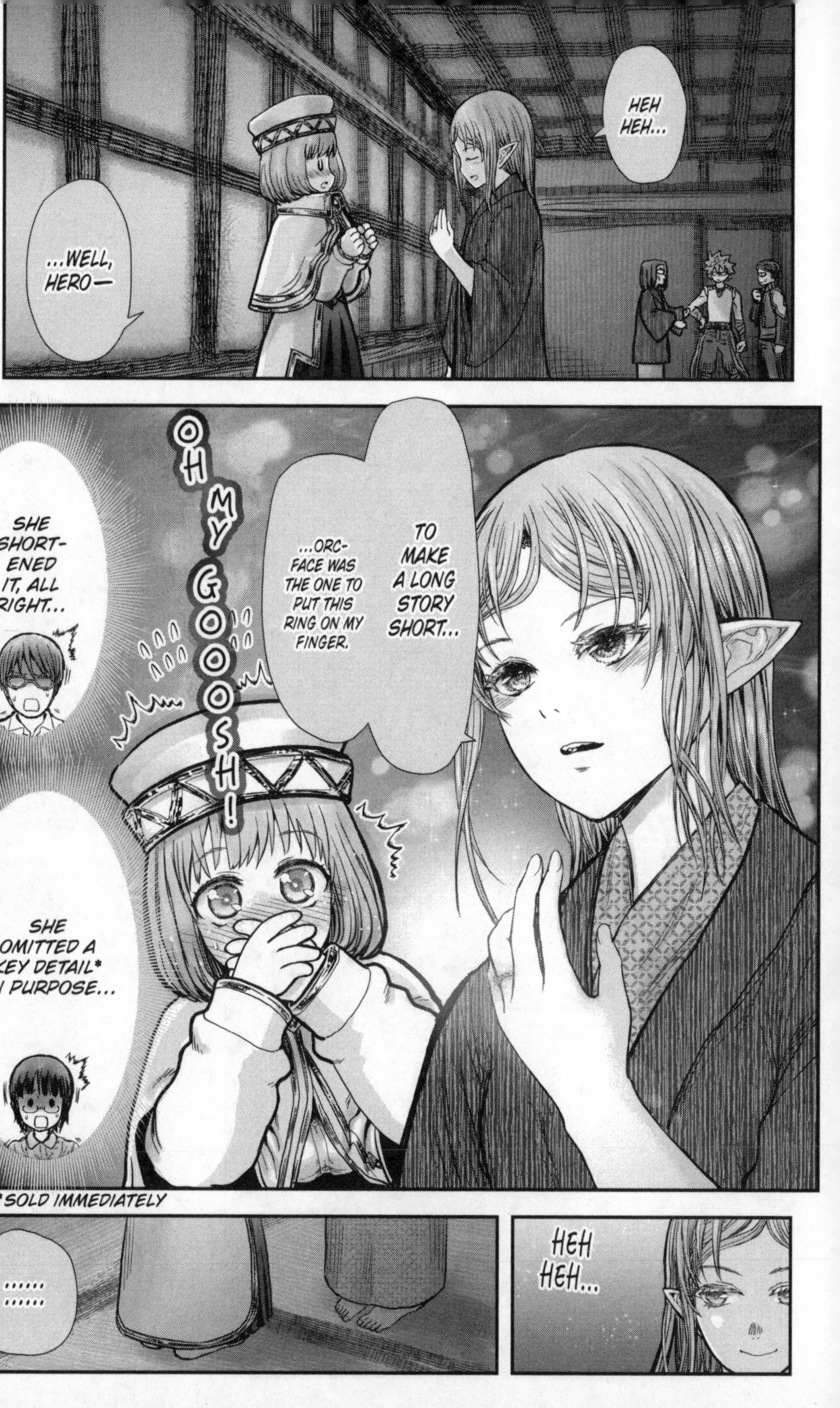
HEH HEH...
...WELL, HERO—
TO MAKE A LONG STORY SHORT...
...ORC-FACE WAS THE ONE TO PUT THIS RING ON MY FINGER.
OH MY GOOOOSH!
SHE SHORTENED IT, ALL RIGHT...
SHE OMITTED A KEY DETAIL* ON PURPOSE...
*SOLD IMMEDIATELY
HEH HEH...
......
......

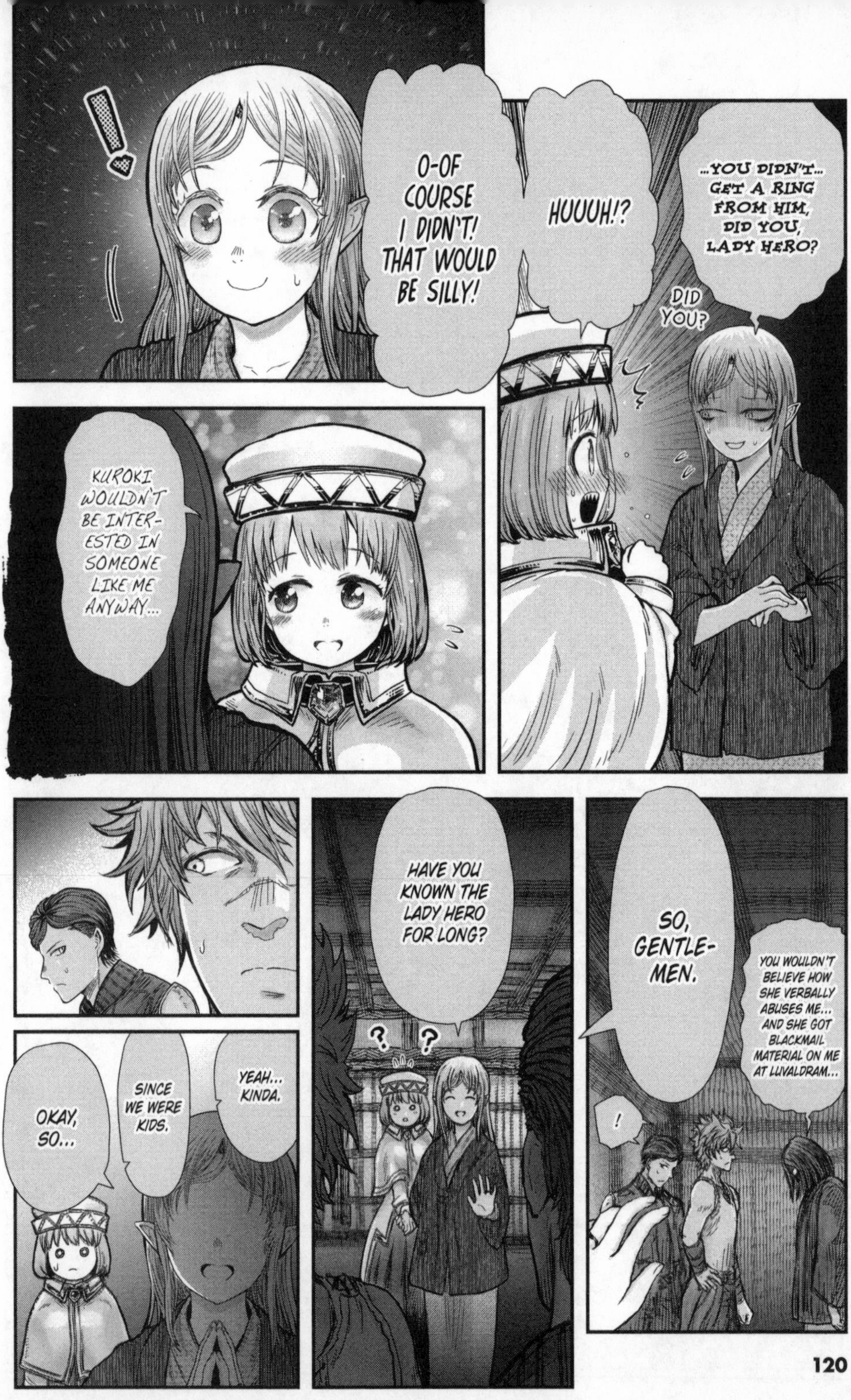
...YOU DIDN'T... GET A RING FROM HIM, DID YOU, LADY HERO?
DID YOU?
HUUUH!?
O-OF COURSE I DIDN'T! THAT WOULD BE SILLY!
KUROKI WOULDN'T BE INTER-ESTED IN SOMEONE LIKE ME ANYWAY...
SO, GENTLE-MEN.
YOU WOULDN'T BELIEVE HOW SHE VERBALLY ABUSES ME... AND SHE GOT BLACKMAIL MATERIAL ON ME AT LUVALDRAM...
!
HAVE YOU KNOWN THE LADY HERO FOR LONG?
YEAH... KINDA.
SINCE WE WERE KIDS.
OKAY, SO...

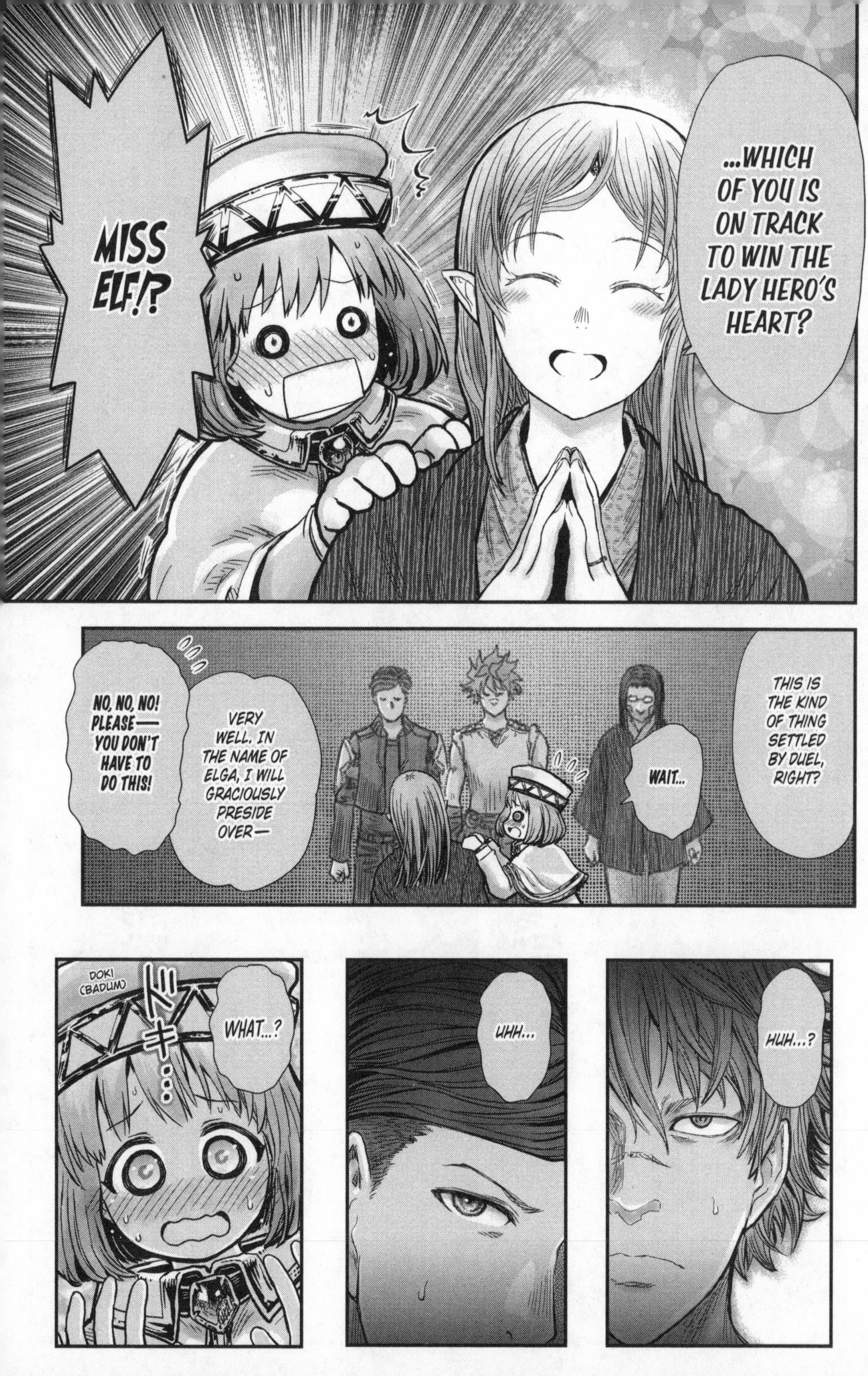
...WHICH OF YOU IS ON TRACK TO WIN THE LADY HERO'S HEART?
MISS ELF!?
THIS IS THE KIND OF THING SETTLED BY DUEL, RIGHT?
WAIT...
VERY WELL. IN THE NAME OF ELGA, I WILL GRACIOUSLY PRESIDE OVER—
NO, NO, NO! PLEASE—YOU DON'T HAVE TO DO THIS!
HUH...?
UHH...
WHAT...?
ドキ...
DOKI (BADUM)

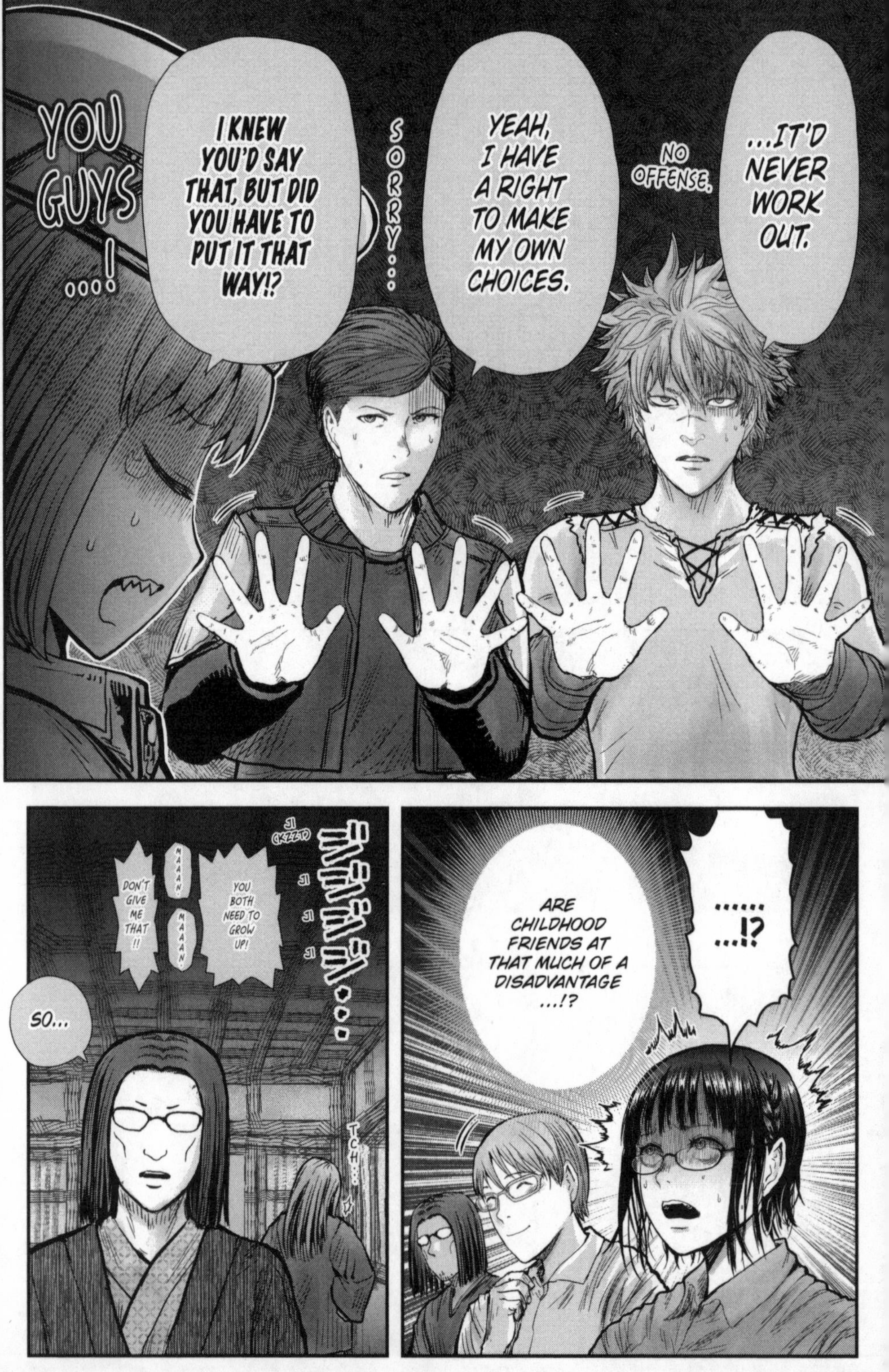
...IT'D NEVER WORK OUT.
NO OFFENSE.
YEAH, I HAVE A RIGHT TO MAKE MY OWN CHOICES.
SORRY...
I KNEW YOU'D SAY THAT, BUT DID YOU HAVE TO PUT IT THAT WAY!?
YOU GUYS...!
......!?
ARE CHILDHOOD FRIENDS AT THAT MUCH OF A DISADVANTAGE ...!?
JI (KZZZT) JI JI JI
YOU BOTH NEED TO GROW UP!
MAAAN. MAAAN.
DON'T GIVE ME THAT!!
SO...
TCH...

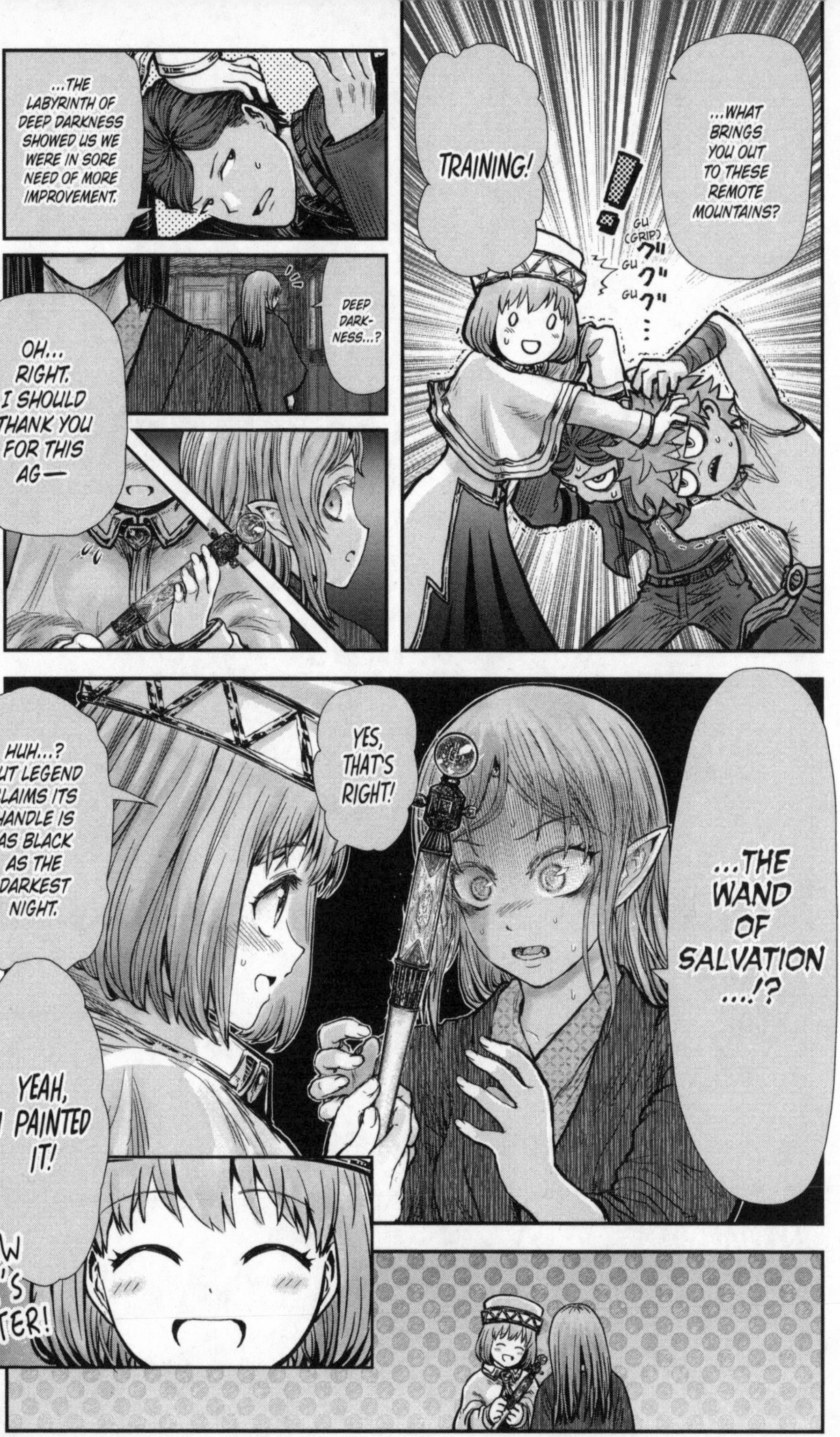
...WHAT BRINGS YOU OUT TO THESE REMOTE MOUNTAINS?
TRAINING!
!
GU (GRIP) グ
GU グ
GU グ
...
...THE LABYRINTH OF DEEP DARKNESS SHOWED US WE WERE IN SORE NEED OF MORE IMPROVEMENT.
DEEP DARK-NESS...?
OH... RIGHT. I SHOULD THANK YOU FOR THIS AG—
...THE WAND OF SALVATION...!?
YES, THAT'S RIGHT!
HUH...? BUT LEGEND CLAIMS ITS HANDLE IS AS BLACK AS THE DARKEST NIGHT.
YEAH, I PAINTED IT!
NOW IT'S CUTER!

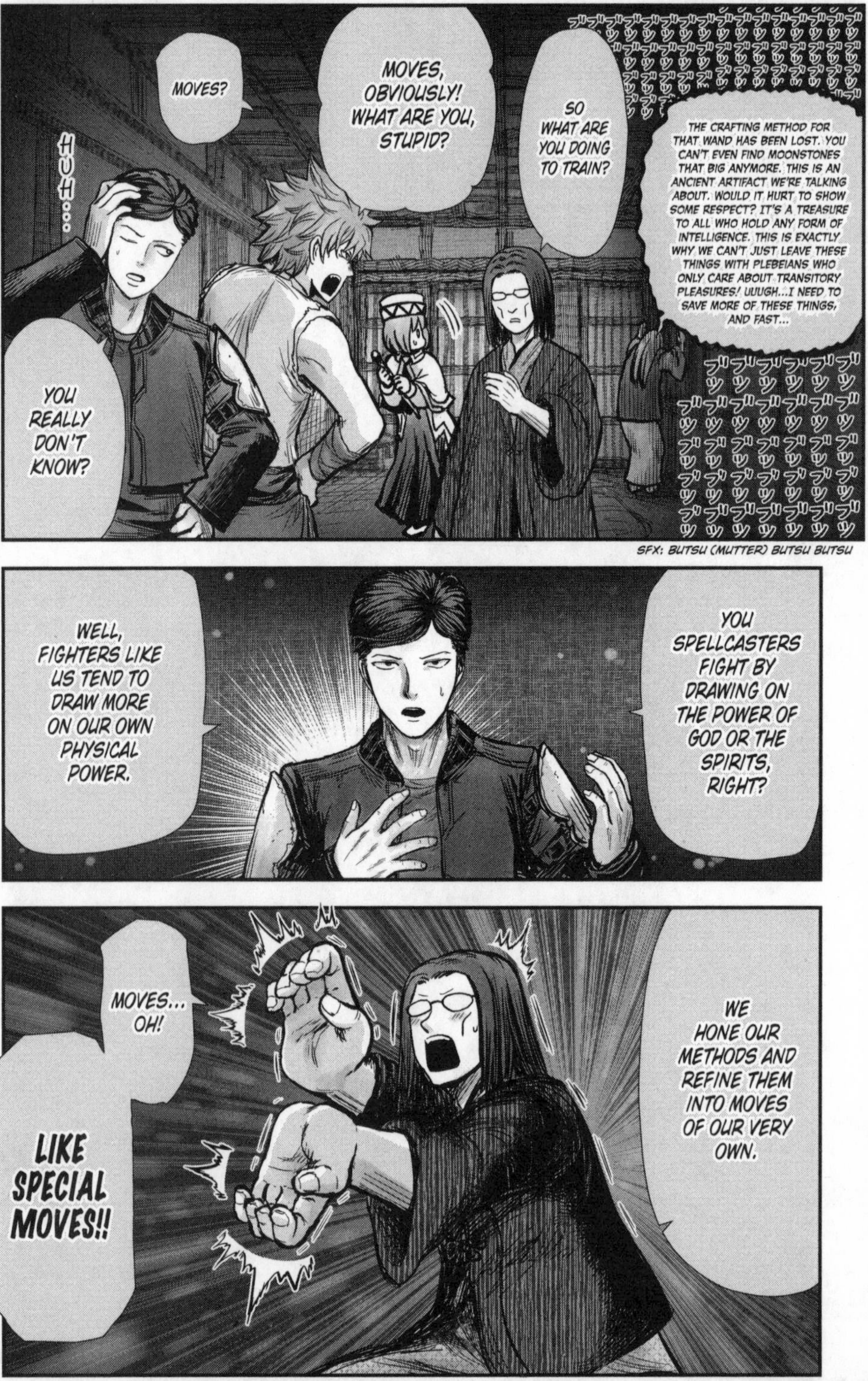
THE CRAFTING METHOD FOR THAT WAND HAS BEEN LOST. YOU CAN'T EVEN FIND MOONSTONES THAT BIG ANYMORE. THIS IS AN ANCIENT ARTIFACT WE'RE TALKING ABOUT. WOULD IT HURT TO SHOW SOME RESPECT? IT'S A TREASURE TO ALL WHO HOLD ANY FORM OF INTELLIGENCE. THIS IS EXACTLY WHY WE CAN'T JUST LEAVE THESE THINGS WITH PLEBEIANS WHO ONLY CARE ABOUT TRANSITORY PLEASURES! UUUGH...I NEED TO SAVE MORE OF THESE THINGS, AND FAST...
SO WHAT ARE YOU DOING TO TRAIN?
MOVES, OBVIOUSLY! WHAT ARE YOU, STUPID?
MOVES?
HUH...
YOU REALLY DON'T KNOW?
SFX: BUTSU (MUTTER) BUTSU BUTSU
YOU SPELLCASTERS FIGHT BY DRAWING ON THE POWER OF GOD OR THE SPIRITS, RIGHT?
WELL, FIGHTERS LIKE US TEND TO DRAW MORE ON OUR OWN PHYSICAL POWER.
WE HONE OUR METHODS AND REFINE THEM INTO MOVES OF OUR VERY OWN.
MOVES... OH!
LIKE SPECIAL MOVES!!

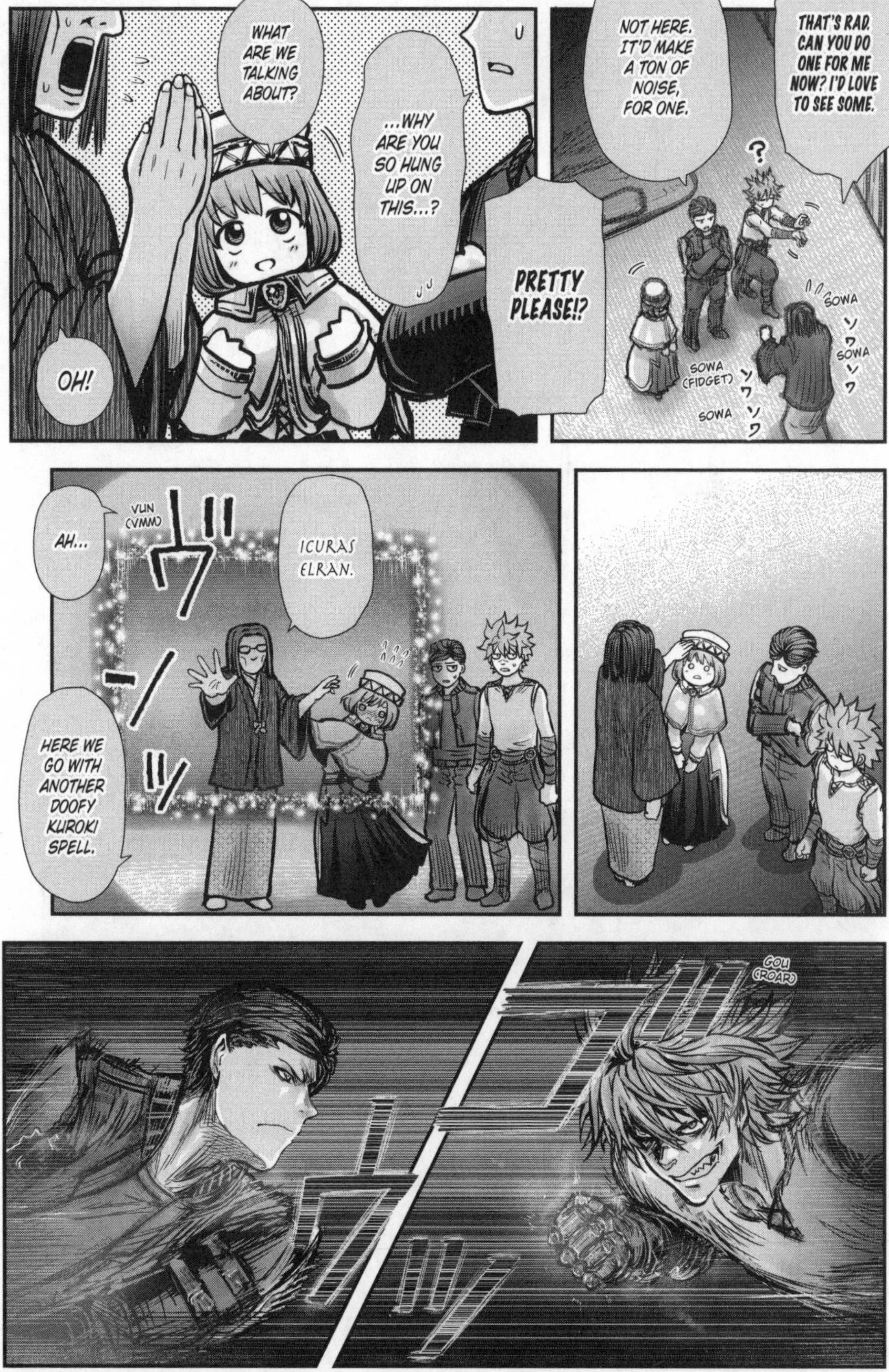
THAT'S RAD. CAN YOU DO ONE FOR ME NOW? I'D LOVE TO SEE SOME.
NOT HERE. IT'D MAKE A TON OF NOISE, FOR ONE.
?
SOWA
SOWA
SOWA (FIDGET)
SOWA
PRETTY PLEASE!?
...WHY ARE YOU SO HUNG UP ON THIS...?
WHAT ARE WE TALKING ABOUT?
OH!
ICURAS ELRAN.
VUN (VMM)
AH...
HERE WE GO WITH ANOTHER DOOFY KUROKI SPELL.
GOU (ROAR)

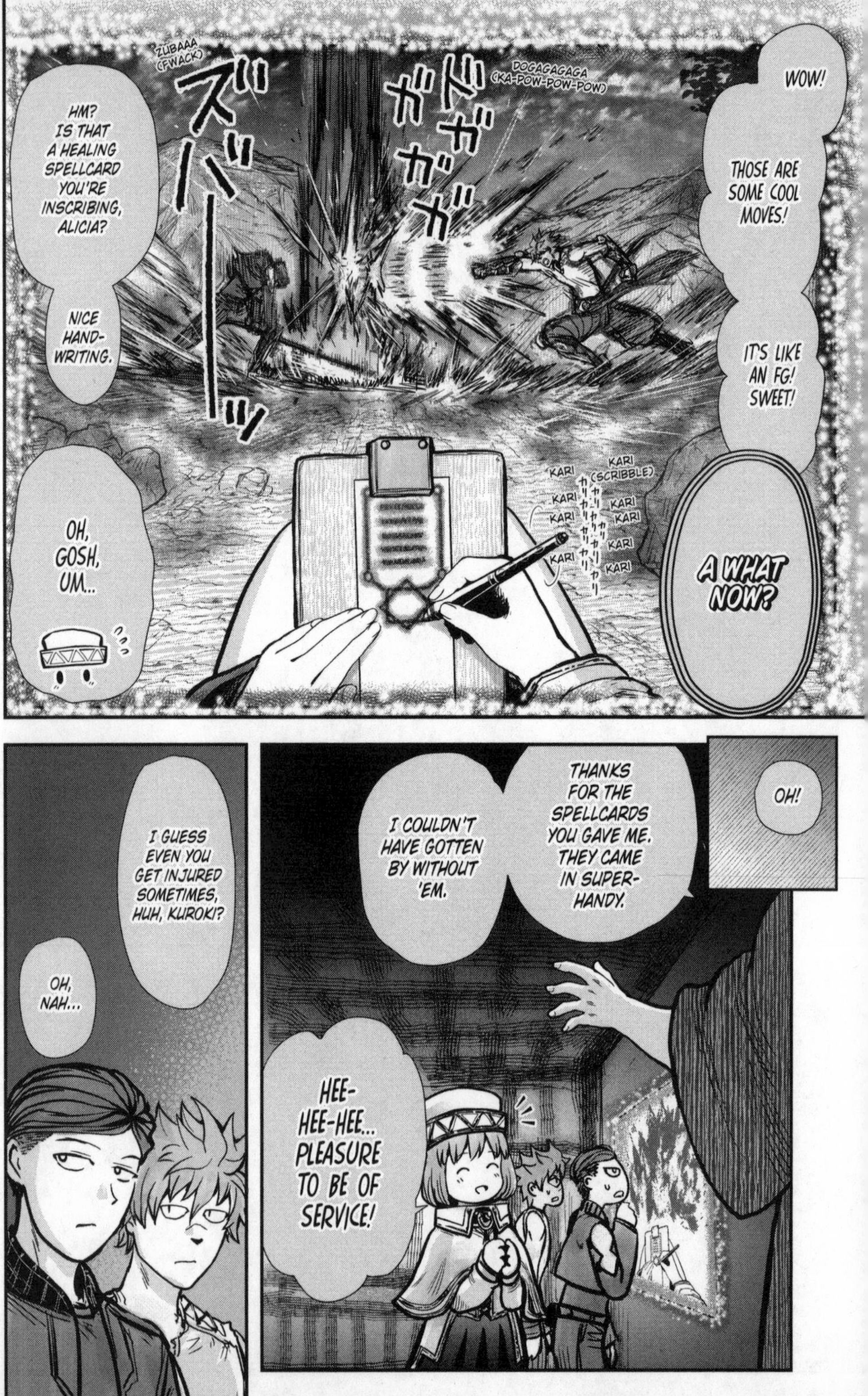
WOW!
THOSE ARE SOME COOL MOVES!
IT'S LIKE AN FG! SWEET!
DOGAGAGAGA (KA-POW-POW-POW)
ZUBAAA (FWACK)
HM? IS THAT A HEALING SPELLCARD YOU'RE INSCRIBING, ALICIA?
NICE HAND-WRITING.
A WHAT NOW?
KARI KARI (SCRIBBLE)
KARI KARI KARI KARI
KARI KARI KARI KARI
OH, GOSH, UM...
OH!
THANKS FOR THE SPELLCARDS YOU GAVE ME. THEY CAME IN SUPER-HANDY.
I COULDN'T HAVE GOTTEN BY WITHOUT 'EM.
HEE-HEE-HEE... PLEASURE TO BE OF SERVICE!
I GUESS EVEN YOU GET INJURED SOMETIMES, HUH, KUROKI?
OH, NAH...

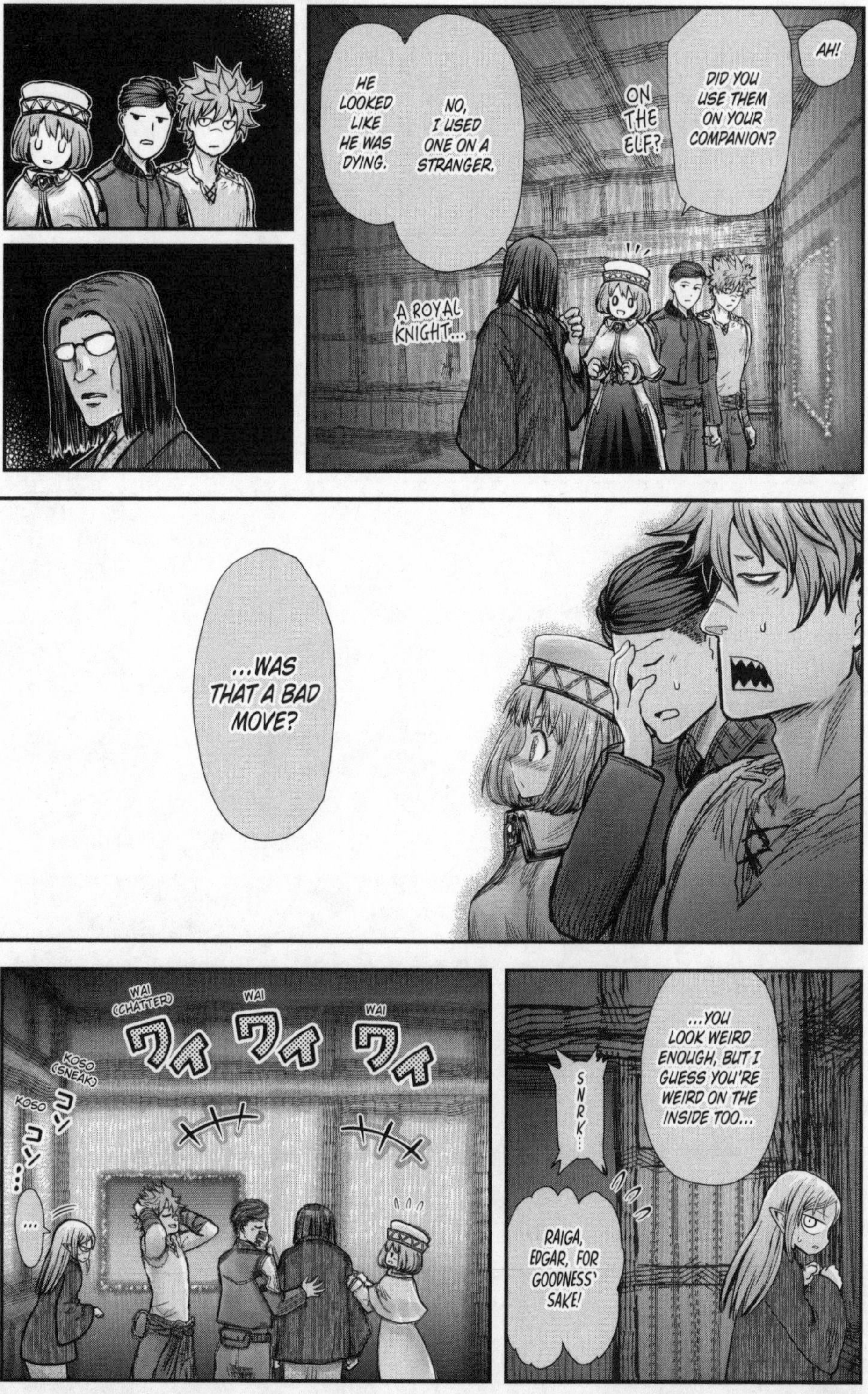
AH!
DID YOU USE THEM ON YOUR COMPANION?
ON THE ELF?
NO, I USED ONE ON A STRANGER.
HE LOOKED LIKE HE WAS DYING.
A ROYAL KNIGHT...
...WAS THAT A BAD MOVE?
...YOU LOOK WEIRD ENOUGH, BUT I GUESS YOU'RE WEIRD ON THE INSIDE TOO...
SNRK...
RAIGA, EDGAR, FOR GOODNESS' SAKE!
WAI (CHATTER) WAI WAI
ワイ ワイ ワイ
KOSO (SNEAK) KOSO
コソ コソ...
...

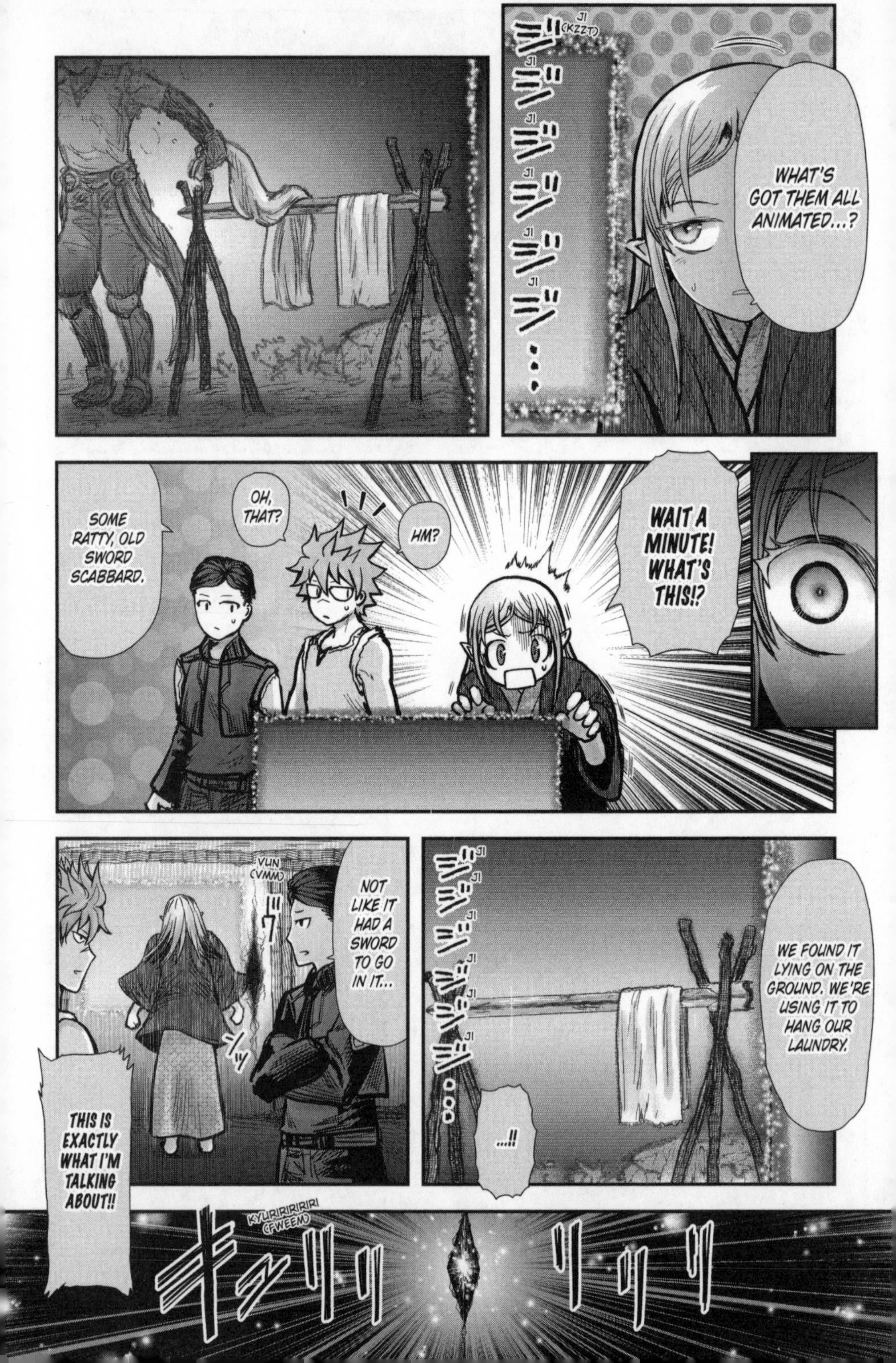
JI (KZZT)
JI
JI
JI
JI
WHAT'S GOT THEM ALL ANIMATED...?
WAIT A MINUTE! WHAT'S THIS!?
HM?
OH, THAT?
SOME RATTY, OLD SWORD SCABBARD.
WE FOUND IT LYING ON THE GROUND. WE'RE USING IT TO HANG OUR LAUNDRY.
JI
JI
JI
JI
JI
...!!
NOT LIKE IT HAD A SWORD TO GO IN IT...
VUN (VMM)
THIS IS EXACTLY WHAT I'M TALKING ABOUT!!
KYURIRIRIRI (FWEEM)

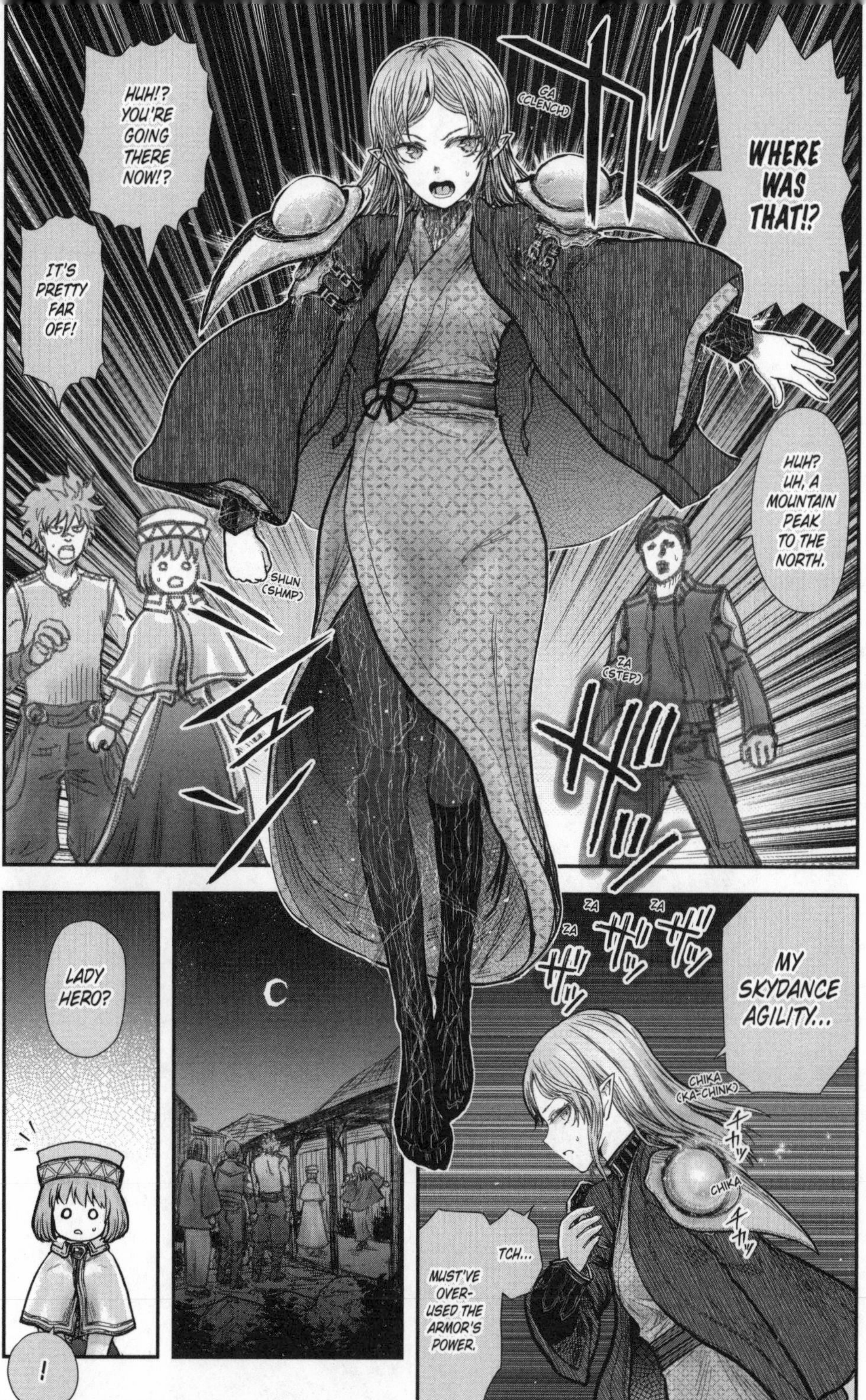
WHERE WAS THAT!?
GA (CLENCH)
HUH? UH, A MOUNTAIN PEAK TO THE NORTH.
HUH!? YOU'RE GOING THERE NOW!?
IT'S PRETTY FAR OFF!
ZA (STEP)
SHUN (SHMP)
ZA
ZA
ZA
MY SKYDANCE AGILITY...
CHIKA (KA-CHINK)
CHIKA
TCH...
MUST'VE OVER-USED THE ARMOR'S POWER.
LADY HERO?
!

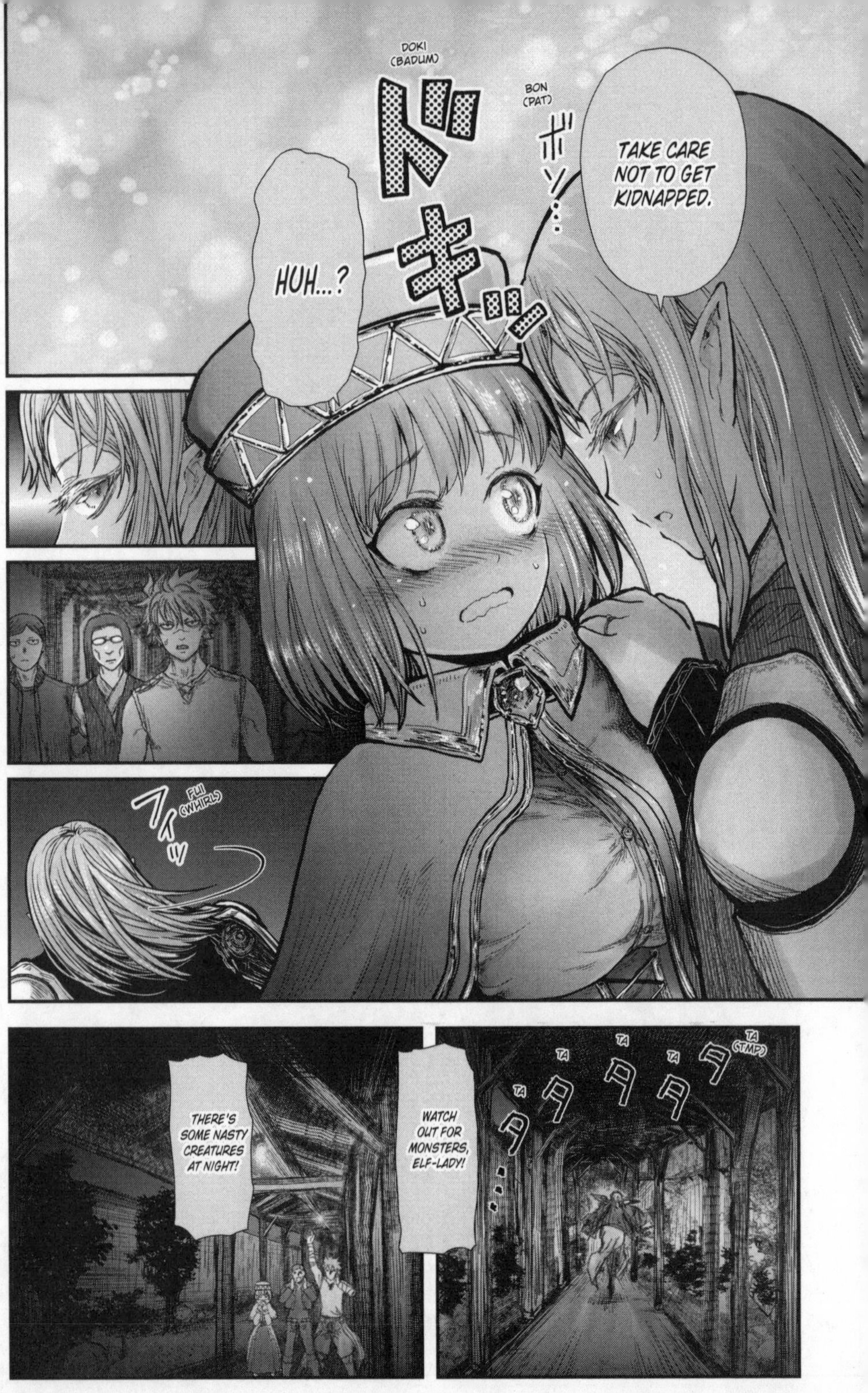
BON (PAT)
TAKE CARE NOT TO GET KIDNAPPED.
DOKI (BADUM)
HUH...?
FUI (WHIRL)
TA TA TA TA TA (TMP)
WATCH OUT FOR MONSTERS, ELF-LADY!
THERE'S SOME NASTY CREATURES AT NIGHT!

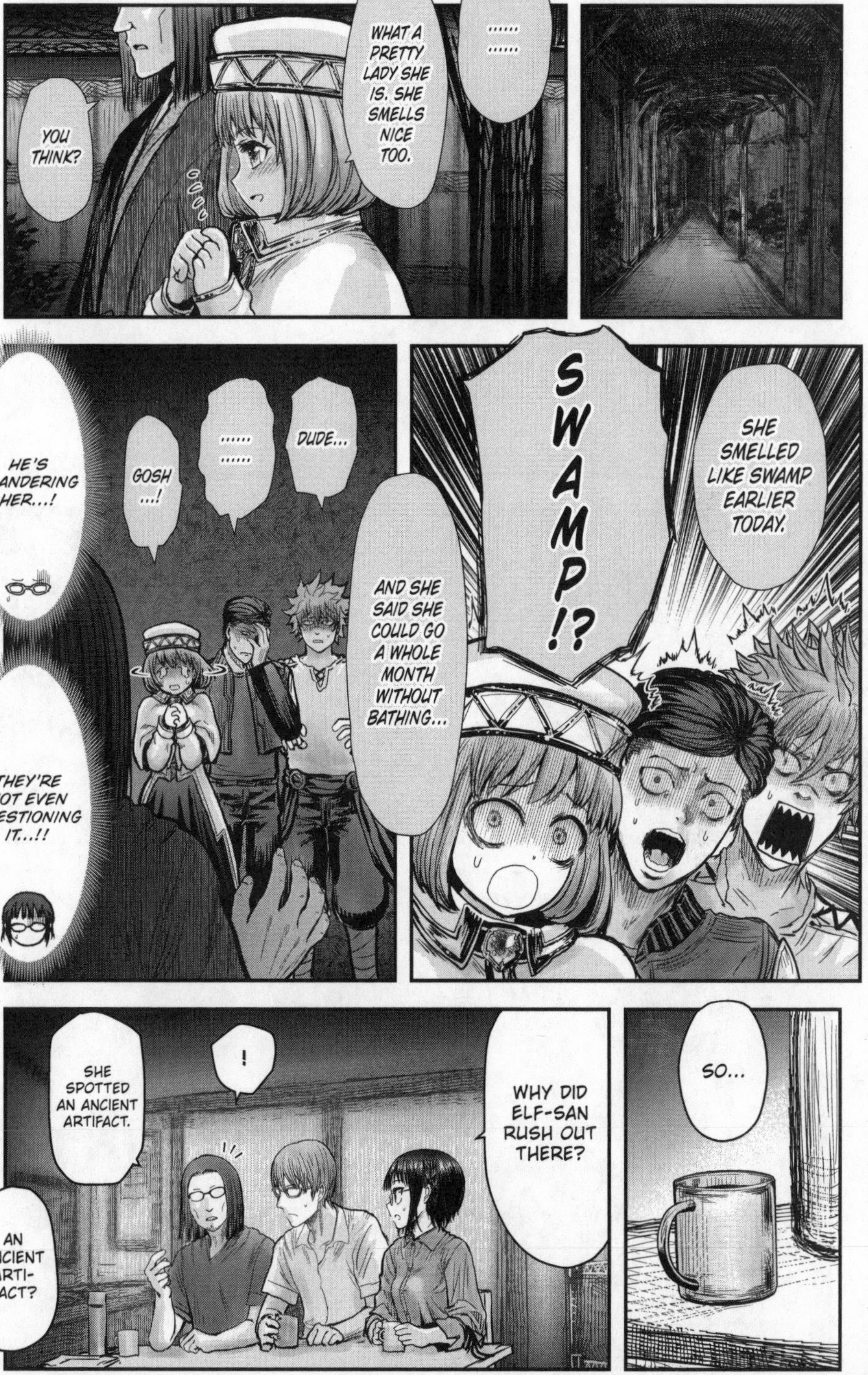

…… ……
WHAT A PRETTY LADY SHE IS. SHE SMELLS NICE TOO.
YOU THINK?
SHE SMELLED LIKE SWAMP EARLIER TODAY.
SWAMP!?
AND SHE SAID SHE COULD GO A WHOLE MONTH WITHOUT BATHING…
DUDE…
…… ……
GOSH …!
HE'S SLANDERING HER…!
THEY'RE NOT EVEN QUESTIONING IT…!!
SO…
WHY DID ELF-SAN RUSH OUT THERE?
!
SHE SPOTTED AN ANCIENT ARTIFACT.
AN ANCIENT ARTI-FACT?

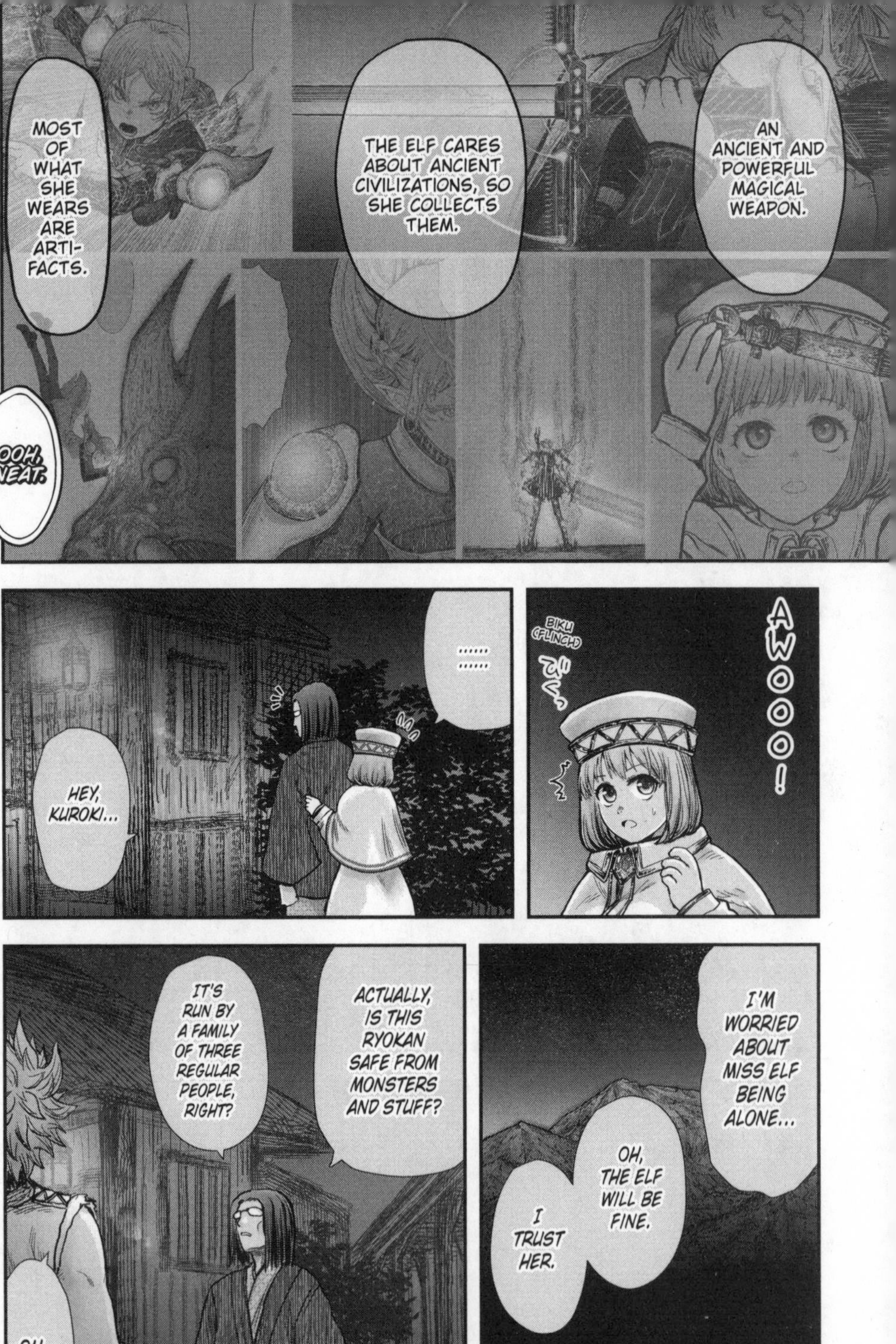
AN ANCIENT AND POWERFUL MAGICAL WEAPON.
THE ELF CARES ABOUT ANCIENT CIVILIZATIONS, SO SHE COLLECTS THEM.
MOST OF WHAT SHE WEARS ARE ARTI-FACTS.
OOH, NEAT.
AWOOOOO!
BIKU (FLINCH)
......
......
HEY, KUROKI...
I'M WORRIED ABOUT MISS ELF BEING ALONE...
OH, THE ELF WILL BE FINE.
I TRUST HER.
ACTUALLY, IS THIS RYOKAN SAFE FROM MONSTERS AND STUFF?
IT'S RUN BY A FAMILY OF THREE REGULAR PEOPLE, RIGHT?
OH...

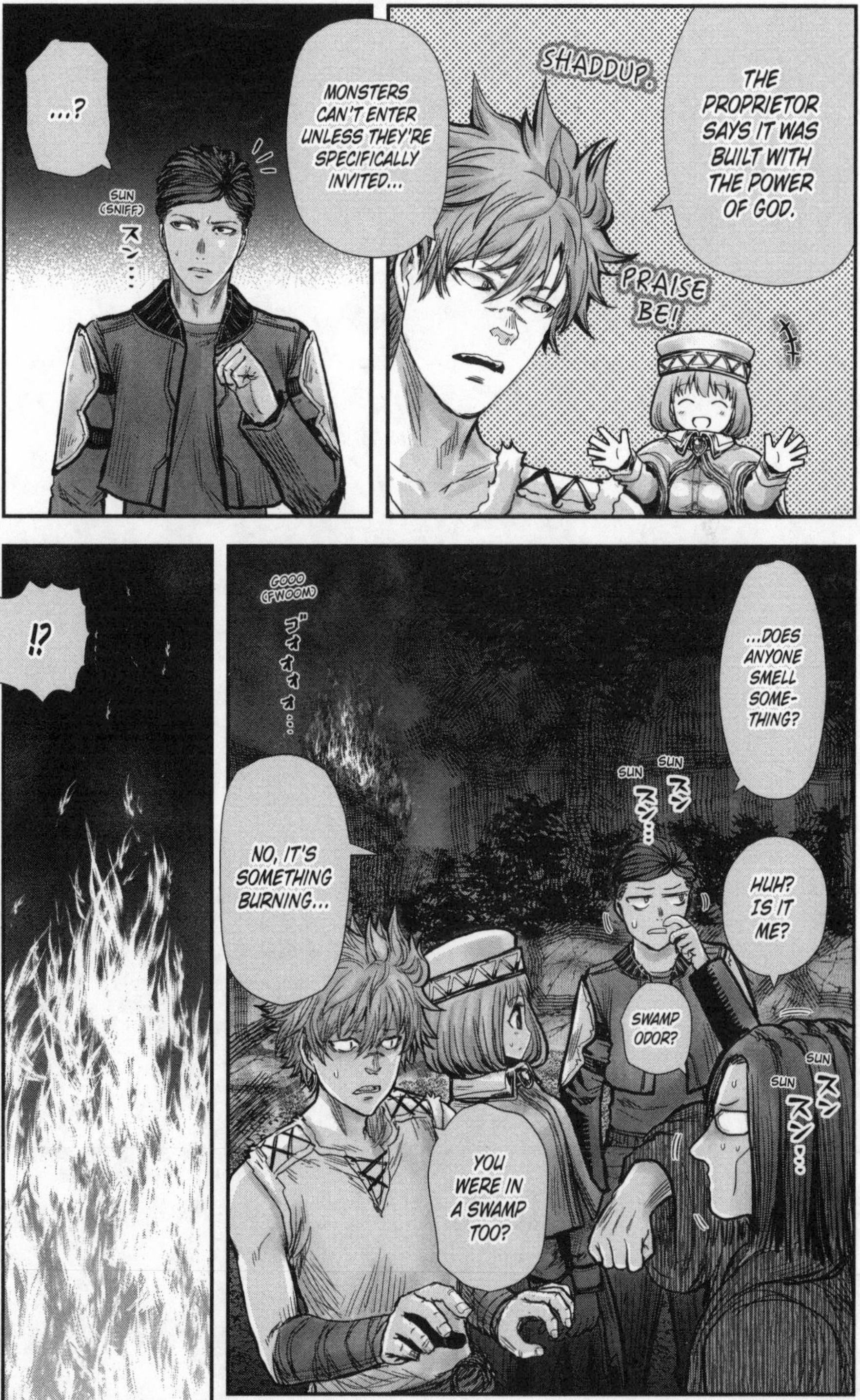
THE PROPRIETOR SAYS IT WAS BUILT WITH THE POWER OF GOD.
PRAISE BE!
SHADDUP.
MONSTERS CAN'T ENTER UNLESS THEY'RE SPECIFICALLY INVITED...
SUN (SNIFF)
スン…
...?
...DOES ANYONE SMELL SOME-THING?
SUN
スン
SUN
スン…
HUH? IS IT ME?
GOOO (FWOOM)
ゴオオオ…
NO, IT'S SOMETHING BURNING...
SWAMP ODOR?
SUN
スン
SUN
スン…
YOU WERE IN A SWAMP TOO?
!?

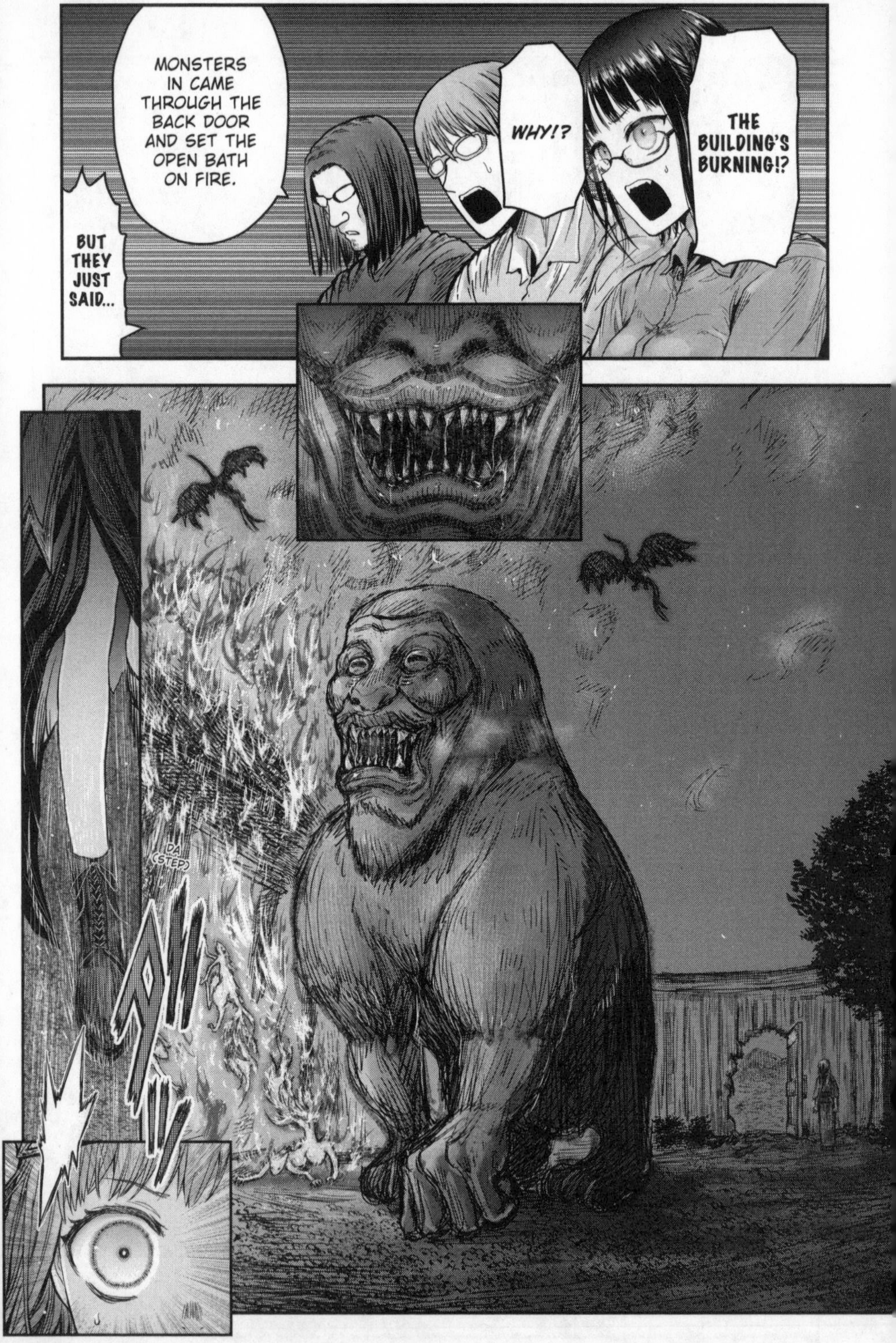
THE BUILDING'S BURNING!?
WHY!?
MONSTERS IN CAME THROUGH THE BACK DOOR AND SET THE OPEN BATH ON FIRE.
BUT THEY JUST SAID...
DA (STEP)

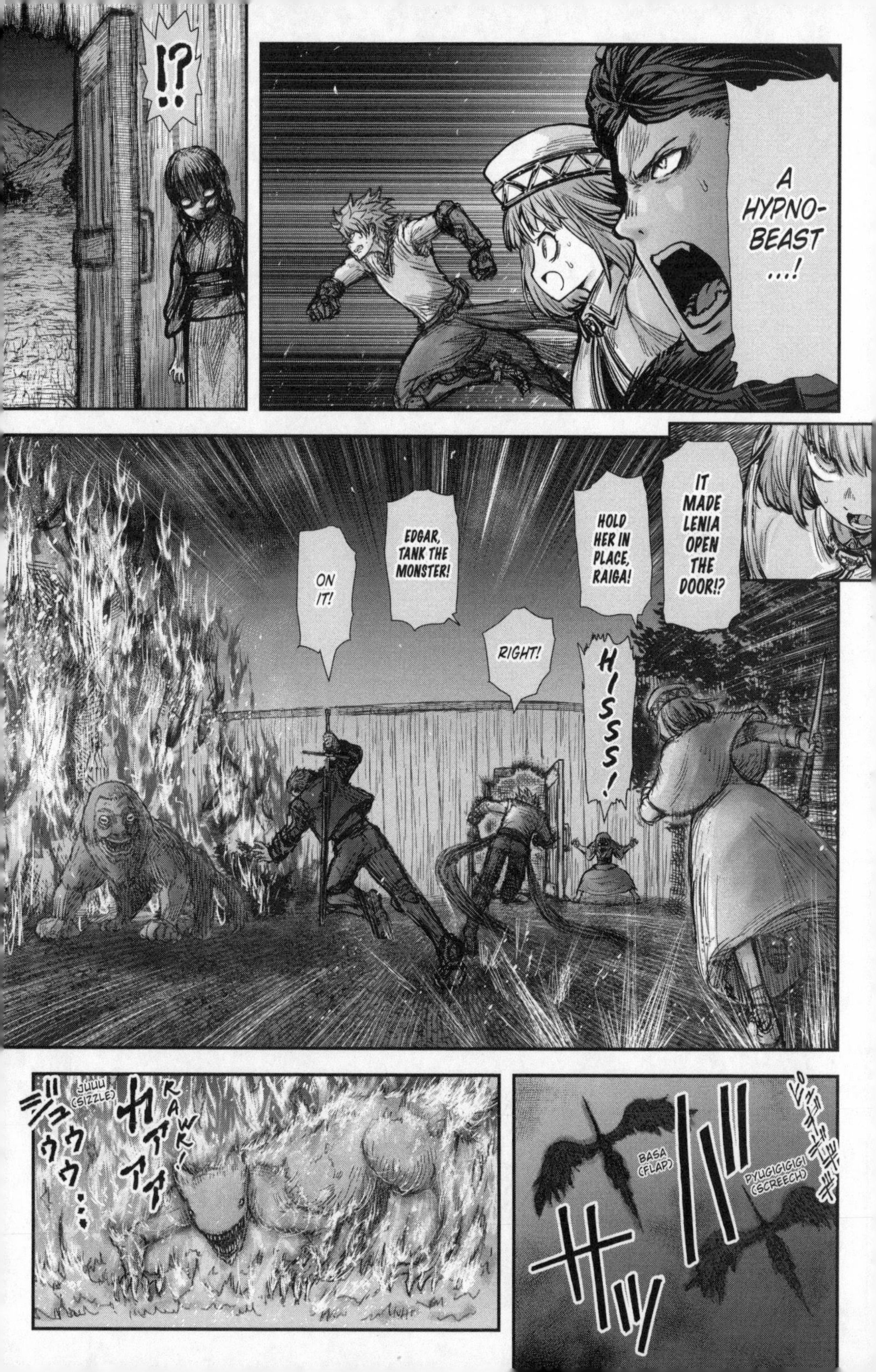
A HYPNO-BEAST ...!
!?
IT MADE LENIA OPEN THE DOOR!?
HOLD HER IN PLACE, RAIGA!
EDGAR, TANK THE MONSTER!
RIGHT!
ON IT!
HISSS!
BASA (FLAP)
PYUGIGIGI (SCREECH)
JUUU (SIZZLE)
RAWK!

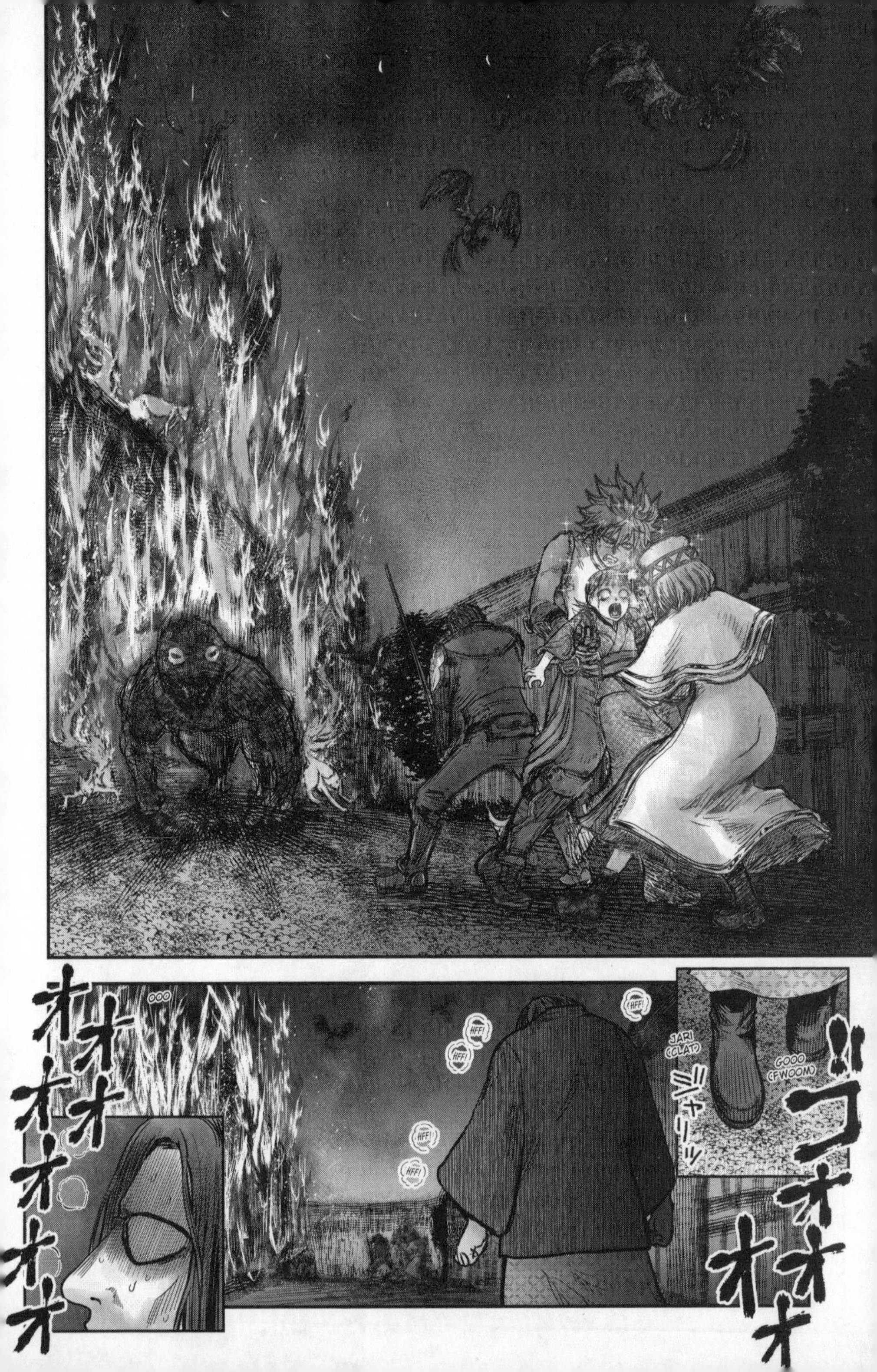

ゴオオオオ
GOOO (FWOOM)
ジャリッ
JARI (CLAT)
HFF!
HFF!
HFF!
HFF!
HFF!
ooo
オオオオオオオ

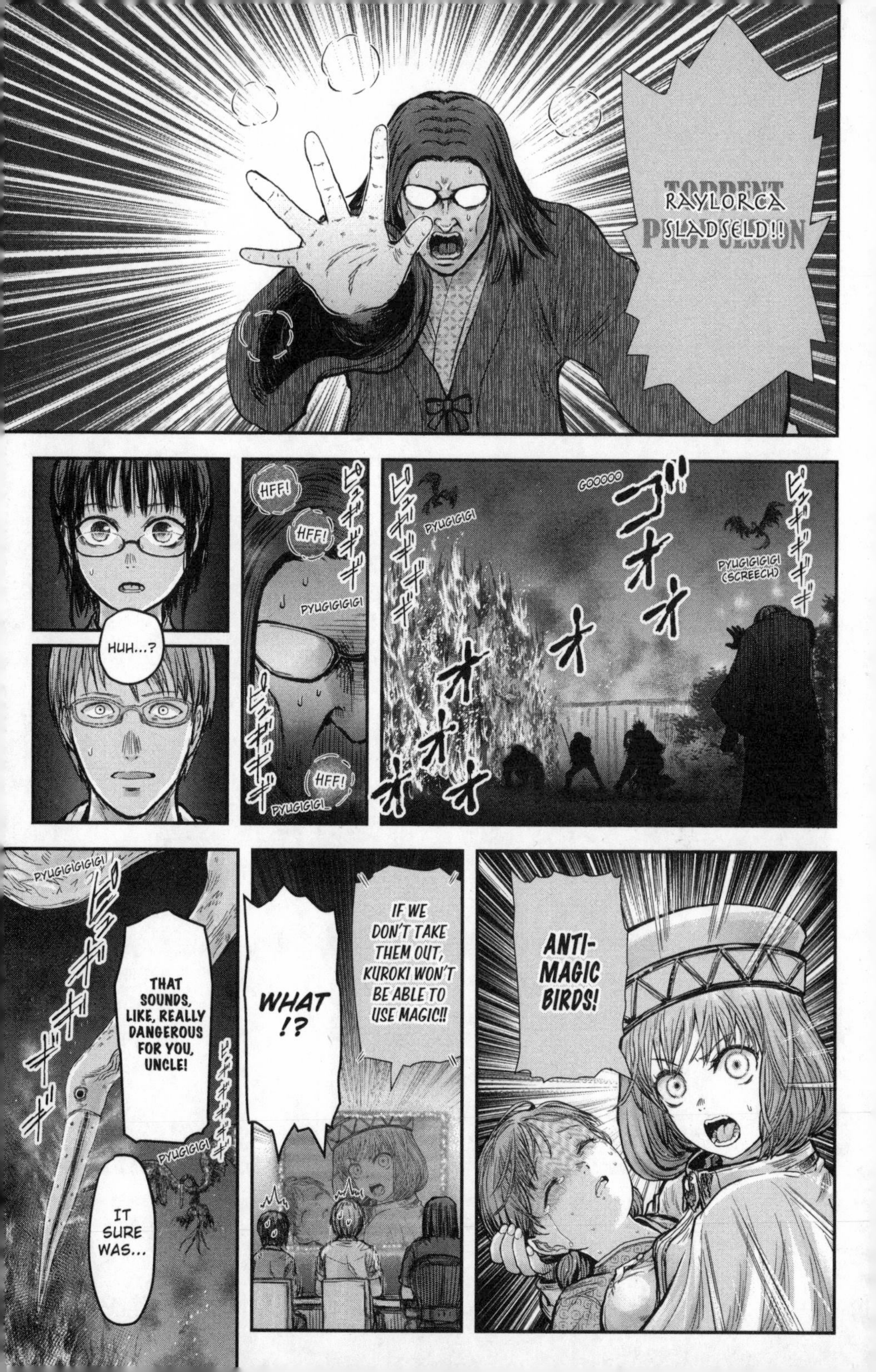
TORRENT PROPULSION
RAYLORCA SLADSELD!!
GOOOOO
PYUGIGIGIGI (SCREECH)
PYUGIGI
HFF!
HFF!
PYUGIGIGI
HFF!
PYUGIGIGI
HUH...?
ANTI-MAGIC BIRDS!
IF WE DON'T TAKE THEM OUT, KUROKI WON'T BE ABLE TO USE MAGIC!!
WHAT!?
PYUGIGIGIGIGI
THAT SOUNDS, LIKE, REALLY DANGEROUS FOR YOU, UNCLE!
PYUGIGIGI
IT SURE WAS...

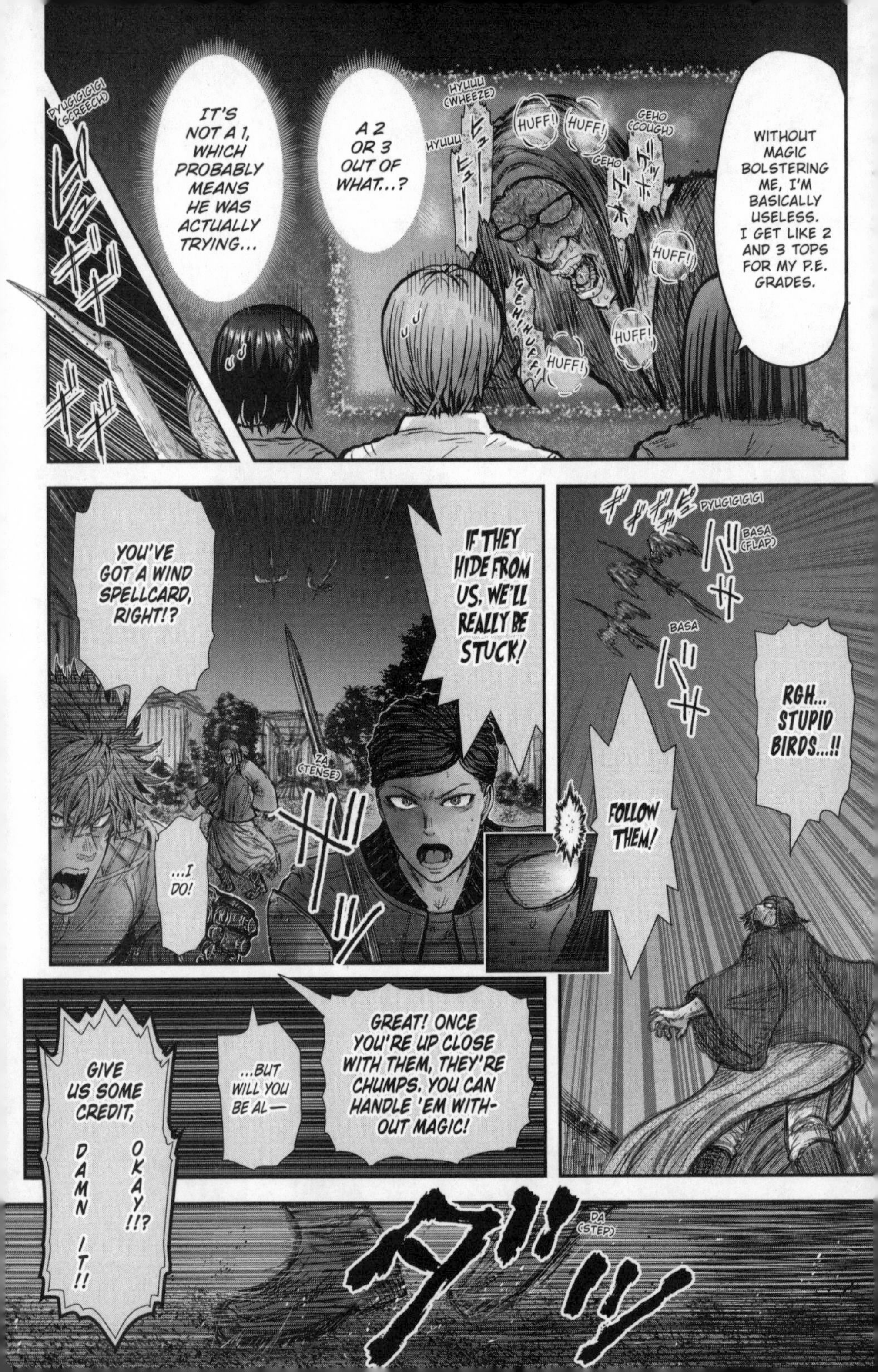
WITHOUT MAGIC BOLSTERING ME, I'M BASICALLY USELESS. I GET LIKE 2 AND 3 TOPS FOR MY P.E. GRADES.
GEHO (COUGH)
GEHO
HUFF!
HUFF!
HYUUU (WHEEZE)
HYUUU
HUFF!
GEHI HUFF!
HUFF!
HUFF!
A 2 OR 3 OUT OF WHAT...?
IT'S NOT A 1, WHICH PROBABLY MEANS HE WAS ACTUALLY TRYING...
PYUGIGIGI (SCREECH)
PYUGIGIGI
BASA (FLAP)
BASA
RGH... STUPID BIRDS...!!
FOLLOW THEM!
IF THEY HIDE FROM US, WE'LL REALLY BE STUCK!
YOU'VE GOT A WIND SPELLCARD, RIGHT!?
ZA (TENSE)
...I DO!
GREAT! ONCE YOU'RE UP CLOSE WITH THEM, THEY'RE CHUMPS. YOU CAN HANDLE 'EM WITHOUT MAGIC!
...BUT WILL YOU BE AL—
GIVE US SOME CREDIT,
OKAY!!?
DAMN IT!!
DA (STEP)

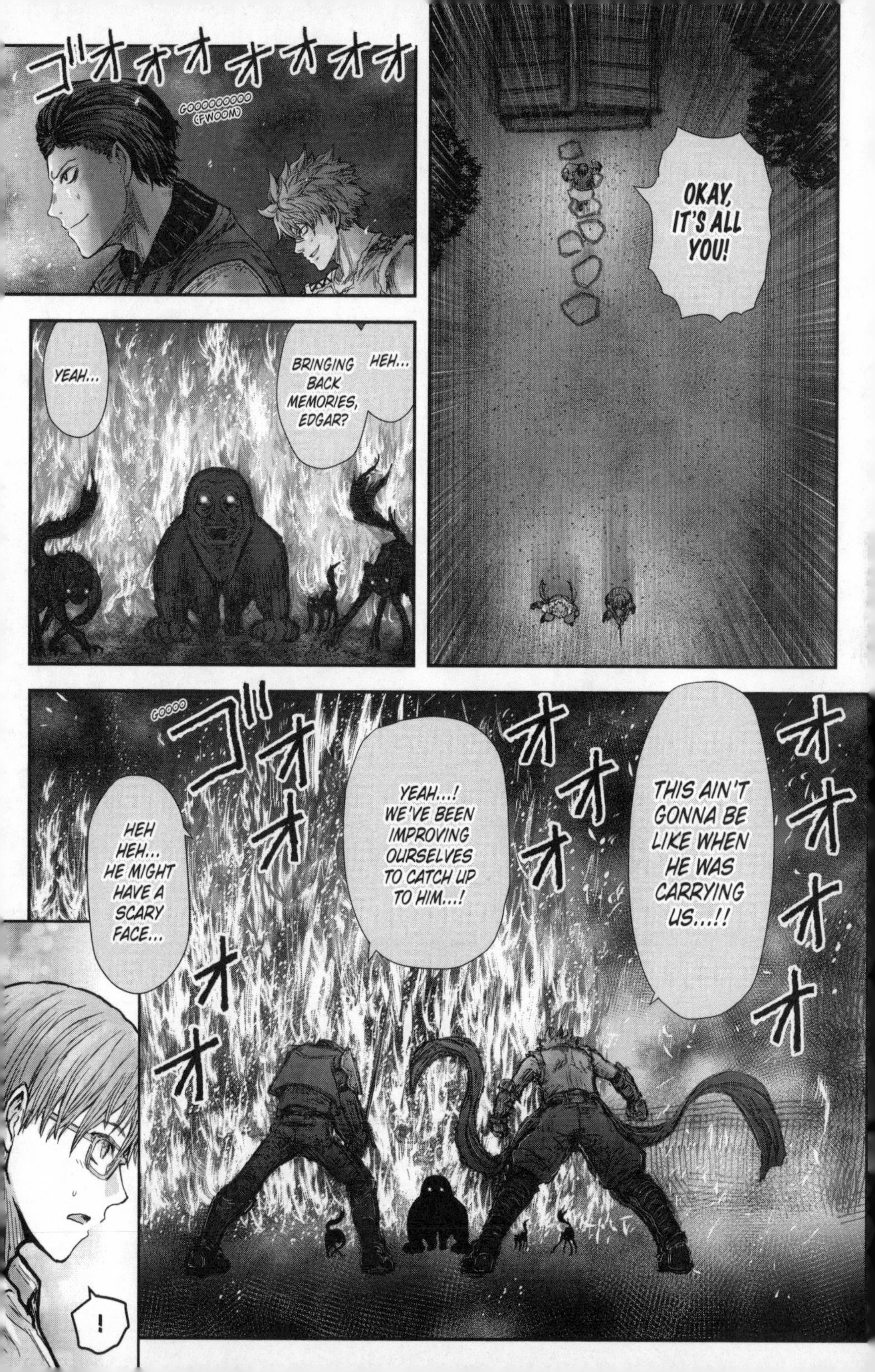
OKAY, IT'S ALL YOU!
GOOOOOOOOO (FWOOM)
HEH...
BRINGING BACK MEMORIES, EDGAR?
YEAH...
GOOOO
THIS AIN'T GONNA BE LIKE WHEN HE WAS CARRYING US...!!
YEAH...! WE'VE BEEN IMPROVING OURSELVES TO CATCH UP TO HIM...!
HEH HEH... HE MIGHT HAVE A SCARY FACE...
!

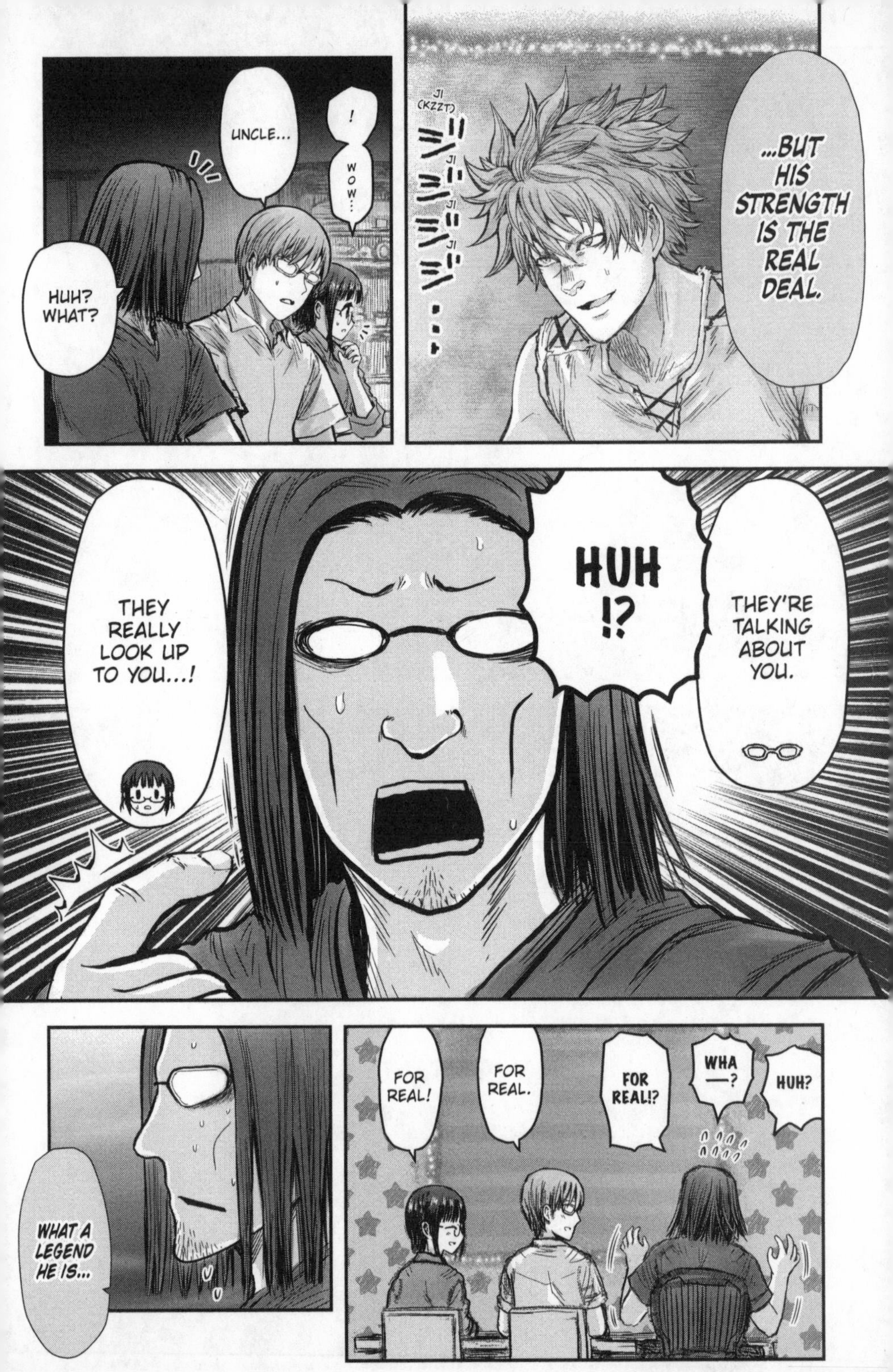
...BUT HIS STRENGTH IS THE REAL DEAL.
JI (KZZT)
!
WOW...
UNCLE...
HUH? WHAT?
THEY'RE TALKING ABOUT YOU.
HUH !?
THEY REALLY LOOK UP TO YOU...!
HUH?
WHA —?
FOR REAL!?
FOR REAL.
FOR REAL!
WHAT A LEGEND HE IS...

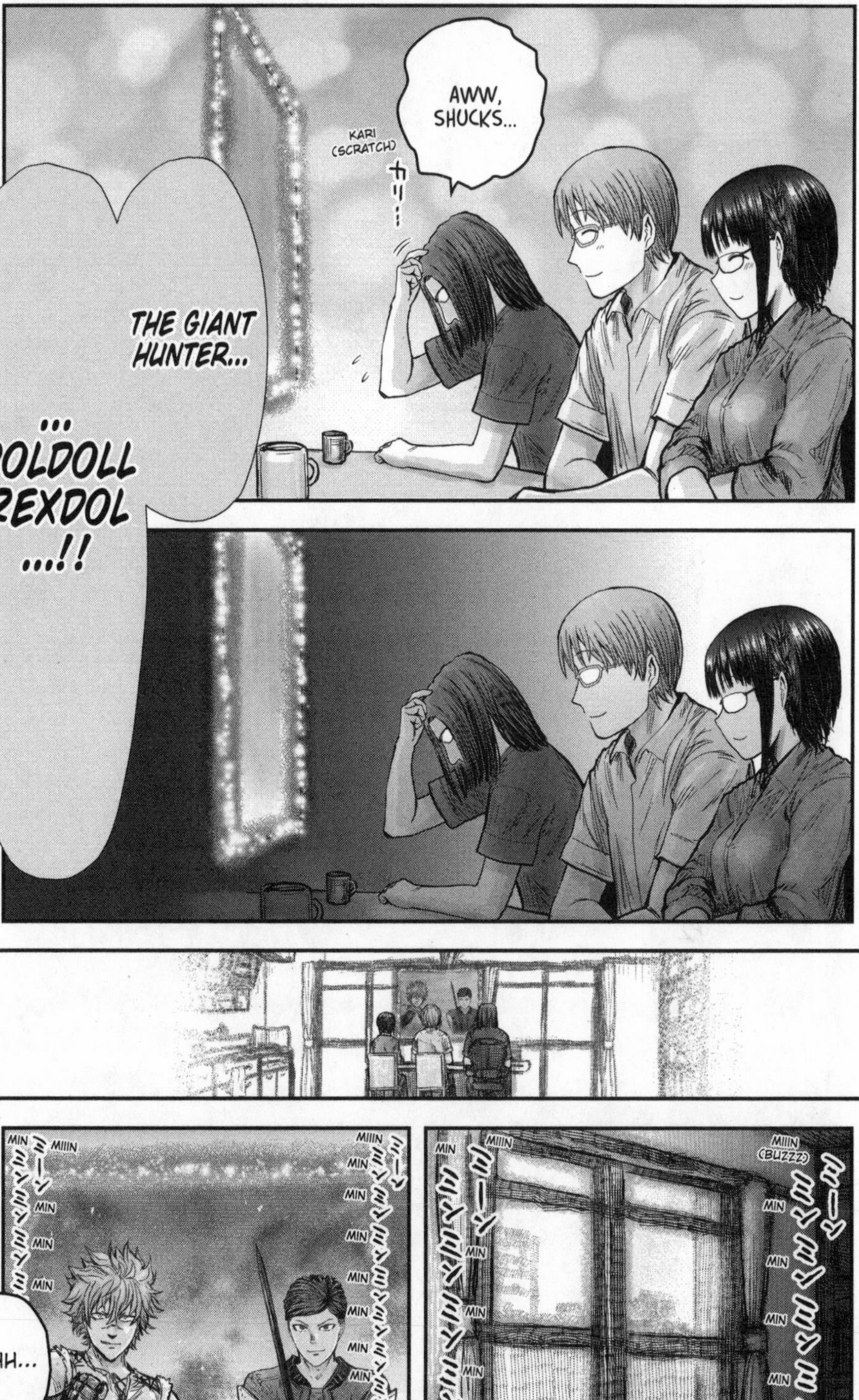
AWW, SHUCKS...
KARI (SCRATCH)
カリ…
THE GIANT HUNTER...
...DOLDOLL REXDOL ...!!
MIIIN (BUZZZ)
MIIIN
MIN MIN MIN MIN MIN MIN MIN
MIIIN
MIN MIN MIN MIN MIN MIN MIN
MIIIN
MIN MIN MIN MIN
UHH...

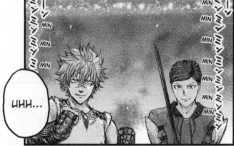

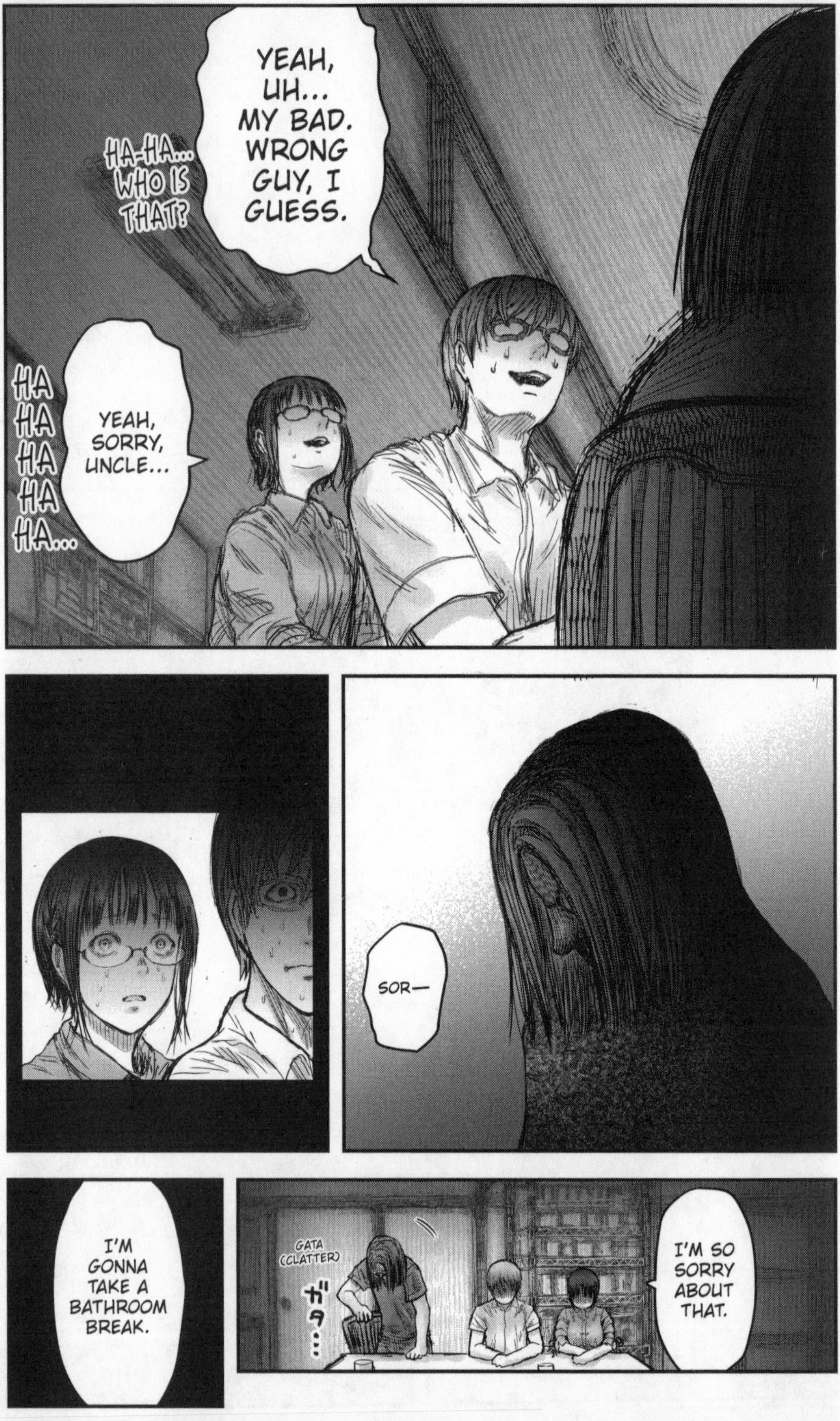
YEAH, UH... MY BAD. WRONG GUY, I GUESS.
HA-HA... WHO IS THAT?
YEAH, SORRY, UNCLE...
HA HA HA HA HA HA...
SOR—
I'M SO SORRY ABOUT THAT.
GATA (CLATTER)
ガタ...
I'M GONNA TAKE A BATHROOM BREAK.

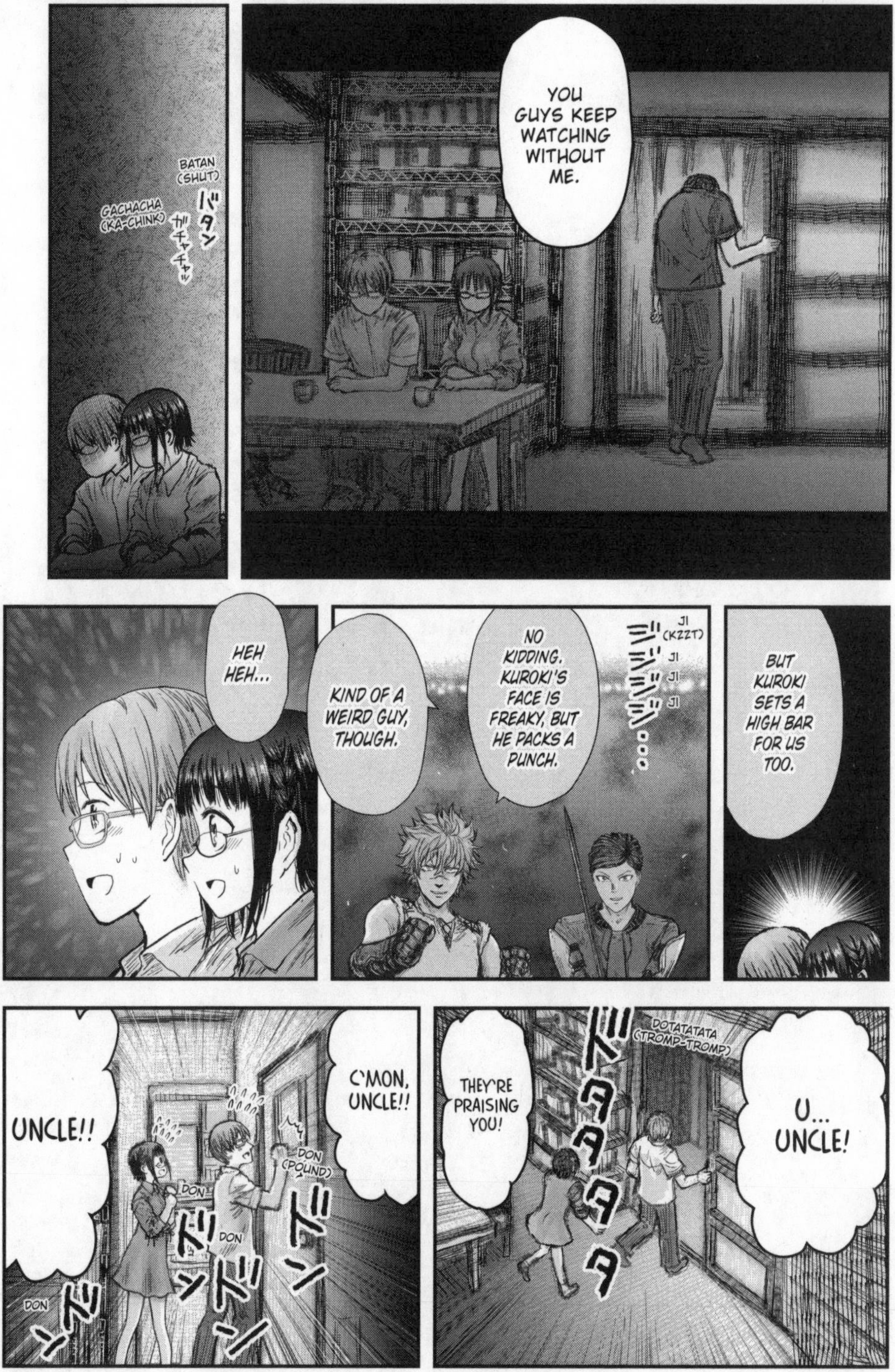
YOU GUYS KEEP WATCHING WITHOUT ME.
BATAN (SHUT)
バタン
GACHACHA (KA-CHINK)
ガチャチャッ
BUT KUROKI SETS A HIGH BAR FOR US TOO.
JI (KZZT) JI JI JI
ジジジジ…
NO KIDDING. KUROKI'S FACE IS FREAKY, BUT HE PACKS A PUNCH.
KIND OF A WEIRD GUY, THOUGH.
HEH HEH...
U... UNCLE!
DOTATATATA (TROMP-TROMP)
ドタタタタタ
THEY'RE PRAISING YOU!
C'MON, UNCLE!!
DON (POUND)
ドン
DON
DON
ドンドン
UNCLE!!
DON
ドン

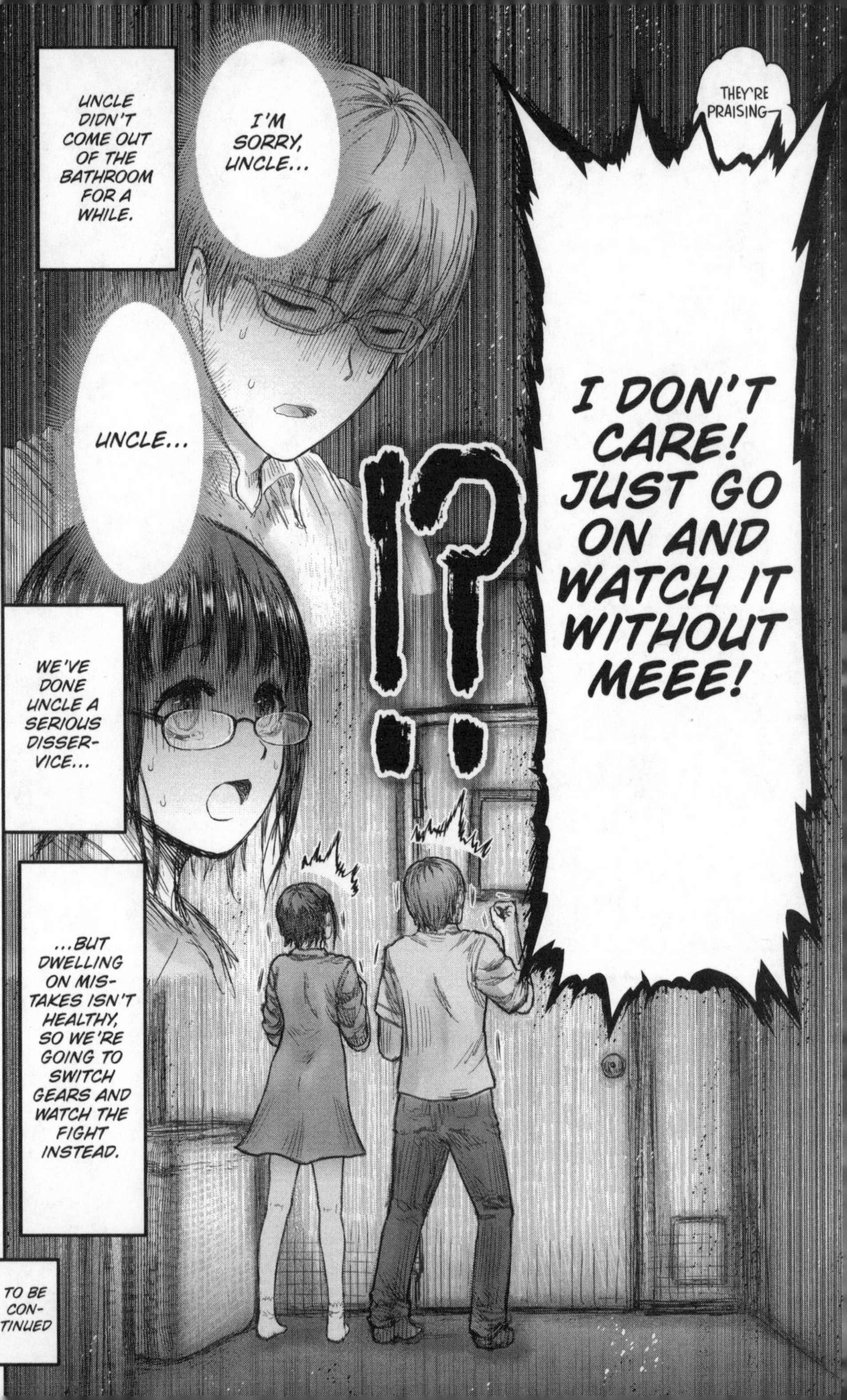
THEY'RE PRAISING—
I DON'T CARE! JUST GO ON AND WATCH IT WITHOUT MEEE!
!?
UNCLE DIDN'T COME OUT OF THE BATHROOM FOR A WHILE.
I'M SORRY, UNCLE...
UNCLE...
WE'VE DONE UNCLE A SERIOUS DISSER-VICE...
...BUT DWELLING ON MIS-TAKES ISN'T HEALTHY, SO WE'RE GOING TO SWITCH GEARS AND WATCH THE FIGHT INSTEAD.
TO BE CON-TINUED

Moves/Special Moves

Terms used to refer to fighting techniques in pro wrestling and fictional media such as video games and manga.
The Japanese term for these moves is *hissatsu waza*, which is written to mean "move that kills with certainty," but it rarely ever kills the target, much less with any sort of certainty.
There is also a variant called *chou hissatsu waza* ("super technique that kills with certainty,") but this also rarely ever kills with certainty.

TIPS

UNCLE from ANOTHER WORLD

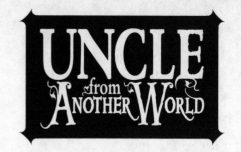

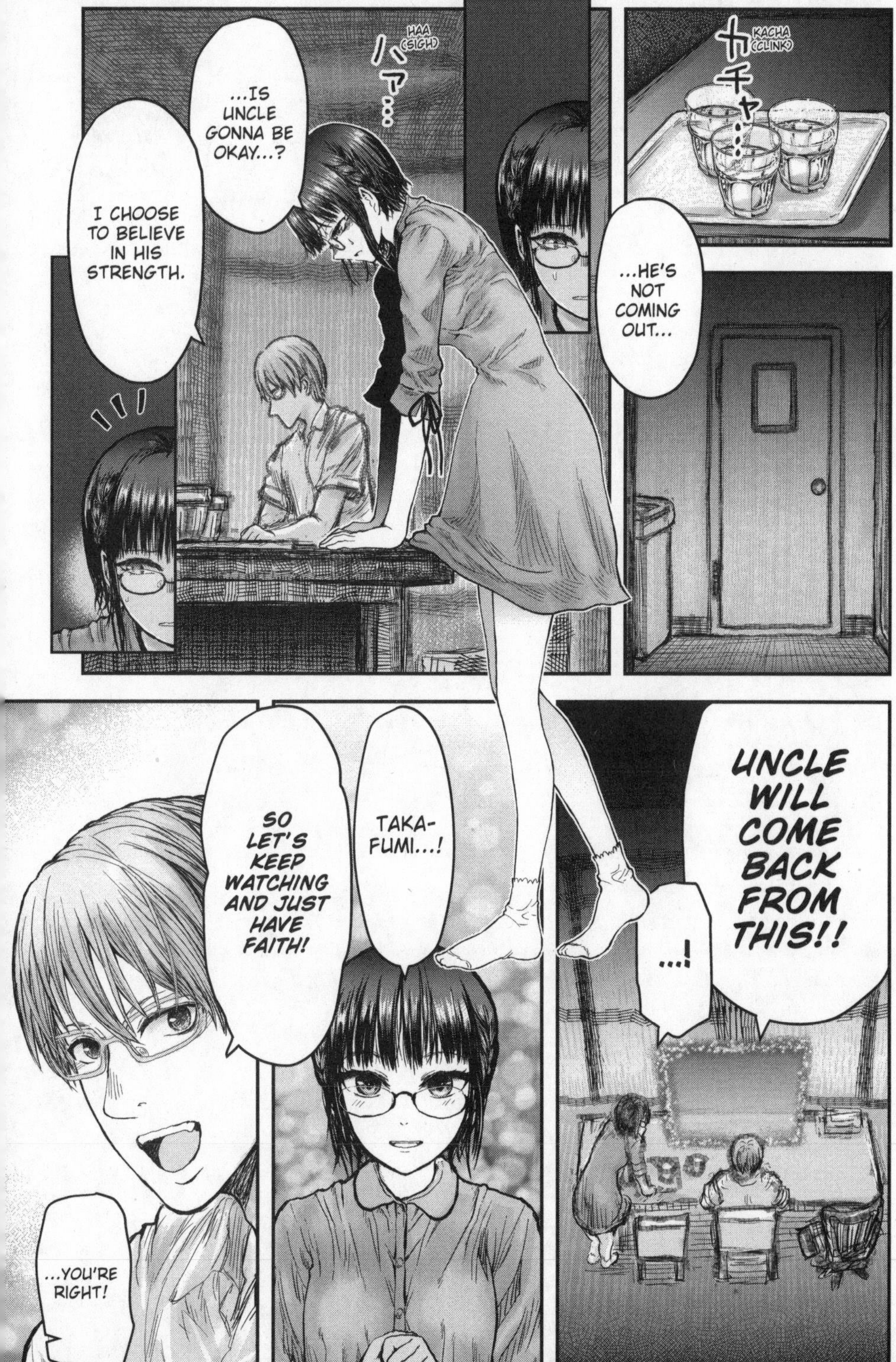
カチャ…
KACHA (CLINK)
...HE'S NOT COMING OUT...
ハア…
HAA (SIGH)
...IS UNCLE GONNA BE OKAY...?
I CHOOSE TO BELIEVE IN HIS STRENGTH.
UNCLE WILL COME BACK FROM THIS!!
...!
TAKA-FUMI...!
SO LET'S KEEP WATCHING AND JUST HAVE FAITH!
...YOU'RE RIGHT!

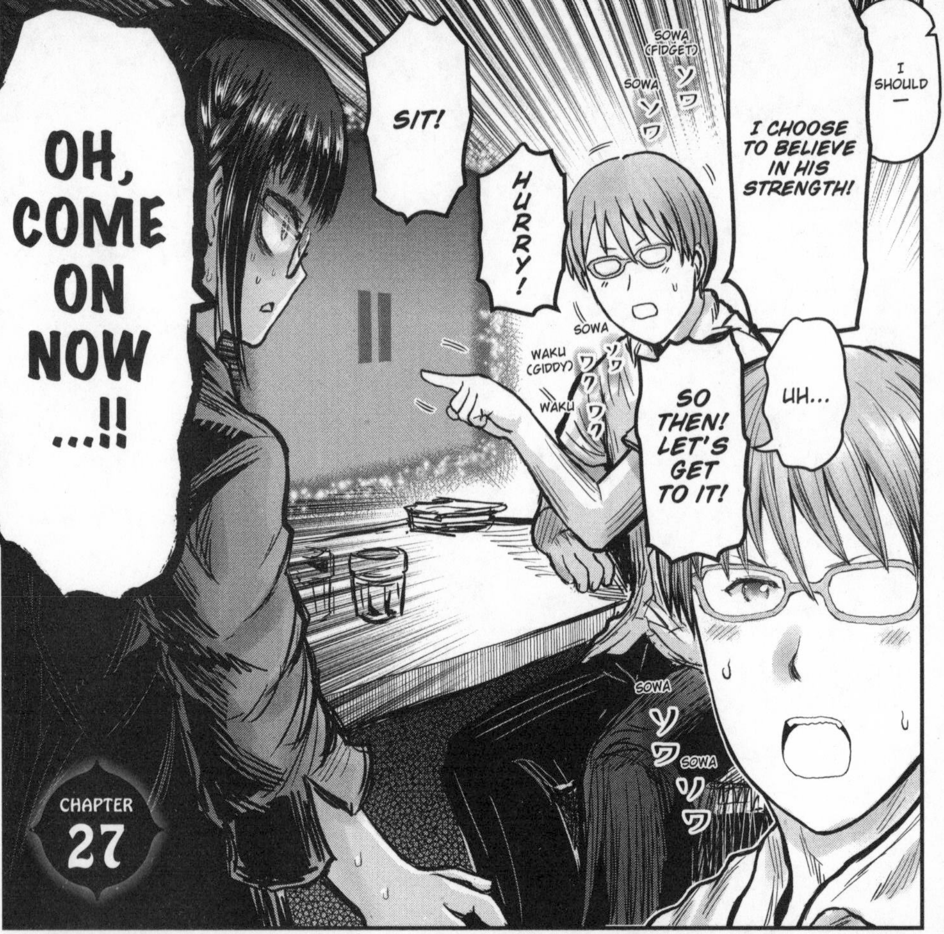
I SHOULD —
I CHOOSE TO BELIEVE IN HIS STRENGTH!
SOWA (FIDGET)
SOWA
UH...
SO THEN! LET'S GET TO IT!
SOWA
WAKU (GIDDY)
WAKU
HURRY!
SIT!
SOWA
SOWA
OH, COME ON NOW ...!!
CHAPTER 27

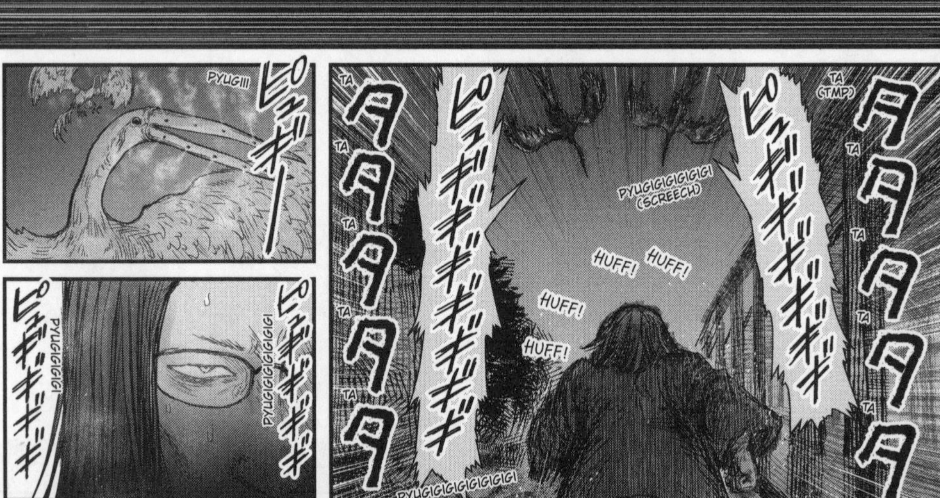
TA (TMP)
TA
TA
TA
TA
PYUGIGIGIGIGI (SCREECH)
HUFF!
HUFF!
HUFF!
HUFF!
TA
TA
TA
TA
TA
PYUGIGIGIGIGIGIGI
PYUGIII
PYUGIGIGIGI

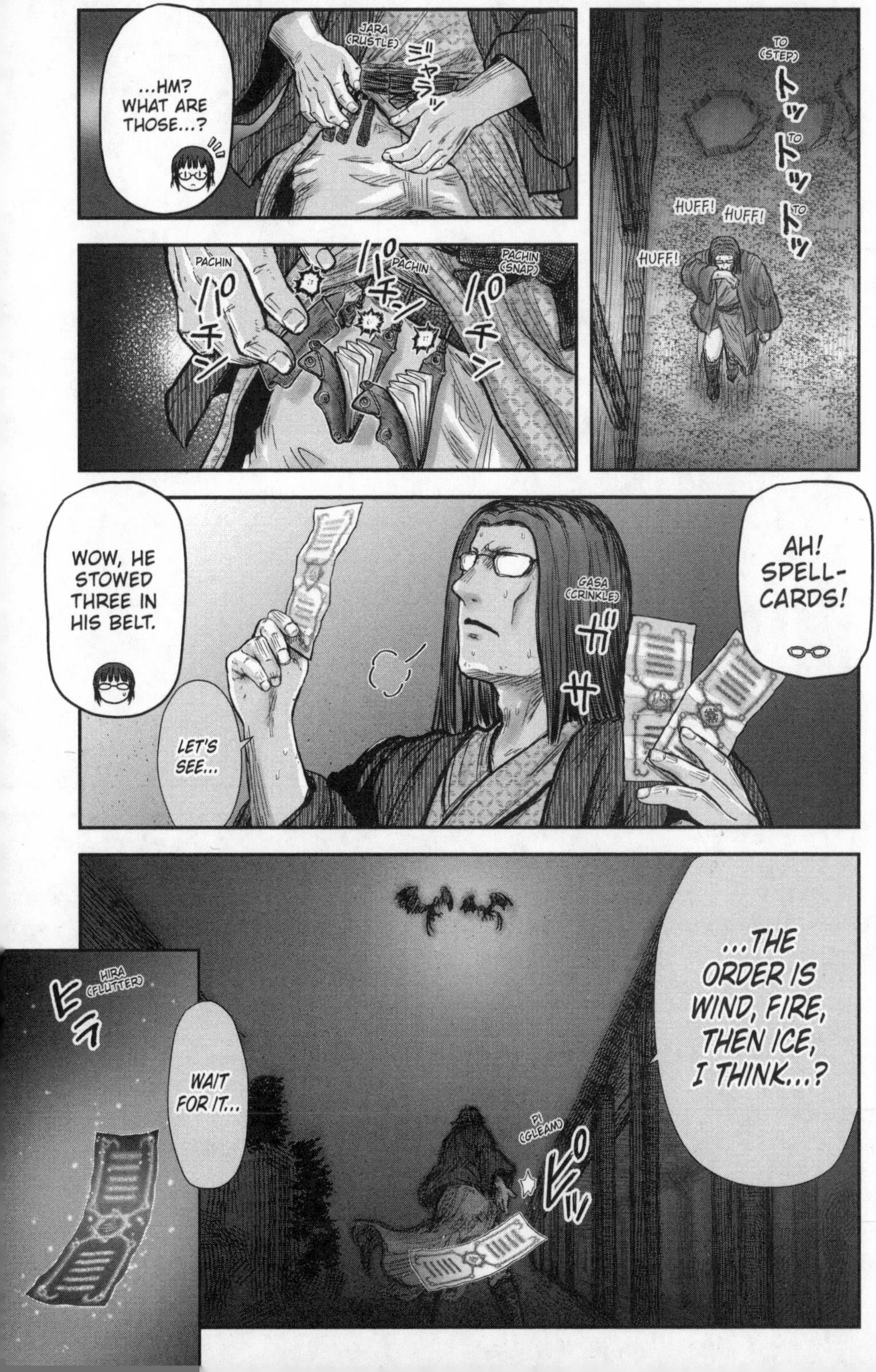
TO (STEP) トッ
TO トッ
TO トッ
HUFF! HUFF!
HUFF!
JARA (RUSTLE) ジャラッ
...HM? WHAT ARE THOSE...?
PACHIN (SNAP) パチン
PACHIN パチン
PACHIN パチン
AH! SPELL-CARDS!
GASA (CRINKLE) ガサ
WOW, HE STOWED THREE IN HIS BELT.
LET'S SEE...
...THE ORDER IS WIND, FIRE, THEN ICE, I THINK...?
PI (GLEAM) ピッ
WAIT FOR IT...
HIRA (FLUTTER) ヒラ

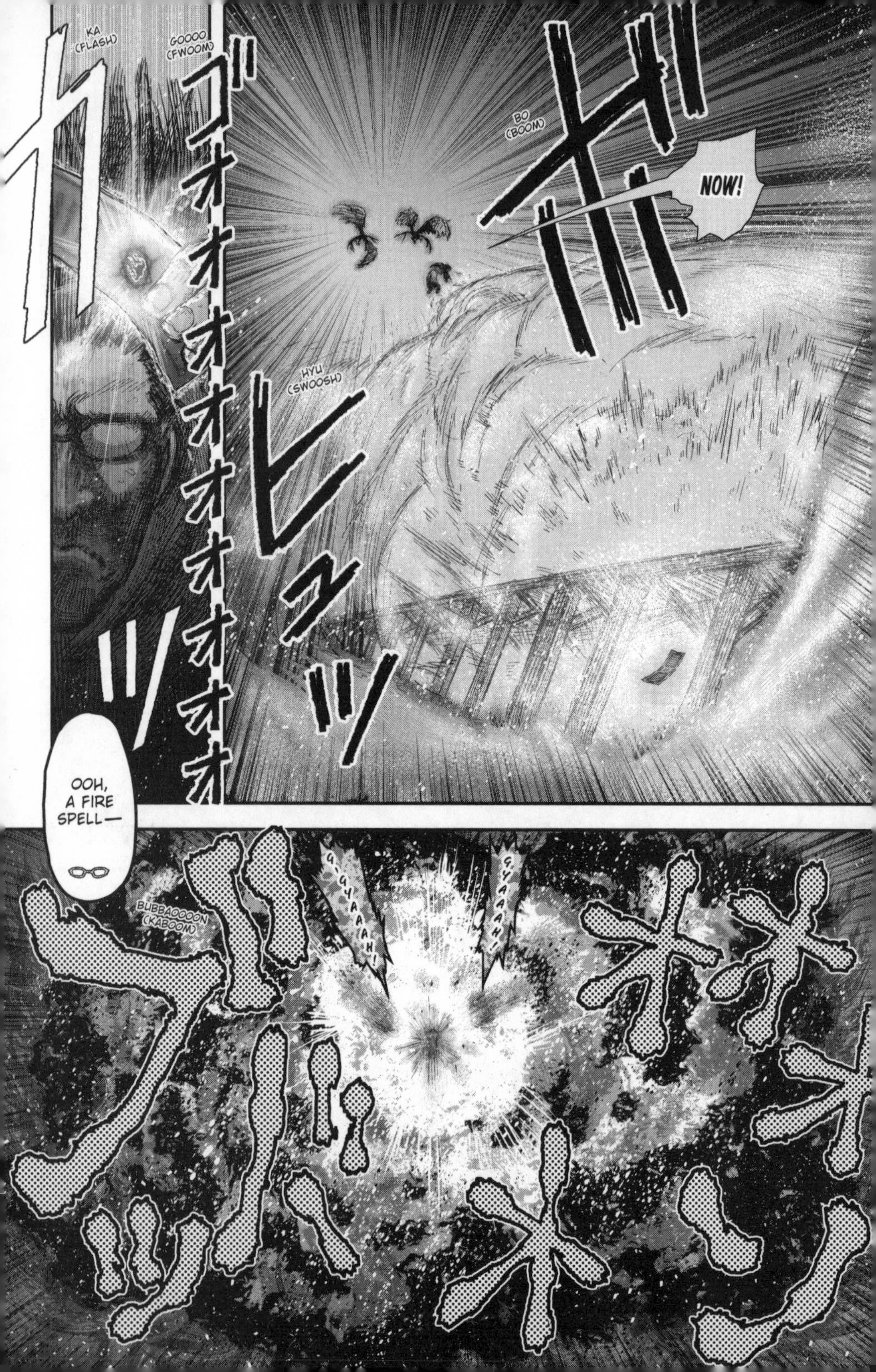
BO (BOOM)
NOW!
GOOOO (FWOOM)
KA (FLASH)
HYU (SWOOSH)
OOH, A FIRE SPELL—
GYAAAAH!
G-GYAAAAH!
BUBBAOOOON (KABOOM)

GOOOO
ゴォォォォ
オォ

BWHA!?

HUH!?

IS HE
DEAD
!?

HE'S
ALIVE!

GUN
(CLENCH)
グッ

FOO
(FWOOSH)
フォォォ
オ

WHOA,
SMOOTH!

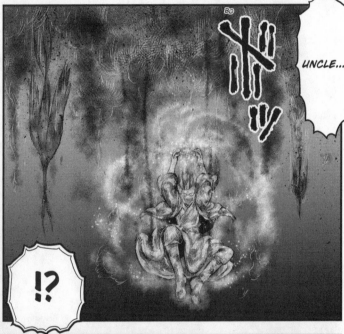

BO
メリッ

UNCLE...

!?

HE
BLOCKED
IT WITH
AN ICE
SPELL-
CARD!

ZUDAN
(WHAM)
ズダン

GISHISHISHI
(PSSHH)

DOCHA
(THUMP)
ドチャ

SHUUU
(FSSHH)
シュウウウウウ...

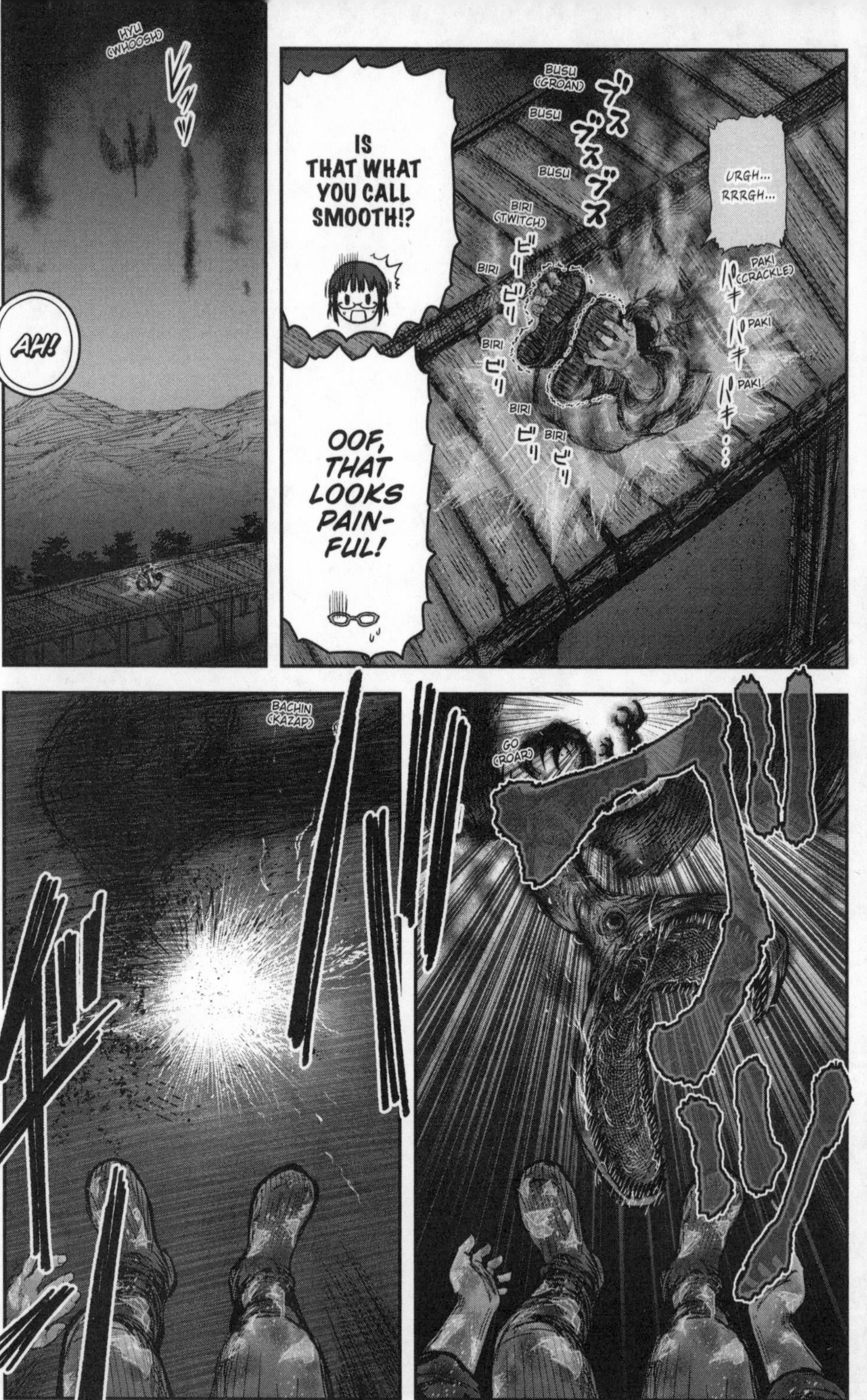
URGH... RRRGH...
BUSU (GROAN)
BUSU
BUSU
ブスブスブス
PAKI (CRACKLE)
PAKI
PAKI
パキパキパキ…
BIRI (TWITCH)
BIRI
BIRI
BIRI
BIRI
IS THAT WHAT YOU CALL SMOOTH!?
OOF, THAT LOOKS PAIN-FUL!
HYU (WHOOSH)
AH!
GO (ROAR)
BACHIN (KAZAP)

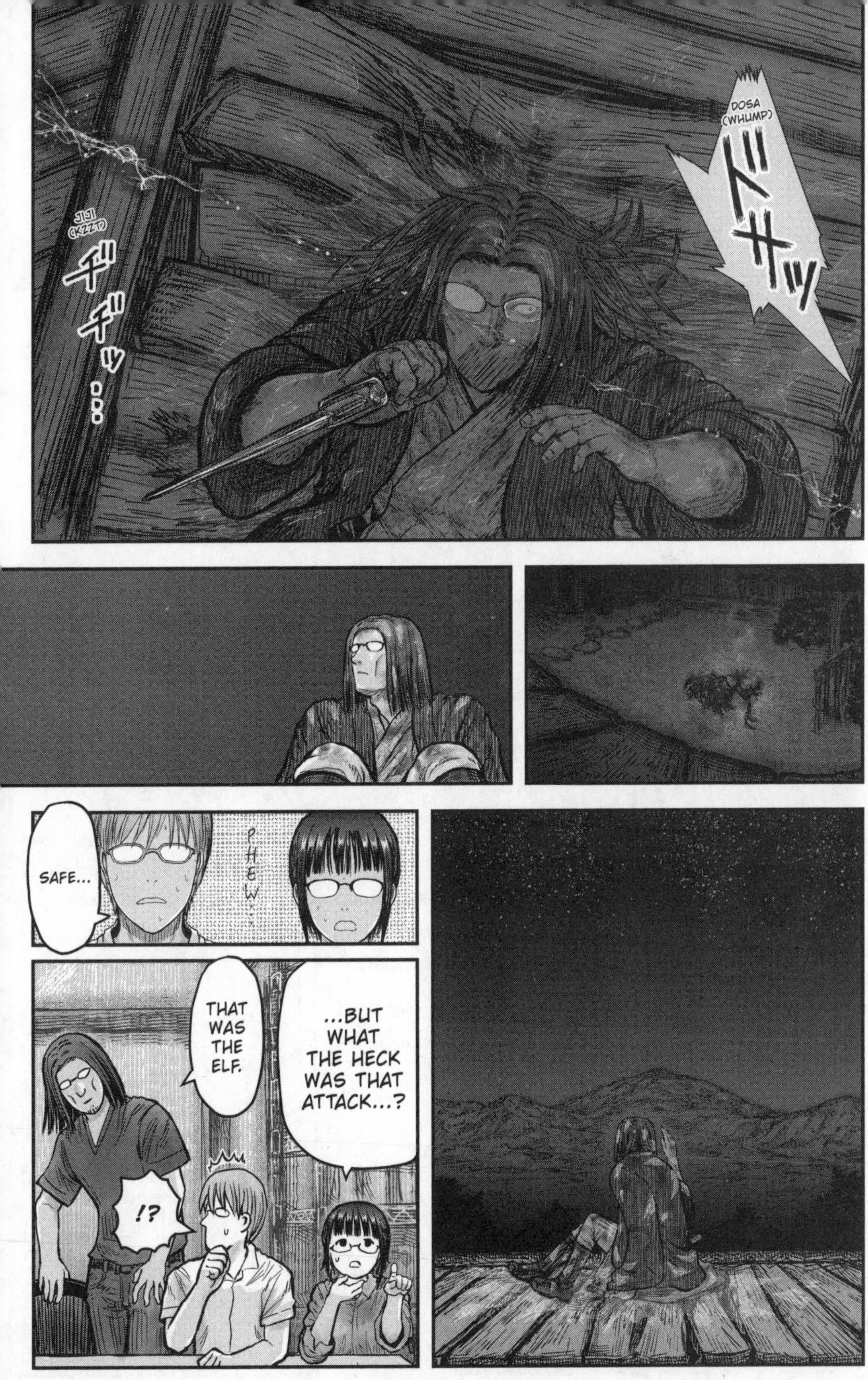
DOSA (WHUMP)
JIJI (KZZT)
PHEW...
SAFE...
...BUT WHAT THE HECK WAS THAT ATTACK...?
THAT WAS THE ELF.
!?

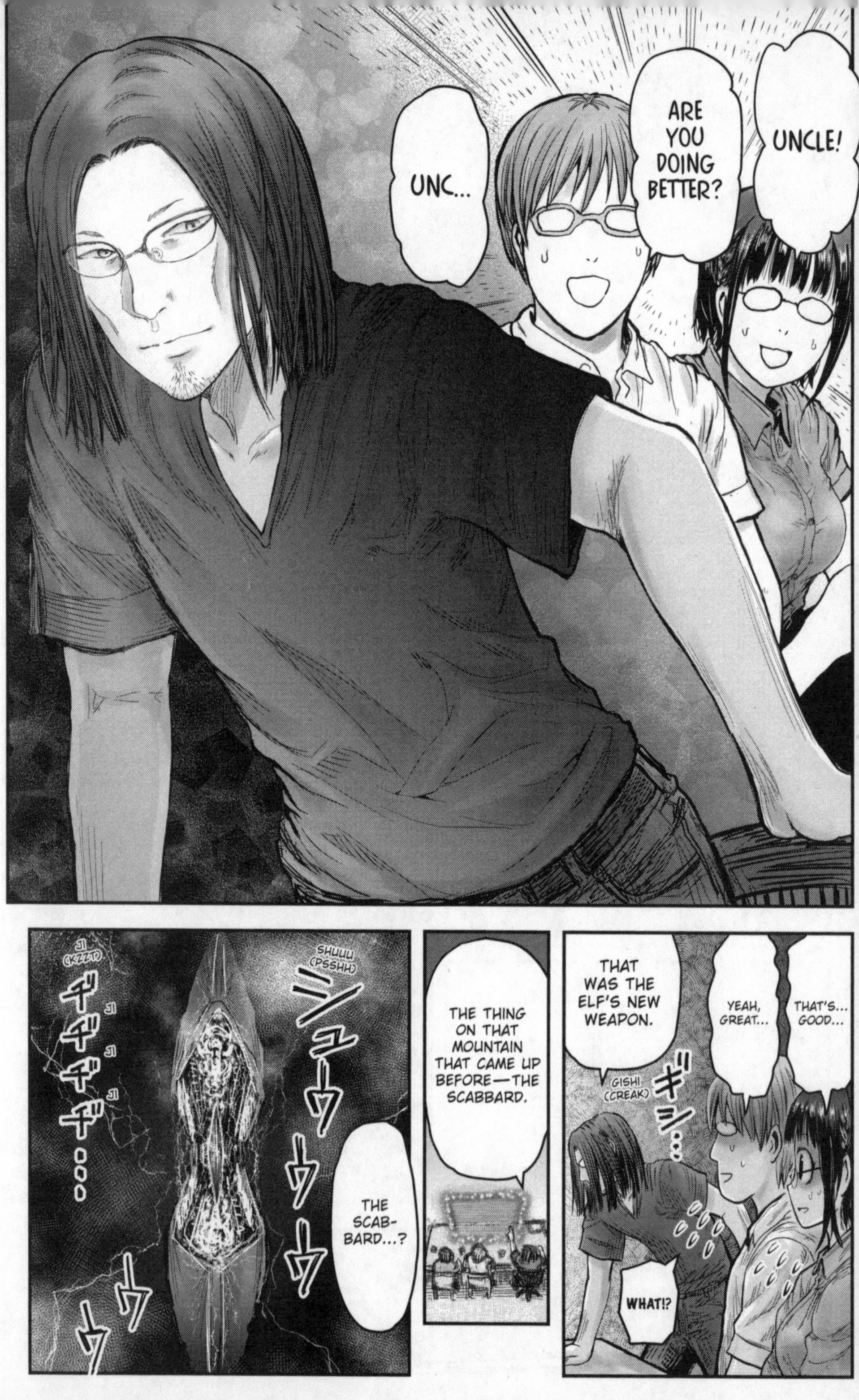
UNCLE!
ARE YOU DOING BETTER?
UNC...
THAT'S... GOOD...
YEAH, GREAT...
THAT WAS THE ELF'S NEW WEAPON.
GISHI (CREAK)
WHAT!?
THE THING ON THAT MOUNTAIN THAT CAME UP BEFORE—THE SCABBARD.
SHUUU (PSSHH)
JI (KZZT)
THE SCAB-BARD...?

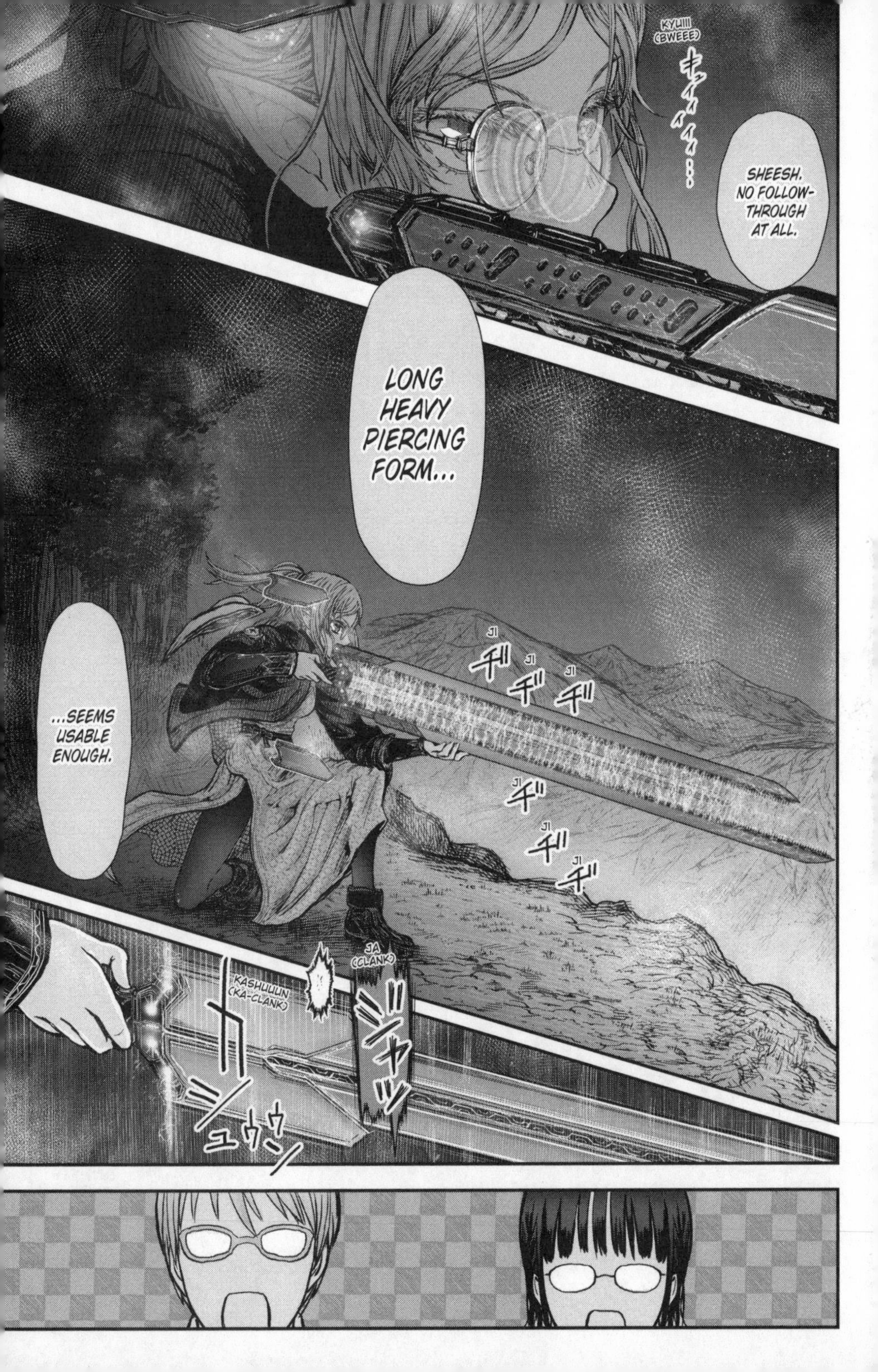
KYUIII (BWEEE)
SHEESH. NO FOLLOW-THROUGH AT ALL.
LONG HEAVY PIERCING FORM...
...SEEMS USABLE ENOUGH.
JI
JI
JI
JI
JI
JI
JA (CLANK)
KASHUUUN (KA-CLANK)

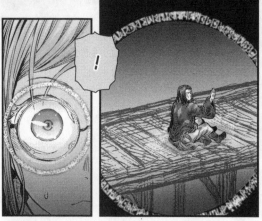

A MONOCLE!
AND PONY-TAIL!
THE SHEATH GUN'S PRETTY BADASS, BUT WHAT'S UP WITH THE MONOCLE?
PROBABLY ANOTHER ANCIENT ARTIFACT.
IS THAT WHAT YOU'RE FOCUSED ON HERE?
!
NO, ORC-FACE.
HEY!
HEEEEY!
FURI
FURI (WAVE)
FURI
OVER HERE, GEEZ!
SILLY BOY.
HERE!
JAKA (SPARK)
KYUUUN (BWEEE)
BASU (BZAM)
OVER HERE!
BASU
BASU
AH! HE RAN!
BASU
HEY, WHAT'S HIS PROB-LEM!?
BASU
AWW, NOW HE'S OUT OF SIGHT! SOME PEOPLE!
AS YOU CAN SEE, THE ELF HUNTS HUMANS FOR SPORT.
IS IT BECAUSE SHE'S ROYAL-TY...?
...THIS ONE'S ELF-SAN'S FAULT.
ELF-SAN'S GOT COM-MUNICATION ISSUES. SHE'S STILL CALLING HIM ORC, FOR ONE THING.
OH...
SAY, UNCLE.

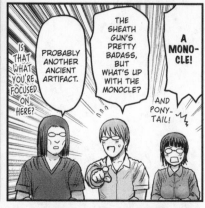

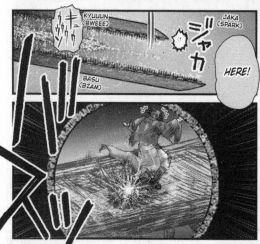

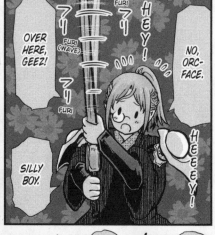

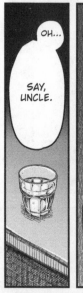

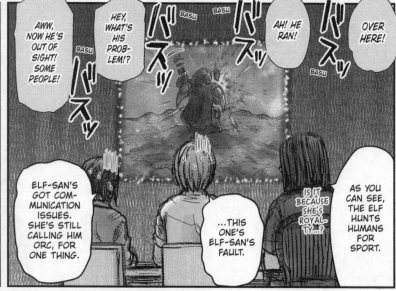

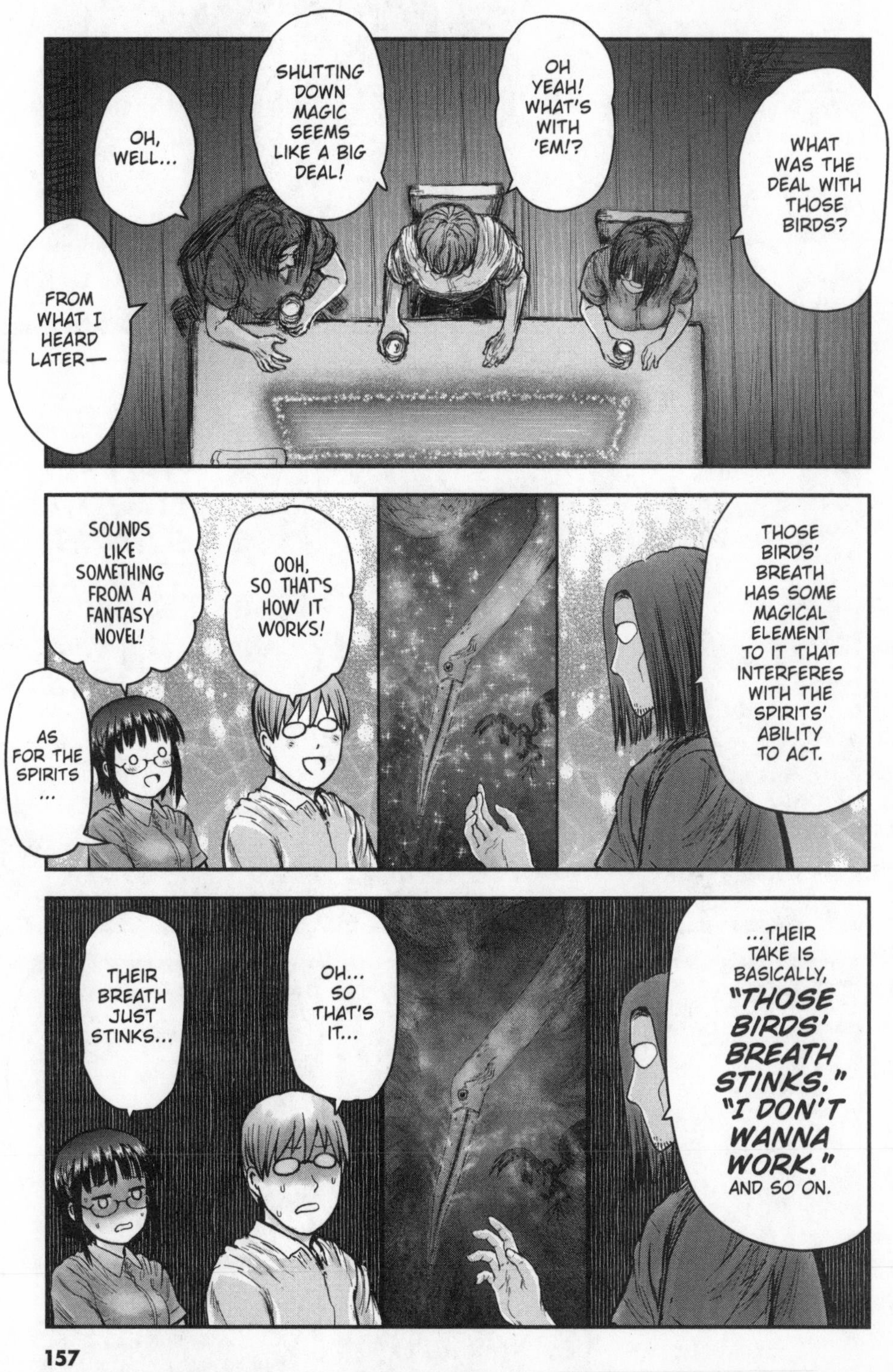
WHAT WAS THE DEAL WITH THOSE BIRDS?
OH YEAH! WHAT'S WITH 'EM!?
SHUTTING DOWN MAGIC SEEMS LIKE A BIG DEAL!
OH, WELL...
FROM WHAT I HEARD LATER—
THOSE BIRDS' BREATH HAS SOME MAGICAL ELEMENT TO IT THAT INTERFERES WITH THE SPIRITS' ABILITY TO ACT.
OOH, SO THAT'S HOW IT WORKS!
SOUNDS LIKE SOMETHING FROM A FANTASY NOVEL!
AS FOR THE SPIRITS...
...THEIR TAKE IS BASICALLY, "THOSE BIRDS' BREATH STINKS." "I DON'T WANNA WORK." AND SO ON.
OH... SO THAT'S IT...
THEIR BREATH JUST STINKS...

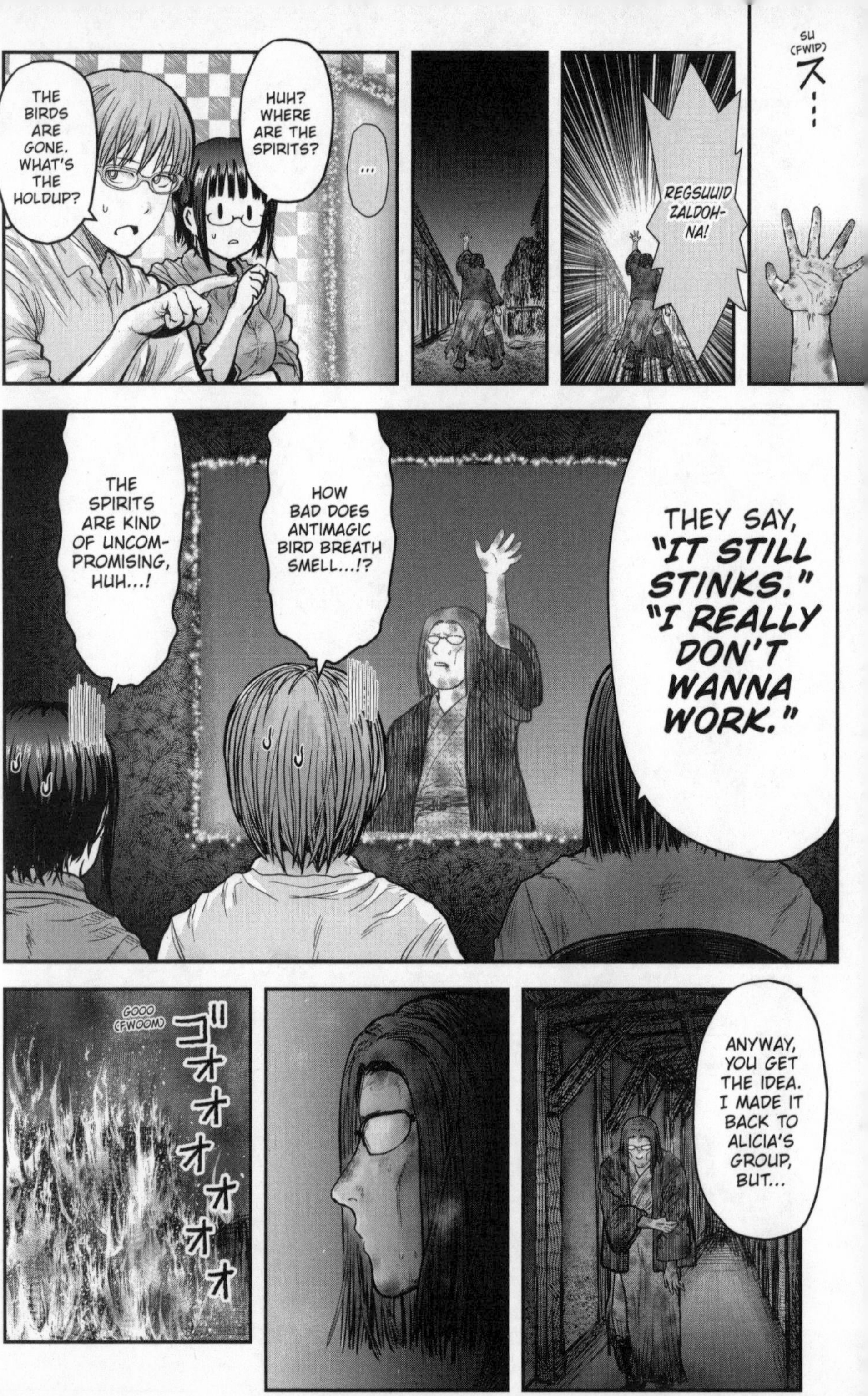
SU (FWIP)
ス…
REGSUUID ZALDOH-NA!
HUH? WHERE ARE THE SPIRITS?
…
THE BIRDS ARE GONE. WHAT'S THE HOLDUP?
THEY SAY, "IT STILL STINKS." "I REALLY DON'T WANNA WORK."
HOW BAD DOES ANTIMAGIC BIRD BREATH SMELL…!?
THE SPIRITS ARE KIND OF UNCOMPROMISING, HUH…!
ANYWAY, YOU GET THE IDEA. I MADE IT BACK TO ALICIA'S GROUP, BUT…
GOOO (FWOOM)
ゴオオオオオ

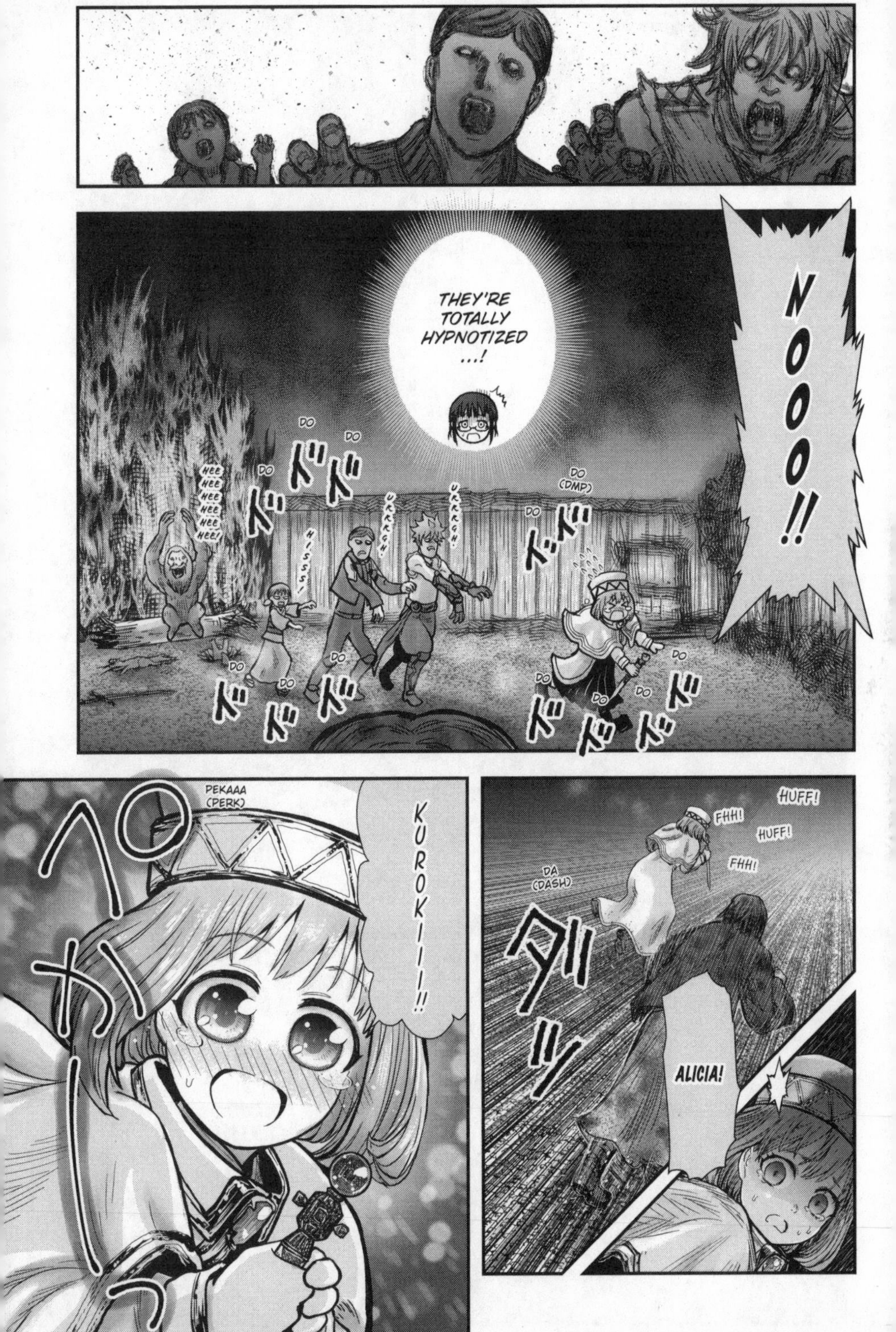
NOOOO!!
THEY'RE TOTALLY HYPNOTIZED...!
DO (DMP)
DO
URRRGH
URRRGH
HISSS!
DO
DO
DO
HEE HEE HEE HEE HEE HEE!
DO
DO
DO
DO
DO
DO
DO
HUFF!
FHH!
HUFF!
FHH!
DA (DASH)
ALICIA!
KUROKIIII!!
PEKAAA (PERK)

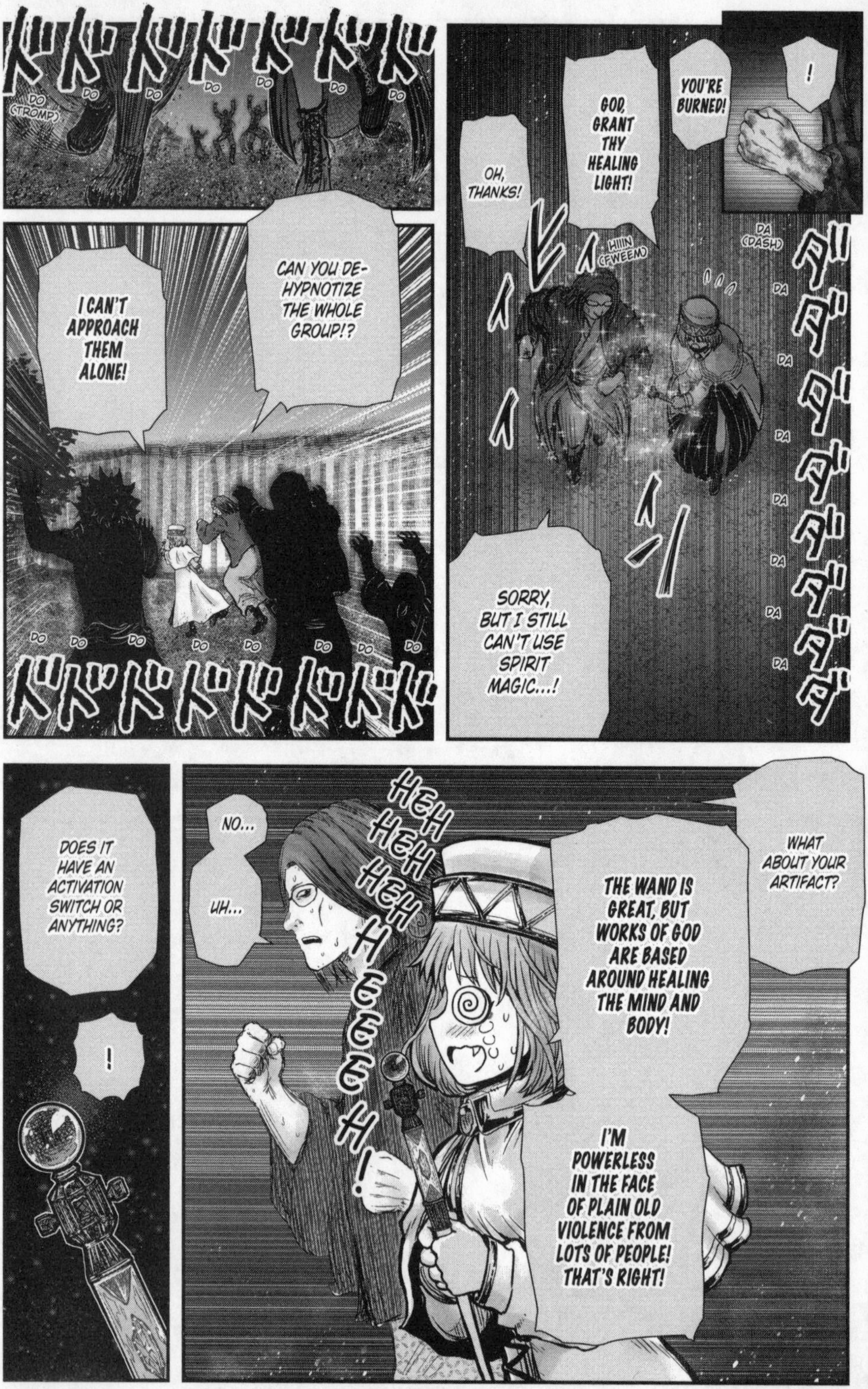
!
YOU'RE BURNED!
GOD, GRANT THY HEALING LIGHT!
OH, THANKS!
HIIIN (FWEEM)
DA (DASH) DA DA DA DA DA DA
SORRY, BUT I STILL CAN'T USE SPIRIT MAGIC...!
DO (TROMP) DO DO DO DO
CAN YOU DE-HYPNOTIZE THE WHOLE GROUP!?
I CAN'T APPROACH THEM ALONE!
DO DO DO DO DO DO
WHAT ABOUT YOUR ARTIFACT?
THE WAND IS GREAT, BUT WORKS OF GOD ARE BASED AROUND HEALING THE MIND AND BODY!
I'M POWERLESS IN THE FACE OF PLAIN OLD VIOLENCE FROM LOTS OF PEOPLE! THAT'S RIGHT!
HEH HEH HEH HEEEEH!
NO...
UH...
DOES IT HAVE AN ACTIVATION SWITCH OR ANYTHING?
!

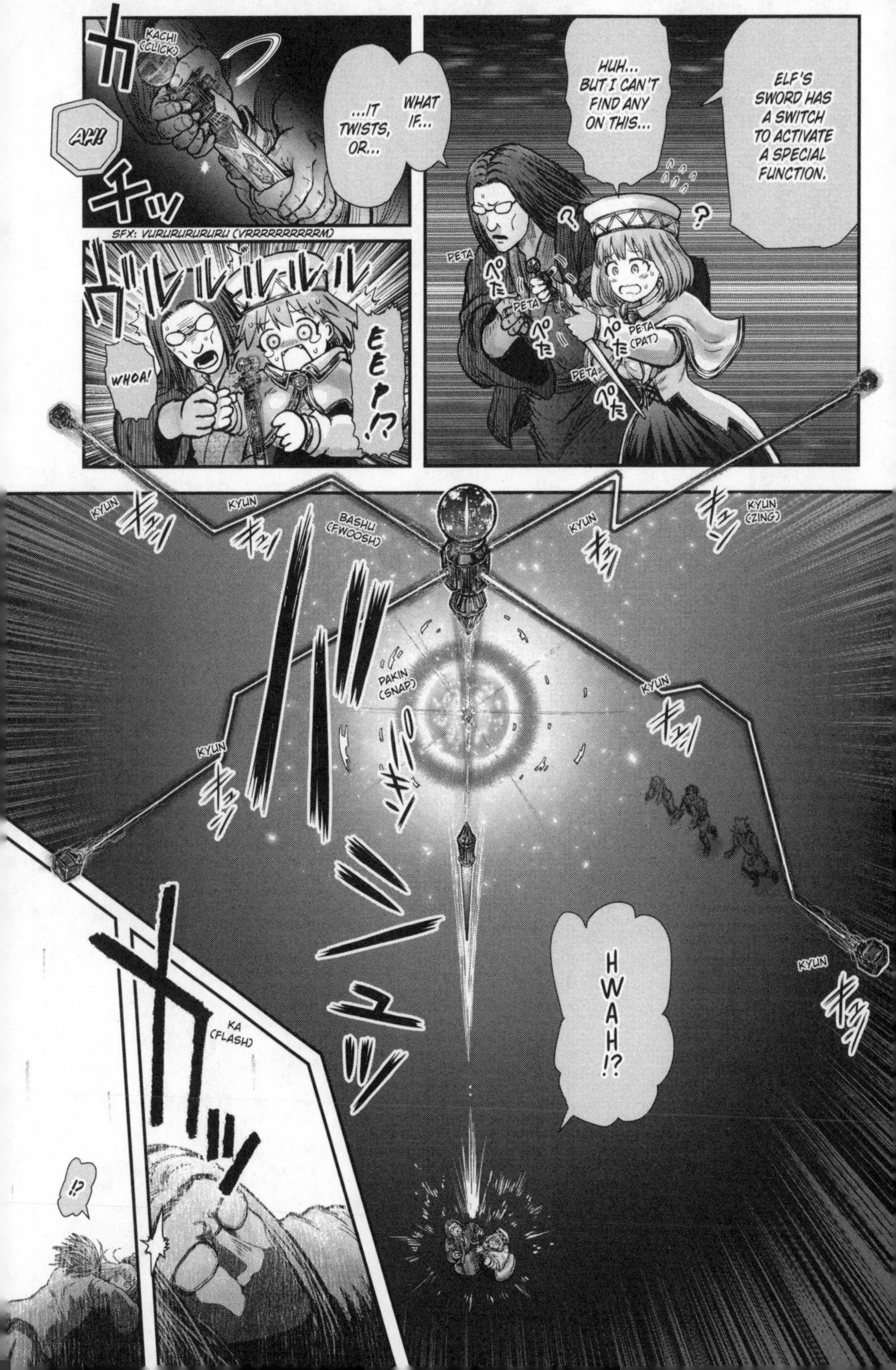
ELF'S SWORD HAS A SWITCH TO ACTIVATE A SPECIAL FUNCTION.
HUH... BUT I CAN'T FIND ANY ON THIS...
?
?
PETA
PETA
PETA (PAT)
PETA
WHAT IF...
...IT TWISTS, OR...
KACHI (CLICK)
AH!
SFX: VURURURURURU (VRRRRRRRRRRM)
WHOA!
EEP!?
KYUN (ZING)
KYUN
BASHU (FWOOSH)
KYUN
KYUN
PAKIN (SNAP)
KYUN
KYUN
HWAH!?
KA (FLASH)
!?

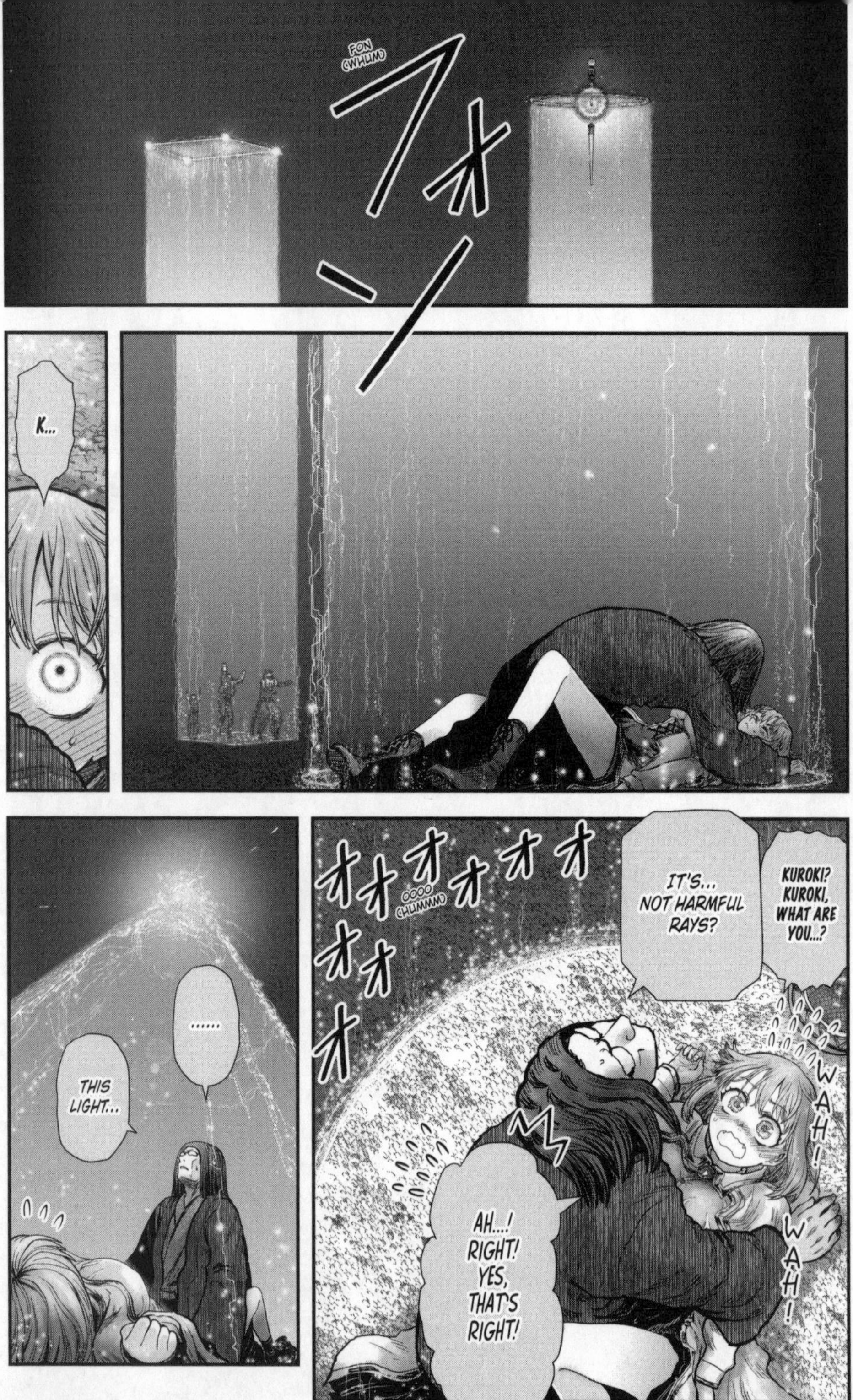
FON (WHUM)
K...
KUROKI? KUROKI, WHAT ARE YOU...?
IT'S... NOT HARMFUL RAYS?
OOOO (HUMMM)
WAH! WAH!
AH...! RIGHT! YES, THAT'S RIGHT!
......
THIS LIGHT...

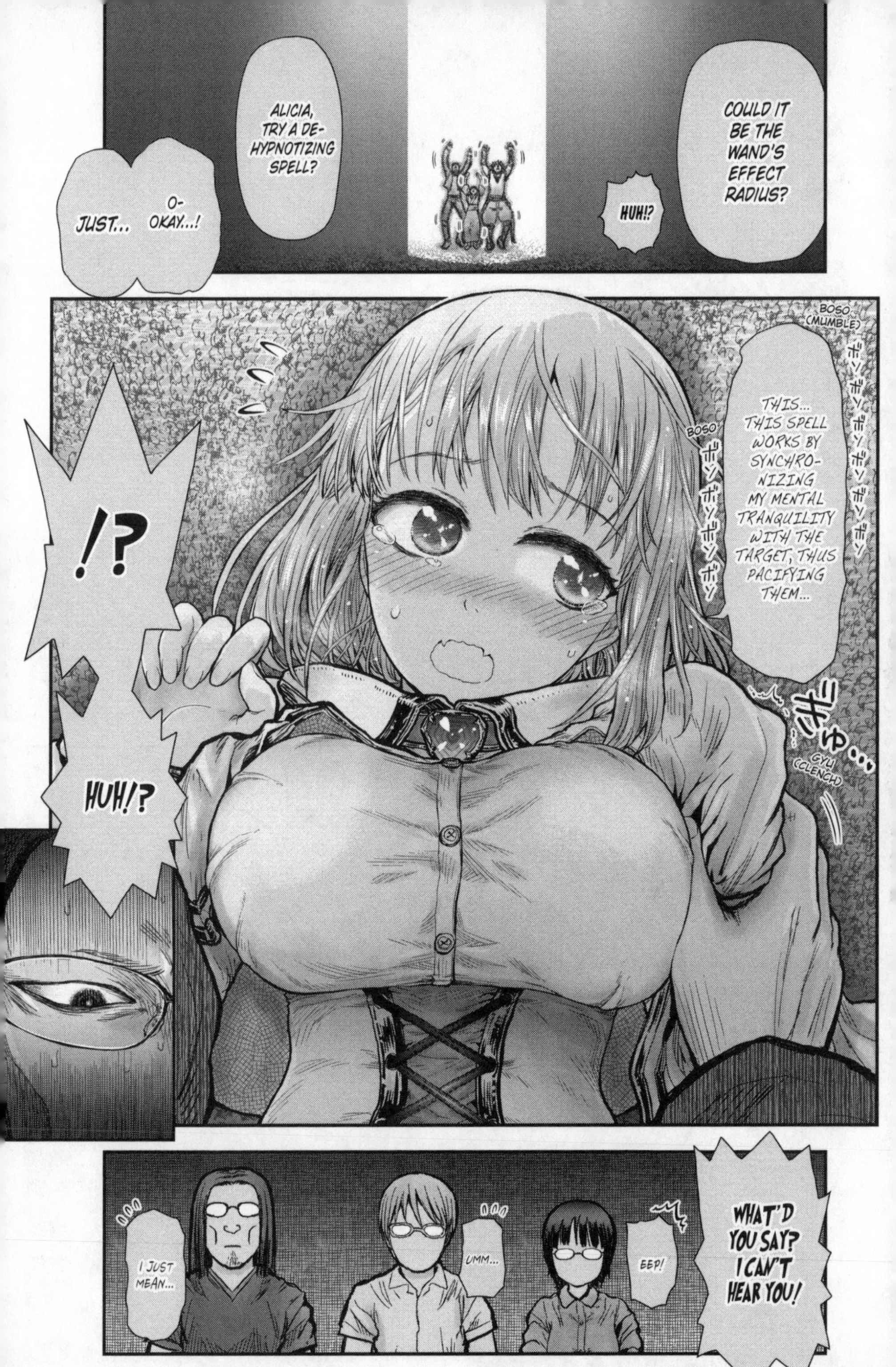
COULD IT BE THE WAND'S EFFECT RADIUS?
HUH!?
ALICIA, TRY A DE-HYPNOTIZING SPELL?
O-OKAY...!
JUST...
BOSO (MUMBLE)
THIS... THIS SPELL WORKS BY SYNCHRO-NIZING MY MENTAL TRANQUILITY WITH THE TARGET, THUS PACIFYING THEM...
BOSO
GYU (CLENCH)
!?
HUH!?
WHAT'D YOU SAY? I CAN'T HEAR YOU!
EEP!
UMM...
I JUST MEAN...

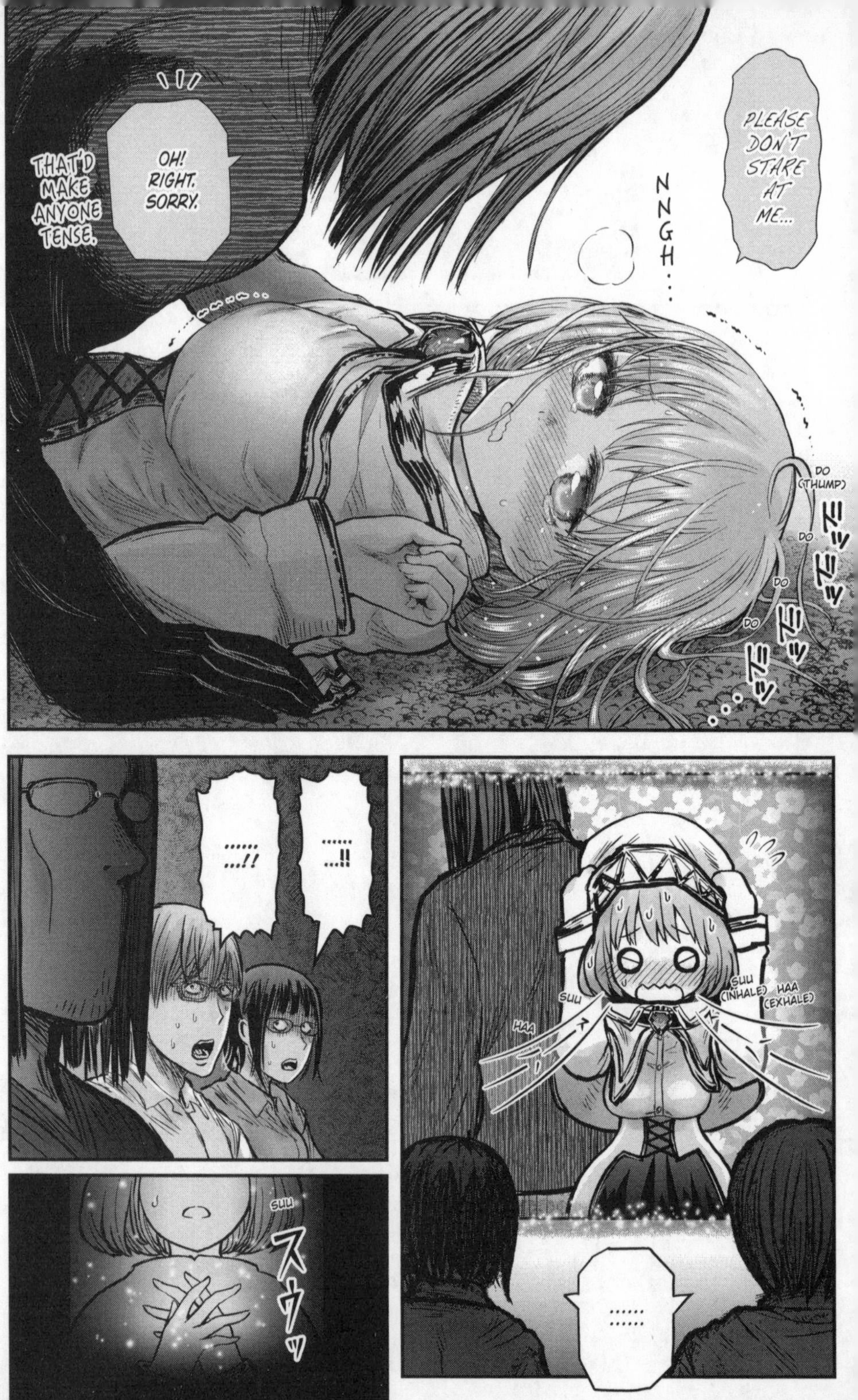
PLEASE DON'T STARE AT ME...
NNGH...
OH! RIGHT. SORRY.
THAT'D MAKE ANYONE TENSE.
DO (THUMP) DO DO DO
SUU (INHALE) HAA (EXHALE)
SUU
HAA
......
......
......!!
......!!
SUU

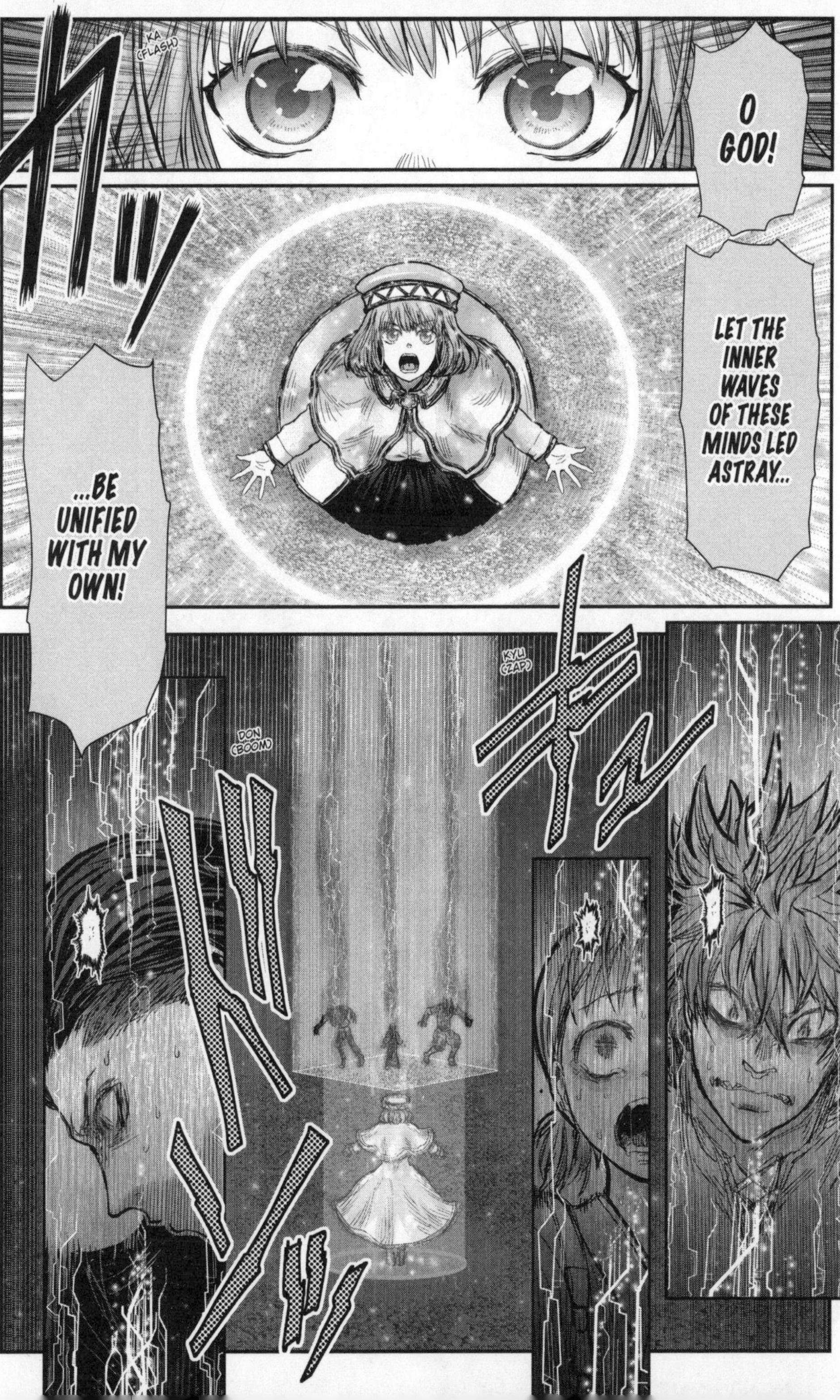
O GOD!
KA (FLASH)
LET THE INNER WAVES OF THESE MINDS LED ASTRAY...
...BE UNIFIED WITH MY OWN!
KYU (ZAP)
DON (BOOM)

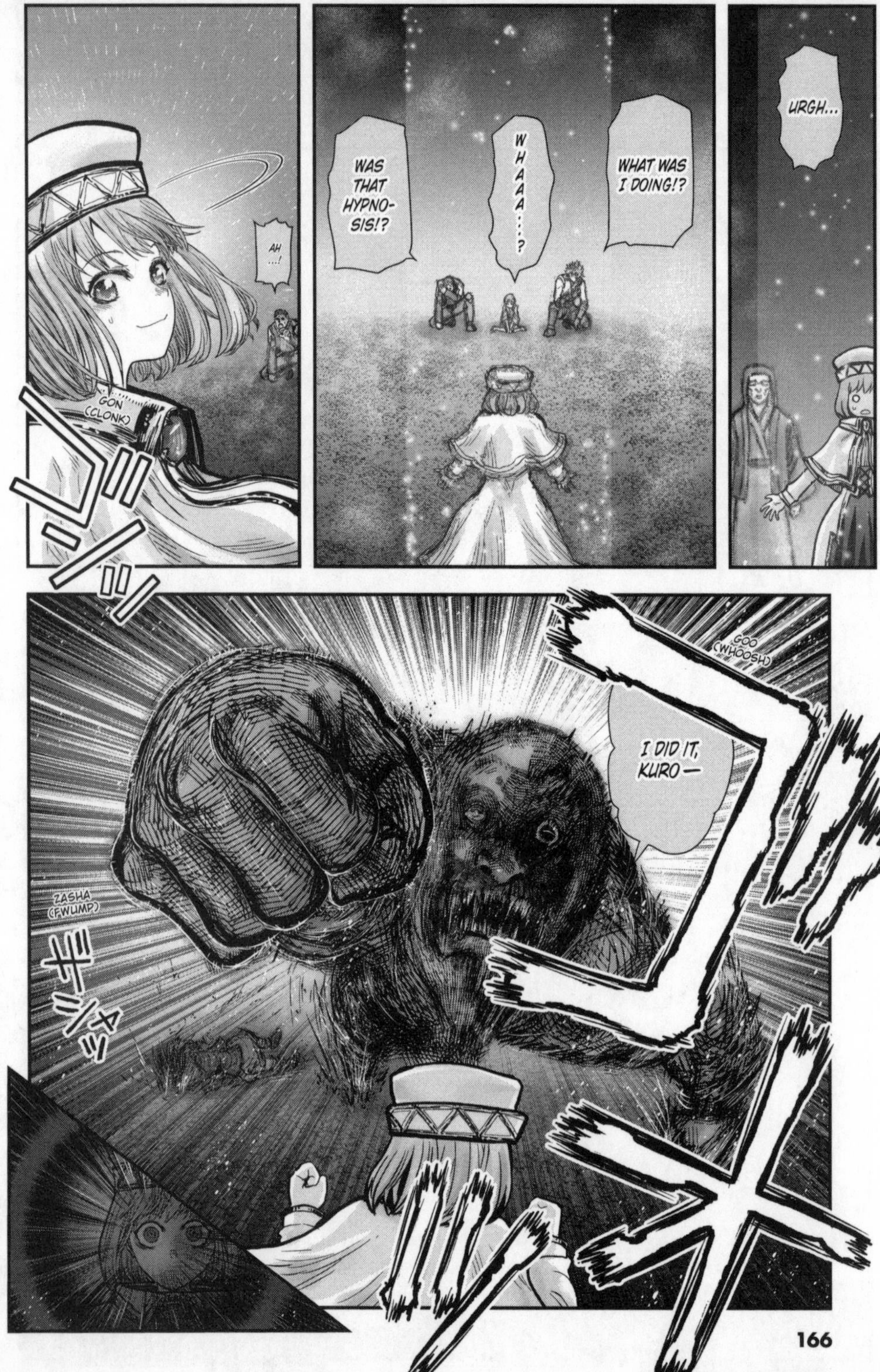
URGH...
WHAT WAS I DOING!?
WHAAAA...?
WAS THAT HYPNO-SIS!?
AH ...!
GON (CLONK)
GOO (WHOOSH)
I DID IT, KURO—
ZASHA (FWUMP)

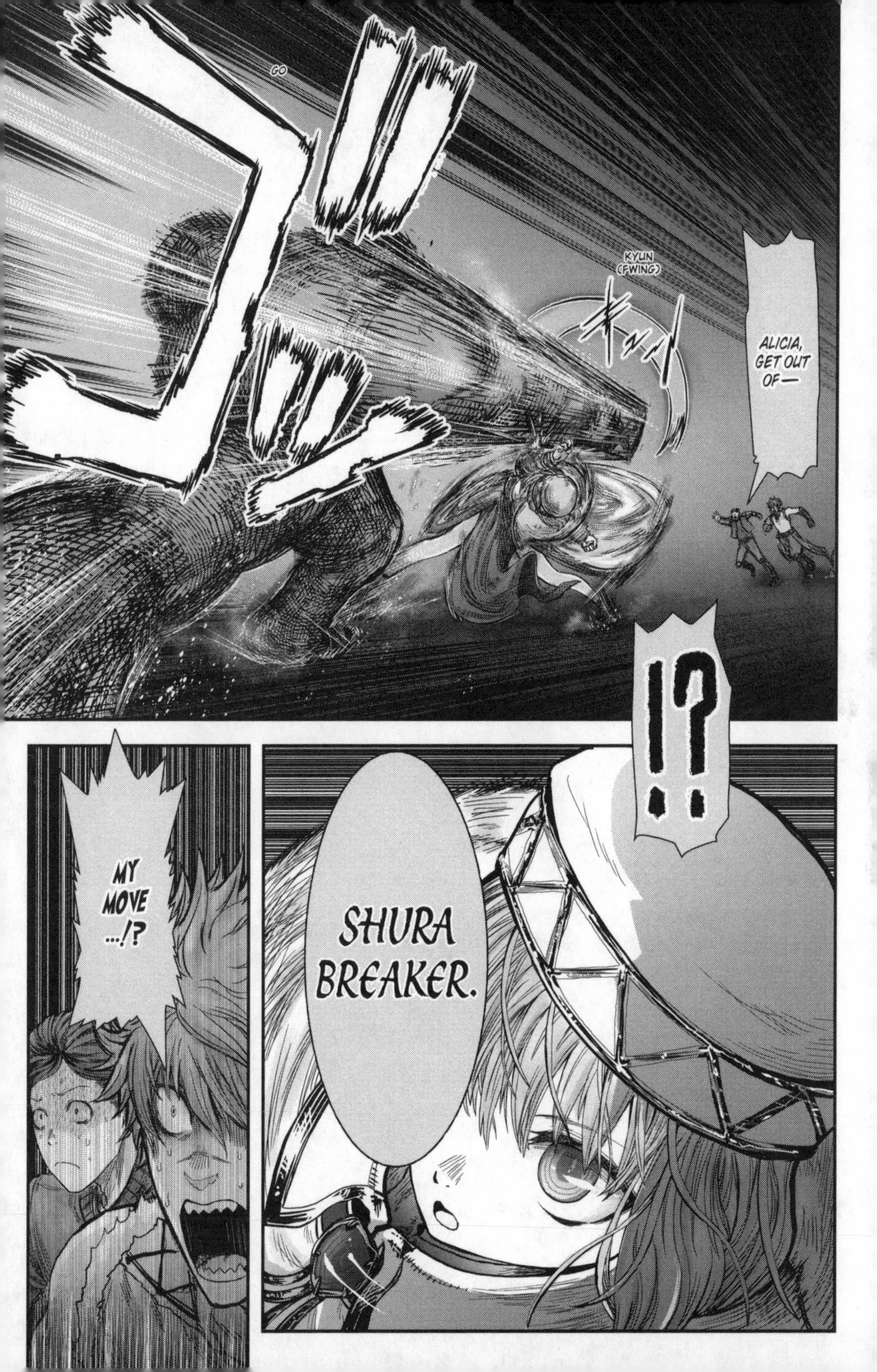
ALICIA, GET OUT OF—
KYUN (FWING)
GO
!?
SHURA BREAKER.
MY MOVE ...!?

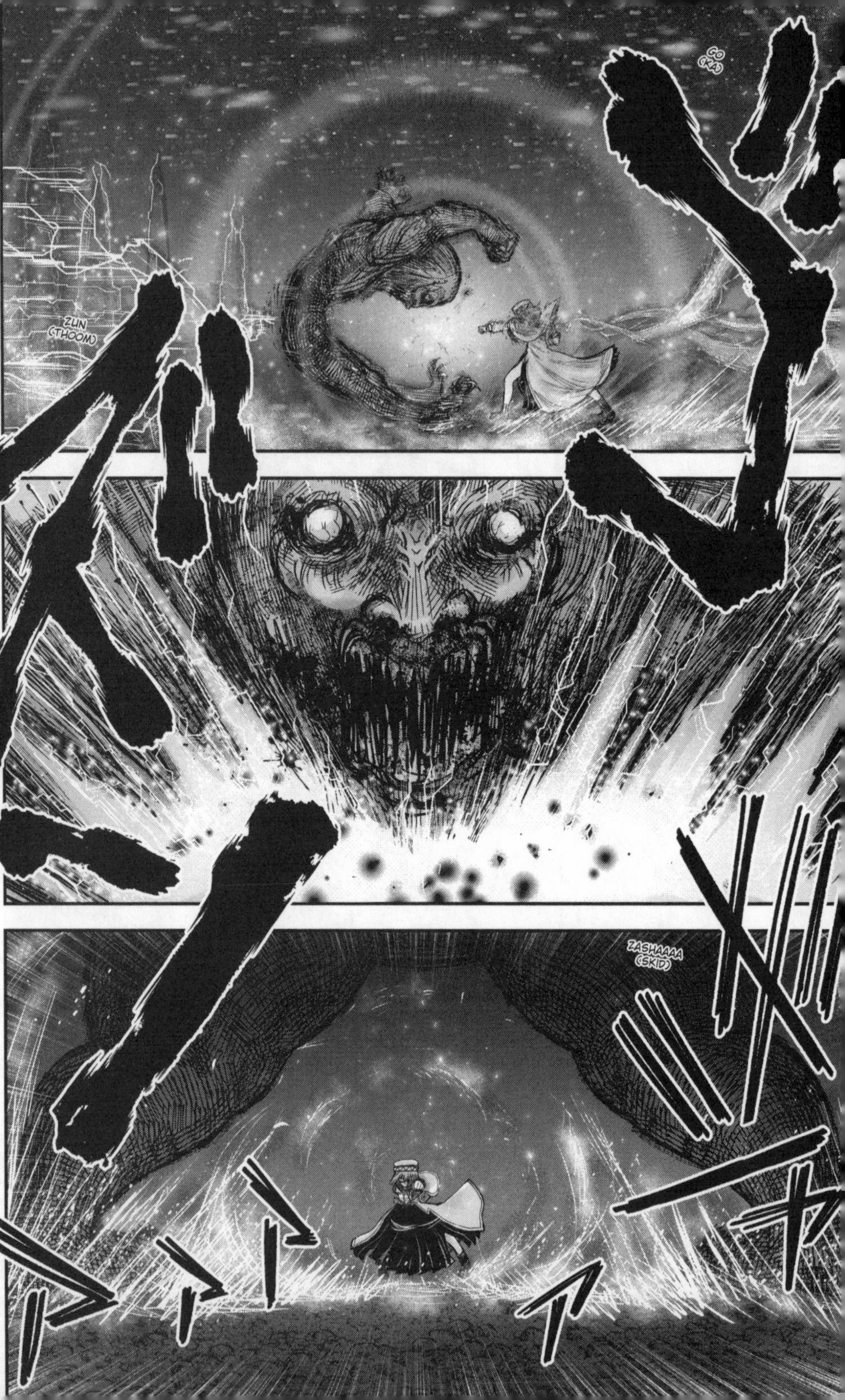
GO (KA)
ZUN (THOOM)
ZASHAAAA (SKID)

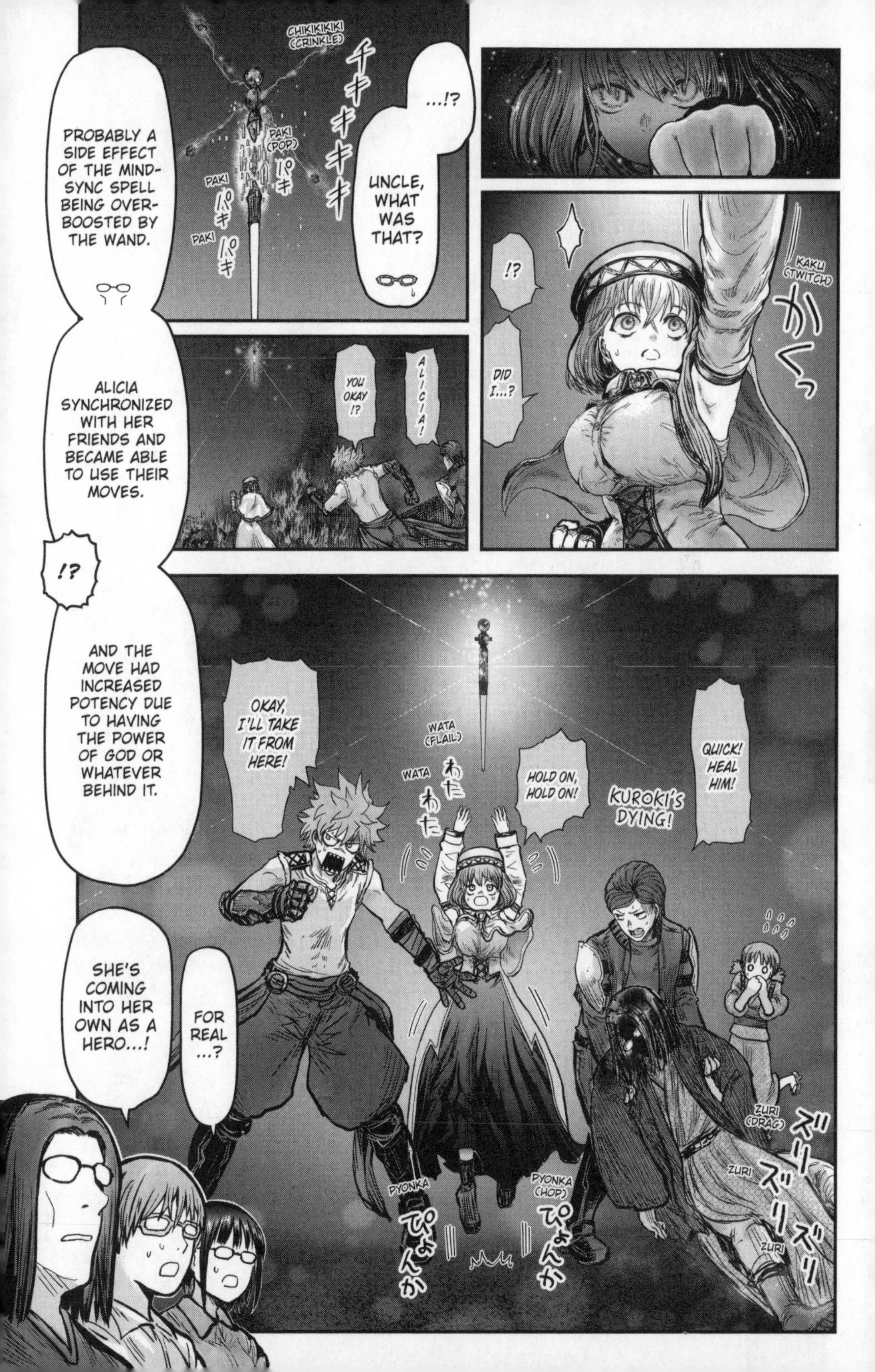
!?
DID I...?
KAKU (TWITCH)
かくっ
...!?
UNCLE, WHAT WAS THAT?
CHIKIKIKIKI (CRINKLE)
チキキキキ
PAKI (POP)
パキ
PAKI
パキ
PAKI
パキ
PROBABLY A SIDE EFFECT OF THE MIND-SYNC SPELL BEING OVER-BOOSTED BY THE WAND.
ALICIA!
YOU OKAY!?
ALICIA SYNCHRONIZED WITH HER FRIENDS AND BECAME ABLE TO USE THEIR MOVES.
!?
AND THE MOVE HAD INCREASED POTENCY DUE TO HAVING THE POWER OF GOD OR WHATEVER BEHIND IT.
QUICK! HEAL HIM!
KUROKI's DYING!
HOLD ON, HOLD ON!
WATA (FLAIL)
わた
WATA
わた
OKAY, I'LL TAKE IT FROM HERE!
ZURI (DRAG)
ズリー
ZURI
ズリ
ZURI
ズリ
PYONKA (HOP)
ぴょんか
PYONKA
ぴょんか
FOR REAL...?
SHE'S COMING INTO HER OWN AS A HERO...!

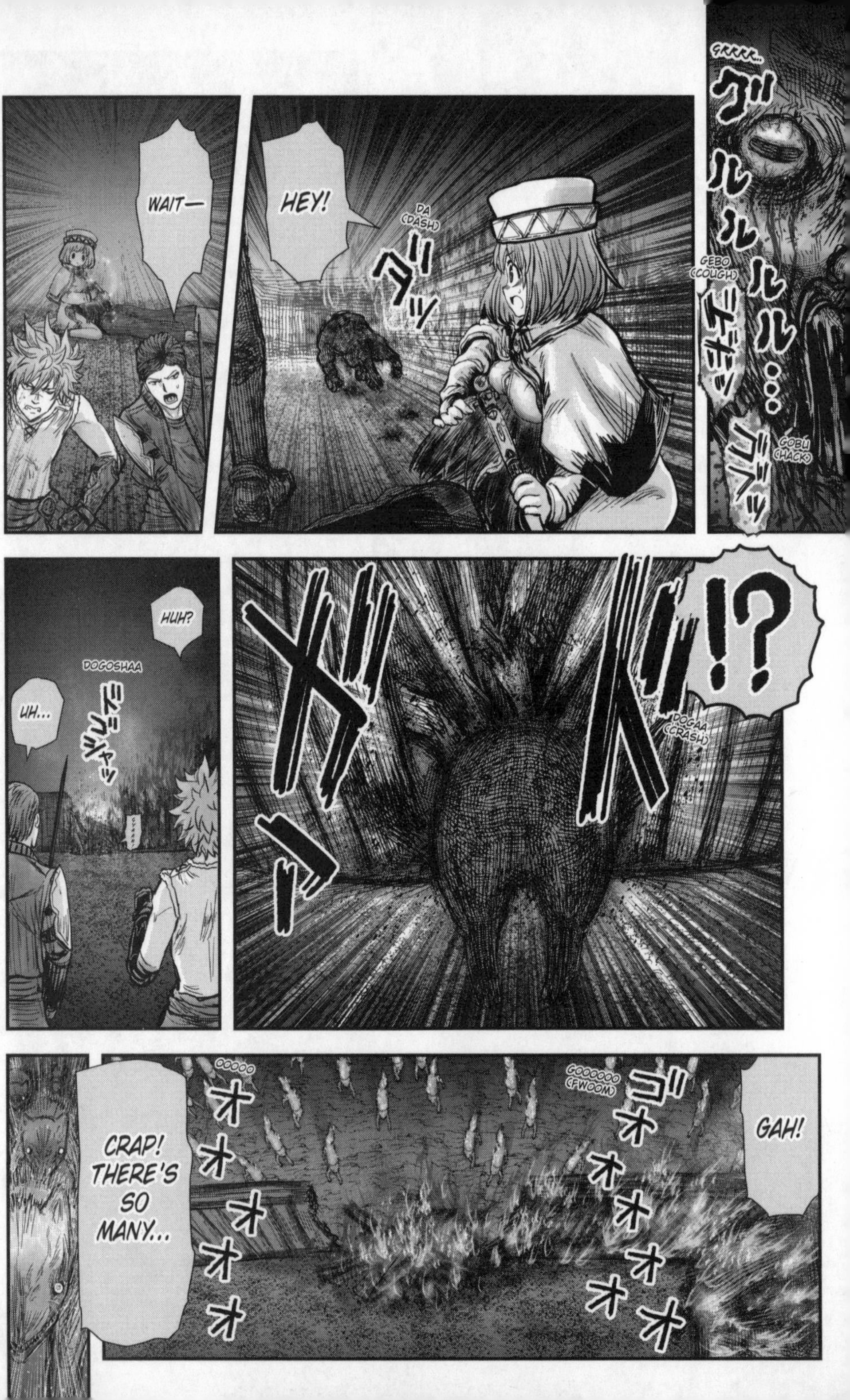
GRRRR...
GEBO (COUGH)
GOBU (HACK)
HEY!
DA (DASH)
WAIT—
!?
DOGAA (CRASH)
HUH?
DOGOSHAA
UH...
GAH!
GOOOOOO (FWOOM)
OOOOO
CRAP! THERE'S SO MANY...

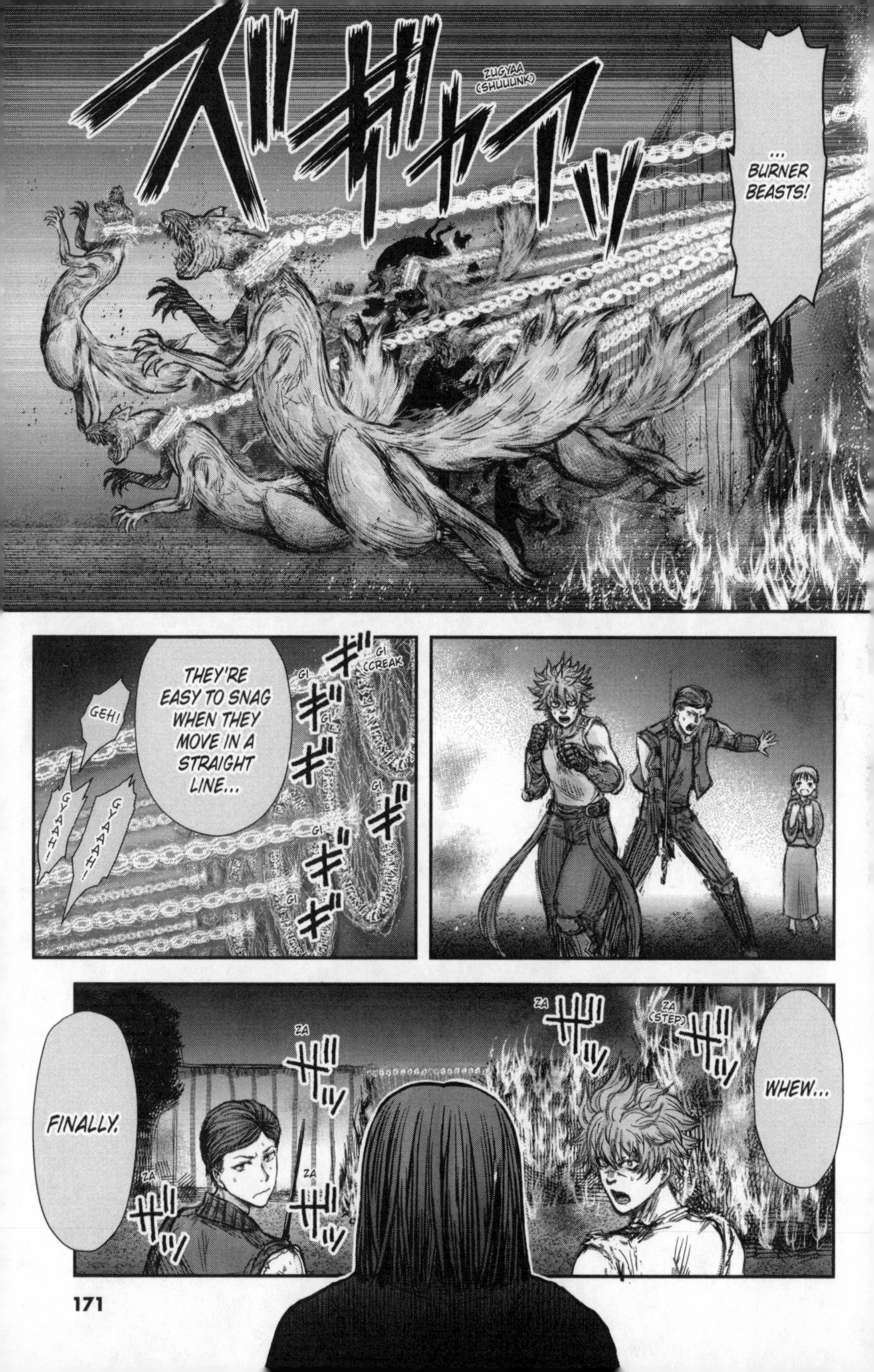

... BURNER BEASTS!
ZUGYAA (SHUUUNK)
GI (CREAK
GI
GI
GI
GI
GI
THEY'RE EASY TO SNAG WHEN THEY MOVE IN A STRAIGHT LINE...
GEH!
GYAAAH!
GYAAAH!
WHEW...
ZA (STEP)
ZA
ZA
ZA
ZA
FINALLY.

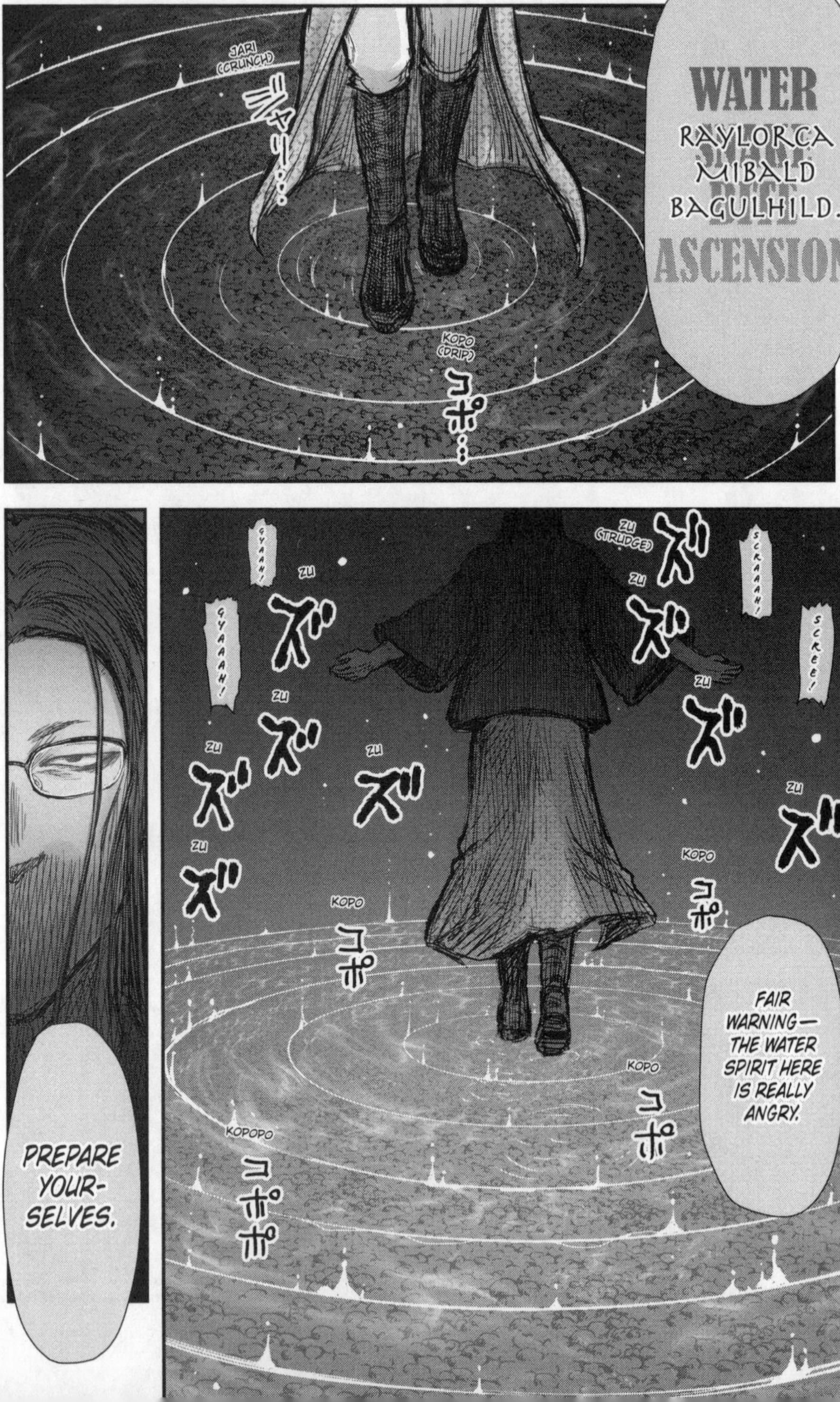
WATER
RAYLORCA MIBALD BAGULHILD.
ASCENSION
JARI (CRUNCH)
ジャー…
KOPO (DRIP)
コポ…
ZU (STRUDGE)
ズ
SCRAAAH!
ZU
ズ
SCREE!
ZU
ズ
ZU
ズ
GYAAN!
ZU
ズ
GYAAAH!
ZU
ズ
ZU
ズ
ZU
ズ
ZU
ズ
KOPO
コポ
KOPO
コポ
FAIR WARNING— THE WATER SPIRIT HERE IS REALLY ANGRY.
KOPO
コポ
KOPOPO
コポポ
PREPARE YOUR-SELVES.

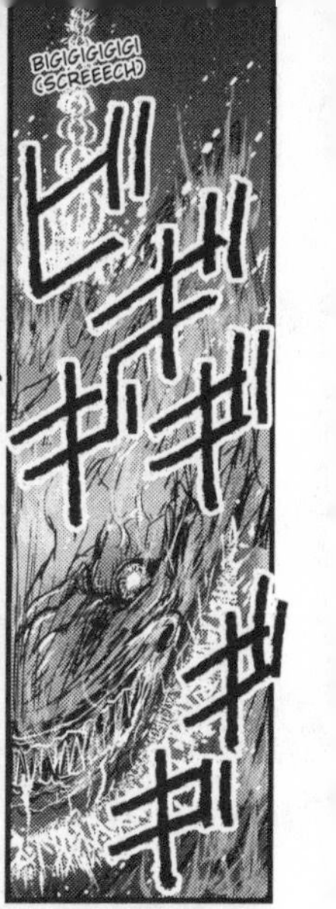
BIGIGIGIGIGI (SCREEECH)
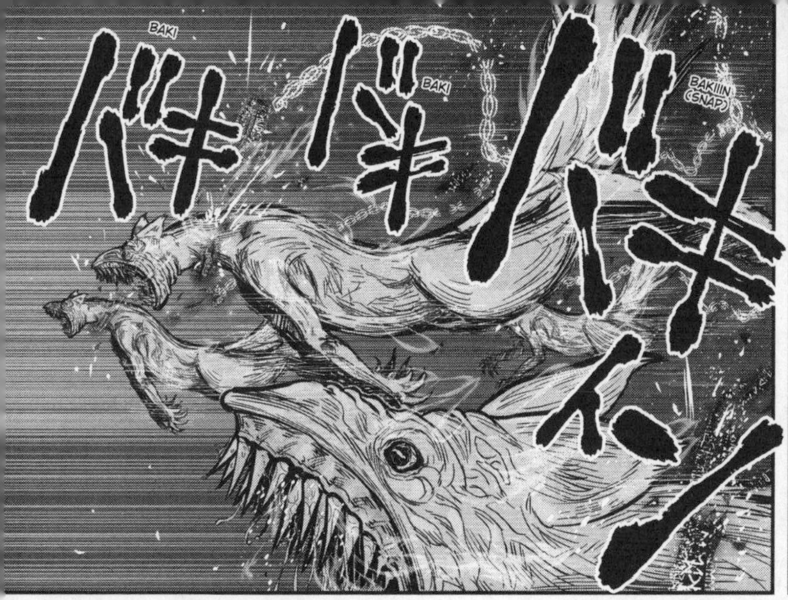
BAKIIIN (SNAP)
BAKI
BAKI
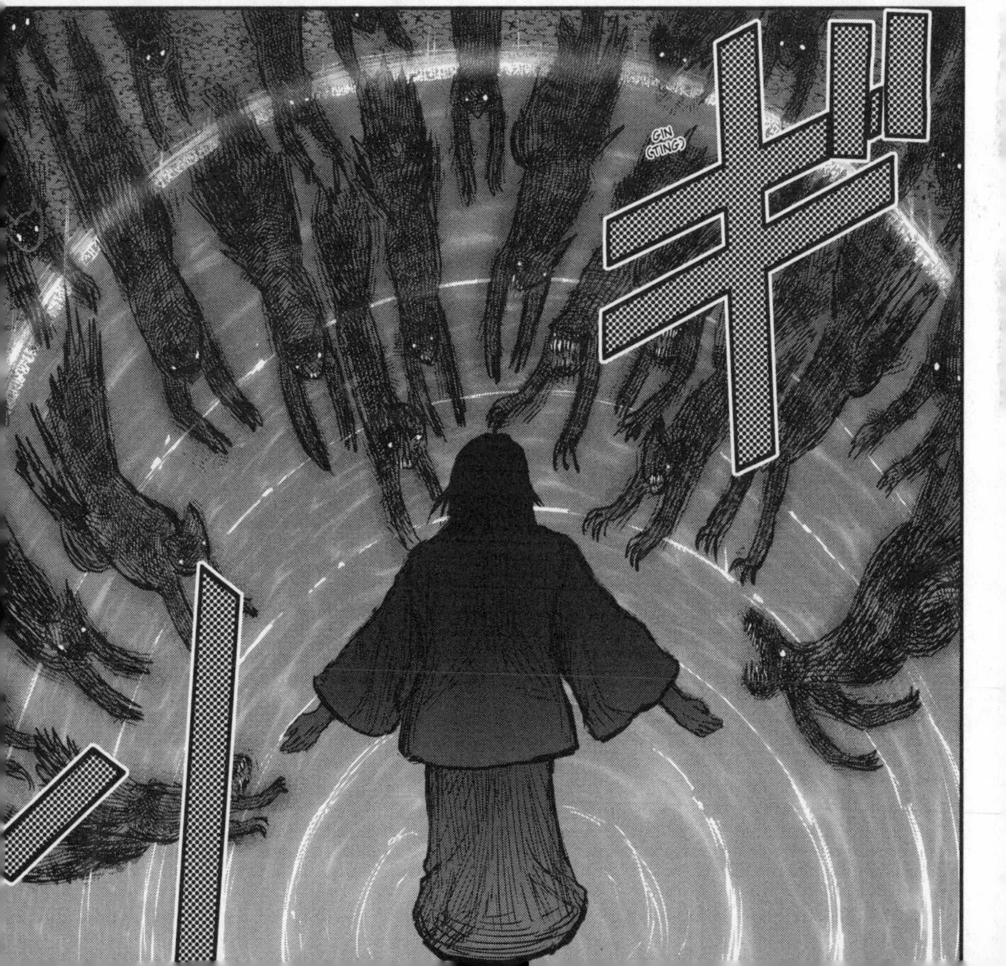
GIN (TING)

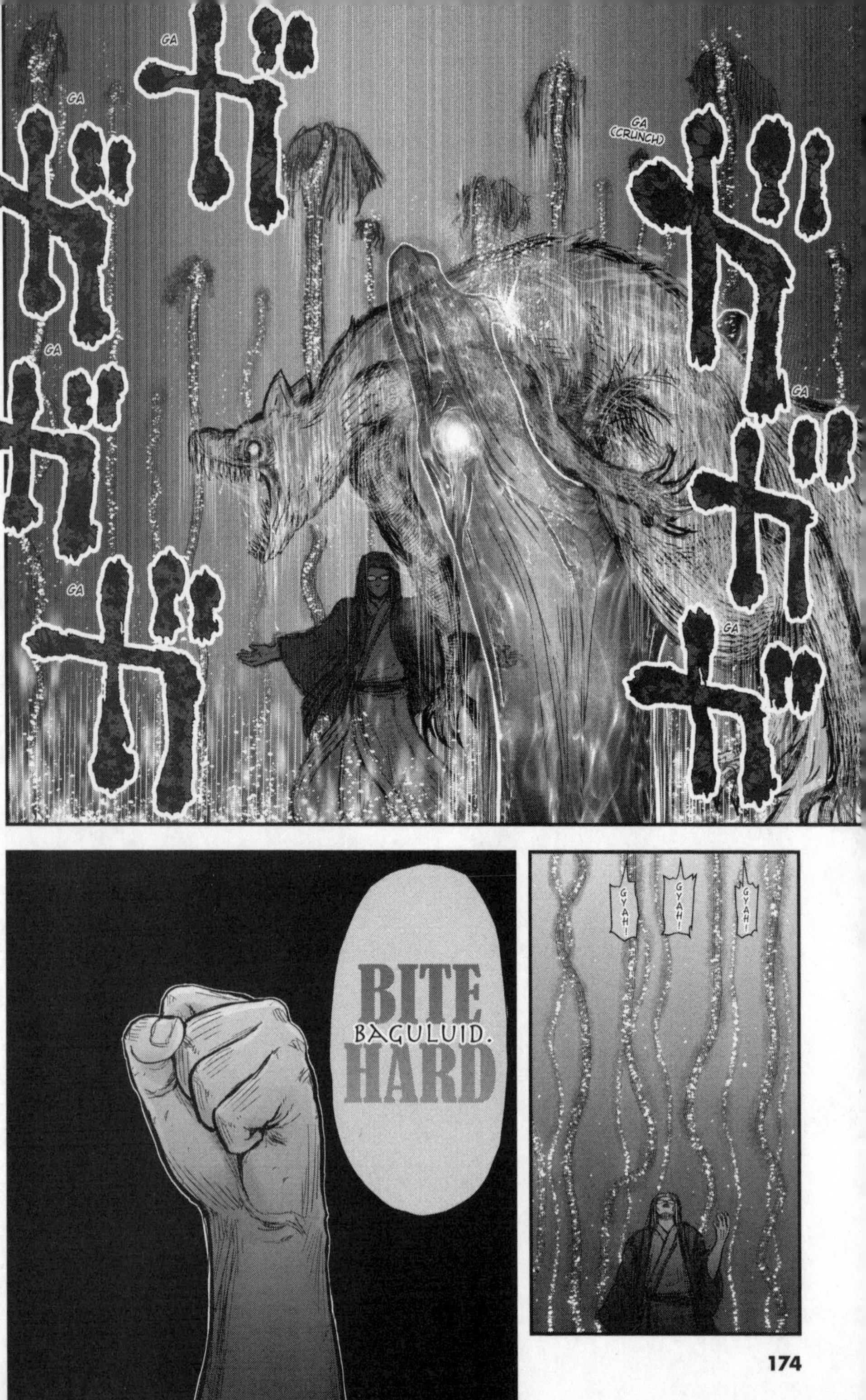
GA
(CRUNCH)
GA
GA
GA
GA
GA
GA
GYAH!
GYAH!
GYAH!
BITE HARD
BAGULUID.

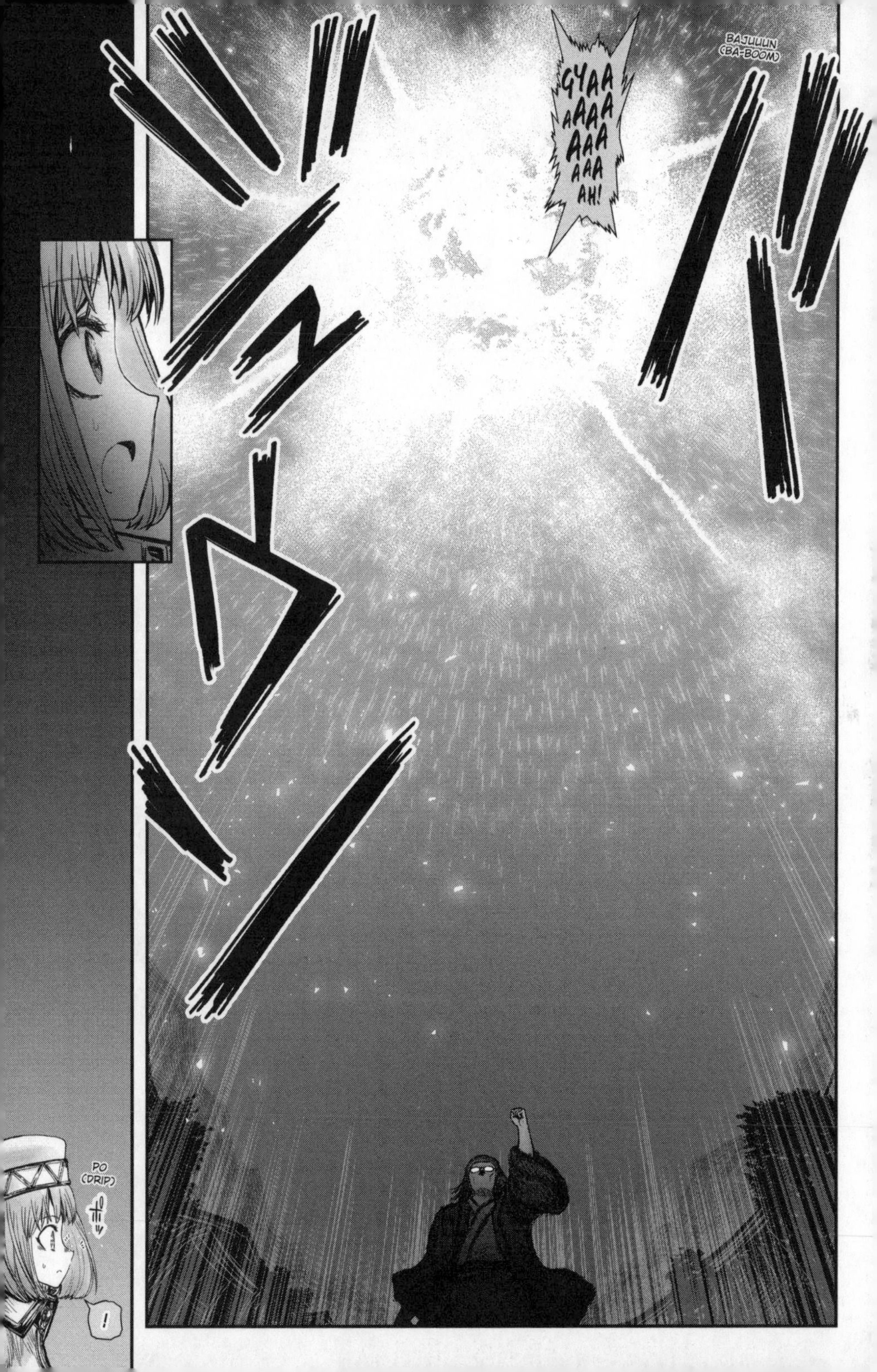
BAJUUUN
(BA-BOOM)
GYAAAAAAAAAAAAAH!
PO
(DRIP)
!

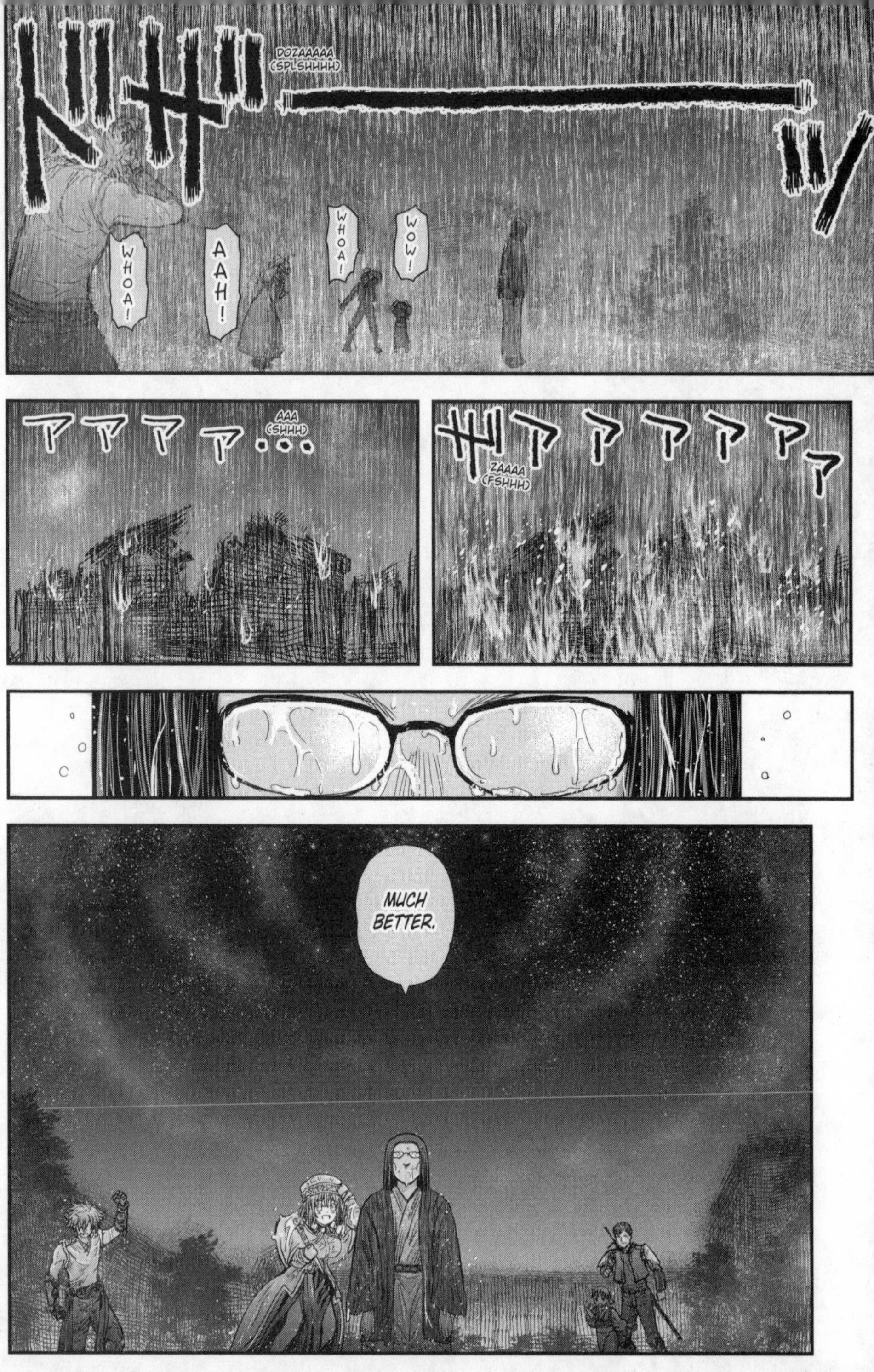
DOZAAAAA (SPLSHHHH)
WOW!
WHOA!
AAH!
WHOA!
ZAAAA (FSHHH)
AAA (SHHH)
MUCH BETTER.

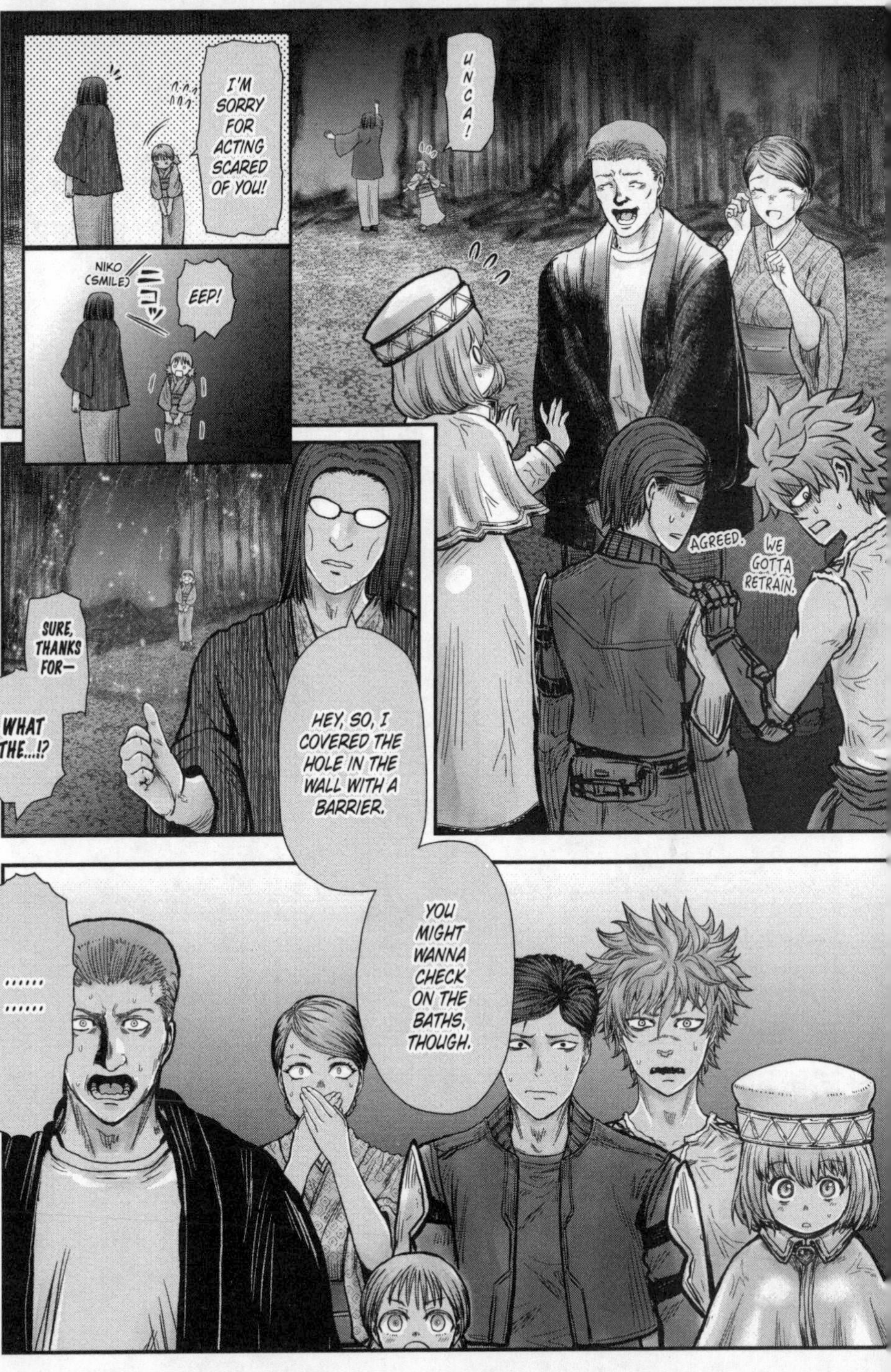
UNCA!
WE GOTTA RETRAIN.
AGREED.
I'M SORRY FOR ACTING SCARED OF YOU!
NIKO (SMILE)
EEP!
HEY, SO, I COVERED THE HOLE IN THE WALL WITH A BARRIER.
YOU MIGHT WANNA CHECK ON THE BATHS, THOUGH.
SURE, THANKS FOR—
WHAT THE...!?
......
......

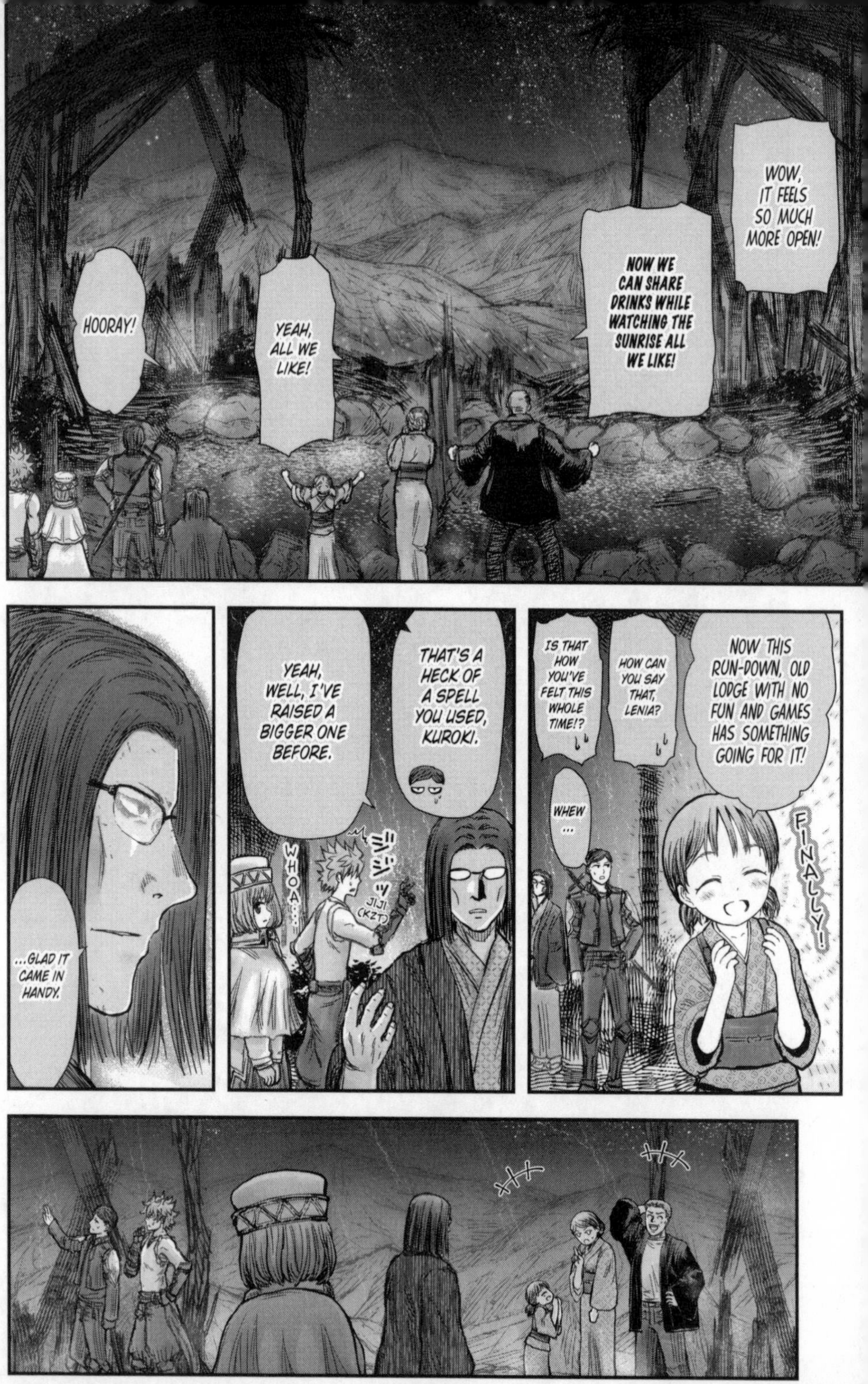
WOW, IT FEELS SO MUCH MORE OPEN!
NOW WE CAN SHARE DRINKS WHILE WATCHING THE SUNRISE ALL WE LIKE!
YEAH, ALL WE LIKE!
HOORAY!
NOW THIS RUN-DOWN, OLD LODGE WITH NO FUN AND GAMES HAS SOMETHING GOING FOR IT!
FINALLY!
HOW CAN YOU SAY THAT, LENIA?
IS THAT HOW YOU'VE FELT THIS WHOLE TIME!?
WHEW...
THAT'S A HECK OF A SPELL YOU USED, KUROKI.
YEAH, WELL, I'VE RAISED A BIGGER ONE BEFORE.
WHOA...
JIJI (KZT)
...GLAD IT CAME IN HANDY.

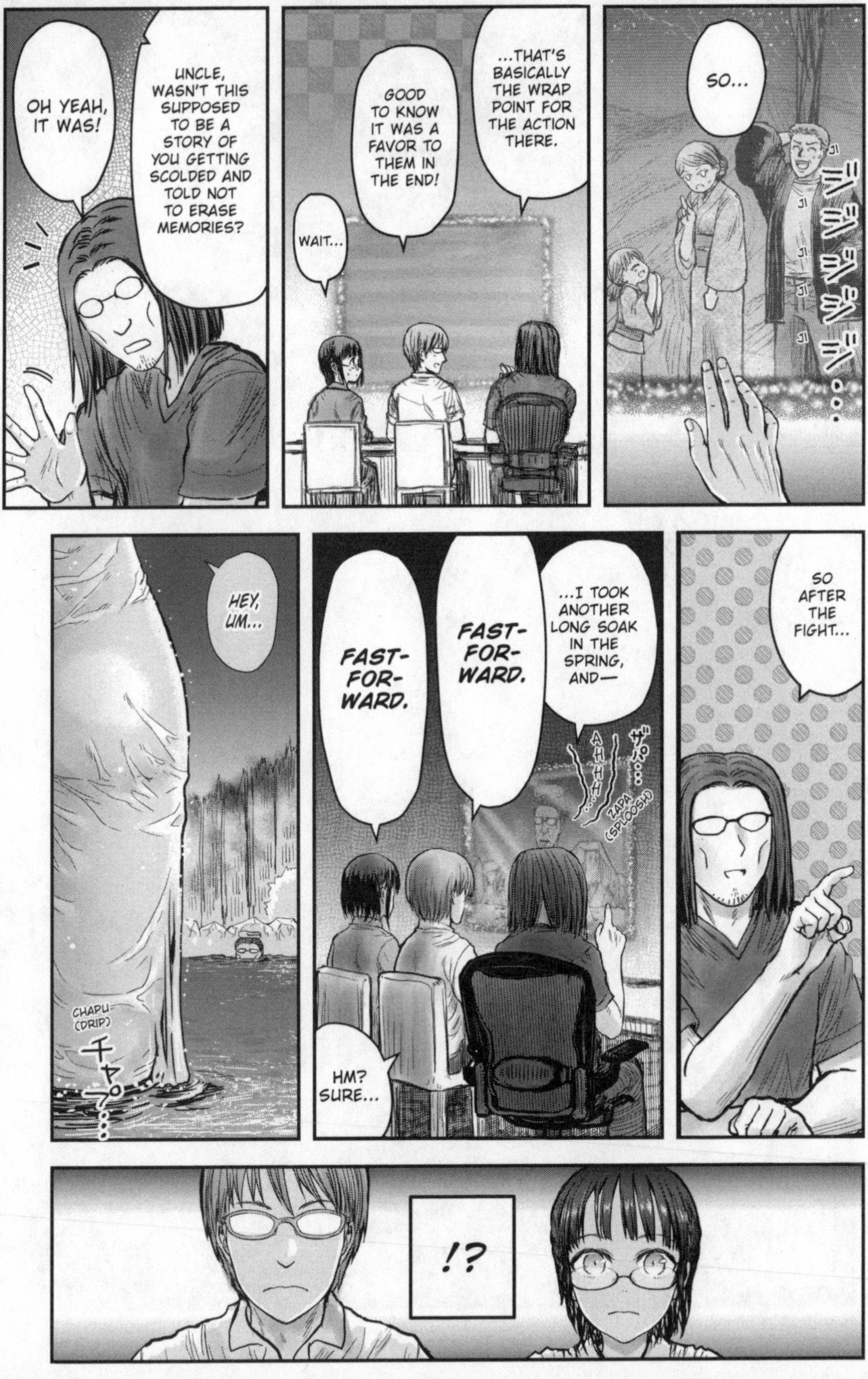
SO...
JI
...THAT'S BASICALLY THE WRAP POINT FOR THE ACTION THERE.
GOOD TO KNOW IT WAS A FAVOR TO THEM IN THE END!
WAIT...
UNCLE, WASN'T THIS SUPPOSED TO BE A STORY OF YOU GETTING SCOLDED AND TOLD NOT TO ERASE MEMORIES?
OH YEAH, IT WAS!
SO AFTER THE FIGHT...
...I TOOK ANOTHER LONG SOAK IN THE SPRING, AND—
FAST-FOR-WARD.
FAST-FOR-WARD.
AHHHH...
ZAPA (SPLOOSH)
HM? SURE...
HEY, UM...
CHAPU (DRIP)
!?

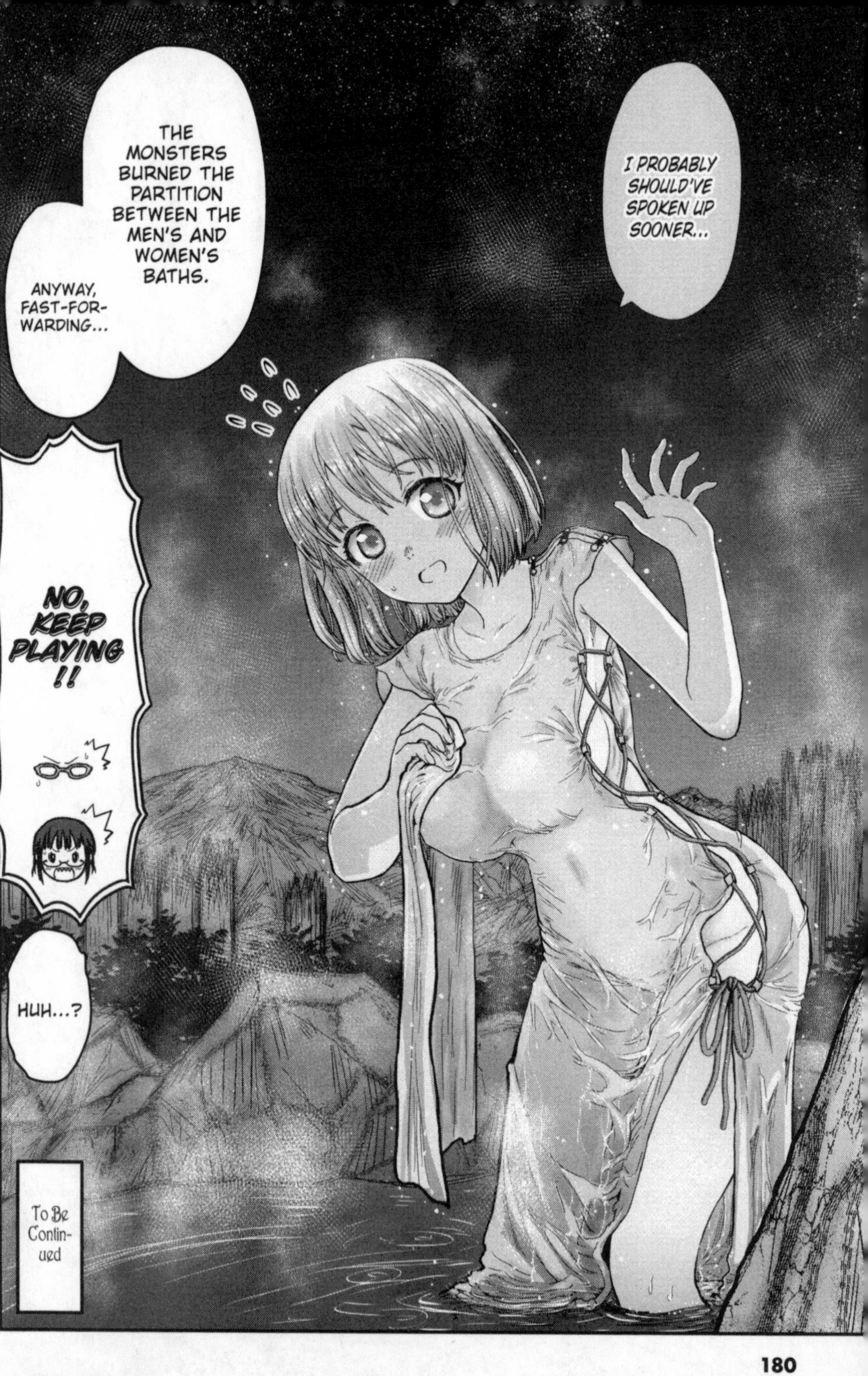

I PROBABLY SHOULD'VE SPOKEN UP SOONER...
THE MONSTERS BURNED THE PARTITION BETWEEN THE MEN'S AND WOMEN'S BATHS.
ANYWAY, FAST-FOR-WARDING...
NO, KEEP PLAYING!!
HUH...?
To Be Contin-ued

Hot Spring

A term used to describe the phenomenon of water getting heated underground and spouting out aboveground, as well as the hot water produced by this phenomenon.

In Japan, the standards for hot springs (*onsen*) are established by a legal code called the Onsen Code, which states that hot springs must either be at least 25°C (about 77°F) or contain a certain amount of key components.

Fun fact: Japan has more naturally occurring hot springs than any other country in the world.

TIPS

UNCLE from ANOTHER WORLD

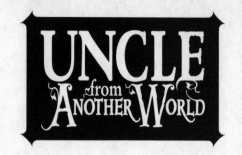

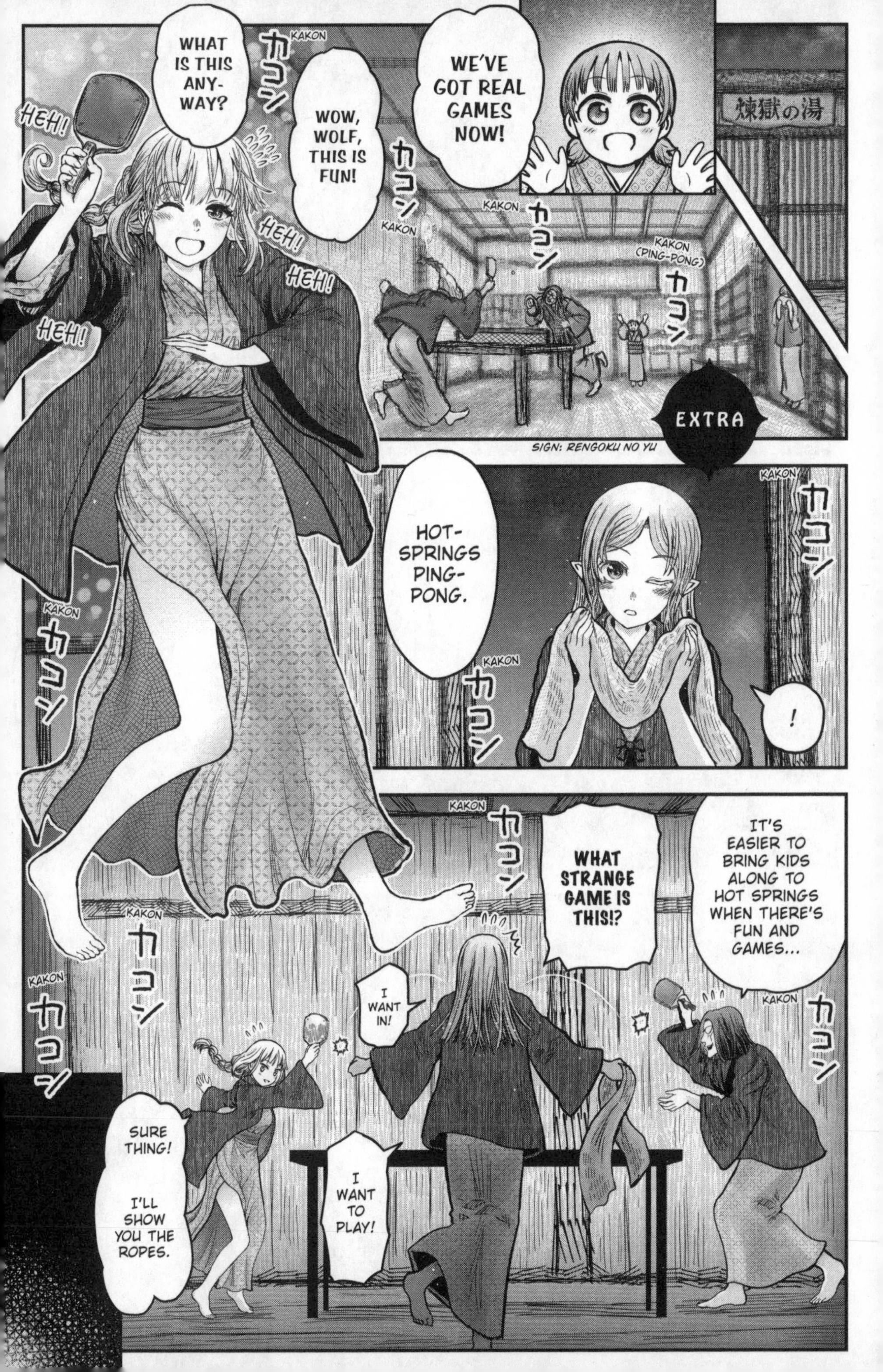
煉獄の湯
WE'VE GOT REAL GAMES NOW!
KAKON
カコン
KAKON (PING-PONG)
カコン
EXTRA
SIGN: RENGOKU NO YU
WOW, WOLF, THIS IS FUN!
WHAT IS THIS ANY-WAY?
HEH! HEH! HEH! HEH!
KAKON
カコン
HOT-SPRINGS PING-PONG.
!
KAKON
カコン
IT'S EASIER TO BRING KIDS ALONG TO HOT SPRINGS WHEN THERE'S FUN AND GAMES...
WHAT STRANGE GAME IS THIS!?
I WANT IN!
I WANT TO PLAY!
SURE THING!
I'LL SHOW YOU THE ROPES.

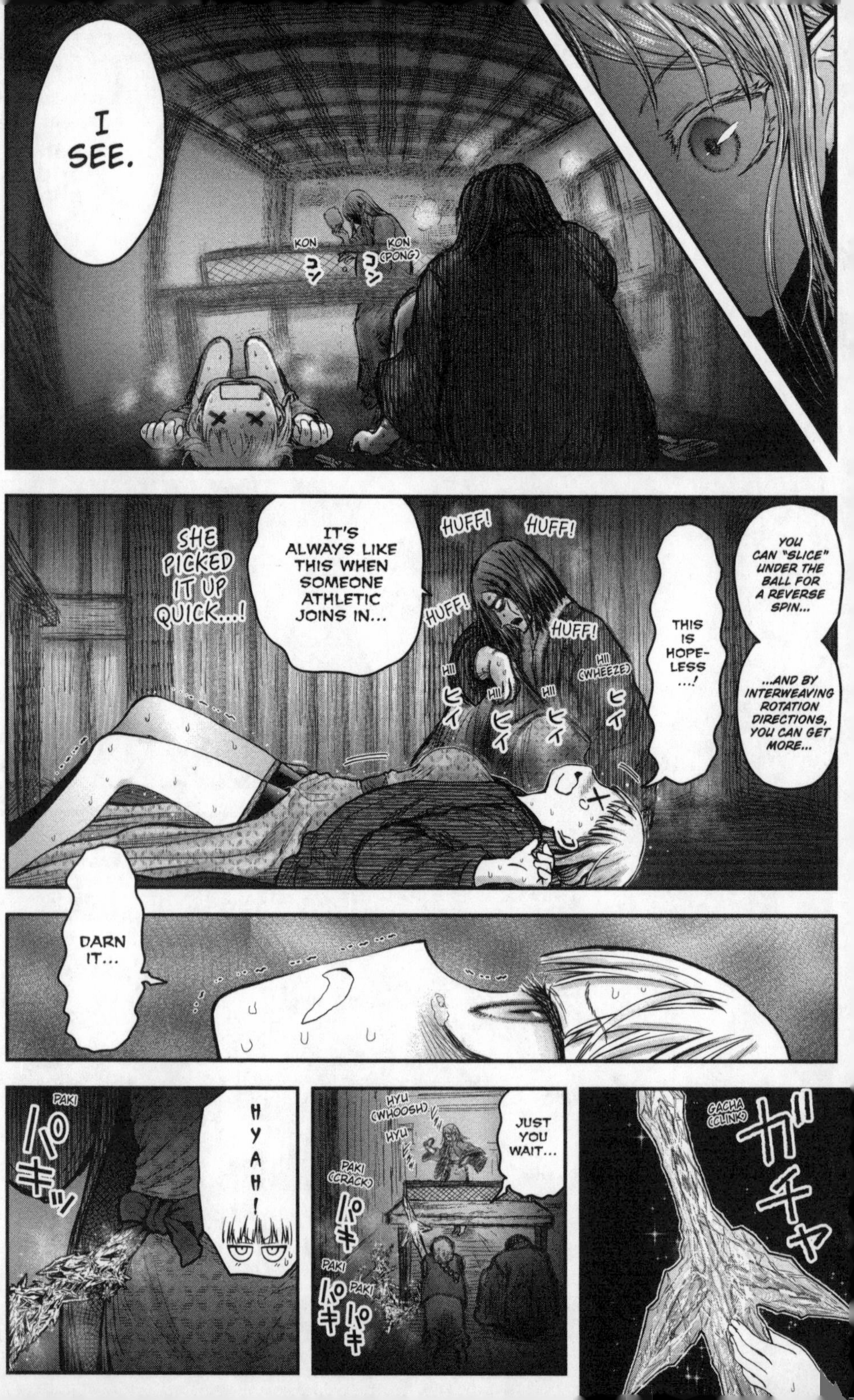
I SEE.
KON (PONG)
コン
KON
コン
YOU CAN "SLICE" UNDER THE BALL FOR A REVERSE SPIN...
...AND BY INTERWEAVING ROTATION DIRECTIONS, YOU CAN GET MORE...
THIS IS HOPE-LESS ...!
HUFF!
HUFF!
HUFF!
HUFF!
HII (WHEEZE)
ヒイ
HII
ヒイ
HII
ヒイ
HII
ヒイ
IT'S ALWAYS LIKE THIS WHEN SOMEONE ATHLETIC JOINS IN...
SHE PICKED IT UP QUICK...!
DARN IT...
GACHA (CLINK)
ガチャ
JUST YOU WAIT...
HYU (WHOOSH)
HYU
PAKI (CRACK)
パキ
PAKI
パキ
PAKI
パキ
HYAH!
PAKI
パキッ

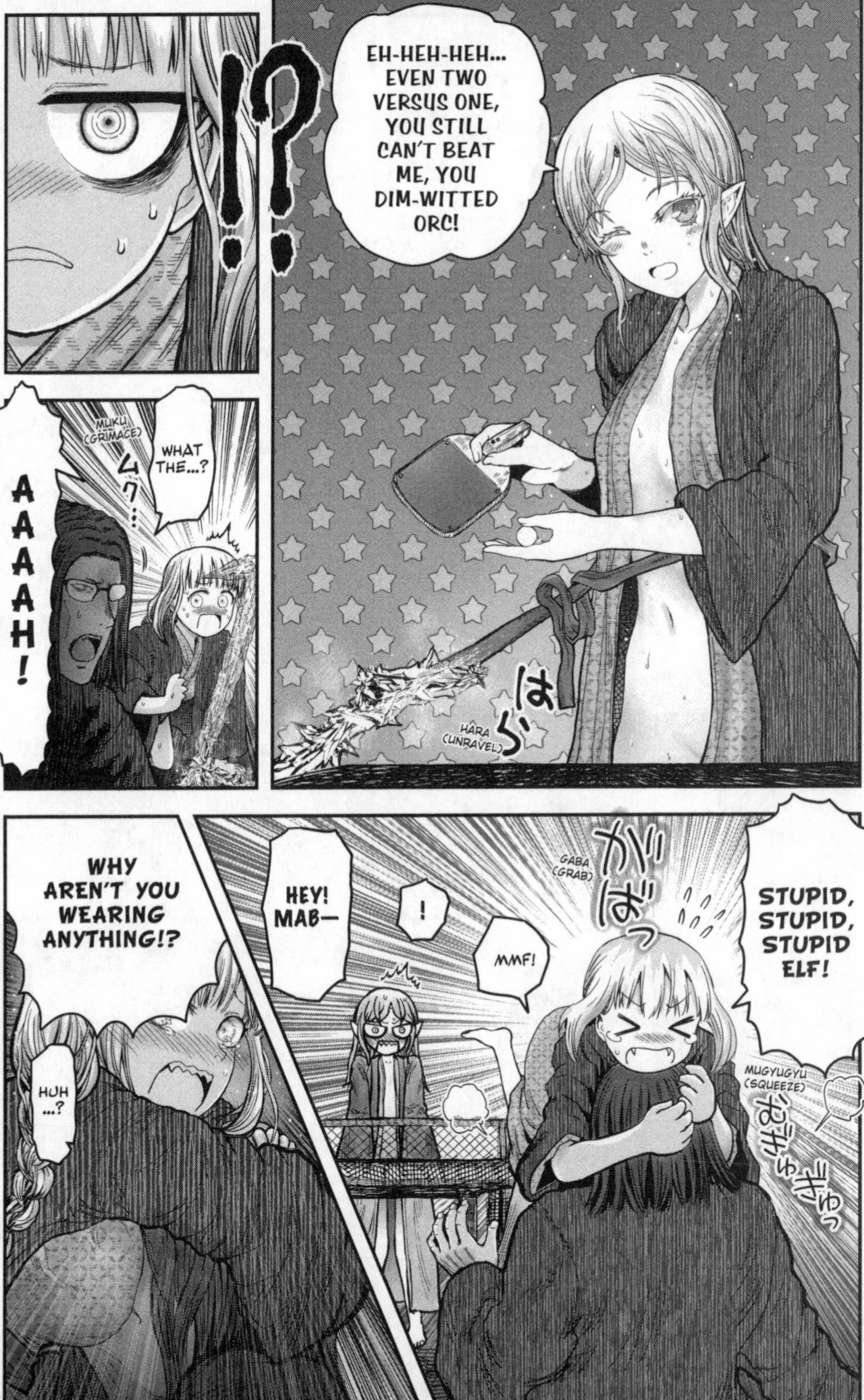

EH-HEH-HEH... EVEN TWO VERSUS ONE, YOU STILL CAN'T BEAT ME, YOU DIM-WITTED ORC!
はら
HARA (UNRAVEL)
!?
WHAT THE...?
MUKU (GRIMACE)
ムク…
AAAAAH!
STUPID, STUPID, STUPID ELF!
がばっ
GABA (GRAB)
HEY! MAB—
!
MMF!
MUGYUGYU (SQUEEZE)
むぎゅぎゅっ
WHY AREN'T YOU WEARING ANYTHING!?
HUH ...?

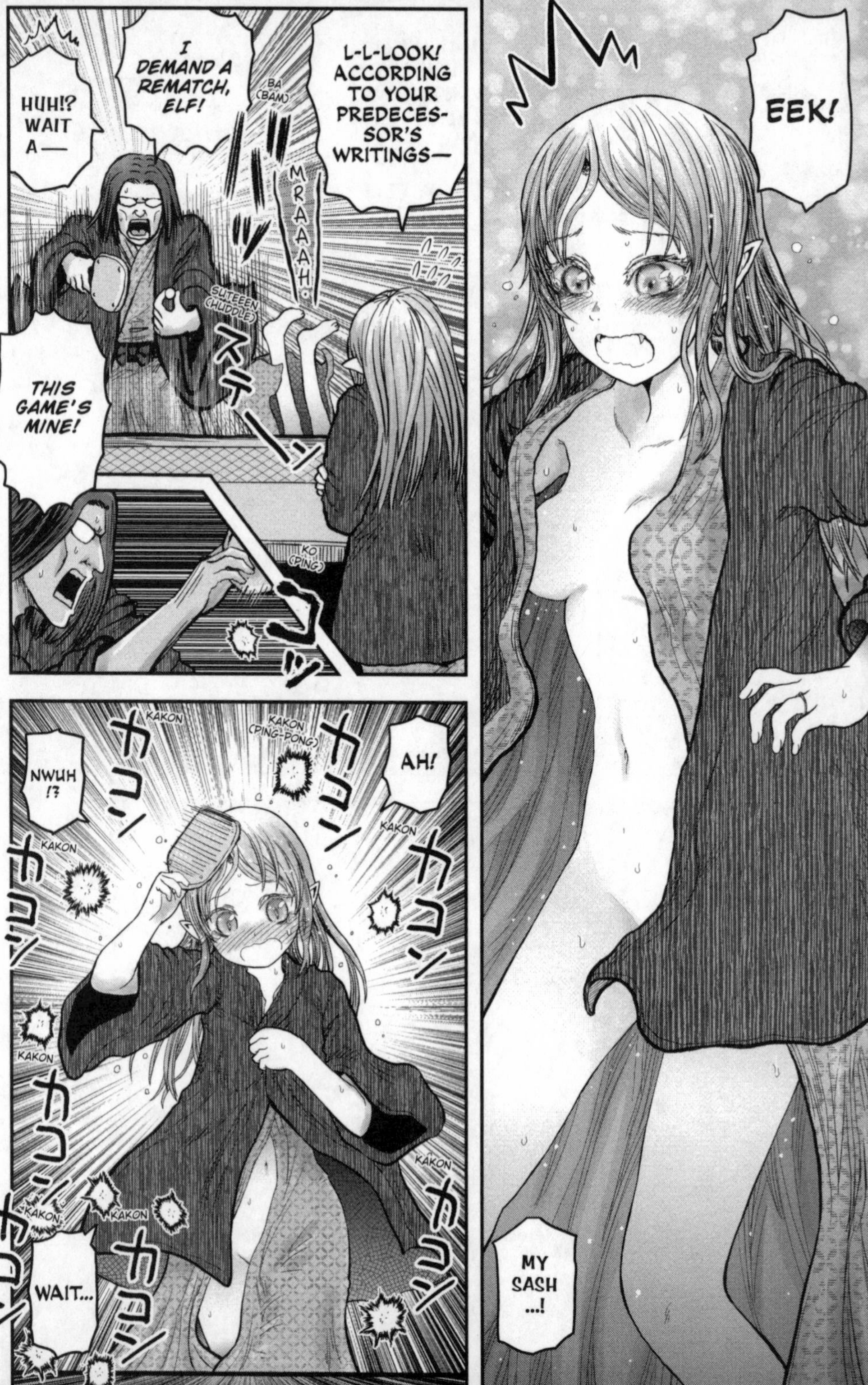
EEK!
MY SASH ...!
L-L-LOOK! ACCORDING TO YOUR PREDECES-SOR'S WRITINGS—
I DEMAND A REMATCH, ELF!
BA (BAM)
HUH!? WAIT A—
MRAAAH.
SUTEEEN (HUDDLE)
THIS GAME'S MINE!
KO (PING)
AH!
KAKON (PING-PONG)
KAKON
KAKON
NWUH !?
KAKON
KAKON
KAKON
KAKON
KAKON
WAIT...

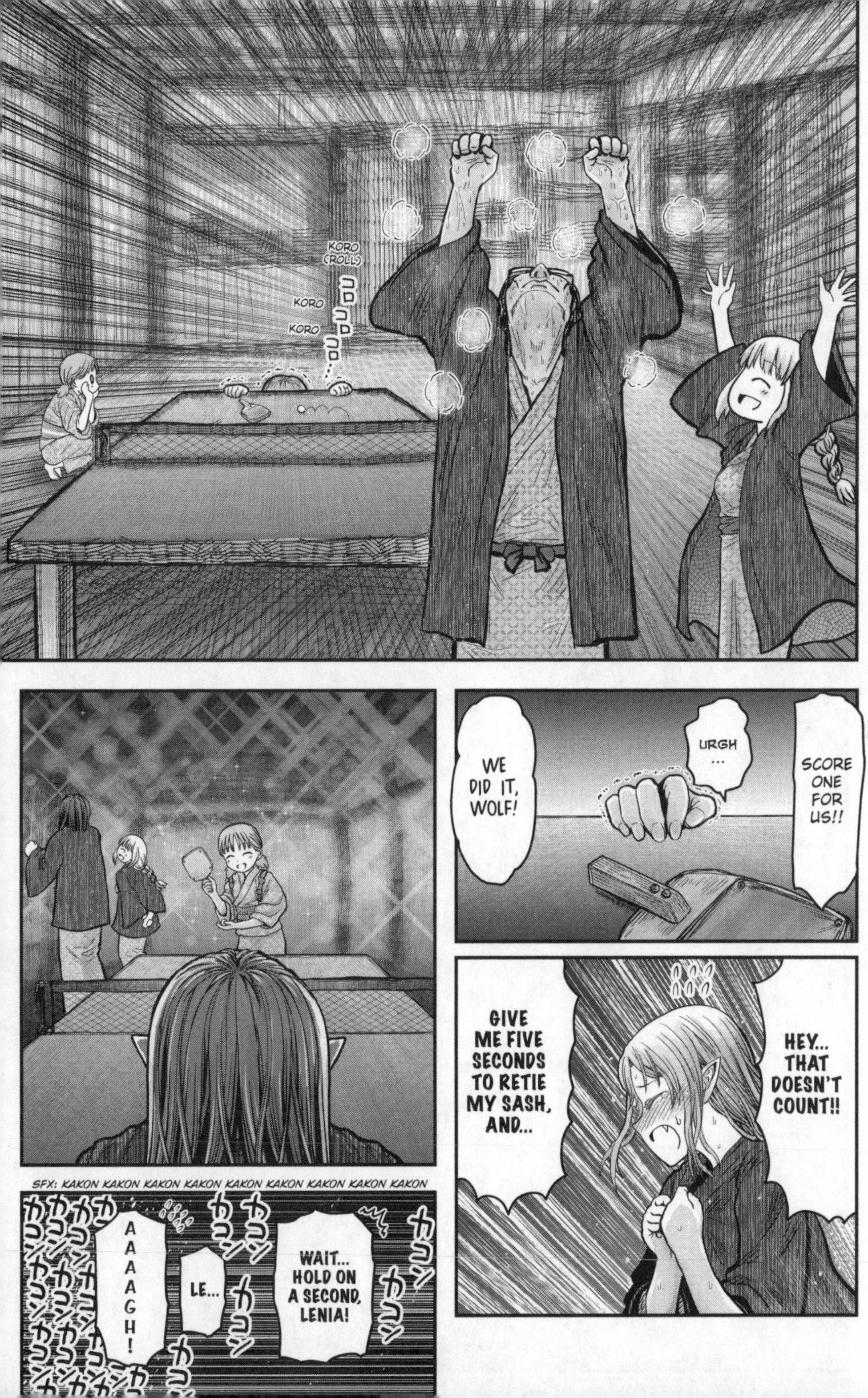
KORO (ROLL)
コロ
KORO
コロ
KORO
コロ…
SCORE ONE FOR US!!
URGH…
WE DID IT, WOLF!
HEY… THAT DOESN'T COUNT!!
GIVE ME FIVE SECONDS TO RETIE MY SASH, AND…
SFX: KAKON KAKON KAKON KAKON KAKON KAKON KAKON KAKON KAKON
WAIT… HOLD ON A SECOND, LENIA!
LE…
AAAAGH!

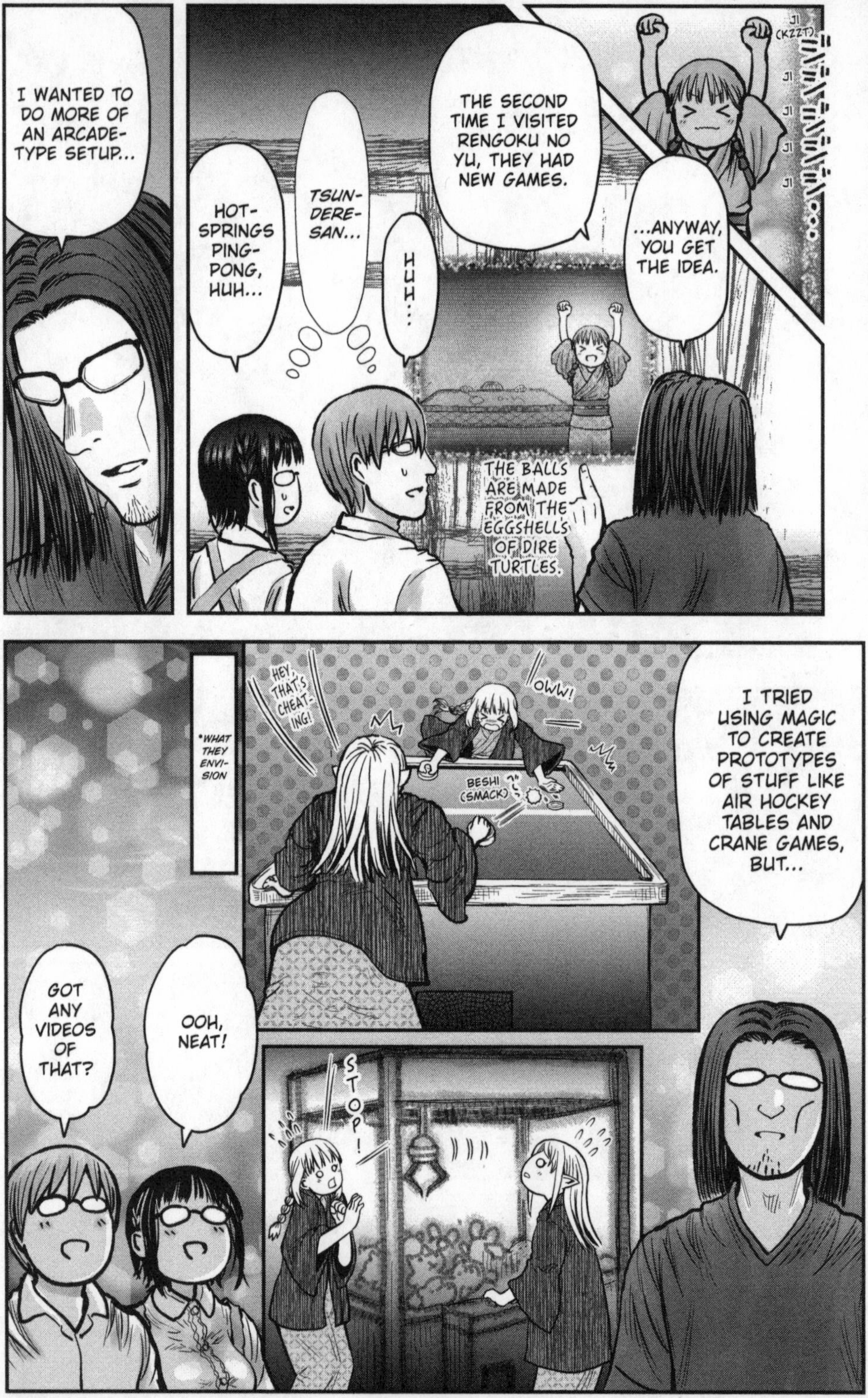

THE SECOND TIME I VISITED RENGOKU NO YU, THEY HAD NEW GAMES.
JI (KZZT) JI JI JI JI
...ANYWAY, YOU GET THE IDEA.
THE BALLS ARE MADE FROM THE EGGSHELLS OF DIRE TURTLES.
HUH...
TSUNDERE-SAN...
HOT-SPRINGS PING-PONG, HUH...
I WANTED TO DO MORE OF AN ARCADE-TYPE SETUP...
I TRIED USING MAGIC TO CREATE PROTOTYPES OF STUFF LIKE AIR HOCKEY TABLES AND CRANE GAMES, BUT...
*WHAT THEY ENVISION
OWW!
HEY, THAT'S CHEATING!
BESHI (SMACK)
STOP!
OOH, NEAT!
GOT ANY VIDEOS OF THAT?

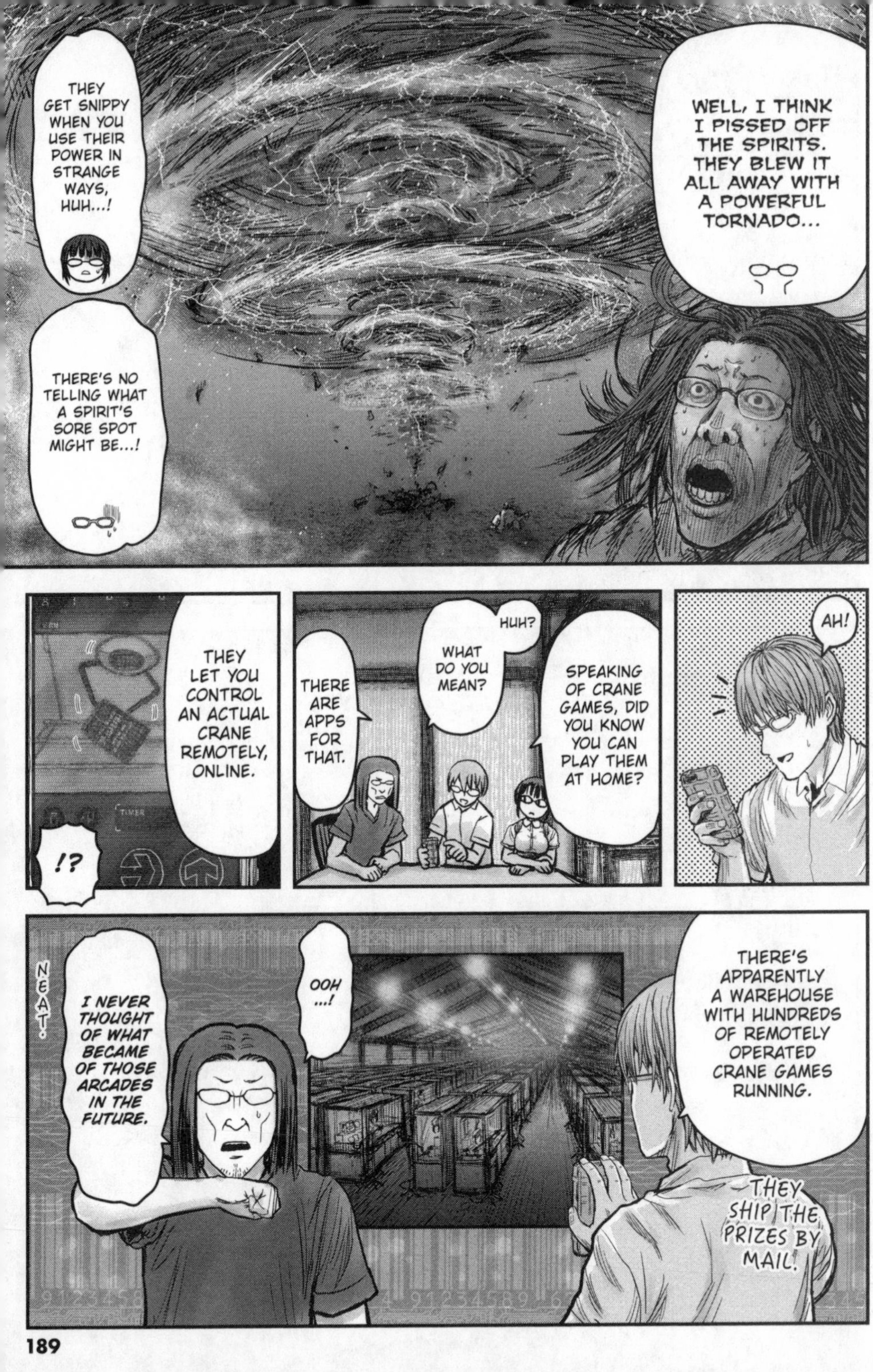
WELL, I THINK I PISSED OFF THE SPIRITS. THEY BLEW IT ALL AWAY WITH A POWERFUL TORNADO...
THEY GET SNIPPY WHEN YOU USE THEIR POWER IN STRANGE WAYS, HUH...!
THERE'S NO TELLING WHAT A SPIRIT'S SORE SPOT MIGHT BE...!
AH!
SPEAKING OF CRANE GAMES, DID YOU KNOW YOU CAN PLAY THEM AT HOME?
HUH?
WHAT DO YOU MEAN?
THERE ARE APPS FOR THAT.
THEY LET YOU CONTROL AN ACTUAL CRANE REMOTELY, ONLINE.
!?
THERE'S APPARENTLY A WAREHOUSE WITH HUNDREDS OF REMOTELY OPERATED CRANE GAMES RUNNING.
THEY SHIP THE PRIZES BY MAIL.
OOH ...!
I NEVER THOUGHT OF WHAT BECAME OF THOSE ARCADES IN THE FUTURE.
NEAT.

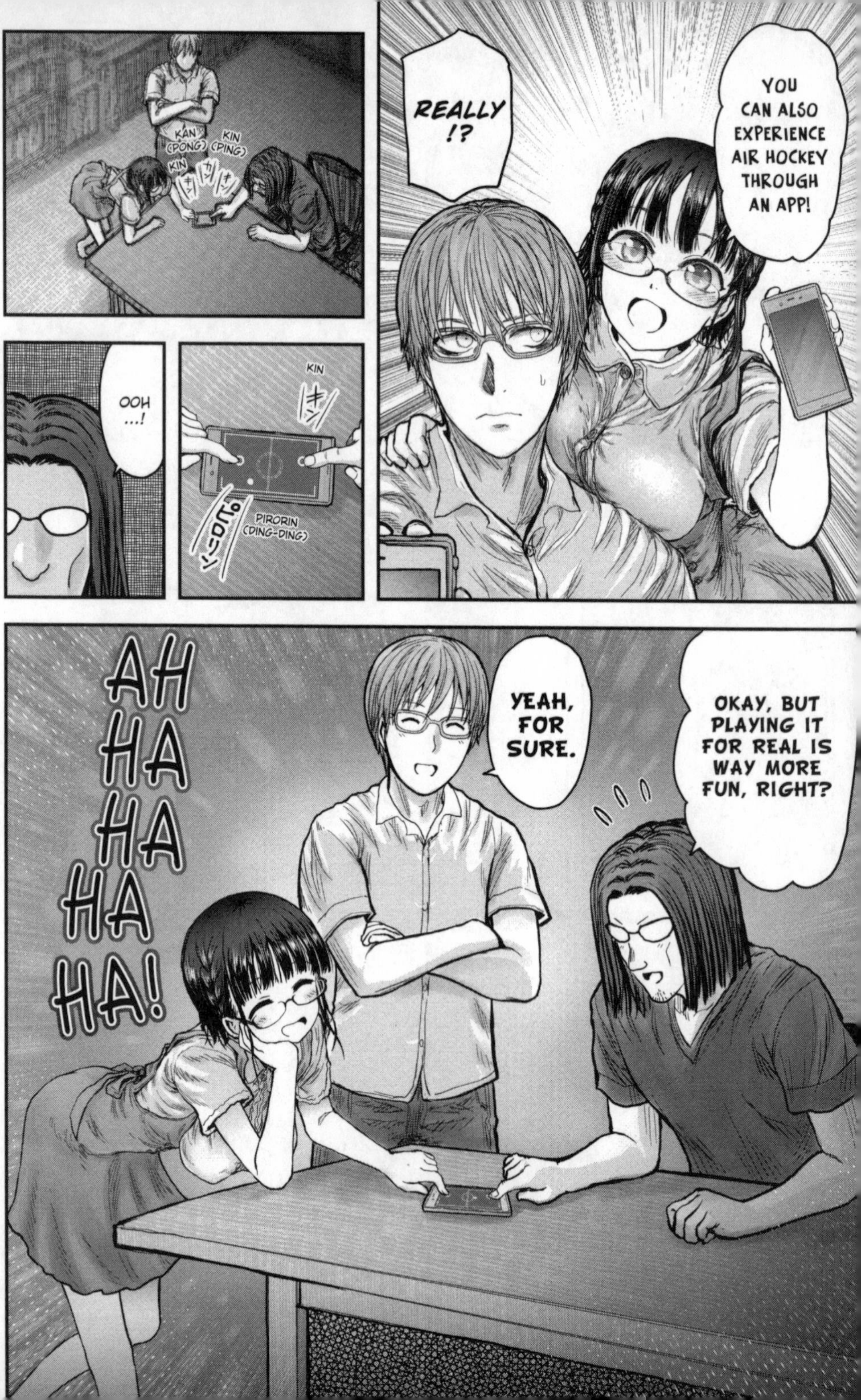
YOU CAN ALSO EXPERIENCE AIR HOCKEY THROUGH AN APP!
REALLY !?
KIN (PING)
KAN (PONG)
KIN
KIN
PIRORIN (DING-DING)
OOH ...!
OKAY, BUT PLAYING IT FOR REAL IS WAY MORE FUN, RIGHT?
YEAH, FOR SURE.
AH HA HA HA HA HA!

Translation Notes

COMMON HONORIFICS

no honorific: Indicates familiarity or closeness; if used without permission or reason, addressing someone in this manner would constitute an insult.

-san: The Japanese equivalent of Mr./Mrs./Miss. If a situation calls for politeness, this is the fail-safe honorific.

-sama: Conveys great respect; may also indicate that the social status of the speaker is lower than that of the addressee.

-dono: Roughly equivalent to "master" or "milord."

-kun: Used most often when referring to boys, this indicates affection or familiarity. Occasionally used by older men among their peers, but it may also be used by anyone referring to a person of lower standing.

-chan: An affectionate honorific indicating familiarity used mostly in reference to girls; also used in reference to cute persons or animals regardless of gender.

-senpai: An honorific for one's senior classmate, colleague, etc., although not as senior or respected as a *sensei* (teacher).

¥100 is approximately $1 USD.

A●ien Soldier, Uncle's favorite game, is an action title from 1995 known for its extreme emphasis on elaborate boss fights and for being impossibly ambitious in scope.

PAGE 2
Tsundere is an archetype common to anime and manga where a character either grows from hating someone to loving someone, or acts especially prickly toward a character they have feelings for.

PAGE 14
Valgar and Serena are characters from *G.H.*, the game that Uncle considers the #1 title for the Saturn. Initially, neither can be used in singleplayer, but Serena can be unlocked by completing the game.

PAGE 35
10.6°C is approximately 51.08°F.

PAGE 47
The **trashy women's porn manga** is referred to as *lady-comi* in the original Japanese. Though once used to refer to manga for older women in general, today it typically refers to a specific type of sex-focused women's manga.

PAGE 49
Obon is a Japanese holiday of Buddhist origins meant to commemorate one's ancestors.

PAGE 55
Uncle from an Underworld was *Osekkai Oji-san* ("Nosy Uncle") in the original Japanese as a play on this series's original title, *Isekai Oji-san.*

PAGE 69
S●ny is an electronics company that is also in the console gaming market.

PAGE 74
A *ryokan* is a type of inn or lodge that emphasizes Japanese cultural and architectural qualities such as sleeping in Japanese-style futons on bamboo mats, soaking in communal baths, and wearing traditional clothing such as the *yukata*—a light cotton *kimono*.

PAGE 79
The N●o Geo was a 1990s video game system that actually used the same hardware for both arcade and console machine, making it the first time players could experience arcade-perfect games at home. The console and its games were enormously expensive as a result, with a 1990s cost comparable to the most powerful modern consoles even when not accounting for inflation.

PAGE 85
YuY● Hakusho: Makyou Touitsusen is a 1994 fighting game based on a popular 1990s battle manga about a middle school delinquent who becomes a spirit detective. Hi●i is a demonic foe and eventual ally to the lead character.

PAGE 89
"Grandpa Kanon" refers to a powerful wizard character in the game *G.H.*

PAGE 92
The **sen** is an obsolete denomination of Japanese currenc. One **sen** was worth one hundredth of a yen.

PAGE 115
Kuroki, the false name Alicia's group knows Uncle by, is a reference to the character Kuroki Tenma from A●ien Soldier. In him resides the evil Epsilon-1, the counterpart to the heroic player character, Epsilon-2.

PAGE 138
Japanese high schools use a grading system of 1 through 5, with 1 being the lowest and 5 being the highest.

PAGE 183
Wolf, the false name Elf knows Uncle by, is based on Wolfgunblood (one word), a boss character from A●ien Soldier.

INSIDE COVER (FRONT)
Gun●tar Heroes is a 1993 run-and-gun shooter game where players can combine different weapon types together to create powerful attacks. It's from the creators of A●ien Soldier and G.H., and—like them—features elaborate boss fights. Many aspects of this title, such as the bosses Seven Force and Golden Silver, would be referenced in those later games.

INSIDE COVER (BACK)
La●dstalker is a 1992 action-adventure game starring a treasure hunter named Nigel and featuring an isometric view.

Hotondoshindeiru

TRANSLATOR: **Christina Rose**
LETTERER: **Phil Christie**

ISEKAI OJI-SAN, Vol. 5
©Hotondoshindeiru 2020
©SEGA

First published in Japan in 2020 by KADOKAWA CORPORATION, Tokyo.
English translation rights arranged with KADOKAWA CORPORATION, Tokyo through TUTTLE-MORI AGENCY, Inc.

English translation © 2022 by Yen Press, LLC

Yen Press
150 West 30th Street, 19th Floor
New York, NY 10001

Visit us at yenpress.com + facebook.com/yenpress
twitter.com/yenpress + yenpress.tumblr.com + instagram.com/yenpress

First Yen Press Edition: July 2022
Edited by Yen Press Editorial: Carl Li
Designed by Yen Press Design: Andy Swist

Yen Press is an imprint of Yen Press, LLC.
The Yen Press name and logo are trademarks of Yen Press, LLC.

Library of Congress Control Number: 2021932161

ISBNs: 978-1-9753-4061-2 (paperback)
978-1-9753-4062-9 (ebook)

10 9 8 7 6 5 4 3 2 1

WOR

Printed in the United States of America